Econophysics and Financial Economics

Econophysics and Financial Economics

An Emerging Dialogue

Franck Jovanovic

and

Christophe Schinckus

OXFORD
UNIVERSITY PRESS

OXFORD
UNIVERSITY PRESS

Oxford University Press is a department of the University of Oxford. It furthers the University's objective of excellence in research, scholarship, and education by publishing worldwide. Oxford is a registered trade mark of Oxford University Press in the UK and certain other countries.

Published in the United States of America by Oxford University Press
198 Madison Avenue, New York, NY 10016, United States of America.

CIP data is on file at the Library of Congress
ISBN 978–0–19–020503–4

CONTENTS

ACKNOWLEDGMENTS

This book owes a lot to discussions that we had with Anna Alexandrova, Marcel Ausloos, Françoise Balibar, Jean-Philippe Bouchaud, Gigel Busca, John Davis, Xavier Gabaix, Serge Galam, Nicolas Gaussel, Yves Gingras, Emmanuel Haven, Philippe Le Gall, Annick Lesne, Thomas Lux, Elton McGoun, Adrian Pagan, Cyrille Piatecki, Geoffrey Poitras, Jeroen Romboust, Eugene Stanley, and Richard Topol. We want to thank them. We also thank Scott Parris. We also want to acknowledge the support of the CIRST (Montréal, Canada), CEREC (University St-Louis, Belgium), GRANEM (Université d'Angers, France), and LÉO (Université d'Orléans, France). We also thank Annick Desmeules Paré, Élise Filotas, Kangrui Wang, and Steve Jones. Finally, we wish to acknowledge the financial support of the Social Sciences and Humanities Research Council of Canada, the Fonds québécois de recherche sur la société et la culture, and TELUQ (Fonds Institutionnel de Recherche) for this research. We would like to thank the anonymous referees for their helpful comments.

INTRODUCTION

Stock market prices exert considerable fascination over the large numbers of people who scrutinize them daily, hoping to understand the mystery of their fluctuations. Science was first called in to address this challenging problem 150 years ago. In 1863, in a pioneering way, Jules Regnault, a French broker's assistant, tried for the first time to "tame" the market by creating a mathematical model called the "random walk" based on the principles of social physics (chapter 1 in this book; Jovanovic 2016). Since then, many authors have tried to use scientific models, methods, and tools for the same purpose: to pin down this fluctuating reality. Their investigations have sustained a fruitful dialogue between physics and finance. They have also fueled a common history. In the mid-1990s, in the wake of some of the most recent advances in physics, a new approach to dealing with financial prices emerged. This approach is called *econophysics*. Although the name suggests interdisciplinary research, its approach is in fact multidisciplinary. This field was created outside financial economics by statistical physicists who study economic phenomena, and more specifically financial markets. They use models, methods, and concepts imported from physics. From a financial point of view, econophysics can be seen as the application to financial markets of models from particle physics (a subfield of statistical physics) that mainly use stable Lévy processes and power laws. This new discipline is original in many points and diverges from previous works. Although econophysicists concretized the project initiated by Mandelbrot in the 1960s, who sought to extend statistical physics to finance by modeling stock price variations through Lévy stable processes, econophysicists took a different path to get there. Therefore, they provide new perspectives that this book investigates.

Over the past two decades, econophysics has carved out a place in the scientific analysis of financial markets, providing new theoretical models, methods, and results. The framework that econophysicists have developed describes the evolution of financial markets in a way very different from that used by the current standard financial models. Today, although less visible than financial economics, econophysics influences financial markets and practices. Many "quants" (quantitativists) trained in statistical physics have carried their tools and methodology into the financial world. According to several trading-room managers and directors, econophysicists' phenomenological approach has modified the practices and methods of analyzing financial data. Hitherto, these practical changes have concerned certain domains of finance: hedging, portfolio management, financial crash predictions, and software dedicated to finance. In the coming decades, however, econophysics could contribute to profound changes in the entire financial industry. Performance measures, risk management, and all financial decisions are likely to be affected by the framework econophysicists have developed. In this context, an investigation of the interface between econophysics and financial economics is required and timely.

Paradoxically, although econophysics has already contributed to change practices on financial markets and has provided numerous models, dialogue between econophysicists and financial economists is almost nonexistent. On the one hand, econophysics faces strong resistance from financial economists (chapter 4), while on the other hand, econophysicists largely ignore financial economics (chapters 4 and 5). Moreover, the potential contributions of econophysics to finance (theory and practices) are far from clear. This book is intended to give readers interested in econophysics an overview of the situation by supplying a comparative analysis of the two fields in a clear, homogenous framework.

The lack of dialogue between the two scientific communities is manifested in several ways. With some rare exceptions, econophysics publications criticize (sometimes very forcefully) the theoretical framework of financial economics, while frequently ignoring its contributions (chapters 5 and 6). In addition, econophysicists are parsimonious with their explanations regarding their contribution in relation to existing works in financial economics or to existing practices in trading rooms. In the same vein, econophysicists criticize the hypothetico-deductive method used by financial economists, starting from postulates (i.e., a hypothesis accepted as true without being demonstrated) rather than from empirical phenomena (chapter 4). However, econophysicists seem to overlook the fact that they themselves implicitly apply a quite similar approach: the great majority of them develop mathematical models based on the postulate that the empirical phenomenon studied is ruled by a power-law distribution (chapter 3). Many econophysicists suggest a simple importing of statistical physics concepts into financial economics, ignoring the scientific constraints specific to each of the two disciplines that make this impossible (chapters 1–4). Econophysicists are driven by a more phenomenological method where visual tests are used to identify the probability distribution that fits with observations. However, most econophysicists are unaware that such visual tests are considered unscientific in financial economics (chapters 1, 4, and 5). In addition, econophysics literature largely remains silent on the crucial issues of the validation of the power-law distribution by existing tests. Similarly, financial economists have developed models (autoregressive conditional heteroskedasticity [ARCH] -type models, jump models, etc.) by adopting a phenomenological approach similar to that propounded by econophysicists (chapters 2, 4, and 5). However, although these models are criticized in econophysics literature, econophysicists have overlooked the fact that these models are rooted in scientific constraints inherent in financial economics (chapters 4 and 5).

This lack of dialogue and its consequences can be traced to three main causes.

The first is reciprocal ignorance, strengthened by some differences in disciplinary language. For instance, while financial economists use the term "Lévy processes" to define (nonstable) jump or pure-jump models, econophysicists use the same term to mean "stable Lévy processes" (chapter 2). Consequently, econophysicists often claim that they offer a new perspective on finance, whereas financial economists consider that this approach is an old issue in finance. Many examples of this situation can be observed in the literature, with each community failing to venture beyond its own perspective. A key point is that the vast majority of econophysics publications are written by econophysicists for physicists, with the result that the field is not easily accessible to other scholars or readers. This context highlights the necessity to clarify the differences and similarities between the two disciplines.

The second cause is rooted in the way each discipline deals with its own scientific knowledge. Contrary to what one might think, how science is done depends on disciplinary processes. Consequently, the ways of producing knowledge are different in econophysics and financial economics (chapter 4): econophysicists and financial economists do not build their models in the same way; they do not test their models and hypotheses with the same procedures; they do not face the same scientific constraints even though they use the same vocabulary (in a different manner), and so on. The situation is simply due to the fact that econophysics remains in the shadow of physics and, consequently, outside of financial economics. Of course there are advantages and disadvantages in such an institutional situation (i.e., being outside of financial economics) in terms of scientific innovations. A methodological study is proposed in this book to clarify the dissimilarities between econophysics and financial economics in terms of modeling. Our analysis also highlights some common features regarding modeling (chapter 5) by stressing that the scientific criteria any work must respect in order to be accepted as scientific are very different in these two disciplines. The gaps in the way of doing science make reading literature from the other discipline difficult, even for a trained scholar. These gaps underline the needs for clear explanations of the main concepts and tools used in econophysics and how they could be used on financial markets.

The third cause is the lack of a framework that could allow comparisons between results provided by models developed in the two disciplines. For a long time, there have been no formal statistical tests for validating (or invalidating) the occurrence of a power law. In finance, satisfactory statistical tools and methods for testing power laws do not yet exist (chapter 5). Although econophysics can potentially be useful in trading rooms and although some recent developments propose interesting solutions to existing issues in financial economics (chapter 5), importing econophysics into finance is still difficult. The major reason goes back to the fact that econophysicists mainly use visual techniques for testing the existence of a power law, while financial economists use classical statistical tests associated with the Gaussian framework. This relative absence of statistical (analytical) tests dedicated to power laws in finance makes any comparison between the models of econophysics and those of financial economics complex. Moreover, the lack of a homogeneous framework creates difficulties related to the criteria for choosing one model rather than another. These issues highlight the need for the development of a common framework between these two fields. Because econophysics literature proposes a large variety of models, the first step is to identify a generic model unifying key econophysics models. In this perspective, this book proposes a generalized model characterizing the way econophysicists statistically describe the evolution of financial data. Thereafter, the minimal condition for a theoretical integration in the financial mainstream is defined (chapter 6). The identification of such a unifying model will pave the way for its potential implementation in financial economics.

Despite this difficult dialogue, a number of collaborations between financial economists and econophysicists have occurred, aimed at increasing exchanges between the two communities.[1] These collaborations have provided useful contributions. However, they also underline the necessity for a better understanding of the disciplinary constraints specific to both fields in order to ease a fruitful association. For instance, as the physicist Dietrich Stauffer explained, "Once we [the economist Thomas Lux and Stauffer] discussed whether to do a Grassberger-Procaccia analysis of some financial data . . . I realized that in this case he, the economist, would have to explain to me, the physicist, how to apply this physics method" (Stauffer 2004, 3). In the same vein, some practitioners are aware of the constraints and perspectives specific to each discipline. The academic and quantitative analyst Emanuel Derman (2001, 2009) is a notable example of this trend. He has pointed out differences in the role of models within each discipline: while physicists implement causal (drawing causal inference) or phenomenological (pragmatic analogies) models in their description of the physical world, financial economists use interpretative models to "transform intuitive linear quantities into non-linear stable values" (Derman 2009, 30). These considerations imply going beyond the comfort zone defined by the usual scientific frontiers within which many authors stay.

This book seeks to make a contribution toward increasing dialogue between the two disciplines. It will explore *what* econophysics is and *who* econophysicists are by clarifying the position of econophysics in the development of financial economics. This is a challenging issue. First, there is an extremely wide variety of work aiming to apply physics to finance. However, some of this work remains outside the scope of econophysics. In addition, as the econophysicist Marcel Ausloos (2013, 109) claims, investigations are heading in too many directions, which does not serve the intended research goal. In this fragmented context, some authors have reviewed existing econophysics works by distinguishing between those devoted to "empirical facts" and those dealing with agent-based modeling (Chakraborti et al. 2011a, 2011b). Other authors have proposed a categorization based on methodological aspects by differentiating between statistical tools and algorithmic tools (Schinckus 2012), while still others have kept to a classical micro/macro opposition (Ausloos 2013). To clarify the approach followed in this book, it is worth mentioning the historical importance of the Santa Fe Institute in the creation of econophysics. This institution introduced two computational ways of describing complex systems that are relevant for econophysics: (1) the emergence of macro statistical regularity characterizing the evolution of systems; (2) the observation of a spontaneous order emerging from microinteractions between components of systems (Schinckus 2017). Methodologically speaking, studies focusing on the emergence of macro regularities consider the description of the system as a whole as the target of the analysis, while works dealing with an emerging spontaneous order seek to reproduce (algorithmically) microinteractions leading the system to a specific configuration. These two approaches have led to a methodological scission in the literature between statistical econophysics and agent-based econophysics (Schinckus 2012). While econophysics was originally defined as the extension of statistical physics to financial economics, agent-based modeling has recently been associated with econophysics. This book mainly focuses on the original way of defining econophysics by considering the applications of statistical physics to financial markets.

Dealing with econophysics raises another challenging issue. The vast majority of existing books on econophysics are written by physicists who discuss the field from their own perspective. Financial economists, for their part, do not usually clarify their implicit assumptions, which does not facilitate collaboration with outsider scientists. This is the first book on econophysics to be written solely by financial economists. It does not aspire to summarize the state of the art on econophysics, nor to provide an exhaustive presentation of econophysics models or topics investigated; many books already exist.[2] Rather, its aim is to analyze the crucial issues at the interface of financial economics and econophysics that are generally ignored or not investigated by scholars involved in either field. It clarifies the scientific foundations and criteria used in each discipline, and makes the first extensive analytic comparison between models and results from both fields. It also provides keys for understanding the resistance each discipline has to face by analyzing what has to be done to overcome these resistances. In this perspective, this book sets out to pave the way for better and useful collaborations between the two fields. In contrast with existing literature dedicated to econophysics, the approach developed in this book enables us to initiate a framework and models common to financial economics and econophysics.

This book has two singular characteristics.

The first is that it deals with the scientific foundations of econophysics and financial economics by analyzing their development. We are interested not only in the presentation of these foundational principles but also in the study of the implicit scientific and methodological criteria, which are generally not studied by authors. After explaining the contextual factors that contributed to the advent of econophysics, we discuss the key concepts used by econophysicists and how they have contributed to a new way of using power-law distributions, both in physics and in other sciences. As we demonstrate, comprehension of these foundations is crucial to an understanding of the current gap between the two areas of knowledge and, consequently, to breaking down the barriers that separate them conceptually.

The second particular feature of this book is that it takes a very specific perspective. Unlike other publications dedicated to econophysics, it is written by financial economists and situates econophysics in the evolution of modern financial theory. Consequently, it provides an analysis in which econophysics makes sense for financial economists by using the vocabulary and the viewpoint of financial economics. Such a perspective is very helpful for identifying and understanding the major advantages and drawbacks of econophysics from the perspective of financial economics. In this way, the reasons why financial economists have been unable to use econophysics models in their field until now can also be identified. Adopting the perspective of financial economics also makes it possible to develop a common framework enabling synergies and potential collaborations between financial economists and econophysicists to be created. This book thus offers conceptual tools to surmount the disciplinary barriers that currently limit the dialogue between these two disciplines. In accordance with this purpose, the book gives econophysicists an opportunity to have a specific disciplinary (financial) perspective on their emerging field.

The book is divided into three parts.

The first part (chapters 1 and 2) focuses on financial economics. It highlights the scientific constraints this discipline has to face in its study of financial markets. This part investigates a series of key issues often addressed by econophysicists (but also by scholars working outside financial economics): why financial economists cannot easily drop the efficient-market hypothesis; why they could not follow Mandelbrot's program; why they consider visual tests unscientific; how they deal with extreme values; and, finally, why the mathematics used in econophysics creates difficulties in financial economics.

The second part (chapters 3 and 4) focuses on econophysics. It clarifies econophysics' position in the development of financial economics. This part investigates econophysicists' scientific criteria, which are different from those of financial economists, implying that the scientific benchmark for acceptance differs in the two communities. We explain why econophysicists have to deal with power laws and not with other distributions; how they describe the problem of infinite variance; how they model financial markets in comparison with the way financial economists do; why and how they can introduce innovations in finance; and, finally, why econophysics and financial economics can be looked on as similar.

The third part (chapters 5 and 6) investigates the potential development of a common framework between econophysics and financial economics. This part aims at clarifying some current issues about such a program: what the current uses of econophysics in trading rooms are; what recent developments in econophysics allow possible contributions to financial economics; how the lack of statistical tests for power laws can be solved; what generative models can explain the appearance of power laws in financial data; and, finally, how a common framework transcending the two fields by integrating the best of the two disciplines could be created.

1

FOUNDATIONS OF FINANCIAL ECONOMICS
THE KEY ROLE OF THE GAUSSIAN DISTRIBUTION

This chapter scrutinizes the theoretical foundations of financial economics. Financial economists consider that stock market variations[1] are ruled by stochastic processes (i.e., a mathematical formalism constituted by a sequence of random variables). The random-walk model is the simplest one. While the random nature of stock market variations is not called into question in the work of econophysicists, the use of the Gaussian distribution to characterize such variations is firmly rejected. The strict Gaussian distribution does not allow financial models to reproduce the substantial variations in prices or returns that are observed on the financial markets. A telling illustration is the occurrence of financial crashes, which are more and more frequent. One can mention, for instance, August 2015 with the Greek stock market, June 2015 with the Chinese stock market, August 2011 with world stock markets, May 2010 with the Dow Jones index, and so on. Financial economists' insistence on maintaining the Gaussian-distribution hypothesis meets with incomprehension among econophysicists. This insistence might appear all the more surprising because financial economists themselves have long been complaining about the limitations of the Gaussian distribution in the face of empirical data. Why, in spite of this drawback, do financial economists continue to make such broad use of the normal distribution? What are the reasons for this hypothesis's position at the core of financial economics? Is it fundamental for financial economists? What benefits does it give them? What would dropping it entail?

The aim of this chapter is to answer these questions and understand the place of the normal distribution in financial economics. First of all, the chapter will investigate the historical roots of this distribution, which played a key role in the construction of financial economics. Indeed, the Gaussian distribution enabled this field to become a recognized scientific discipline. Moreover, this distribution is intrinsically embedded in the statistical framework used by financial economists. The chapter will also clarify the links between the Gaussian distribution and the efficient-market hypothesis. Although the latter is nowadays well established in finance, its links with stochastic processes have generated many confusions and misunderstandings among financial economists and consequently among econophysicists. Our analysis will also show that the choice of a statistical distribution, including the Gaussian one, cannot be reduced to empirical considerations. As in any scientific discipline, axioms and postulates[2] play an important role in combination with scientific and methodological constraints with which successive researchers have been faced.

1.1. FIRST INVESTIGATIONS AND EARLY ROOTS OF FINANCIAL ECONOMICS: THE KEY ROLE OF THE GAUSSIAN DISTRIBUTION

Financial economics' construction as a scientific discipline has been a long process spread over a number of stages. This first part of our survey looks back at the origins of financial tools and concepts that were combined in the 1960s to create financial economics. These first works of modern finance will show the close association between the development of financial ideas, probabilities theory, physics, statistics, and economics. This perspective will also provide reading keys in order to understand the scientific criteria on which financial economics was created. Two elements will get our attention: the Gaussian distribution and the use of stochastic processes for studying stock market variations. This analysis will clarify the major theoretical and methodological foundations of financial economics and identify justifications for the use of the normal law and the random character of stock market variations produced by early theoretical works.

1.1.1. The First Works of Modern Finance

1863: Jules Regnault and the First Stochastic Modeling of Stock Market Variations

Use of a random-walk model to represent stock market variations was first proposed in 1863 by a French broker's assistant (*employé d'agent de change*), Jules Regnault.[3] His only published work, *Calculation of Chances and Philosophy of the Stock Exchange* (*Calcul des chances et philosophie de la bourse*), represents the first known theoretical work whose methodology and theoretical content relates to financial economics. Regnault's objective was to determine the laws of nature that govern stock market fluctuations and that statistical calculations could bring within reach.

Regnault produced his work at a time when the Paris stock market was a leading place for derivative trading (Weber 2009); it also played a growing role in the whole economy (Arbulu 1998; Hautcœur and Riva 2012; Gallais-Hamonno 2007). This period was also a time when new ideas were introduced into the social sciences. As we will detail in chapter 4, such a context also contributed to the emergence of financial economics and of econophysics. The changes on the Paris stock market gave rise to lively debates on the usefulness of financial markets and whether they should be restricted (Preda 2001, 2004; Jovanovic 2002, 2006b). Regnault published his work partly in response to these debates, using a symmetric random-walk model to demonstrate that the stock market was both fair and equitable, and that consequently its development was acceptable (Jovanovic 2006a; Jovanovic and Le Gall 2001). In conducting his demonstration, Regnault took inspiration from Quételet's work on the normal distribution (Jovanovic 2001). Adolphe Quételet was a Belgian mathematician and statistician well known as the "father of social physics."[4] He shared with the scientists of his time the idea that the average was synonymous with perfection and morality (Porter 1986) and that the normal distribution,[5] also known as "the law of errors," made it possible to determine errors of observation (i.e., discrepancies) in relation to the true value of the observed object, represented by the average. Quételet, like Regnault, applied the Gaussian distribution, which was considered as one of the most important scientific results founded on the central-limit theorem (which explains the occurrence of the normal distribution in nature),[6] to social phenomena.

Precisely, the normal law allowed Regnault to determine the true value of a security that, according to the "law of errors," is the security's long-term mean value. He contrasted this long-term determination with a short-term random walk that was mainly due to the shortsightedness of agents. In Regnault's view, short-term valuations of a security are subjective and subject to error and are therefore distributed in accordance with the normal law. As a result, short-term valuations fall into two groups spread equally about a security's value: the "upward" and the "downward." In the absence of new information, transactions cause the price to gravitate around this value, leading Regnault to view short-term speculation as a "toss of a coin" game (1863, 34).

In a particularly innovative manner, Regnault likened stock price variations to a random walk, although that term was never employed.[7] On account of the normal distribution of short-term valuations, the price had an equal probability of lying above or below the mean value. If these two probabilities were different, Regnault pointed out, actors could resort to arbitrage[8] by choosing to systematically follow the movement having the highest probability (Regnault 1863, 41). Similarly, as in the toss of a coin, rises and falls of stock market prices are independent of each other. Consequently, since neither a rise nor a fall can anticipate the direction of future variations (Regnault 1863, 38), Regnault explained, there could be no hope of short-term gain. Lastly, he added, a security's current price reflects all available public information on which actors base their valuation of it (Regnault 1863, 29–30). Therefore, with Regnault, we have a perfect representation of stock market variations using a random-walk model.[9]

Another important contribution from Regnault is that he tested his hypothesis of the random nature of short-term stock market variations by examining a mathematical property of this model, namely that deviations increase proportionately with the square root of time. Regnault validated this property empirically using the monthly prices from the French 3 percent bond, which was the main bond issued by the government and also the main security listed on the Paris Stock Exchange. It is worth mentioning that at this time quoted prices and transactions on the official market of Paris Stock Exchange were systematically recorded,[10] allowing statistical tests. Such an obligation did not exist in other countries. In all probability the inspiration for this test was once again the work of Quételet, who had established the law on the increase of deviations (1848, 43 and 48). Although the way Regnault tested his model was different from the econometric tests used today (Jovanovic 2016; Jovanovic and Le Gall 2001; Le Gall 2006), the empirical determination of this law of the square root of time thus constituted the first result to support the random nature of stock market variations.

It is worth mentioning that Regnault's choice of the Gaussian distribution was based on three factors: (1) empirical data; (2) moral considerations, because this law allowed him to demonstrate that speculation necessarily led to ruin, whereas investments that fostered a country's development led to the earning of money; and (3) the importance at the time of the "law of errors" in the development of social sciences, which was due to the work of Quételet based on the central-limit theorem.

In conclusion, contemporary intuitions and mainstream ideas about the random character of stock market prices and returns informed Regnault's book.[11] Its pioneering aspect is also borne out with respect to portfolio analysis, since the diversification strategy and the concept of correlation were already in use in the United Kingdom and in France at the end of the nineteenth century (Edlinger and Parent 2014; Rutterford and Sotiropoulos 2015). Although Regnault introduced foundational intuitions about the description of financial data, his idea of a random walk had to wait until Louis Bachelier's thesis in 1900 to be formalized.

1900: Louis Bachelier and the First Mathematical Formulation of Brownian Motion

The second crucial actor in the history of modern financial ideas is the French mathematician Louis Bachelier. Although the whole of Bachelier's doctoral thesis is based on stock markets and options pricing, we must remember that this author defended his thesis in a field called at this time mathematical physics—that is, the field that applies mathematics to problems in physics. Although his research program dealt with mathematics alone—his aim was to construct a general, unified theory of the calculation of probabilities exclusively on the basis of continuous time[12]—the genesis of Bachelier's program of mathematical research most certainly lay in his interest in financial markets (Taqqu 2001, 4–5; Bachelier 1912, 293). It seems clear that stock markets fascinated him, and his endeavor to understand them was what stimulated him to develop an extension of probability theory, an extension that ultimately turned out to have other applications.

His first publication, *Théorie de la spéculation*, which was also his doctoral thesis, introduced continuous-time probabilities by demonstrating the equivalence between the results obtained in discrete time and in continuous time (an application of the central-limit theorem). Bachelier achieved this equivalence by developing two proofs: one using continuous-time probabilities, the other with discrete-time probabilities completed by a limit approximation using Stirling's formula. In the second part of his thesis he proved the usefulness of this equivalence through empirical investigations of stock market prices, which provided a large amount of data.

Bachelier applied this principle of a double demonstration to the law of stock market price variation, formulating for the first time the so-called Chapman-Kolmogorov-Smoluchowski equation:[13]

$$p(z,t)=\int_{-\infty}^{+\infty} p(x,t_1)\,p(z-x,t_2)\,dx, \text{ with } t=t_1+t_2, \tag{1.1}$$

where P_{z,t_1+t_2} designates the probability that price z will be quoted at time $t_1 + t_2$, knowing that price x was quoted at time t_1. Bachelier then established the probability of transition as σW_t—where W_t is a Brownian movement:[14]

$$p(x,t) = \frac{1}{2\pi k\sqrt{t}} e^{-\frac{x^2}{4\pi k^2 t}}, \tag{1.2}$$

where t represents time, x a price of the security, and k a constant. Bachelier next applied his double-demonstration principle to the "two problems of the theory of speculation" that he proposed to resolve: the first establishes the probability of a given price being reached or exceeded at a given time—that is, the probability of a "prime," which was an asset similar to a European option,[15] being exercised, while the second seeks the probability of a given price being reached or exceeded before a given time (Bachelier 1900, 81)—which amounts to determining the probability of an American option being exercised.[16]

His 1901 article, "Théorie mathématique du jeu," enabled him to generalize the first results contained in his thesis by moving systematically from discrete time to continuous time and by adopting what he called a "hyperasymptotic" point of view. The "hyperasymptotic" was one of Bachelier's central concerns and one of his major contributions. "Whereas the asymptotic approach of Laplace deals with the Gaussian limit, Bachelier's hyperasymptotic approach deals with trajectories," as Davis and Etheridge point out (2006, 84). Bachelier was the first to apply the trajectories of Brownian motion, making a break from the past and anticipating the mathematical finance developed since the 1960s (Taqqu 2001). Bachelier was thus able to prove the results in continuous time of a number of problems in the theory of gambling that the calculation of probabilities had dealt with since its origins.

For Bachelier, as for Regnault, the choice of the normal distribution was not only dictated by empirical data but mainly by mathematical considerations. Bachelier's interest was in the mathematical properties of the normal law (particularly the central-limit theorem) for the purpose of demonstrating the equivalence of results obtained using mathematics in continuous time and those obtained using mathematics in discrete time.

Other Endeavors: A Similar Use of the Gaussian Distribution

Bachelier was not the only person working successfully on premium/option pricing at the beginning of the twentieth century. The Italian mathematician Vinzenz Bronzin published a book on the theory of premium contracts in 1908. Bronzin was a professor of commercial and political arithmetic at the Imperial Regia Accademia di Commercio e Nautica in Trieste and published several books (Hafner and Zimmermann 2009, chap. 1). In his 1908 book, Bronzin analyzed premiums/options and developed a theory for pricing them. Like Regnault and Bachelier, Bronzin assumed the random character of market fluctuations and zero expected profit. Bronzin did no stochastic modeling and was uninterested in stochastic processes (Hafner and Zimmermann 2009, 244), but he showed that "applying Bernoulli's theorem to market fluctuations leads to the same result that we had arrived at when supposing the application of the law of error [i.e., the normal law]" (Bronzin 1908, 195). In other words, Bronzin used the normal law in the same way as Regnault, since it allowed him to determine the probability of price fluctuations (Bronzin 1908 in Hafner and Zimmermann 2009, 188). In all these pioneering works, it appears that the Gaussian distribution and the hypothesis of random character of stock market variations were closely linked with the scientific tools available at the time (and particularly the central-limit theorem).

The works of Bachelier, Regnault, and Bronzin have continued to be used and taught since their publication (Hafner and Zimmermann 2009; Jovanovic 2004, 2012, 2016). However, despite these writers' desire to create a "science of the stock exchange," no research movement emerged to explore the random nature of variations. One of the reasons for this was the opposition of economists to the mathematization of their discipline (Breton 1991; Ménard 1987). Another reason lay in the insufficient development of what is called modern probability theory, which played a key role in the creation of financial economics in the 1960s (we will detail this point later in this chapter).

Development of continuous-time probability theory did not truly begin until 1931, before which the discipline was not fully recognized by the scientific community (Von Plato 1994). However, a number of publications aimed at renewing this theory emerged between 1900 and 1930.[17] During this period, several authors were working on random variables and on the generalization of the central-limit theorem, including Sergei Natanovich Bernstein, Alexandre Liapounov, Georges Polya, Andrei Markov,[18] and Paul Lévy. Louis Bachelier (Bachelier 1900, 1901, 1912), Albert Einstein (1905), Marian von Smoluchowski (1906),[19] and Norbert Wiener (1923)[20] were the first to propose continuous-time results, on Brownian motion in particular. However, up until the 1920s, during which decade "a new and powerful international progression of the mathematical theory of probabilities" emerged (due above all to the work of Russian mathematicians such as Kolmogorov, Khintchine, Markov, and Bernstein), this work remained known and accessible only to a few specialists (Cramer 1983, 8). For example, the work of Wiener (1923) was difficult to read before the work of Kolmogorov published during the 1930s, while Bachelier's publications (1901, 1900, 1912) were hardly readable, as witnessed by the error that Paul Lévy (one of the rare mathematicians working in this field) believed he had detected.[21] The 1920s were a period of very intensive research into probability theory—and into continuous-time probabilities in particular—that paved the way for the construction of modern probability theory.

Modern probability theory was properly created in the 1930s, in particular through the work of Kolmogorov, who proposed its main founding concepts: he introduced the concept of probability space, defined the concept of the random variable as we know it today, and also dealt with conditional expectation in a totally new manner (Cramer 1983, 9; Shafer and Vovk 2001, 39). Since his axiom system is the basis of the current paradigm of the discipline, Kolmogorov can be seen as the father of this branch of mathematics. Kolmogorov built on Bachelier's work, which he considered the first study of stochastic processes in continuous time, and he generalized on it in his 1931 article.[22] From these beginnings in the 1930s, modern probability theory became increasingly influential, although it was only after World War II that Kolmogorov's axioms became the dominant paradigm in the discipline (Shafer and Vovk 2005, 54–55).

It was also after World War II that the American probability school was born.[23] It was led by Joseph Doob and William Feller, who had a major influence on the construction of modern probability theory, particularly through their two main books, published in the early 1950s (Doob 1953; Feller 1957), which proved, on the basis of the framework laid down by Kolmogorov, all results obtained prior to the 1950s, enabling their acceptance and integration into the discipline's theoretical corpus (Meyer 2009; Shafer and Vovk 2005, 60).

In other words, modern probability theory was not accessible for analyzing stock markets and finance until the 1950s. Consequently, it would have been exceedingly difficult to create a research movement before that time, and this limitation made the possibility of a new discipline such as financial economics prior to the 1960s unlikely. However, with the emergence of econometrics in the United States in the 1930s, an active research movement into the random nature of stock market variations and their distribution did emerge, paving the way for financial econometrics.

1.1.2. The Emergence of Financial Econometrics in the 1930s

The stimulus to conduct research on the hypothesis of the random nature of stock market variations arose in the United States in the 1930s. Alfred Cowles, a victim of the 1929 stock market crash, questioned the predictive abilities of the portfolio management firms who gave advice to investors. This led him into contact with the newly founded Econometric Society—an "International Society for the Advancement of Economic Theory in its Relation with Statistics and Mathematics." In 1932, he offered the society financial support in exchange for statistical treatment of his problems in predicting stock market variations and the business cycle. On September 9 of the same year, he set up an innovative research group: the Cowles Commission.[24]

Research into application of the random-walk model to stock market variations was begun by two authors connected with this institution, Cowles himself (1933, 1944) and Holbrook Working (1934, 1949).[25] The failure to predict the 1929 crisis led them to entertain the possibility that stock market variations were unpredictable. Defending this perspective led these researchers to oppose the chartist theories, very influential at the time, that claimed to be able to anticipate stock market variations based on the history of stock market prices. Cowles and Working undertook to show that these theories, which had not foreseen the 1929 crisis, had no predictive power. It was through this postulate of unpredictability that the random nature of stock market variations was reintroduced into financial theory, since it allowed this unpredictability to be modeled. Unpredictability became a key element of the first theoretical works in finance because they were associated with econometrics.

The first empirical tests were based on the normal distribution, which was still considered the natural attractor for the sum of a set of random variables. For example,

Working (1934) started from the notion that the movements of price series "are largely random and unpredictable" (1934, 12). He constructed a series of random returns with random drawings generated by a Tippett table[26] based on the normal distribution. He assumed a Gaussian distribution because of "the superior generality of the 'normal' frequency distribution" (1934, 16). This position was common at this time for authors who studied price fluctuations (Cover 1937; Bowley 1933): the normal distribution was viewed as the starting point of any work in econometrics. This presumption was reinforced by the fact that all existing statistical tests were based on the Gaussian framework. Working compared his random series graphically with the real series, and noted that the artificially created price series took the same graphic shapes as the real series. His methodology was similar to that used by Slutsky ([1927] 1937) in his econometric work, which aimed to demonstrate that business cycles could be caused by an accumulation of random events (Armatte 1991; Hacking 1990; Le Gall 1994; Morgan 1990).[27] Slutsky proposed a graphical comparison between a random series and an observed price series. Slutsky and Working considered that, if price variations were random, they must be distributed according to the Gaussian distribution.

The second researcher affiliated with the Cowles Commission, Cowles himself, followed the same path: he tested the random character of returns (price variations), and he postulated that these price variations were ruled by the normal distribution. Cowles (1933), for his part, attempted to determine whether stock market professionals (financial services and chartists) were able to predict stock market variations, and thus whether they could realize better performance than the market itself or than random management. He compared the evolution of the market with the performances of fictional portfolios based on the recommendations of 16 professionals. He found that the average annual return of these portfolios was appreciably inferior to the average market performance; and that the best performance could have been attained by buying and selling stocks randomly. It is worth mentioning that the desire to prove the unpredictability of stock market variations led authors occasionally to make contestable interpretations in support of their thesis (Jovanovic 2009b).[28] In addition, Cowles and Jones (1937), whose article sought to demonstrate that stock price variations are random, compared the distribution of price variations with a normal distribution because, for these authors, the normal distribution was the means of characterizing chance in finance.[29] Like Working, Cowles and Jones sought to demonstrate the independence of stock price variations and made no assumption about distribution.

The work of Cowles and Working was followed in 1953 by a statistical study by the English statistician Maurice Kendall. Although his work used more technical statistical tools, reflecting the evolution of econometrics, the Gaussian distribution was still viewed as the statistical framework describing the random character of time series, and no other distribution was considered when using econometrics or statistical tests. Kendall in turn considered the possibility of predicting financial-market prices. Although he found weak autocorrelations in series and weak delayed correlations between series, Kendall concluded that "a kind of economic Brownian motion" was operating and commented on the central-limit tendency in his data. In addition, he considered that "unless individual stocks behave differently from the average of similar stocks, there is no hope of being able to predict movements on the exchange for a week ahead without extraneous information" (1953, 11). Kendall's conclusions remained cautious, however. He pointed out at least one notable exception to the random nature of stock market variations and warned that "it is . . . difficult to distinguish by statistical methods between a genuine wandering series and one wherein the systematic element is weak" (1953, 11).

These new research studies had a strong applied, empirical, and practical dimension: they favored an econometric approach without theoretical explanation, aimed at validating the postulate that stock market variations were unpredictable. From the late 1950s on, the absence of theoretical explanation and the weakness of the results were strongly criticized by two of the main proponents of the random nature of stock market prices and returns: Working (1956, 1961, 1958), and Harry V. Roberts (1959), who was professor of statistics at the Graduate School of Business at the University of Chicago.[30] Each pointed out the limitations of the lack of theoretical explanation and the way to move ahead. Roberts (1959, 15) noted that the independence of stock market variations had not yet been established (1959, 13). Working also highlighted the absence of any verification of the randomness of stock market variations. In his view, it was not possible to reject with certainty the chartist (or technical) analysis, which relied on figures or graphics to predict variations in stock market prices. "Although I may seem to have implied that these 'technical formations' in actual prices are illusory," Working said, "they have not been proved so" (1956, 1436).

These early American authors' choice of the randomness of stock market variations derives, then, from their desire to support their postulate that variations were unpredictable. However, although they reintroduced this hypothesis independently of the work of Bachelier, Regnault, and Bronzin and without any "a priori assumptions" about the distribution of stock market prices,[31] their works were embedded in the Gaussian framework. The latter was, at the time, viewed as the necessary scientific tool for describing random time series (chapter 2 will also detail this point). At the end of the 1950s, Working and Roberts called for research to continue, initiating the break in the 1960s that led to the creation of financial economics.

1.2. THE ROLE OF THE GAUSSIAN FRAMEWORK IN THE CREATION OF FINANCIAL ECONOMICS AS A SCIENTIFIC DISCIPLINE

Financial economics owes its institutional birth to three elements: access to the tools of modern probability theory; a new scientific community that extended the analysis framework of economics to finance; and the creation of new empirical data.[32] This birth is inseparable from work on the modeling of stock market variations using stochastic processes and on the efficient-market hypothesis. It took place during the 1960s at a time when American university circles were taking a growing interest in American financial markets (Poitras 2009) and when new tools became available. An analysis of this context provides an understanding of some of the main theoretical and methodological foundations of contemporary financial economics. We will detail this point in the next section when we study how the hard core of this discipline was constituted.

1.2.1. On the Accessibility of the Tools of Modern Probability Theory

As mentioned earlier, in the early 1950s Doob and Feller published two books that had a major influence on modern probability theory (Doob 1953; Feller 1957). These works led to the creation of a stable corpus that became accessible to nonspecialists. Since then, the models and results of modern probability theory have been used in the study of financial markets in a more systematic manner, in particular by scholars trained in economics. The most notable contributions were to transform old results, expressed in a literary language, into terms used in modern probability theory.

The first step in this development was the dissemination of mathematical tools enabling the properties of random variables to be used and uncertainty reasoning to be developed. The first two writers to use tools that came out of modern probability theory to study financial markets were Harry Markowitz and A. D. Roy. In 1952 each published an article on the theory of portfolio choice theory.[33] Both used mathematical properties of random variables to build their model, and more specifically, the fact that the expected value of a weighted sum is the weighted sum of the expected values, while the variance of a weighted sum is not the weighted sum of the variances (because we have to take covariance into account). Their works provided new proof of a result that had long been known (and which was considered as an old adage, "Don't put all your eggs in one basket")[34] using a new mathematical language, based on modern probability theory. Their real contribution lay not in the result of portfolio diversification, but in the use of this new mathematical language.

In 1958, Modigliani and Miller proceeded in the same manner: they used random variables in the analysis of an old question, the capital structure of companies, to demonstrate that the value of a company is independent of its capital structure.[35] Their contribution, like that of Markowitz and Roy, was to reformulate an old problem using the terms of modern probability theory.

These studies launched a movement that would not gain ground until the 1960s: until then, economists refused to accept this new research path. Milton Friedman's reaction to Harry Markowitz's defense of his PhD thesis gives a good illustration since he declared: "It's not economics, it's not mathematics, it's not business administration." Markowitz suffered from this scientific conservatism since his first article was not cited before 1959 (Web of Science). It was also in the 1960s that the development of probability theory enabled economists to discover Bachelier's work, even though it had been known and discussed by mathematicians and statisticians in the United States since the 1920s (Jovanovic 2012). The spread of stochastic processes and greater ease of access to them for nonmathematicians led several authors to extend the first studies of financial econometrics.

The American astrophysicist Maury Osborne suggested an "analogy between 'financial chaos' in a market, and 'molecular chaos' in statistical mechanics" (Osborne

1959b, 808). In 1959, his observation that the distribution of prices did not follow the normal distribution led him to perform a log-linear transformation to obtain the normal distribution. According to Osborne, this distribution facilitated empirical tests and linked with results obtained in other scientific disciplines. He also proposed considering the price-ratio logarithm, $\log\left(\frac{P_{t+1}}{P_t}\right)$, which constitutes a fair approximation of returns for small deviations (Osborne 1959a, 149). He then showed that deviations in the price-ratio logarithm are proportional to the square root of time, and validated this result empirically. This change, which leads to consideration of the logarithmic of returns of stocks rather than of prices, was retained in later work, because it provides an assurance of the stationarity of the stochastic process. It is worth mentioning that such a transformation was already suggested by Bowley (1933) for the same reasons: bringing back the series to the normal distribution, the only one allowing the use of statistical tests at this time. This transformation shows the importance of mathematical properties that authors used in order to keep the normal distribution as the major describing framework.

The random processes used at that time have also been updated in the light of more recent mathematics. Samuelson (1965a) and Mandelbrot (1966) criticized the overly restrictive character of the random-walk (or Brownian-motion) model, which was contradicted by the existence of empirical correlations in price movements. This observation led them to replace it with a less restrictive model: the martingale model. Let us remember that a series of random variables P_t adapted to $(\Phi; 0 \leq n \leq N)$ is a martingale if $E(P_{t+1}/\Phi_t) = P_t$, where $E(./\Phi_t)$ designates the conditional expectation in relation to (Φ_t) which is a filtration.[36] In financial terms, if one considers a set of information Φ_t increasing over time with t representing time and $P_t \in \Phi_t$, then the best estimation—in line with the method of least squares—of the price (P_{t+1}) at the time $t + 1$ is the price (P_t) in t. In accordance with this definition, a random walk is therefore a martingale. However, the martingale is defined solely by a conditional expectation, and it imposes no restriction of statistical independence or stationarity on higher conditional moments—in particular the second moment (i.e., the variance). In contrast, a random-walk model requires that all moments in the series are independent[37] and defined. In other terms, from a mathematical point of view, the concept of a martingale offers a more generalized framework than the original version of random walk for the use of stochastic processes as a description of time series.

1.2.2. A New Community and the Challenge to the Dominant School of the Time

The second element that contributed to the institutional birth of financial economics was the formation in the early 1960s of a community of economists dedicated to the analysis of financial markets. The scientific background of these economists determined their way of doing science by defining specific scientific criteria for this new discipline.

Prior to the 1960s, finance in the United States was taught mainly in business schools. The textbooks used were very practical, and few of them touched on what became modern financial theory. The research work that formed the basis of modern financial theory was carried out by isolated writers who were trained in economics or were surrounded by economists, such as Working, Cowles, Kendal, Roy, and Markowitz.[38] No university community devoted to the new subjects and methods existed prior to the 1960s. During the 1960s and 1970s, training in American business schools changed radically, becoming more "rigorous."[39] They began to "academicize" themselves, recruiting increasing numbers of economics professors who taught in university economics departments, such as Merton H. Miller (Fama 2008). Similarly, prior to offering their own doctoral programs, business schools recruited PhD students who had been trained in university economics departments (Jovanovic 2008; Fourcade and Khurana 2009). The members of this new scientific community shared common tools, references, and problems thanks to new textbooks, seminars, and to scientific journals. The two journals that had published articles in finance, the *Journal of Finance* and the *Journal of Business*, changed their editorial policy during the 1960s: both started publishing articles based on modern probability theory and on modeling (Bernstein 1992, 41–44, 129).

The recruitment of economists interested in questions of finance unsettled teaching and research as hitherto practiced in business schools and inside the American Finance Association. The new recruits brought with them their analysis frameworks, methods, hypotheses, and concepts, and they were also familiar with the new mathematics that arose out of modern probability theory. These changes and their consequences were substantial enough for the American Finance Association to devote part of its annual meeting to them in two consecutive years, 1965 and 1966.

At the 1965 annual meeting of the American Finance Association an entire session was devoted to the need to rethink courses in finance curricula. At the 1966 annual meeting, the new president of the American Finance Association, Paul Weston, presented a paper titled "The State of the Finance Field," in which he talked of the changes being brought about by "the creators of the New Finance [who] become impatient with the slowness with which traditional materials and teaching techniques move along" (Weston 1967, 539).[40] Although these changes elicited many debates (Jovanovic 2008; MacKenzie 2006; Whitley 1986a, 1986b; Poitras and Jovanovic 2007, 2010), none succeeded in challenging the global movement.

The antecedents of these new actors were a determining factor in the institutionalization of modern financial theory. Their background in economics allowed them to add theoretical content to the empirical results that had been accumulated since the 1930s and to the mathematical formalisms that had arisen from modern probability theory. In other words, economics brought the theoretical content that was missing and that had been underlined by Working and Roberts. Working (1961, 1958, 1956) and Roberts (1959) were the first authors to suggest a theoretical explanation of the random character of stock market prices by using concepts and theories from economics. Working (1956) established an explicit link between the unpredictable arrival of information and the random character of stock market price changes. However, this paper made no link with economic equilibrium and, probably for this reason, was not widely circulated. Instead it was Roberts (1959, 7) who first suggested a link between economic concepts and the random-walk model by using the "arbitrage proof" argument that had been popularized by Modigliani and Miller (1958). This argument is crucial in financial economics: it made it possible to demonstrate the existence of equilibrium in uncertainty when there is no opportunity for arbitrage. Cowles (1960, 914–15) then made an important step forward by identifying a link between financial econometric results and economic equilibrium. Finally, two years later, Cootner (1962, 25) linked the random-walk model, information, and economic equilibrium, and set out the idea of the efficient-market hypothesis, although he did not use that expression. It was a University of Chicago scholar, Eugene Fama, who formulated the efficient-market hypothesis, giving it its first theoretical account in his PhD thesis, defended in 1964 and published the next year in the *Journal of Business*. Then, in his 1970 article, Fama set out the hypothesis of efficient markets as we know it today (we return to this in detail in the next section). Thus, at the start of the 1960s, the random nature of stock market variations began to be associated both with the economic equilibrium of a free competitive market and with the building of information into prices.

The second illustration of how economics brought theoretical content to mathematical formalisms is the capital-asset pricing model (CAPM). In finance, the CAPM is used to determine a theoretically appropriate required rate of return for an asset, if the asset is to be added to an already well-diversified portfolio, given the asset's nondiversifiable risk. The model takes into account the asset's sensitivity to nondiversifiable risk (also known as systematic risk or market risk or beta), as well as the expected market return and the expected return of a theoretical risk-free asset. This model is used for pricing an individual security or a portfolio. It has become the cornerstone of modern finance (Fama and French 2004). The CAPM is also built using an approach familiar to economists for three reasons. First, some sort of maximizing behavior on the part of participants in a market is assumed;[41] second, the equilibrium conditions under which such markets will clear are investigated; third, markets are perfectly competitive. Consequently, the CAPM provided a standard financial theory for market equilibrium under uncertainty.

In conclusion, this combination of economic developments with the probability theory led to the creation of a truly homogeneous academic community whose actors shared common problems, common tools, and a common language that contributed to the emergence of a research movement.

1.2.3. The Creation of New Empirical Data

Another crucial advance occurred in the 1960s: the creation of databases containing long-term statistical data on the evolution of stock market prices. These databases allowed spectacular development of empirical studies used to test models and theories in finance. The development of these studies was the result of the creation of new statistical data and the emergence of computers.

Beginning in the 1950s, computers gradually found their way into financial institutions and universities (Sprowls 1963, 91). However, owing to the costs of using them and their limited calculation capacity, "It was during the next two decades, starting in the early 1960s, as computers began to proliferate and programming languages and facilities became generally available, that economists more widely became users" (Renfro 2009, 60). The first econometric modeling languages began to be developed during the 1960s and the 1970s (Renfro 2004, 147). From the 1960s on, computer programs began to appear in increasing numbers of undergraduate, master's, and doctoral theses. As computers came into more widespread use, easily accessible databases were constituted, and stock market data could be processed in an entirely new way thanks to, among other things, financial econometrics (Louçã 2007). Financial econometrics marked the start of a renewal of investigative studies on empirical data and the development of econometric tests. With computers, calculations no longer had to be performed by hand, and empirical study could become more systematic and conducted on a larger scale. Attempts were made to test the random nature of stock market variations in different ways. Markowitz's hypotheses were used to develop specific computer programs to assist in making investment decisions.[42]

In addition, computers allowed the creation of databases on the evolution of stock market prices. They were used as "bookkeeping machines" recording data on phenomena. Chapter 2 will discuss the implications of these new data on the analysis of the probability distribution. Of the databases created during the 1960s, one of the most important was set up by the Graduate School of Business at the University of Chicago, one of the key institutions in the development of financial economics. In 1960, two University of Chicago professors, James Lorie and Lawrence Fisher, started an ambitious four-year program of research into security prices (Lorie 1965, 3). They created the Center for Research in Security Prices (CRSP). Roberts worked with them too. One of their goals was to build a huge computer database of stock prices to determine the returns of different investments. The first version of this database, which collected monthly prices from the New York Stock Exchange (NYSE) from January 1926 through December 1960, greatly facilitated the emergence of empirical studies. Apart from its exhaustiveness, it provided a history of stock market prices and systematic updates.

The creation of empirical databases triggered a spectacular development of financial econometrics. This development also owed much to the scientific criteria propounded by the new community of researchers, who placed particular importance on statistical tests. At the time, econometric studies revealed very divergent results regarding the representation of stock market variations by a random-walk model with the normal distribution. Economists linked to the CRSP and the Graduate School of Business at the University of Chicago—such as Moore (1962) and King (1964)—validated the random-walk hypothesis, as did Osborne (1959a, 1962), and Granger and Morgenstern (1964, 1963). On the other hand, work conducted at MIT and Harvard University established dependencies in stock market variations. For example, Alexander (1961), Houthakker (1961), Cootner (1962), Weintraub (1963), Steiger (1963), and Niederhoffer (1965) highlighted the presence of trends.[43] Trends had already been observed by some of the proponents of the random-walk hypothesis, in particular by Cowles, who, in his 1937 and 1944 articles, had observed a bias that opened up the possibility of predicting future stock market price variations. In response to a remark by Working (1960)[44] concerning the statistical explanation for these "alleged trends," Cowles redid his calculations and once more validated the existence of trends (1960, 914).

These databases changed the perception of stock markets, and it also paved the way to their statistical analysis. However, several drawbacks must be pointed out. First, it must be borne in mind that the incompleteness, the nonstandardization, errors, and misregistrations of data before the 1960s limited empirical investigations as well as the trustworthiness of their results. For instance, many trades took place outside the official markets and therefore were not recorded; the records generally focused on high market value, leading to underevaluated returns because the higher returns offered by firms with low market value are missing (Banz 1981; Annaert, Buelens, and Riva 2015). Second, data recorded were averages of prices (higher and lower day price, for instance) or closing prices. When the first databases were created, they did not collect daily data that are more time consuming than collecting monthly data. For instance, the original CRSP stock file contained month-end prices and returns from the NYSE starting from December 1925, while daily data have only been provided since July 1962. Consequently, the volatility of stock market prices/returns recorded at that time was necessary lower than the volatility observed during a market day. Chapter 2 will detail the implications of these drawbacks on the probability distribution analysis, particularly the choice for the Gaussian distribution by financial economists.

1.3. ROLE AND PLACE OF THE GAUSSIAN DISTRIBUTION IN FINANCIAL ECONOMICS

1.3.1. Stochastic Processes and the Efficient-Market Hypothesis

The overlapping of the mathematical formalisms that emerged from modern probability theory, and economics theory in particular, was a crucial factor in the birth of financial economics. In this movement, the efficient-market hypothesis had a very specific place, which is unclear to most econophysicists and financial economists. Fama developed his intuition that a random-walk model would verify two properties of competitive economic equilibrium: the absence of marginal profit and the equalization of a stock's price and value, meaning that the price perfectly reflects the available information. This project was undeniably a tour de force: creating a hypothesis that made it possible to incorporate econometric results and statistics on the random nature of stock market variations into the theory of economic equilibrium. It is through this link that one of the main foundations of current financial economics was laid down and that the importance of the random-walk model, or Brownian motion, and thus of the normal distribution, can be explained: validating the random nature of stock market variations would in effect establish that prices on competitive financial markets are in permanent equilibrium as a result of the effects of competition. This is what the efficient-market hypothesis should be, but this hypothesis does not really reach this goal.

To establish this link, Fama extended the early theoretical thinking of the 1960s and transposed onto financial markets the concept of free competitive equilibrium on which rational agents would act (1965b, 56). Such a market would be characterized by the equalization of stock prices with their equilibrium value. This value is determined by a valuation model the choice of which is irrelevant for the efficient-market hypothesis.[45] The latter considers that the equilibrium model valued stocks using all available information in accordance with the idea of competitive markets. Thus, on an efficient market, equalization of the price with the equilibrium value meant that all available information was included in prices.[46] Consequently, that information is of no value in predicting future price changes, and current and future prices are independent of past prices. For this reason, Fama considered that, in an efficient market, price variations should be random, like the arrival of new information, and that it is impossible to achieve performances superior to that of the market (Fama 1965a, 35, 98). A random-walk model thus made it possible to simulate dynamic evolution of prices in a free competitive market that is in constant equilibrium.

For the purpose of demonstrating these properties, Fama assumed the existence of two kinds of traders: the "sophisticated traders" and the normal ones. Fama's key assumption was the existence of "sophisticated traders" who, due to their skills, make a better estimate of the intrinsic/fundamental value than other agents do by using all available information. Moreover, Fama assumes that "although there are sometimes discrepancies between actual prices and intrinsic values, sophisticated traders in general feel that actual prices usually tend to move toward intrinsic values" (1965a, 38). According to Fama's hypothesis, "sophisticated traders" are better than other agents at determining the equilibrium value of stocks, and since they share the same valuation model for asset prices and since their financial abilities are superior to those of other agents (Fama 1965a, 40), their transactions will help prices trend toward the fundamental value that these sophisticated traders share. Fama added, using arbitrage reasoning, that any new information is immediately reflected in prices and that the arrival of information and the effects of new information on the fundamental value are independent (1965a, 39). The independence of stock market fluctuations, the independence of the arrival of new information, and the absence of profit made the direct connection with the random-walk hypothesis possible. In other words, on the basis of assumptions about the existence of these sophisticated traders' having financial abilities superior to those of other agents, Fama showed that the random nature of stock market variations is synonymous with dynamic economic equilibrium in a free competitive market.

But when the time came to demonstrate mathematically the intuition of the link between information and the random (independent) nature of stock market variations, Fama became elusive. He explicitly attempted to link the efficient-market hypothesis with the random nature of stock market variations in his 1970 article. Seeking to generalize, he dropped all direct references to fundamental value. The question of the number of "sophisticated traders" required to obtain efficiency (which Fama was unable to answer) was resolved by being dropped. Consequently, all agents were assumed to be perfectly rational and to have the same model for evaluating the price of financial assets (i.e., the representative-agent hypothesis). Finally, he kept the general hypothesis that "the conditions of market equilibrium can (somehow) be stated in terms of expected returns" (1970, 384). He formalized this hypothesis by using the definition of a martingale:

$$E\left(\tilde{P}_{j,t+1}\middle|\Phi_t\right)=\left[1+E\left(\tilde{r}_{j,t+1}\middle|\Phi_t\right)\right]P_{j,t},\quad \text{with}\quad r_{j,t+1}=\frac{P_{j,t+1}-P_{j,t}}{P_{j,t}}, \tag{1.3}$$

where the tilde indicates that the variable is random, P_j and r_j represent the price and return of a period of the asset *j*, *E*(./.) the conditional expectation operator, and Φ_t all information at the time *t*.

This equation implies that "the information Φ_t would be determined from the particular expected return theory at hand" (1970, 384). Fama added that "this is the sense in which Φ_t is 'fully reflected' in the formation of the price $P_{j,t}$" (1970, 384). To test the hypothesis of information on efficiency, he suggested that from this equation one can obtain the mathematical expression of a fair game, which is one of the characteristics of a martingale model and a random-walk model. Demonstration of this link would ensure that a martingale model or a random-walk model could test the double characteristic of efficiency: total incorporation of information into prices and the nullity of expected return.

This is the most well-known and used formulation of the efficient-market hypothesis. However, it is important to mention that the history of the efficient-market hypothesis went beyond the Fama (1970) article. Indeed, in 1976, LeRoy showed that Fama's demonstration is tautological and that his hypothesis is not testable. Fama answered by changing his definition and admitted that any test of the efficient-market hypothesis is a test of both market efficiency and the model of equilibrium used by investors (Fama 1976). Moreover, he modified his mathematical formulation and made his definition of efficiency more precise:

$$E_m\left(\tilde{R}_{j,t}\middle|\Phi^m_{t-1}\right)=E\left(\tilde{R}_{j,t}\middle|\Phi_{t-1}\right), \tag{1.4}$$

where $E_m\left(\tilde{R}_{j,t}\middle|\Phi^m_{t-1}\right)$ is the equilibrium expected return on security *j* implied by the set of information used by the market at *t* – 1, Φ^m_{t-1}, and $E\left(\tilde{R}_{j,t}\middle|\Phi_{t-1}\right)$ is the true expected return implied by the set of information available at *t* – 1, Φ_{t-1}. From then on, efficiency presupposes that, using Fama's own terms, the market "correctly" evaluates the "true" density function conditional on all available information. Thus, in an efficient market, the true model for valuing the equilibrium price is available to agents. To test efficiency, Fama reformulated the expected return by introducing a distinction between price—defined by the true valuation model—and agents' expectations. The test consisted in verifying whether the return expected by the market based on the information used, Φ^m_{t-1}, is equal to the expectation of true return obtained on the basis of all information available, Φ_{t-1}. This true return is obtained by using the "true" model for determining the equilibrium price. Fama proposed testing the efficiency in two ways, both of which relied on the same process. The first test consisted in verifying whether "trading rules with abnormal expected returns do not exist" (1976, 144). In other words, this was a matter of checking that one could obtain the same return as that provided by the true model of assessment of the equilibrium value on the one hand and the set of available information on the other hand. The second test would look more closely at the set of information. It was to verify that "there is no way to use the information Φ_{t-1} available at $t - 1$ as the basis of a correct assessment of the expected return on security j which is other than its equilibrium expected value" (1976, 145).

At the close of his 1976 article, Fama answered LeRoy's criticisms: the new definition of efficiency was a priori testable (we will make this point more precise hereafter). It should be noted, however, that the definition of efficiency had changed: it now referred to the true model for assessing the equilibrium value. For this reason, testing efficiency required also testing that agents were using the true assessment model for the equilibrium value of assets.[47] The test would, then, consist of using a model for setting the equilibrium value of assets—the simplest would be to take the model actually used by operators—and determining the returns that the available information would generate; then to use the same model with the information that agents use. If the same result were obtained—that is, if equation (1.4) was verified—then all the other information would indeed have been incorporated into prices. It is striking to note that this test is independent of the random nature of stock market variations. This is because, in this 1976 article, there is no more talk of random walk or martingale; no connection with a random process is necessary to test efficiency. Despite this important conclusion, Fama's article (1976) is rarely cited. Almost all authors refer to the 1970 article and keep the idea that to validate the random nature of stock market variations means validating market efficiency.

The precise linkage proposed by Fama was, however, only one of many possible linkages, as subsequent literature would demonstrate. LeRoy (1973) and Lucas (1978) provided theoretical proofs that efficient markets and the martingale hypothesis are two distinct ideas: a martingale is neither necessary nor sufficient for an efficient market. In a similar way, Samuelson (1973), who gave a mathematical proof that prices may be permanently equal to the intrinsic value and fluctuate randomly, explained that the making of profits by some agents cannot be ruled out, contrary to the original definition of the efficient-market hypothesis. De Meyer and Saley (2003) showed that stock market prices follow a martingale even if all available information is not reflected in the prices.

A proliferation of theoretical developments combined with the accumulation of empirical work led to a confusing situation. Indeed, the definition of efficient markets has changed depending on the emphasis placed by each author on a particular feature. For instance, Fama et al. (1969, 1) defined an efficient market as "a market that adjusts rapidly to new information"; Jensen (1978, 96) stated that "a market is efficient with respect to information set θ_t if it is impossible to make economic profit by trading on the basis of information set θ_t"; and according to Malkiel (1992), "The market is said to be efficient with respect to some information set ... if security prices would be unaffected by revealing that information to all participants. Moreover, efficiency with respect to an information set . . . implies that it is impossible to make economic profits by trading on the basis of [that information set]." The confusing situation is similar regarding tests: the type of test used depends on the definition used by the authors.

However, it is worth mentioning that all of these tests shared the hypothesis of normality (Gaussian distribution). Indeed, all statistical tests have been based on the central-limit theorem, which cannot be separate from the Gaussian framework. Financial economists, particularly Fama and Mandelbrot, discussed this characteristic and its consequences in the 1960s (as will be explained in chapter 2). Even today, the vast majority of statistical tests are developed in this Gaussian framework (chapters 4 and 5 will come back to this point). Moreover, some authors have used the weakness of theoretical definitions to criticize the very relevance of efficient markets. For instance, Grossman and Stiglitz (1980) argued that because information is costly, prices cannot perfectly reflect all available information. Consequently, they considered perfectly informationally efficient markets to be impossible.

In retrospect it is clear that the theoretical content of the efficient-market hypothesis refers to its suggestion of a link between a mathematical model, some empirical results, and the economic equilibrium. For analyzing the connection between the economic concept of equilibrium and the random character of stock market prices/returns, Fama assumed that information arrives randomly. In this perspective, a stochastic process describing the evolution of prices/returns should be able to test if a financial market is a free competitive market perpetually assumed to be at its equilibrium (such a framework means that the market is efficient). The choice for the Gaussian distribution/framework reflects the will of financial economists to keep statistical tests that make sense with their economic hypotheses (for instance, the fact that a security should have one price and not a set of prices). However, it is important to emphasize that this demonstration of the link between a random-walk model, or Brownian motion, and a competitive market perpetually assumed to be at its equilibrium (as predicted by the efficient-market hypothesis) holds only if information arrives randomly.

Three consequences can be deduced from the previous remarks. First, the random character of stock market prices/returns must be separated from the efficient-market hypothesis. In this context, the impossibility of obtaining returns higher than those of the market (i.e., making a profit) is sufficient for validating the efficient-market hypothesis. Second, statistical tests cannot reject this hypothesis because it is an ideal to strive for. Precisely, in economics a free competitive market is a market that would optimize global welfare; it is a theoretical ideal picture that must respect several conditions (a large number of buyers and sellers; no barriers of entry and exit; no transaction costs, etc.). Financial economists are generally aware that empirical examples contradict the ideal of freely competitive stock markets. However, despite these empirical contradictions, most financial economists hold onto this theoretical ideal. Faced with these contradictions, they try to adopt rules for going through a more free, competitive market. Such apriorism is well documented in the economics literature, where several authors have studied its potential consequences on the financial industry

(Schinckus 2008, 2012; McGoun 1997; Macintosh 2003; Macintosh et al. 2000). Third, the choice of the Gaussian framework is directly related to the need to develop statistical tests, which, due to the state of science, cannot be separated from the Gaussian distribution and the central-limit theorem.

Finally, the efficient-market hypothesis represents an essential result for financial economics, but one that is founded on a consensus that leads to acceptance of the hypothesis independent of the question of its validity (Gillet 1999, 10). The reason is easily understood: by linking financial facts with economic concepts, the efficient-market hypothesis enabled financial economics to become a proper subfield of economics and consequently to be recognized as a scientific field. Having provided this link, the efficient-market hypothesis became the founding hypothesis of the hard core of financial economics.

1.3.2. The Gaussian Framework and the Key Models of Finance

The 1960s and 1970s were years of "high theory" for financial economics (Daemen 2010) in which the hard core of the discipline was laid down.[48] The efficient-market hypothesis was a crucial building block of modern financial economics. If markets are efficient, then techniques for selecting individual securities will not generate abnormal returns. In such a world, the best strategy for a rational person seeking to maximize expected utility is to diversify optimally. Achieving the highest level of expected return for a given level of risk involves eliminating firm-specific risk by combining securities into optimal portfolios. Building on Markowitz (1952, 1959), Treynor (1961), Sharpe (a PhD student of Markowitz's) (1964, 1963), Lintner (1965a, 1965b), and Mossin (1966) made key theoretical contributions to the development of the capital-asset pricing model (CAPM) and the single-factor model, and few years after, Ross (1976a, 1977) suggested the arbitrage pricing theory (APT), which is an important extension of the CAPM. A new definition of risk was provided. It is not the total variance of a security's return that determines the expected return. Rather, only the systematic risk—that portion of total variance which cannot be diversified away—will be rewarded with expected return. An ex ante measure of systematic risk—the beta of a security—is proposed and the single-factor model used to motivate ex post empirical estimation of this parameter. Leading figures of the modern financial economics network, such as Miller, Scholes, and Black, examined the inherent difficulties in determining empirical estimates and developed important techniques designed to provide such estimates. A collection that promoted these important contributions was the volume edited by Jensen (1972).

The combination of these three essential elements—the efficient-market hypothesis, the Markowitz mean-variance portfolio optimization model, and the CAPM—constitutes the core of analytical progress on modern portfolio theory during the 1960s. Just as a decade of improvement and refinement of modern portfolio theory was about to commence, another kernel of insight contained in Cootner (1964) came to fruition with the appearance of Black and Scholes's work (1973).[49] Though the influential paper by Samuelson (1965b) was missing from the edited volume, Cootner (1964) did provide, along with other studies of option pricing, an English translation of Bachelier's 1900 thesis and a chapter by Case Sprenkle (1961) where the partial-differential-equation-based solution procedure employed by Black and Scholes was initially presented (MacKenzie 2003, 2007). With the aim of setting a price for options, Black and Scholes took the CAPM as their starting point, using this model of equilibrium to construct a null-beta portfolio made up of one unit of the underlying asset and a certain quantity of sold options.[50]

Black and Scholes (1973) marked the beginning of another scientific movement—concerned with contingent securities pricing[51]—that was to be larger in practical impact and substantially deeper in analytical complexity. The Black-Scholes-Merton model is based on the creation of a replicating portfolio that, if the model is clearly specified and its hypotheses tested, holds out the possibility of locally eliminating risk in financial markets.[52] From a theoretical point of view, this model allows for a particularly fruitful connection with the Arrow-Debreu general-equilibrium model, giving it a degree of reality for the first time. Indeed, Arrow and Debreu (1954) and later Debreu (1959) were able to model an uncertain economy and show the existence of at least a competitive general equilibrium—which, moreover, had the property of being Pareto-optimal if as many markets as contingent assets were opened. When a market system is in equilibrium according to Arrow-Debreu's framework, it is said to be complete. Otherwise, it is said to be incomplete. Black-Scholes-Merton's model gave reality to this system of complete markets by allowing that any contingent claim asset is replicable by basic assets.[53] This model takes on special theoretical importance, then, because it ties results from financial economics more closely to the concept of equilibrium from economic science.

The theories of the hard core of financial economics have had a very strong impact on the practices of the financial industry (MacKenzie and Millo 2009; Millo and Schinckus 2016). The daily functioning of financial markets today is conducted, around the clock, on concepts, theories, and models that have been defined in financial economics (MacKenzie 2006). What operators on today's financial markets do is based on stochastic calculation, benchmarks, informational efficiency, and the absence of arbitrage opportunities. The theories and models of financial economics have become tools indispensable for professional activities (portfolio management, risk measurement, evaluation of derivatives, etc.). Hereafter we give some examples to illustrate this influence.

According to efficient-market hypothesis, it is impossible to outperform the market. Together with the results of the CAPM, particularly regarding the possibility of obtaining a portfolio lying close to the efficiency frontier, this theory served as the basis for the development, from 1973[54] on, of a new way of managing funds—passive, as opposed to active, management. Funds managed this way create portfolios that mirror the performance of an externally specified index. For example, the well-known Vanguard 500 Index fund is invested in the 500 stocks of Standard & Poor's 500 Index on a market-capitalization basis. "Two professional reports published in 1998 and 1999 [on portfolio management] stated that 'the debate for and against indexing generally hinged on the notion of the informational efficiency of markets' and that 'managers' various offerings and product ranges [note: indexed and nonindexed products] often depended on their understanding of the informational efficiency of markets'" (Walter 2005, 114).[55]

Further examples of the changes brought about by the hard core of financial economics are the development of options and new ways of managing risks. The Chicago Board Options Exchange (CBOE), the first public options exchange, began trading in April 1973, and since 1975, thousands of traders and investors have been using the Black and Scholes formula every day (MacKenzie 2006; MacKenzie and Millo 2009) on the CBOE to price and hedge their option positions. By enabling a distinction to be made between risk takers and hedgers, the Black and Scholes model directly influenced the organization of the CBOE by defining how market makers can be associated with the second category, the hedgers (Millo and Schinckus 2016. Between 1974 and 2014, annual volumes of options exchanged on the CBOE rose from 5.6 million to 1.275 billion (in dollars, from $449.6 million to $579.7 billion billion) in Chicago alone. OTC derivatives notional amounts outstanding totaled $630 trillion at the end of December 2014 (www.bis.org). In 1977 Texas Instruments brought out a handheld calculator specially programmed to produce Black-Scholes options prices and hedge ratios. Merton (1998) pointed out that the influence of the Black-Scholes option theory on finance practice has not been limited to financial options traded in markets or even to derivatives generally. It is also used to price and evaluate risk in a wide array of applications, both financially and nonfinancially.

Moreover, the Black and Scholes model totally changed approaches to appraising risk since it allows risk to be individualized by giving a price to each insurance guarantee rather than mutualizing it, as was done previously. This means that a price can be put on any risk, such as the loss of the use of a famous singer's voice, which would clearly not be possible when risks are mutualized (Bouzoubaa and Osseiran 2010).

Last, we would point out that financial-market regulations increasingly make reference to concepts taken from financial economics, such as the efficiency of markets, that directly influence US legislative policies (Dunbar and Heller 2006)[56] As Hammer and Groeber (2007, 1) explain, the "efficient-market hypothesis is the main theoretical basis for legal policies that impact both Fraud on the Market and doctrines in security regulation litigation." The efficient-market hypothesis was invoked as an additional justification for the existing doctrine of fraud on the market, thereby strengthening the case for class actions in securities-fraud litigation. The efficient-market hypothesis demonstrated that every fraudulent misrepresentation was necessarily reflected in stock prices, and that every investor could rely solely on those prices for transactions (Jovanovic et al. 2016). Chane-Alune (2006) emphasizes the incidence of the efficient-market hypothesis on accounting standardization, while Miburn (2008, 293) notes that the theory directly influences the international practice of certified accountants: "It appears that arguments typically put forward by the International Accounting Standards Board and the FASB for the relevance of fair value for financial reporting purposes do imply a presumption of reasonably efficient markets."

1.3.3. The Mathematical Foundations of the Gaussian Framework

This final section looks at the role of the mathematical properties of Brownian motion (continuity and normal distribution) and their importance in the creation of the hard core of financial economics. The importance of Brownian motion clearly emerges from the work of Harrison, Kreps, and Pliska, who laid down the mathematical framework—using a probability framework based on the measure theory—for much of current financial economics, and for the Black-Scholes-Merton model and the efficient-market hypothesis in particular.

Harrison and Kreps (1979), Kreps (1981), and Harrison and Pliska (1981) proposed a general model for the valuation of contingent claim assets with no arbitrage opportunity. They showed that on any date the price of an asset is the average of its discounted terminal flows, weighted by a so-called risk-neutral probability.[57] In order to obtain a single risk-neutral probability and thus to have a complete market, these authors hypothesized that variations in the underlying asset followed Brownian motion. If the price did not follow Brownian motion, then the market would not be complete, which would imply that the option price was not unique and that exact replication by a self-financing strategy (i.e., there is neither investment nor withdrawal of money) would no longer be possible.[58] Unique price and exact replication are two central hypotheses of financial economics. The uniqueness of the price of a good or asset originates from the "law of one price" in economics, which is a constituent part of financial economics. Exact replication by means of a self-financing strategy is based on the one-price hypothesis associated with arbitrage reasoning that, as we have seen, enables an equilibrium situation on a market to be obtained—thus making the absence of arbitrage opportunity the financial-economics counterpart of equilibrium in economics.

The efficient-market hypothesis also has roots in Brownian motion (section 1.3.1). The definition put forward by Jensen (1978) and found in Malkiel (1992) is without doubt one of the easiest to apply: "A market is efficient with respect to information set θ_t if it is impossible to make economic profit by trading on the basis of information set θ_t." This definition is equivalent to the no-arbitrage principle as defined by Harrison, Kreps, and Pliska, according to which it should not be possible to make a profit with zero net investment and without bearing any risk. The absence of arbitrage opportunities as defined by Harrison, Kreps, and Pliska indeed made it possible to give a mathematical definition of the theory of informational efficiency proposed by Fama. Now, as we have just pointed out, the demonstration by Harrison, Kreps, and Pliska relies on the mathematical properties of Brownian motion.

The capital-asset pricing model, the arbitrage pricing theory, and modern portfolio theory, also components of the hard core of financial economics, were built on the mean-variance optimization developed by Markowitz. This optimization owes its results to the hypothesis that the returns of financial assets are distributed according to the normal distribution. Similarly, assuming that the returns of an efficient stock market are influenced by a large number of firm-specific economic factors that should add up to something resembling the normal distribution, the creators of CAPM took their hypothesis from the central-limit theorem.

Without any question, the normal distribution, and its cousin, Brownian motion, or the Wiener process, are fundamental hypotheses for reasoning within the mathematical framework of financial economics:[59] "While many quantitative financiers would gladly dispose of the Brownian motion, the absence of arbitrage, or a free lunch, is a cornerstone principle few could do without. In the light of these discoveries, the researcher wishing to reject Brownian diffusion as description of the evolution of returns must first invent an alternative mechanism, which would include the concept of arbitrage. This is not impossible but it requires a very radical conceptual revision of our current understanding of financial economics."[60]

1.4. CONCLUSION

This chapter analyzed the theoretical and methodological foundations of financial economics, which are embedded in the Gaussian framework. The historical, mathematical, and practical reasons justifying these foundations were investigated.

Since the first works in modern finance in the 1960s, the Gaussian distribution has been considered to be the law ruling any random phenomena. Indeed, the authors based their stochastic models on results deduced from the central-limit theorem, which led to the systematic use of the Gaussian distribution. In this perspective, the major objective of these developments was to "reveal" the Gaussian distribution in the data. When observations did not fit with the normal distribution or showed some extreme values, authors commonly used a log-linear transformation to obtain the normal distribution. However, it is worth reminding that, in the 1960s, prices were recorded monthly or daily, implying a dilution of price volatility.

In this chapter, we explained that financial econometrics and statistical tests became key scientific criteria in the development of financial economics. Given that the vast majority of statistical tests have been developed in the Gaussian framework, the latter was viewed as a necessary scientific tool for the treatment of financial data.

Finally, this chapter clarified the links between the Gaussian distribution and the efficient-market hypothesis. More precisely, the random character of stock market prices/returns must be separated from the efficient-market hypothesis. In other words, any stochastic process, including the Gaussian one, will not provide an empirical validation for this hypothesis.

For all these reasons, the Gaussian distribution becomes a key element of financial economics. The following chapter will study how financial economists have dealt with extreme values given the scientific constraints dictated by the Gaussian framework.

2

EXTREME VALUES IN FINANCIAL ECONOMICS
FROM THEIR OBSERVATION TO THEIR INTEGRATION INTO THE GAUSSIAN FRAMEWORK

The previous chapter explained how the Gaussian framework played a key role in the development of financial economics. It also pointed out how the choice for the normal distribution was directly related to the kind of data available at that time. Given the inability of the Gaussian law to capture the occurrence of extreme values, chapter 2 studies the techniques financial economists use to deal with extreme variations on financial markets. This point is important for the general argument of this book because the existence of large variations in the stock prices/returns is often presented by econophysicists as the major justification for the importation of their models in finance. While financial economists have mainly used stochastic processes with Gaussian distribution to model stock variations, one must not assume that they have ignored extreme variations. On the contrary, this chapter will show that the possibility of modeling extreme variations has been sought since the creation of financial economics in the early 1960s. From an econophysics viewpoint, this statement may surprise: there are countless publications on extreme values in finance. However, few econophysicists seem to be aware of them, since they usually ignore or misunderstand the solutions that financial economists have implemented. Indeed, statistical analysis of extreme variations is at the heart of econophysics, and the integration of these variations into stochastic processes is the main purpose of this discipline, as will be shown in chapter 3. From this perspective, a key question is, how does financial economics combine Gaussian distribution with other statistical frameworks in order to characterize the occurrence of extreme values?

This chapter aims to investigate this question and the reasons that financial economists decided to keep the Gaussian distribution. First of all, this chapter will review the first observations of extreme values made by economists. Afterward, we will analyze their first attempts to model these observations by using stable Lévy processes. The difficulties in using these processes will be detailed by emphasizing the reasons that financial economists did not follow this path. We will then study the alternative paths that were developed to consider extreme values. Two major alternatives will be considered here: the ARCH-type models and the jump-diffusion processes. To sum up, this chapter shows that although financial economists have integrated extreme variations into their models, they use different stochastic processes than econophysicists.

2.1. EMPIRICAL EVIDENCES

2.1.1. Extreme Values in the Current Stock Price Variations

Although anyone who looks at stock current movements will observe some extreme variations, they are relatively rare. Their occurrence can be observed in all kinds of listed companies (public or state-owned) and over any time scale. For example, monthly variations of returns for the private company IBM listed on the New York Stock Exchange (NYSE) show several such extreme variations (figure 2.1).

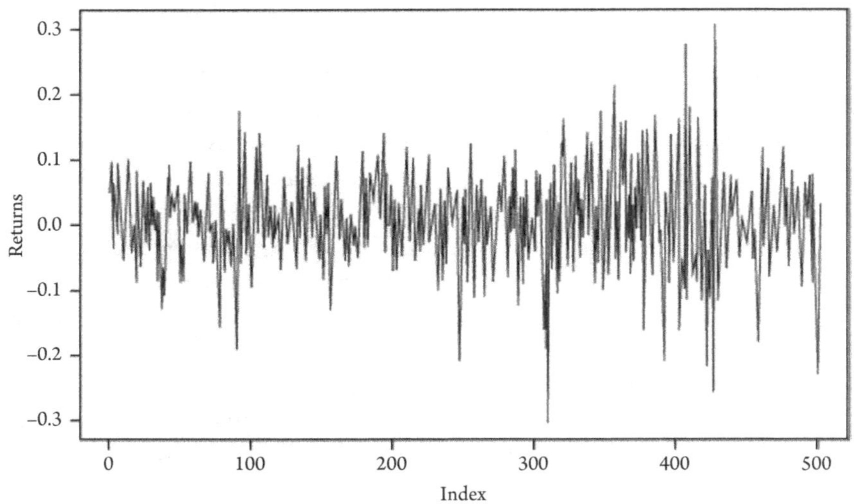

Figure 2.1 Time plot of monthly log returns of IBM stock from March 1967 to December 2012
Source: Google Finance.

Extreme variations are also present in daily returns of the same stock (figure 2.2).

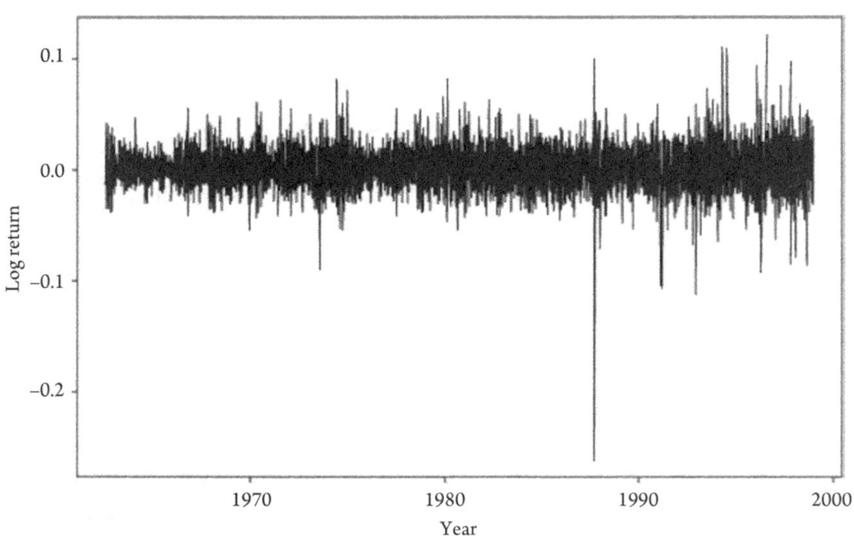

Figure 2.2 Time plot of daily log returns of IBM stock from July 1962 until December 1998
Source: Google Finance.

Similar observations exist for most stocks, currencies, and other commodities listed on any financial market around the world. The challenge for theoreticians is therefore to find the most appropriate statistical framework for describing variations as observed empirically.

From a statistical point of view, the occurrence of these extreme values is generally associated with what statisticians call the leptokurticity of empirical distribution. Schematically, leptokurtic distributions (such as the dotted line in figure 2.3) have higher peaks (characterized by long tails on both sides of the mean) around the mean than does the normal distribution (the solid line in figure 2.3), which has short statistical tails.

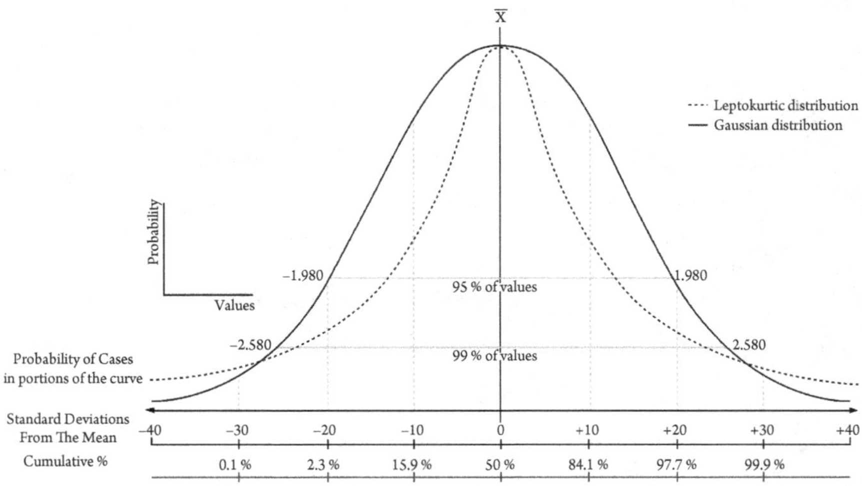

Figure 2.3 Visual comparison between the Gaussian distribution (solid line) and a more leptokurtic distribution (dotted line) for an infinity of observations

Long tails observed in leptokurtic distributions signify that portion of the distribution which has a large number of occurrences far from the mean. For instance, with the Gaussian distribution the probability of a fluctuation 2.6 times the standard deviation is less than 1 percent. This implies that extreme values are extremely rare. By contrast, with the more leptokurtic distribution represented in figure 2.3, such a fluctuation is more probable and therefore more important (depending on the value of parameters associated with the distribution), meaning that the possibility of large variations is greater in the distribution. In other words, long tails in a distribution describe the behavior of a variable for which extreme variations occur more often than in the case of the Gaussian distribution. For illustrative purposes, consider that the occurrence of a financial crash is equivalent to a fluctuation five times the standard deviation suggested by the Gaussian framework, in which a financial crash has a probability of less than 0.000057 percent (that would mean a crash every 10,000 years, according to Mandelbrot 2004).[1]

Although the Gaussian distribution has been widely used by financial economists, mainly for its interesting statistical and mathematical properties (chapter 1), it does not provide a full description of empirical data (figure 2.4a). In contrast, a leptokurtic distribution implies that small changes are less frequent than in the Gaussian case, but that extreme moves are more likely to occur and are potentially much larger than in the Gaussian distribution, as shown in figure 2.4b.

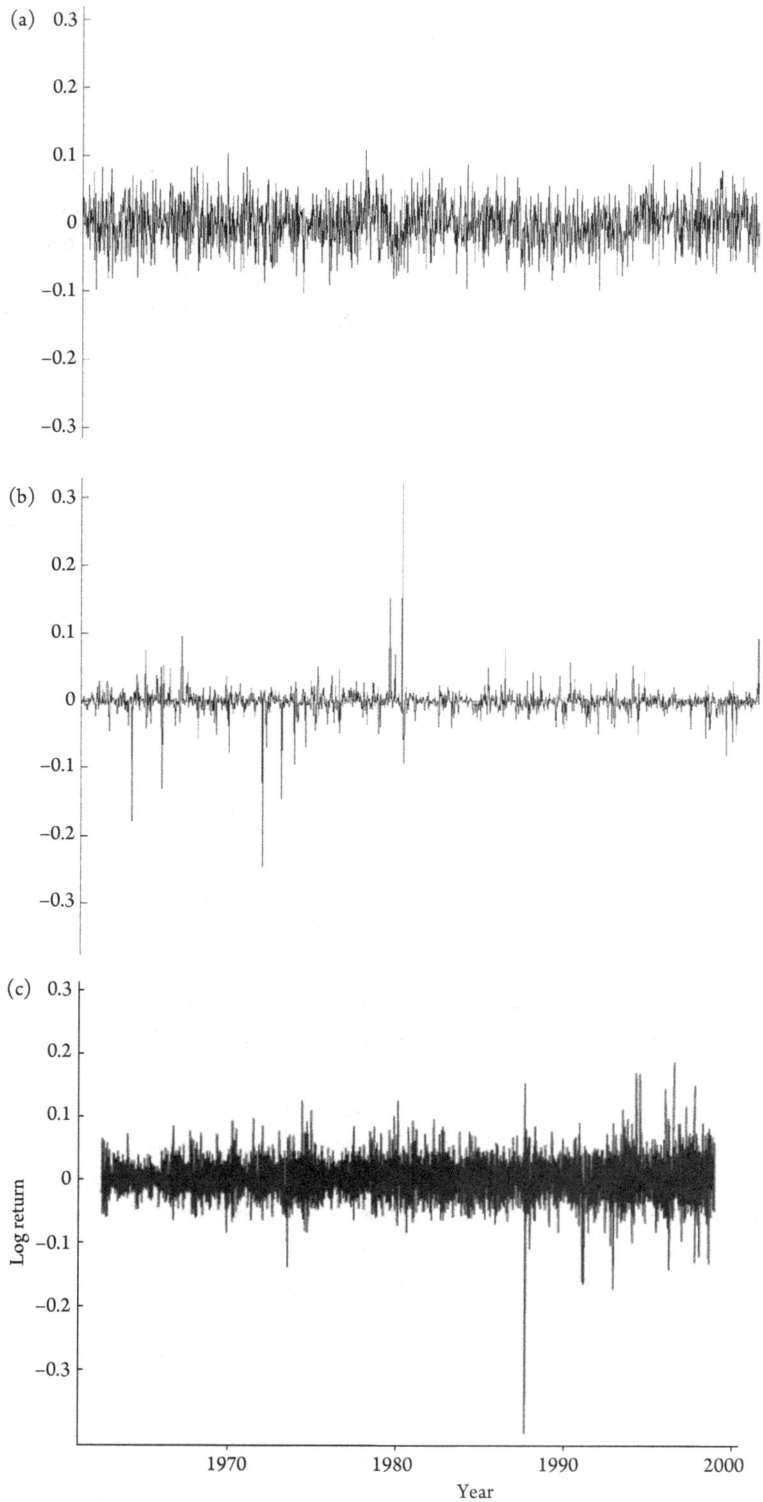

Figure 2.4 (a) Gaussian simulation describing the dynamics of financial data
(b) Paretian simulation (based on a leptokurtic distribution) describing the dynamics of financial data
(c) Empirical evolution of financial data (time plot of daily log returns of IBM stock from July 1962 until December 1998)
Source: Google Finance and authors.

In this figure we see that using a stochastic process with a Gaussian distribution (figure 2.4a) does not allow extreme variations of stock prices or returns to be reproduced (figure 2.4c). In contrast, a Paretian simulation opens a room for the statistical characterization of extreme variations (figure 2.4b). Obviously, this inability to capture the occurrence of extreme variations is a major limitation of the Gaussian framework for reproducing stock variations and consequently for analyzing risk or for theoretical models. In this challenging context, financial economists had to find a way to capture the occurrence of extreme values in the evolution of stock prices/returns.

2.1.2. Early Evidence of Extreme Values

Chapter 1 pointed out that the first authors to study stock price fluctuations did not perform systematic analysis of the distribution.[2] The Gaussian distribution was for them simply the most obvious distribution to use, first because it was commonly used in science at the time, and second because of its mathematical properties, particularly the fact that Gaussian law was seen as the asymptotic limit of statistical laws in common use. In 1863, Regnault introduced the Gaussian distribution because it was the "scientific law" in social sciences, and also for ethical reasons. Regnault is one of the authors studied in chapter 1 who analyzed the distribution of stock price variations as such. The empirical data he had were imprecise (the highest and lowest price for each month), but they were sufficient to confirm the normal distribution and the fact that stock price variations followed the square root of time. In 1900, Louis Bachelier in turn used the normal distribution for mathematical reasons, this distribution having the right mathematical properties for the demonstration he wished to make. Bachelier did not study the distribution of stock prices as such; he used the same data as Regnault (the French 3 percent bond) to validate his mathematical demonstration. In 1908, Vinzenz Bronzin justified the Gaussian distribution for modeling stock price variations for the same reason as Bachelier: "Total mathematical expectations of gains and losses are equal to one another at the moment when the respective deals are struck" (Hafner and Zimmermann 2009, 156). Like Bachelier, he did not study the distribution of stock prices as such. Finally, the first authors (Working, Cowles) to make empirical studies on stock prices in the United States in the 1930s sought to demonstrate the independence of stock price variations. Here again, except for the work of Cowles and Jones (1937),[3] research was not focused on the distribution but aimed at confirming the independence of stock price variations. Paradoxically, the first analyses of the distribution of stock market fluctuations were not developed by these authors, but by macroeconomists and statisticians whose research was conducted independently of early research dedicated to financial markets.

From the late nineteenth century until the outbreak of World War I, there was massive development of measurement techniques.[4] As Morgan and Klein (2001) showed, this "age of economic measurement" involved the use of various instruments to describe empirical phenomena. Inside this movement, economists who were interested in macroeconomic forecasts via barometers studied stock price variations and their distribution too.[5] The first American economic barometers, designed for the study and forecasting of business cycles, appeared in the early twentieth century (Armatte 1992,

2003; Chancelier 2006b, 2006a; Morgan 1990). The leader was Harvard's forecasting barometer, created in 1916 by the Economic Office of Harvard and supervised by Professor Warren Persons.[6] Harvard's barometer became famous for its three curves (labeled A, B, and C), representing stock prices, the level of business, and the interest rate on the money market. This approach spread to Europe in the 1920s, when French statistician Lucien March constructed a French business barometer based on index numbers that was seen as an equivalent to the Harvard barometer (Jovanovic and Le Gall 2001). With the development of barometers, economists—for example Fisher[7] and Mitchell[8] (Armatte 1992; Banzhaf 2001; Diewert 1993)—became increasingly interested in the construction of indices, among them the stock price index. According to barometer analysis, stock price movements were an important indicator of economic activity, and this belief led economists to study stock price variations and their distributions. Economists interested in barometers were among the first to notice that stock price variations were not necessarily distributed according to the normal distribution. Among them, Mitchell (1915) seems to have been the first to empirically detect and describe extreme variations in wholesale price time series. He found that distribution of percentage changes in prices consistently deviated from normal distribution (Mitchell 1915, 19–21). Mills (1927, chap. 3) also stressed the leptokurtic character of financial distributions. However, two points must be underlined here: first, neither Mitchell nor Mills studied stock prices per se (they were more interested in the direction of the prices than in the volatility of the series); second, the distribution was not the core of their analysis, which, like business barometers, focused on macroeconomic predictions.

Three other authors deserve our attention. Irving Fisher (1922) did some analysis of stock market prices in his book on index numbers; he noted in particular the absence of correlation in stock prices (Dimand and Geanakoplos 2005; Dimand 2007). Moore must also be mentioned. In his book, published in October 1917, he analyzed the price of cotton quoted on the stock market and compared the actual distribution of spot cotton prices to the theoretical normal distribution (Le Gall 1999, 2006). Even though the histogram created from real price changes has high peaks and fat tails compared to the Gaussian distribution (Moore 1917, 26), Moore ignored these observations and considered that the variations in cotton prices were normally distributed. Later, Arthur Lyon Bowley (1933) discussed the distribution of prices, particularly stock prices, taking the length of time studied into account. He found that for short periods (e.g., one year), a normal distribution provides a good approximation of stock prices, but that "when we take the longer period 1924 to 1930, resemblance to the normal curve is not present" (Bowley 1933, 369). To circumvent this difficulty while preserving the Gaussian distribution (and consequently its mathematical properties), he proposed considering the logarithm of the price in some cases (Bowley 1933, 370).[9]

These were not the only authors of the period to identify the leptokurtic nature of the distribution of stock market fluctuations. This finding was shared by a number of statisticians and French engineers (known at the time as *ingénieurs économistes*). As explained by Jovanovic and Le Gall (2001), these *ingénieurs économistes* developed an indisputable talent for measurement in economics. Their involvement in measurement and more generally in statistics became particularly apparent around 1900: Statistique Générale de la France (SGF), the main government statistical agency at that time, became something of an engineers' fortress. Although the SGF remained small in comparison with other European statistical bureaus, its early-twentieth-century achievements—in data collection and in formulating explanations of what had been measured—remain impressive. A large part of its work can be attributed to Lucien March (Huber 1937). March (1921) was the first author to analyze whether the probability calculus and the law of large numbers were relevant for studying, in particular, whether relative prices are distributed around their mean according to Gaussian law. He pointed out that that distribution did not conform to Gaussian law: occurrences far from the mean occurred too frequently and were too large. In addition, during the 1910s, SGF statisticians under Marcel Lenoir became interested in the effects of stock market fluctuations on economic activity (Chaigneau and Le Gall 1998). In 1919 Lenoir developed the first long-term indices for the French stock market. These examples should not cause us to forget that analysis of price distribution was still rare when another author, Maurice Olivier, published his doctoral thesis in 1926, wherein he correctly pointed out that "a series of indices should never be published unless the distribution of the data used to calculate the index is published at the same time" (1926, 81). Olivier can be considered to have provided the first systematic analysis of price distribution. He obtained the same result as March: the distribution of price variations did not fit with normal distribution. Several decades later, Kendall (1953) studied a number of price series by analyzing their variations (see chapter 1) and pointed out that some of them were leptokurtic.

Although these authors noted the fact that distributions of stock price variations were not strictly Gaussian, there was no systematic research into this topic at the time. Distributions were only a matter of observation and were not mathematically modeled by a specific statistical framework. Econometrics was in its beginnings and not yet organized as a discipline (Le Gall 1994, 2006; Morgan 1990), and economists were interested in empirical investigations into dynamic business cycles (i.e., barometers). Moreover, even Vilfredo Pareto (1848–1923), who was widely known for his research on the leptokurtic nature of distribution of wealth in Italy at the beginning of the twentieth century (Barbut 2003), did not analyze the dynamics of price variations (he made a static analysis). Only one exception to this pattern can be mentioned, since Luigi Amoroso used a Paretian distribution in a dynamic analysis of incomes (Tusset 2010).

2.1.3. Confirmations in the 1960s and the 1970s

These early findings had very little impact because financial economics was not yet established as a scientific discipline. Moreover, econometrics was a very young discipline and the data collected had several drawbacks. With some exceptions, each author worked with his own empirical data. Consequently, standard data did not exist and a comparison between results was difficult. The low quality of the data was also a real problem. For instance, the volume and price of all transactions were not compulsorily recorded. Moreover, on the NYSE, when the volume of transactions was exceptionally large, successive transactions made at the same price were recorded as a single transaction (Godfrey, Granger, and Morgenstern 1964, 7). In addition, it is worth mentioning that available data were computed as a monthly average, which dilutes the volatility. Although weekly data were collected beginning in the 1920s (1921 in the United

Kingdom and 1923 in the United States), they were available only for the wholesale prices of a small number of foods.[10] Finally, the quantity of data was limited, and consequently the opportunity to observe extreme values or rare events was very limited.

The situation changed completely in the 1960s, as discussed in chapter 1. The creation of financial economics as a scientific discipline, on the one hand, and the building of the first comprehensive database (through the creation of the CRSP), on the other, made the development of work in financial econometrics possible. Moreover, with the creation of financial economics, empirical validation became a prerequisite for publication of research. The introduction of computers into university departments also facilitated changes. Thus, from the 1960s onward, financial economists and especially MA and PhD students systematically tested the statistical indicators of the random character of stock market fluctuations, such as the independence, the distribution, and the stability of the process. Some of them also developed new tests to validate the models used in "hard core" financial economics.[11] However, as Jovanovic (2008) has shown, empirical results indicating the random character of stock market prices are inseparable from the underlying theoretical assumptions guiding the gathering and interpretation of data, especially the assumption of perfect markets, defended at the Chicago Graduate School of Business, or of imperfect markets, defended at MIT. Opinion on the randomness of stock market fluctuations was far from unanimous: authors from the Chicago Graduate School of Business validated randomness empirically, while authors from the MIT did not. The same was true of the identification and analysis of extreme values: while econometric studies established several important results, there was no universally shared result regarding leptokurtic distributions.

Some authors pointed out extreme values in stock market fluctuations. For instance, Larson (1960, 380) identified "an excessive number of extreme values" that did not accord with a Gaussian process. Houthakker (1961, 168) concluded that "the distribution of day-to-day changes in the logarithms of prices does not conform to the normal curve. It is not significantly skew, but highly leptokurtic. . . . The variance of price changes does not seem to be constant over time. . . . The leptokurticity mentioned above may be related to the changing variance." Studying a sample of 85,000 observations, Brada, Ernst, and van Tassel observed that "the distributions, in all cases, are excessively peaked. However . . . there are no fat tails. At this point we suggest that stock prices differenced across single transactions are not normally distributed, not because they have fat tails, but because they are too peaked" (1966, 337). Let us also mention Sprenkle (1961, 1964), who also noted that the stock price distribution was not Gaussian.

It is clear that with the creation of financial economics and the development of stock price databases, the distribution of stock price variations, and their leptokurtic character in particular, began to be apparent and widely analyzed by financial economists. Although each author presented his empirical results with confidence, these results should primarily be considered as statistical indices, because empirical data and tests were still new at that time. However, this field of study underwent a radical change when the leptokurtic nature of changes in stock prices became the subject of mathematical investigations from 1962 onward.

2.2. FINANCIAL ECONOMISTS AND PARETO-LÉVY DISTRIBUTIONS

Mathematical treatment of extreme variations in financial economics gained impetus from Benoit Mandelbrot's work on stable Lévy processes.

2.2.1. Interesting Properties of Stable Lévy Processes for Extreme Variations

As we saw in chapter 1, various authors subscribed, explicitly or implicitly, to the normal-distribution hypothesis on account of its mathematical properties and more particularly of its links with the central-limit theorem, according to which distribution of a set of identically distributed independent random variables will converge toward a Gaussian distribution. But this was not the only mathematical property of interest to these authors. The Gaussian framework implies that distribution of the process is "stable" (by addition) over time.

The stability of a random process means that any linear combination of the independent and identically distributed random variables of this process will generate a random variable that has the same probability distribution. For instance, the sum of any number of Gaussian random variables is itself a Gaussian random variable.[12] This statistical property is very useful for financial modeling because it allows data to be analyzed independently from the time scale: if variables are independent and distributed in accordance with normal law, the estimate of statistical characteristics observed at a given time scale (monthly) can be applied to another analysis time scale (annual or daily). Thus, the stability of the process makes it possible to analyze the monthly return of a stock as the sum of its daily returns.

In his efforts to model extreme values, the mathematician Benoit Mandelbrot noted that these mathematical properties are not specific to Gaussian processes, as the French mathematician Paul Lévy had shown in the 1920s. Mandelbrot was a student of Lévy and worked on the mathematical infinity of empirical phenomena assuming infinite divisibility of observations. Lévy had defined a category of stochastic processes, $X = X(t)$ with $t \geq 0$, that have right-continuous paths whose increments are independent and identically distributed (i.i.d.), and that satisfy the following conditions:

(1) X has independent and stationary increments.
(2) $X(0) = 0$ with a probability one.
(3) X is stochastically continuous, that is, $\forall t > 0$ and $\forall s \geq 0$,

$$\lim_{t \to s} P\big((X(t) - X(s)) > 0\big) = 0.$$

The general characteristic function $\Phi(t)$ of these processes is[13]

$$\log \Phi(t) = \begin{cases} -\sigma^{\alpha}|t|^{\alpha}\left\{1 - i\beta sign(t)\tan\frac{\pi\alpha}{2}\right\} + i\gamma t, \alpha \neq 1 \\ -\sigma^{\alpha}|t|\left\{1 - i\beta sign(t)\frac{2}{\pi}\log|t|\right\} + i\gamma t, \alpha = 1 \end{cases}. \tag{2.1}$$

This function requires four parameters (α, β, γ, δ) to be described; the parameter δ does not need to be shown here.[14] Lévy's definition makes it possible to define a great number of processes (Gauss, Poisson, Cauchy, Pareto, Gamma, generalized hyperbolic processes), depending on the distribution.

Through this definition, one can show that the stability of the distribution of the stochastic process depends on the value of these four parameters: a stochastic process is said to be stable if $0 < \alpha \leq 2$, $\gamma \geq 0$, $-1 \leq \beta \leq 1$, $\delta \in \mathfrak{R}$. As Nolan (2009) reminded the only necessary condition concerns the value of the α:[15] all Lévy processes with $0 < \alpha \leq 2$ are said to be stable. Consequently, following Feller (1971), the definition of a stable process can simply be formulated in terms of distribution (rather than in terms of characteristic function): a random variable X has a stable distribution if, for n independent copies X_i of X, there exists a positive number C_n and a real number D_n such that the following relationship is valid for $0 < \alpha \leq 2$:

$$X_1 + X_2 + \cdots + X_n \overset{d}{=} C_n X + D_n. \tag{2.2}$$

Finally, Lévy's work made it possible to introduce a set of stable stochastic processes that can be used to model stock price variations from an empirical estimate of the four parameters (α, β, γ, δ). Here is a brief reminder of the interpretation of these parameters. The parameter α (called the "characteristic exponent") is the index of stability of the distribution. The value of this exponent determines the shape of the distribution: the smaller this exponent is, the fatter the tails are (extreme events have a higher probability of occurring). In other words, the lower α is, the more often extreme events are observed. In financial terms, this parameter is an indicator of risk, since it describes how often substantial variations can occur. The parameter β, termed "skewness," provides information about the symmetry of the distribution. If $\beta = 0$, the distribution is symmetric. If $\beta < 0$ it is skewed toward the left (totally asymmetric toward the left if $\beta = -1$) while $\beta > 0$ indicates a distribution skewed towards the right (totally asymmetric towards the left if $\beta = -1$). The parameter γ is the scale factor, which can be any positive number. It refers to the "random size," that is, the size of variance whose regularity is given by the exponent α. This parameter describes the size of the variations (whose regularity is given by α). Finally, the parameter δ is a localization factor: it shifts the distribution right if $\delta > 0$ and left if $\delta < 0$.

Thanks to the value of these parameters, stable Lévy distribution provides a general framework that makes it possible to characterize both the Gaussian distribution (one that does not include extreme values) and a Paretian distribution (one that includes extreme values).

2.2.2. The First Attempts to Model Extreme Variations with Pareto-Lévy Distributions

The first attempts to model extreme stock market price variations using stable Lévy processes were the work of Mandelbrot. After graduating in France, he left for the

United States permanently in 1958 and began working for IBM. From the beginning of his research, Mandelbrot aimed to extend statistical physics to other fields, including social sciences. In his 1957 report, he set out his "interdisciplinary" project: "It appears that the author's activity has by now been durably oriented along the lines of a long-range program, having two aspects: the study of physical and non-physical applications of thermodynamics, and the study of the 'universal' foundations" (1957, 4). His approach was "to distinguish the part of thermodynamics, which is so general that it could also conceivably apply to systems more general than sets of molecules" (1957, 2). Mandelbrot started his ambitious program of investigations (nonphysical applications of thermodynamics) with the structure of language, texts, and communication, moving on to distributions of species, and then to income distributions. In this perspective, he proposed to expand Pareto's work on income distributions by representing these distributions by Lévy distribution in the late 1950s.[16] In 1961, he was invited to present his work on income distribution at a Harvard University seminar. On this occasion, Mandelbrot entered Hendrik Houthakker's office and came face to face with a graphical representation of the distribution of changes in cotton prices that was similar to the results he had obtained with incomes: "Houthakker's cotton chart looked like my income chart. The math was the same" (Mandelbrot 1963, 394 n. *). This parallelism led him to apply the stable Lévy process to cotton prices, which was the longest, most complete time series with daily quotations available at the time, and then to stock price movements. He published a first article on the topic in 1962 and gave lectures at Harvard in 1962, 1963, and 1964.

Mandelbrot's starting point was to postulate an infinite variance. It is clear that infinite variance cannot be observed in the real world:

> In practice, it is of course impossible to ever attain any limit corresponding to an infinitely large T, or to ever verify any condition relative to an infinitely large u. Hence, in practice, one must consider that a month or a year are [*sic*] infinitely long, and that the largest observed daily changes of log Z(t) are infinitely large." (Mandelbrot 1962b, 28)

Mandelbrot justified his postulate by the need to distinguish physical infinity, which cannot be observed, from mathematical infinity, which can be postulated to model real-world phenomena: "Let me begin by reassuring you that an infinite variance is not the consequence of my mistakenly taking the logarithm of zero. The concept of infinity, as used in engineering and physics, is not the same as the mathematician's infinity.... there is a range of cases where a variance that is really finite can be safely considered infinite.... I was led to postulate an 'infinite variance' as the simplest way of mathematically describing the outliers, and of emphasizing their very strong contribution and their very erratic behavior from one year to the next" (Mandelbrot 1966b, 2).

Since we cannot observe infinite variance in practice, we can conceive it by assuming that time is infinitely divisible and that this infinite divisibility does not affect the properties of a distribution. In other words, the distribution of a random process must be stable (or "invariant").[17] For stock prices, this means that the distribution of the result of changes in prices of a given frequency (hour, day, week, etc.) remains the same regardless of the length of time considered (one day, several weeks, one year) or, in other words, whatever the number of observations. Thus, thanks to the stability of probability distributions, a daily observation can be thought of as 24 hourly observations or 1,440 per-minute observations or even 86,400 per-second observations, and so on. By conceptualizing the infinite divisibility of time, one can give real meaning to the mathematical hypothesis of infinity.

In sum, drawing on Lévy's work (1924) on the stability of probability distributions and that of Gnedenko and Kolmogorov (1954)[18] on the generalization of the central-limit theorem, Mandelbrot used a Pareto-Lévy distribution for two reasons (Mandelbrot 1960, 80):

1. It is a possible limit distribution with infinite variance of the sums of random independent and identically distributed variables (i.e., generalized central-limit theorem).
2. It is stable (i.e., it is time invariant) in its Pareto form.

Mandelbrot pointed out several advantages of using stable Pareto-Lévy processes with infinite variance. First, these processes can characterize the leptokurticity of stock price or return distributions. Second, they can explain some dependence in stock price variations, particularly the "dependencies" detected by Alexander (1961). Third, they can explain some breaks in the structure of stock price variations (the Noah effect). Fourth, they can be used even though the Gaussian distribution seems to represent some empirical observations quite well. This last advantage would have been of interest to most financial economists during the 1960s and the 1970s. Because the Gaussian distribution is the only stable distribution with a finite variance, Mandelbrot necessarily had to reject it. However, because most financial economists of the time used the Gaussian distribution, Mandelbrot took time to explain why it is a specific case of the Pareto-Lévy distribution. In particular, he explained that while, for a small sample, the observed distribution can be approximated by a Gaussian distribution, extending the sample will necessitate dropping it in favor of a Pareto-Lévy distribution. In other words, from Mandelbrot's perspective, as the amount of stock market data increased, empirical validation of the Pareto-Lévy distribution becomes essential. The lack of data at that time made the approach adopted by Mandelbrot prospective. However, he had a clear theory: a growing amount of data would necessarily cause a sample to converge toward a Pareto-Lévy distribution.[19] We will return to this prediction in chapter 4.

Fama (1963) was the first author to attempt to connect Mandelbrot's work with the core of financial economics. In his first paper, Fama presented the statistical properties of Pareto-Lévy processes from an economic point of view. Two years later, he developed a general model for portfolio analysis in a market where stock returns can be described with a Pareto-Lévy distribution. While he gave a mathematical reinterpretation of the modern portfolio theory developed by Markowitz (together with Sharpe's diagonal model), he was unable to provide a complete economic interpretation of his work because a clear computational definition of all parameters did not exist (Fama 1965b, 405). However, in his article, Fama aimed to give an economic meaning to diversification in a Pareto-Lévy framework, even if the parameter related to the dispersion of the return on the portfolio could no longer be described by the variance. From this perspective, he observed that a general increase in diversification has a direct impact on the evolution of the scale factor (γ) of the stable distribution. More precisely, increasing diversification reduces the scale of the distribution of the return on a portfolio (only when the characteristic exponent $\alpha > 1$).[20] Fama proposed, therefore, to replace variance with the scale factor (γ) of a stable distribution in order to approximate the dispersion of financial distributions. It is worth mentioning that Fama's work on the stable Lévy framework in the 1960s does not conflict with his efficient-market hypothesis (which we discussed in chapter 1), because this hypothesis assumes the perfect integration of information in financial prices with no particular hypothesis regarding the statistical process describing the evolution of financial returns. Basically, the only necessary condition for a statistical process to be consistent with the efficient-market hypothesis is the use of independent variables (and by extension i.i.d. variables), ensuring that past information is not necessary for forecasting the future evolution of variables. This is the case for stable Lévy processes.

In the same vein, Samuelson (1967) provided an "efficient portfolio selection for Pareto-Lévy investments" in which the scale factor (γ) was used as an approximation of variance (because the scale parameter is proportional to the mean absolute deviation). Samuelson presented the computation of the efficiency frontier as a problem of nonlinear programming solvable by Kuhn-Tucker techniques. However, even though he demonstrated the theoretical possibility of finding an optimal solution for a stable Lévy distribution, Samuelson gave no example or application of his technique. Other economists followed the path opened by Fama and Mandelbrot toward stable Lévy processes: Fama and Roll (1968, 1971), Blattberg and Sargent (1971), Teichmoeller (1971), Clark (1973), and Brenner (1974) were among them. Moreover, following the publications by Mandelbrot and Fama, the hypothesis of the Pareto-Lévy processes was frequently tested during the 1960s and the 1970s (Brada, Ernst, and van Tassel 1966; Godfrey, Granger, and Morgenstern 1964; Officer 1972) as explained in the following section.

2.3. MATHEMATICAL TREATMENTS OF EXTREME VALUES BY FINANCIAL ECONOMISTS

2.3.1. Difficulties Encountered with Stable Lévy Processes in the 1960s and 1970s

While research into Pareto-Lévy processes in financial economics began to gather momentum in the 1960s, the subject rapidly lost its importance among financial economists, who identified four major limitations on the use of stable Lévy processes.

First, empirical tests did not validate with certainty either infinite variance or the Pareto-Lévy processes. Not everyone found infinite variance a convincing postulate.

According to Godfrey, Granger, and Morgenstern, "No evidence was found in any of these series [of the NYSE prices] that the process by which they were generated behaved as if it possessed an infinite variance" (1964, 6). Brada, Ernst, and van Tassel observed that "the distributions [of the stock price differences], in all cases, are excessively peaked. However, contrary to The Stable Paretian hypothesis, there are no fat tails" (Brada, Ernst, and van Tassel 1966, 337). Officer (1972) wrote that stock markets have some characteristics of a non-Gaussian process but also emphasized that there was a tendency for sums of daily stock returns to become "thinner-tailed" for large sums, even though he acknowledged that the normal distribution did not approximate the distribution of his sample. Blattberg and Gonedes (1974) showed that while stable Pareto-Lévy distributions had better descriptive properties than the Gaussian one, the Student distribution[21] fit the data better. Even Mandelbrot's student, Fama, reached a similar conclusion: "Distributions of monthly returns are closer to normal than distributions of daily returns. This finding was first discussed in detail in Officer 1971, and then in Blattberg and Gonedes 1974. This is inconsistent with the hypothesis that return distributions are non-normal symmetric stable, which implies that distributions of daily and monthly returns should have about the same degree of leptokurtosis" (Fama 1976, 38).

Nor did stability of the distribution, which is one of the major statistical properties of stable Lévy processes, appear certain.[22] In the 1950s, Kendall (1953, 15) had already noticed that variance was not always stationary. Investigations carried out in the 1960s and 1970s seemed to confirm this point. Officer (1972) explained that the sum of independently distributed random variables from a stable process did not give a stable distribution with the same characteristic exponent, as required by the stability property.[23] Financial data "have some but not all properties of a stable process," and since several "inconsistencies with the stable hypothesis were observed," the evolution of financial markets cannot be described through a stable Lévy process (Officer 1972, 811). Even Fama seemed to share this view: "Contrary to the implications of the hypothesis that daily and monthly returns conform roughly to the same type of stable non-normal distribution, monthly returns have distributions closer to normal than daily returns" (Fama 1976, 33). Upton and Shannon (1979) also confirmed that stable processes were not appropriate for the analysis of empirical of time series.[24]

The second limitation to the use of stable Lévy processes in finance was the fact that, until the end of the 1970s, the theory of probability related to stable Lévy processes was still unformed (Nolan 2009). Several developments were necessary in order to apply these processes to the study of stock market fluctuations and to test them adequately. While Mandelbrot opened up a stimulating avenue for research, the formulation of the mathematical hypothesis (i.e., the Pareto-Lévy process) was not immediately followed by the development of statistical tools. A direct result of this unformed knowledge on stable Lévy processes was the absence, at the time, of statistical tests to check the robustness of results provided by these processes. Therefore, authors focused on visual tests to validate the hypothesis of non-Gaussian distribution. This situation is very similar to the first empirical work that suggested the random character of stock prices before the creation of financial economics (chapter 1). However, without appropriate statistical tests, it is simply impossible to evaluate to what extent these outcomes are statistically reliable (chapters 4 and 5 will come back to this point). Available statistical tests at the time either were constructed for the Gaussian distribution or assumed normality: examples are the Pearson test (also known as the chi-square test), which was used to test the compliance of the observed distribution with a theoretical distribution; and Student's t-test, which was used for comparing parameters such as the mean and for estimating the parameters of a population from data on a sample. Similarly, as Mandelbrot (1962, 35) explained, methods based upon the minimization of the sum of squares of sample deviations, or upon the minimization of the expected value of the square of the extrapolation error, cannot be reasonably used for non-Gaussian Lévy processes. This was true for the test of the distribution as well as for the other components of the hard core of financial economics, as Fama pointed out:

> ". . . There are admittedly difficult problems involved in applying [portfolio models with stable Paretian distributions] to practical situations. Most of these difficulties are due to the fact that economic models involving stable Paretian generating processes have developed more rapidly than the statistical theory of stable Paretian distributions." (Fama 1965b, 418)

For this reason, authors such as Mandelbrot and Fama insisted on the need "to develop more adequate statistical tools for dealing with stable Paretian distributions" (Fama 1965b, 429). Even in 1976, 14 years after Mandelbrot's first publication, Fama considered that "statistical tools for handling data from non-normal stable distributions are [still] primitive relative to the tools that are available to handle data from normal distribution" (Fama 1976, 26). It is worth keeping in mind the importance that statistical tests hold for financial economists since they founded their approach on the use of such tests, in opposition to the visual techniques used by chartists or the accounting-based analysis adopted by fundamentalists.

The third reason for explaining the meager use of stable Lévy processes in finance in the 1970s refers to the difficulty of estimating their parameters. Indeed, the use of these processes requires the identification of the four parameters that define the stable distribution. This is done by using parameterization techniques. Unfortunately, parameterization techniques were nonexistent in the 1960s and still in their infancy in the 1970s (Borak, Hardle, and Weron 2005). As Fama explained,

> The acceptability of the stable Paretian hypothesis will be improved not only by further empirical documentation of its applicability but also by making the distributions themselves more tractable from a statistical point of view. At the moment very little is known about the sampling behavior of procedures for estimating the parameters of these distributions. (1963, 428–29)

For instance, Fama (1965b, 414) emphasized that the application of stable Lévy processes in practical situations is very complicated because "the difficulty at this stage is that the scale parameter of a stable Paretian distribution is, for most values of α, a theoretical concept." That is, the mathematical statistics of stable Paretian distribution was not yet sufficiently developed to give operational or computational meaning to γ in all cases. The first estimation for symmetric stable Lévy processes was proposed by Fama and Roll (1968), who, for simplicity, assumed symmetry of stable distributions, meaning that three parameters could be equal to zero ($\mu = 0, \beta = 0, \gamma = 0$), while α was given by the following approximate formula:

$$\alpha = 1 + n\left[\sum_{i=1}^{n} \ln \frac{x_i}{x_{\min}}\right], \tag{2.3}$$

where x_i are the quantiles-based measures and $x_{\min}$ is the minimum value of x. This formula is an approximation, because the parameterization of factors depends on the size of the sample. It is worth mentioning that this parameterization technique[25] was the only one available at the end of the 1960s. Because results given by quantiles-based methods depend directly on the size of the sample, Press (1972) proposed a second method based on their characteristic function. Given that the generalized central-limit theorem requires a huge (theoretically an infinite) amount of data, Press combined observations from the empirical samples with extrapolations made from these data. He was therefore able to generate a large quantity of data.[26]

All the methods that emerged in the 1970s for parameterizing these stable Lévy processes had one serious drawback: while quantiles-based (called nonparametric) methods directly depended on the size of the sample, the characteristic-function-based (called spectral) methods depended on the extrapolation technique used to minimize the difference between empirical results given by the sample and theoretical results. The impossibility of parameterizing stable Lévy processes explained why financial economists were not inclined to use them.

Finally, the fourth barrier to the use of stable Lévy processes in finance concerns the infinity of variance, which has no theoretical interpretation congruent with the theoretical framework of financial economics. As discussed in chapter 1, variance and the expected mean are two of the main variables for the theoretical interpretations of financial economists, which associated risk with variance and return with the mean.[27] From this perspective, if variance is infinite, it is impossible to understand the notion of risk as financial economists define it. In other words, the statistical characteristics of stable Lévy processes could not be integrated into the theoretical framework of financial economics, which provided significant operational results. Financial economists focused on statistical solutions that were theoretically compatible with the Gaussian framework. Fama and Roll (1971, 337) emphasized this difficulty of working with a non-Gaussian framework in the social sciences, where "economists, psychologists and sociologists frequently dismiss non-normal distributions as data models because they cannot believe that processes generating prices, breakdowns, or riots, can fail to have second moments."

It is worth mentioning that, in the beginning of the 1970s, financial economics was a young field trying to assert its ability to provide scientific reasoning about financial reality, and financial economists did not necessarily want to deal with a scientific puzzle (the interpretation of infinite variance) that could discredit the scientific reputation of their emerging field. Knowing these limitations, and because the Gaussian framework had allowed the development of financial economics while achieving remarkable theoretical and practical results (chapter 1), several authors,[28] including Fama, proposed acceptance of the Gaussian framework as a good approximation:

> Although the evidence also suggests that distributions of monthly returns are slightly leptokurtic relative to normal distributions, let us tentatively accept the normal model as a working approximation for monthly returns. . . . If the model does well on this score [how well it describes observed relationships between average returns and risk], we can live with the small observed departures from normality in monthly returns, at least until better models come along. (Fama 1976, 38)

Fama added:

> Although most of the models of the theory of finance can be developed from the assumption of stable non-normal return distributions . . . the cost of rejecting normality for securities returns in favor of stable non-normal distributions are substantial." (Fama 1976, 26)

In other words, at the end of the 1970s, Mandelbrot's hypothesis could not yet be applied for modeling extreme values in financial markets. However, as Mandelbrot (1962) had already pointed out, the four major limitations evoked above do not necessarily contradict the Pareto-Lévy framework; they simply made it impossible to use this approach in the 1970s. This conclusion can also be drawn from the paper by Officer (1972), who mentioned that his sample was not large enough to justify the use of a nonnormal distribution, as observed by Borak et al. (2005, 13). Parameterization techniques also directly depends on the size of the sample used in the statistical analysis. The bigger the sample, the better the estimation of the parameters. Despite such conclusions, research on integrating the leptokurtic character of distributions was continued by financial economists, who developed alternative models in order to describe the occurrence of extreme values.

2.3.2. Alternative Paths Explored to Deal with Extreme Values

Financial economists have taken extreme variations into account without jettisoning the Gaussian framework. Two methods have been explored giving rise to two literatures, thereby allowing the Gaussian approach to persist in financial economics: jump-diffusion and ARCH (autoregressive conditional heteroskedasticity)-type models. These two types of models arose from two different methodologies: jump-diffusion models characterize extreme values by combining the statistical properties of different distributions, while ARCH models deal with extreme values by modeling the residues observed in the Gaussian framework. Technically, the former propose a mathematical solution for the analysis of extreme values, while the latter propose econometric processing of these values.

2.3.2.1. Jump-Diffusion Processes

Jump-diffusion processes were the first class of models developed by financial economists to take extreme variations into account. These models start from the premise that increments of process are independent but not identically distributed. They attempt to reproduce empirical observations by breaking stock price variations into frequent variations of small amplitude and rare variations of very great amplitude. The leptokurtic nature of price distributions is therefore a reflection of this double movement. The response of these financial economists was the hypothesis that the observed distribution of prices can be divided into two: a Gaussian and a non-Gaussian distribution. The non-Gaussian distribution (referring to variations) can be described through any distribution for which the mean is finite, including a Pareto-Lévy distribution.[29] Conceptually, we can use the graph in figure 2.5 in order to summarize this reasoning.

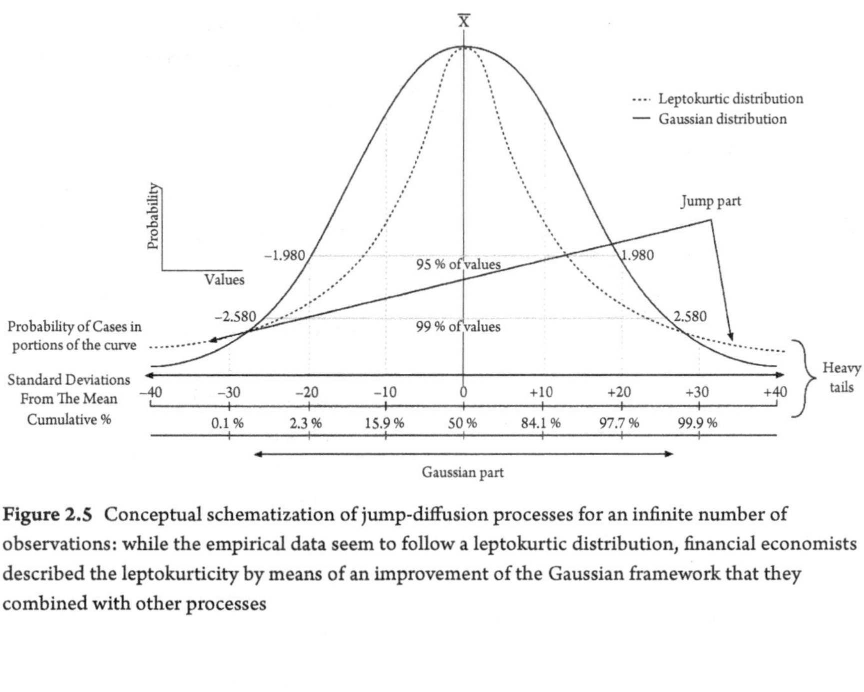

Figure 2.5 Conceptual schematization of jump-diffusion processes for an infinite number of observations: while the empirical data seem to follow a leptokurtic distribution, financial economists described the leptokurticity by means of an improvement of the Gaussian framework that they combined with other processes

The statistical description of a long-tails distribution can be decomposed into two blocks: a Gaussian description (solid line) of the middle part of the main part of the distribution (the trend or the diffusion) and a "jump part" (associated with the dotted line distribution) describing the heavy tails that are not in the Gaussian regime. So doing, financial economists opened a window for modeling the occurrence of extreme variations on the financial markets. The three graphs in figure 2.6 respectively compare a Gaussian simulation characterizing the dynamics of financial data with a jump process-based simulation and the empirical data recorded on the financial markets.

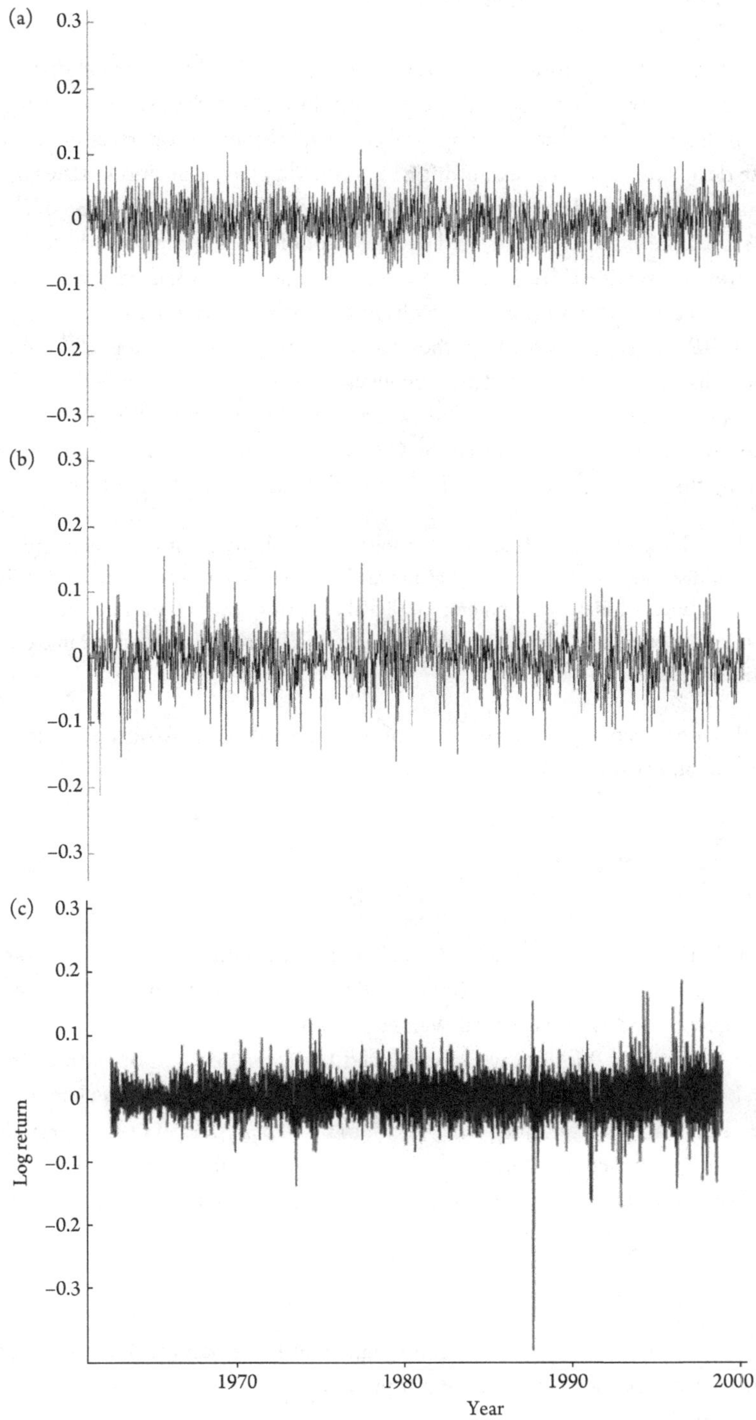

Figure 2.6 (a) Gaussian simulation describing the dynamics of financial data
(b) Jump-process-based simulation based on a combination of the Gaussian distribution with a Poisson law for the description of the jump part of the process
(c) Empirical evolution of financial data (time plot of daily log returns of IBM stock from July 1962 until December 1998)
Source: Google Finance and authors.

The first models, introduced by Press (1967), combined the normal distribution with a Poisson law (figure 2.6b). Although the combination of these two distributions does not describe accurately the empirical data (figure 2.6c), it offers, at least, a possibility to deal with a dynamics exhibiting a high volatility (by opposition to the Gaussian distribution reproduced on figure 2.6a). Press was a PhD student in the GBS of Chicago at the same time as Fama and opened debates about Mandelbrot's hypothesis (evoked in the previous section). He wanted to solve the issue of leptokurticity while keeping finite variance, in line with the data he observed: "Sample evidence cogently reported by Fama (1965a) supports the hypothesis of non-zero mean, long-tailed, peaked, non-Gaussian distributions for logged price changes. However, there is no need to conclude, on the basis of this evidence, that the variance is infinite" (Press 1967, 319). Within this framework, Press explained that the Gaussian distribution was not appropriate for describing the empirical data.[30] To address this shortfall, he built a model in which

> the logged price changes are assumed to follow a distribution that is a Poisson mixture of normal distributions. It is shown that the analytical characteristics of such a distribution agree with what has been found empirically. That is, this distribution is in general skewed, leptokurtic, [and] more peaked at its mean than the distribution of a comparable normal variate. (Press 1967, 317)

From this perspective, the occurrence of extreme values is associated with jumps whose probability follows a Poisson law:

$$X_t = C + \sum_{k=1}^{N(t)} Y_k + W_t, \tag{2.4}$$

where C is the initial price $X(0)$, $(Y_1, \ldots Y_k)$ are independent random variables following a common law $N(0, \sigma_t^2)$, $N(t)$ is a Poisson process counting the number of random events, and W_t is a classical Weiner process.

Some years later, Merton, who introduced the term "jump," popularized this approach by applying it to the analysis of option pricing, which is a major element in the hard core of financial economics (chapter 1). In his paper, Merton (1976) provided an extension of Black, Scholes, and Merton's 1973 option-pricing model with a two-block model. The evolution of stock prices was therefore described by the following process:

$$S_t = S_0 e^{X_t}, \tag{2.5}$$

where X_t was characterized with a combination of Brownian motion and a Poisson process to describe the occurrence of jumps, which took the following form:

$$X_t = \mu t + \sigma B_t + \sum_{i=1}^{N_t} Y_i, \tag{2.6}$$

where μ is the mean (drift) of the process, σ is the variance, and B_t is a Brownian motion with $B_t = B_t - B_0 \sim N(0,t)$. $\{Y_i\}$ refers to the jumps block modeled with a compound Poisson process with $t \geq 0$. In his article, Merton explained the need to develop a model "consistent with the general efficient market hypothesis of Fama (1970) and Samuelson (1965b)" (Merton 1976, 128) by taking "the natural process for the continuous component of the stock-price change: the Wiener process" (128). In other words, Merton founded his reasoning on the Gaussian framework since the Wiener process is also called Brownian motion (Doob 1953).

The methodology used by Press and Merton opened the path to a vast literature on what are now called "jump-process models." A large category of models were developed, using different kinds of statistical processes.[31] From this category of models emerged another kind of model, called "pure-jump processes," introduced by Cox and Ross in 1976. They do not describe the occurrence of jumps through a double-block model but rather through a single block in which a high rate of arrival of jumps of different sizes obviates the need to use a diffusion component.[32] Over two decades, these processes have generated a prolific literature in which the number of models is important: the generalized hyperbolic distribution (Eberlein and Keller 1995), the variance gamma model (Madan, Carr, and Chang 1998), and the CGMY process (named after the authors of Carr, Geman, Madan, and Yor 2002).[33]

This category of models allowed financial economics to characterize extreme values in an improved Gaussian framework even though they are by definition nonstable. Indeed, all these pure-jump processes are related to Brownian motion because of its properties of normality and continuity (Geman 2002). In other terms, the randomness in operational time is supposed to generate randomness in the evolution of financial returns. By associating the process describing the evolution of financial returns with the evolution of volume characterized by Brownian motion, Clark (1973) showed that the variance characterizing the extreme values observed in the dynamics of financial returns is always finite. Consequently, pure-jump models offer very technical solutions for describing the occurrence of extremes values while maintaining an improved Gaussian framework.

2.3.2.2. ARCH-Type Models

The second category of financial economic models that take into account extreme variations is ARCH-type models.

As we have seen, some of the first empirical investigations during the 1960s and 1970s pointed out that the variance of stock price fluctuations appeared not to be stable over time and that some dependence in price variations seemed to exist. Mandelbrot (1963, 1962) had already discussed this empirical result and had suggested in 1966 (as did Samuelson 1965) replacing Brownian motion with a martingale model (see chapter 1). This is because martingale models, unlike Gaussian processes, allow a process with a variance that is not independent. The first exhaustive empirical study of this kind of dependence was by McNees in 1979, who showed that variance "associated with different forecast periods seems to vary widely over time" (1979, 52). To solve this problem, Engle (1982) introduced ARCH-types models based on statistical processes whose variance directly depends on past information. Within this framework, variance is considered a random variable with its own distribution that can be estimated through a defined average of its past values. Such models can therefore reproduce extreme variations, as figure 2.7 suggests.

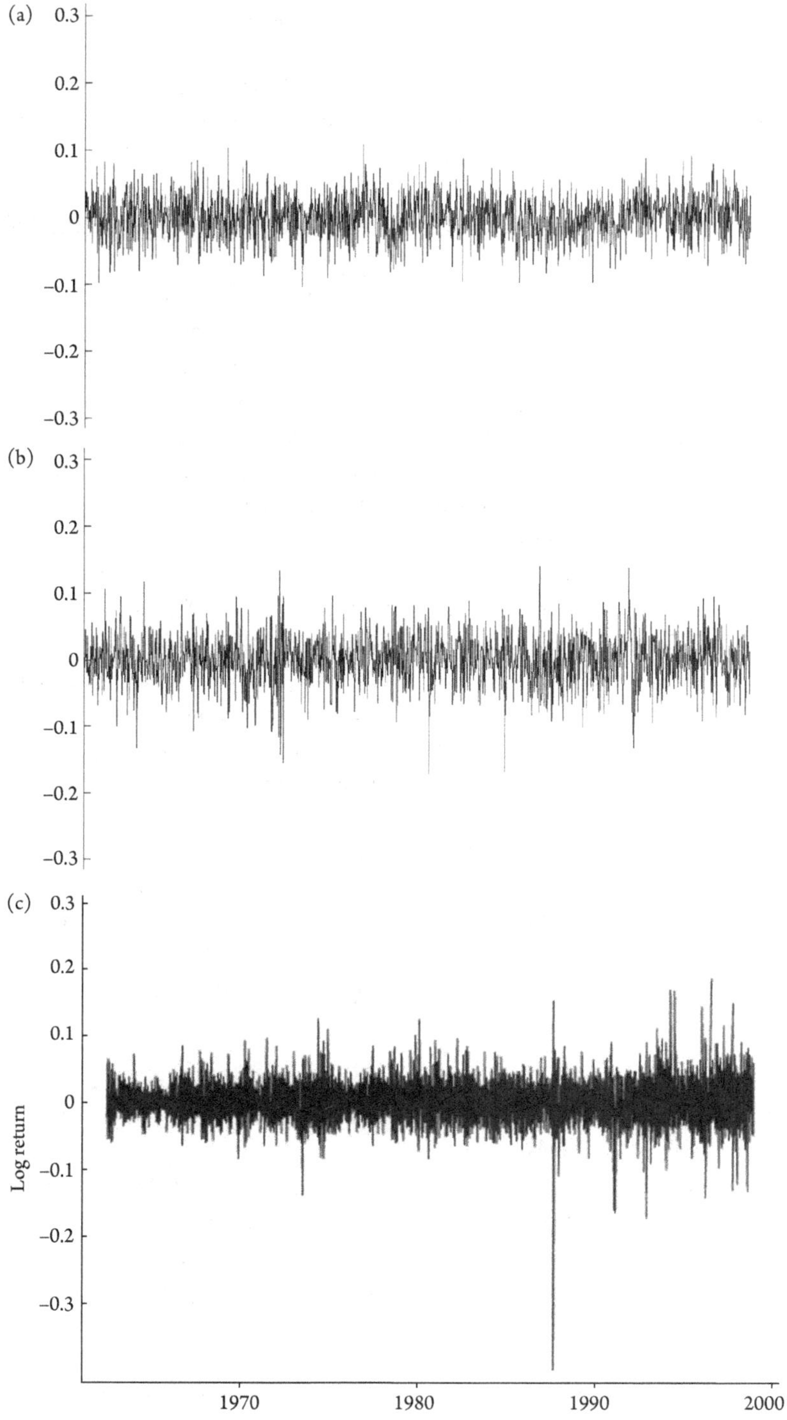

Figure 2.7 (a) Gaussian simulation describing the dynamics of financial data
(b) ARCH model-based simulation characterizing the dynamics of financial data
(c) Empirical evolution of financial data (time plot of daily log returns of IBM stock from July 1962 until December 1998)
Source: Google Finance and authors.

These representations indicate that an ARCH-based simulation provides a better estimate of the dynamics ruling the evolution of financial data. However, figure 2.7b also shows that this kind of model does not capture the occurrence of large variations that sporadically appear in reality (figure 2.7c). While ARCH-type models are based on a non-Gaussian property (time dependence), financial economists aimed to describe the occurrence of extreme values in a Gaussian perspective. Indeed, they still postulate that financial returns follow a Gaussian framework. The distribution of these returns is therefore considered as granted (for this reason it is called unconditional distribution). The variability of this unconditional distribution can be described through a new distribution (called conditional distribution) derived from specific time-dependent dynamics.[34] From a statistical point of view, it is important to emphasize that only the variable referring to the variance is not independent and identically distributed. In other words, variables (financial returns) associated with the unconditional distribution are still assumed to have a Gaussian behavior. More formally, the evolution of financial returns is described through the following unconditional normal law:

$$X_t = N(\mu + \sigma_t^2) + \varepsilon_t, \tag{2.7}$$

where μ is the mean, σ^2 is the variance, and $\mathcal{E}$ is the statistical error. This statistical equation can also be expressed as

$$X_t = \mu t + \bar{\sigma}_t^2 + \varepsilon_t. \tag{2.8}$$

ARCH-type models focus on the variance and statistical errors that they decompose into an unconditional and conditional part. The first ARCH model was introduced by Engle (1982), who characterized the variance as follows:

$$\bar{\sigma}_t^2 = \alpha\bar{\sigma} + (1-\alpha)\frac{1}{n}\sum_{i=1}^{n} R_i^2. \tag{2.9}$$

The unconditional dimension of variance is defined by the statistical parameter $\alpha > 0$ and the long-term variance σ, while the conditional part is characterized by the weighted sum of the last n returns, $R_i^2 = \frac{S_i - S_{t-1}}{S_i}$. This model was improved through GARCH (generalized autoregressive conditional heteroscedasticity) models by Bollerslev (1986), who showed that all last n returns did not influence the current variance in the same way, by using an exponentially weighted moving average estimate in which greater weight is assigned to the more recent returns. Statistically, this dependence of conditional variance on the past (which refers to the distribution of statistical errors or innovation in statistical terms) can be characterized using various potential statistical processes (Kim et al. 2008) that generated a huge literature providing a variety of time-dependence dynamics. Depending on this specific dynamic, one finds in the literature several types of ARCH models (IGARCH, EGARCH,

GARCH, NGARCH, etc.).[35] Moreover, notice that, in line with the literature on jump processes, ARCH models can describe the occurrence of extreme variations within a Gaussian framework.

2.4. CONCLUSION

This chapter showed that financial economists have considered extreme variations in the analysis of stock prices/returns by using three statistical approaches: Pareto-Lévy, jump diffusion, and ARCH types. In the 1960s, the Pareto-Lévy model was the first alternative proposed for characterizing the occurrence of extreme values in finance. However, as explained, this path of research was not investigated further for technical and theoretical reasons. Consequently, since the beginning of the 1980s, only the jump-diffusion and the ARCH-types models have been developed in financial economics. As discussed, these two approaches are totally embedded in the Gaussian framework. This point is important because chapter 1 showed that the latter defines the foundations of financial economics (modern portfolio theory, the capital-asset pricing model, the arbitrage pricing theory, the efficient-market hypothesis, and the Black and Scholes model).

It is interesting to note that the Gaussian framework was also shared by alternative approaches that emerged in financial economics. For instance, extreme-values analysis was the starting point for one of the major theoretical alternatives developed in financial economics: behavioral finance. In 1981, Shiller showed that market volatility was too high to be compatible with a Gaussian process and that, therefore, it could not describe the occurrence of extremes values. However, although behavioral finance offers a psychological explanation for the occurrence of extreme values, it does not question the Gaussian statistical framework (Schinckus 2009).

The first two chapters highlighted the foundations of financial economics and how this field deals with the extreme variations. Similarly, the two following chapters will introduce econophysics and investigate its foundations.

3

NEW TOOLS FOR EXTREME-VALUE ANALYSIS
STATISTICAL PHYSICS GOES BEYOND ITS BORDERS

The previous chapter studied how financial economists deal with extreme values given the constraints imposed by their theoretical and methodological framework, the major constraint being variance as a measure of risk. In this context, we explained that stable Lévy distributions, which generate an infinite variance, considerably complicate their application in finance. Surprisingly, since the 1990s statistical physicists have found a way to apply stochastic models based on stable Lévy distributions to deal with extreme values in finance. Many financial economists have found the incursion from statistical physics for the study of finance difficult to accept. How can this reluctance be explained? It appears that the major reason comes from the divergence in terms of scientific criteria, and a way of "doing science" that differs from financial economists' practices. Moreover, other differences can be mentioned, including approach, methodology, and concepts used. In the same vein, the core mathematics used in econophysics models are still not easily accessible for noninitiated scholars.

The aim of this chapter is to outline the theoretical and methodological foundations of statistical physics, which led some physicists to apply their approach and models to finance. This clarification is a crucial step in the understanding of econophysics from an economic point of view. This chapter will trace the major developments in statistical physics, explaining why physicists extended their new methods out of their field. This extension is justified by four key physical notions: critical points, universality class, renormalization group theory, and the Ising model. These elements will be clarified through an intuitive presentation. We will then explain how the combination of these key notions leads statistical physicists to consider their framework as the most appropriate one to describe the occurrence of extreme values in some phenomena. In finance, econophysicists describe the observation of extreme variations with a power law. This chapter will show the connections between these power laws and the current knowledge in financial economics. As chapter 2 explained, financial economists abandoned stable Lévy processes due to a technical issue related to the infinity of variance. This chapter will explain how physicists solve this problem by introducing truncation techniques. Their original motivation was to make stable Lévy distributions physically plausible, simply because all physical systems have finite parameters and therefore finite measures. To sum up, this chapter studies the theoretical tools developed since the 1970s in statistical physics that led to the creation of econophysics.

3.1. WHY DID STATISTICAL PHYSICS GO BEYOND ITS BORDERS?

For most economists, including most financial economists, it is not perfectly clear why statistical physicists find it obvious that their recent models can be applied to financial markets or other areas of economics.

The influence of physics on economics—and on social science in general—is nothing new. A number of writers studied the "physical attraction"[1] exerted by economics on hard sciences: Mirowski (1989) extensively highlighted contributions of physics to the development of marginalist economics and mathematical economics. Ingrao and Israel (1990) drew renewed attention to the influences of mechanics in the conceptualization of equilibrium in economics. Ménard (1981), Schabas (1990), and Maas (2005) also highlighted the role of physics in the economic works of Cournot and of Jevons. Similarly, we saw in chapters 1 and 2 that financial economics, and more generally finance, is also subject to the influence of physics. Yet despite these theoretical and historical links, econophysics is a fundamentally new approach. Its practitioners are not economists taking their inspiration from the work of physicists to develop their discipline, as has been seen repeatedly in the history of economics. This time, it is physicists who are going beyond the boundaries of their discipline, using their methods and models to study various problems thrown up by economics.

The current movement involves statistical physics. It is rooted in changes that occurred in physics but also in other scientific disciplines, including social sciences, in the 1970s. We will analyze these changes in order to understand the origins and the theoretical foundations of econophysics.

3.1.1. Statistical Physics' Golden Age

A turning point in the recent history of physics took place in the 1970s: it concerns the new connection between the theories of statistical mechanics—also called statistical physics—and particle physics. Statistical physics' main purpose is to explain the macroscopic behavior of a system and its evolution, in terms of physical laws governing the motion of the microscopic constituents (atoms, electrons, ions, spins, etc.) that make it up. Statistical physics (which is the contemporary label used to characterize thermodynamics) distinguishes itself from other fields of physics by its methodology based on statistics. This is due to the enormous number of variables with which statistical physicists have to work. As Fitzpatrick (2012)[2] explains, in areas of physics other than thermodynamics, physicists are able to formulate some exact, or nearly exact, set of equations—resulting from physical laws and theories—that govern the system under investigation. Therefore, they are able to analyze the system by solving these equations, either exactly or approximately. In thermodynamics, physicists have no problem in formulating the governing equations and writing down the exact laws of motion, including all the interatomic forces. Their problem is the gigantic number of variables—as many as Avogadro's number, 6×10^{23}—and therefore the gigantic number of equations of motion that have to be resolved.[3] This enormous number of relationships makes an analysis strictly based on equations unworkable, even for a computer. "Quite plainly, this is impossible [to solve the system of equations] . . . [the] subject is so difficult that [physicists] are forced to adopt a radically different approach to that employed in other areas of physics" (Fitzpatrick 2012, 4).

Fortunately, physicists are not interested in knowing the position and velocity of every particle in a system at any time. Instead, they want to know the properties of the system (volume, temperature, density distribution, etc.) at a given moment. Therefore, the number of pieces of information they require is minuscule compared to the number of pieces of information that would be needed to completely specify the internal motion of all single elements. In this perspective, the quantities that physicists are interested in do not depend on the motions of individual particles. They rather depend on the average motions of all the particles in the system combined with the correlations between these movements in a spatiotemporal description. In other words, these quantities depend on the statistical properties of each particle's motion. Moreover, the gigantic quantity of data makes it possible to use most statistical laws and theorems generally founded on asymptotic calculus (Batterman 2002).[4] The methods used in statistical physics are thus essentially dictated by the complexity of the systems due to the enormous number of constituents. This situation leads statistical physicists to start with statistical information about the motions of the microconstituent properties of the system in order to infer statistically some macro properties for this system. The statistical approach is so common that "in most situations physicists can forget that the results are statistical at all, and treat them as exact laws of physics" (Fitzpatrick 2012, 6).[5] The turning point that occurred in the 1970s is a direct result of this problematic of extremely voluminous data.

In 1982, the (high-energy or elementary-particle-trained) physicist Kenneth Wilson received the Nobel Prize in Physics for his contribution to the connection between macroscopic and microscopic levels. More precisely, Wilson was awarded the prize for having developed the renormalization group theory for critical phenomena in connection with phase transitions.[6] The systematic study of such critical phenomena emerged in the 1960s when physicists observed the emergence of macroregularities in the evolution of complex systems. Before going further, it is worth explaining what physicists mean by "critical phenomena." This concept is used to describe systems whose configuration evolves through a dynamics of critical states. A critical state is a particular configuration of the system in which two phases (or two states) are about to become one. The most telling example is water. Water is commonly known to be liquid in a room condition, but when the temperature or the pressure of this environment changes, the state of water changes as well (figure 3.1).

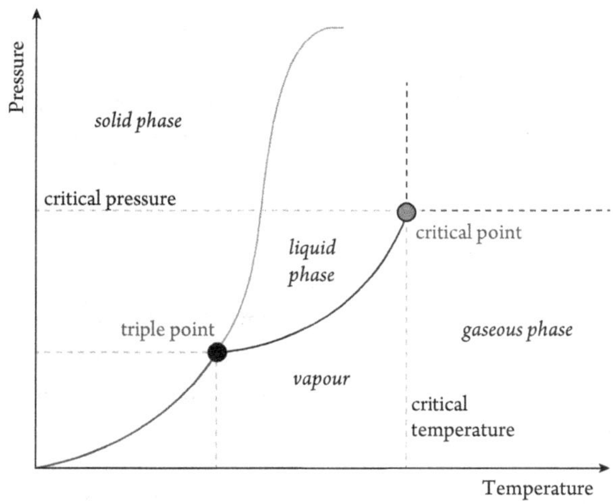

Figure 3.1 Temperature-pressure phase diagram for a fluid
Source: Adapted from Batterman 2002, 38. Reproduced by permission of Oxford University Press, USA.

The transition of a state into another one is due to the gradual change of an external variable (temperature or pressure); it is simply called "phase transition" in physics. This transformation can be likened to the passage from one equilibrium (phase)[7] to another. When this passage occurs in a continuous way (for instance, a continuous variation of temperature), the system passes through a critical point defined by a critical pressure and a critical temperature and at which neither of the two states is realized (figure 3.1). This is a kind of nonstate situation with no real difference between the two configurations of the phenomenon—both gas and liquid coexist in a homogenous phase. Indeed, physicists have observed that at the critical point, the liquid water, before becoming a gas, becomes opalescent and is made up of liquid water droplets, made up of a myriad of bubbles of steam, themselves made up of a myriad of droplets of liquid water, and so on. This is called *critical opalescence*. In other words, at the critical point, the system appears the same at all scales of analysis. This property is called "scale invariance," which means that no matter how closely one looks, one sees the same properties. In contrast, when this passage occurs in a discontinuous way (i.e., the system "jumps" from one state to another), there is no critical point. Phenomena for which this passage is continuous are called *critical phenomena* (in reference to the critical points).

Since the 1970s, critical phenomena have captured the attention of physicists due to several important conceptual advances in the characterization of scale invariance through the theory of renormalization,[8] on the one hand, and to the very interesting properties that define them, on the other. Among these properties, the fact that the dynamics of critical states can be characterized by a power law deserved special attention, because this law is a key element in econophysics' literature (the next part of this chapter will come back to this point). As Serge Galam (2004) explains in his personal testimony, the years 1975–80 appeared to be a buoyant period for statistical physics, which was blossoming with the exact solution of the enigma of critical phenomena, one of the toughest problems in physics. The so-called modern theory of phase transitions, along with renormalization group techniques, brought condensed-matter physics into its golden age, leading hundreds of young physicists to enter the field with a great deal of excitement.

As previously mentioned, Wilson won the Nobel Prize for his method of renormalization, used to demonstrate mathematically how phase transitions occur in critical phenomena. His approach provides a conceptual framework explaining critical phenomena in terms of phase transitions and enabling exact resolutions.

> The development of [the renormalization group] technique undoubtedly represents the single most significant advance in the theory of critical phenomena and one of the most significant in theoretical physics generally since the 1970s. (Alastair and Wallace 1989, 237)

The renormalization group theory has been applied in order to describe critical phenomena. As explained above, the latter are characterized by the existence of a critical state in which the phenomenon shows the same properties independently of the scale of analysis. The major idea of the renormalization group theory is to describe mathematically these common features through a power-law dependence. As we will show, this theory played a key role in the extension of statistical physics to other social sciences. Therefore, we will introduce this method in order to understand some of the connections econophysicists make with finance.[9] As mentioned above, the renormalization method deals with scale invariance. While the concept of invariance refers to the observation of recurrent characteristics independently of the context, the notion of scale invariance describes a particular property of a system/object or law that does not change when scales of length, energy, or other variables are multiplied by a common factor. In other words, this idea of scale invariance means that one recurrent feature (or more than one) can be found at every level of analysis. Concretely, this means that a macroscopic configuration can be described without describing all microscopic details. This aspect is a key point in the renormalization theory developed by Wilson, who extended Widom's (1965a, 1965b) and Kadanoff's (1966) discovery of "the importance of the notion of scale invariance which lies behind all renormalisation methods" (Lesne 1998, 25). More precisely, his method considers each scale separately and progressively connects contiguous scales to one another. This makes it possible to establish a connection between the microscopic and the macroscopic levels by decreasing the number of interacting parts at the microscopic level until one obtains the macroscopic level (ideally a system with one part only). In this perspective, the idea of scaling invariance allows physicists to capture the essence of a complex phenomenon by identifying key features that are not dependent on the scale of analysis.

Consider a phenomenon whose combination of microcomponents can be described with the sequence $X = X_1 + X_2 + \cdots + X_{kn}$, composed of *kn* random independent variables and identically distributed by a stable Lévy distribution (i.e., power law) such as that used in finance. The renormalization group method consists in using a scaling transformation to group the kn random variables into n blocks of k random variables. The transformation S_n takes the sequence X into a new sequence of random variables—still independent and identically distributed by a Lévy distribution and therefore still stable. This transformation becomes truly fruitful when it is iterated, when each renormalization leads to a reduction in the number of variables, leading to a system that contains fewer variables while keeping the characteristics of the original system—thanks to the fact that the system stays independent, identically distributed, and stable.[10] For instance, considering the previous sequence X with $kn = 8$, $n = 4$, and $k = 2$, we can renormalize the sequence three times in order to obtain a single random variable that characterizes the initial sequence (figure 3.2).

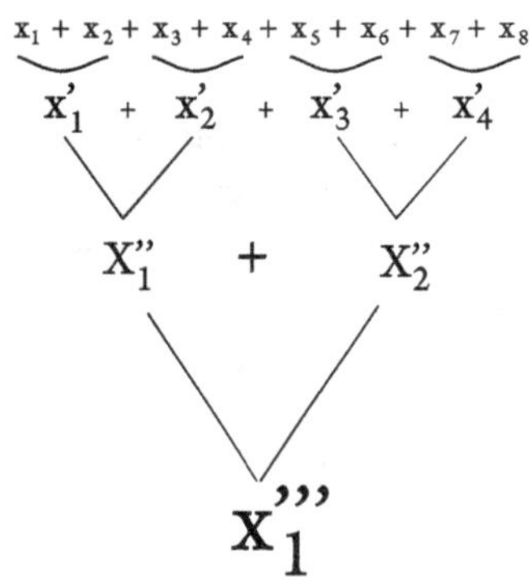

Figure 3.2 Renormalization group method applied to a stochastic process
Source: Sornette 2006, 53. Reproduced by permission of the author.

When applied several times, this pairing method allows modelers to "climb" the scales by reducing the number of variables (kn) without losing key features of the phenomena, which are captured in the scaling invariance of the process. In other words, this technique allows us to group random variables into (n) blocks of variables in order to reduce the initial complexity of the phenomenon. Roughly speaking, the technique can be summarized by the equation

$$S_n([X],\alpha) = n^{-\alpha}\sum_{j=1}^{n} X_j,$$

where S_n is the sequence at a specific scale of analysis describing the phenomena, while X_j refers to the number variables used at that level of analysis. The a quantity is called the "critical exponent" and describes the scale invariance of the phenomena. In other terms, this exponent describes a universal property observed without regard for scale. Considering the renormalization group method, the system at one scale is said to consist of self-similar copies of itself when viewed at a smaller scale, but with different ("rescaled") parameters describing the components of the system. In other words, at the end of the 1970s, statistical physics had established precise calculation methods for analyzing phenomena characterized by scale invariance.

The scale-invariance assumption was not new in physics,[11] but the properties allowing the mathematical demonstration of invariance were only established at the end of the 1970s. This demonstration makes it possible to study mathematically macroscopic regularities that occur as a result of microscopic random interactions without having to study these microscopic interactions.[12] The focus is therefore on the macroscopic level, which is directly observable for physical phenomena. In other words, since the 1970s, thanks to scale invariance, physicists can infer from microscopic constituents some key parameters that allow the capture and description of the dynamics of macroscopic behaviors without studying, in detail, what happens at the microscopic level. For these reasons, scale invariance is the foundation of any modern approach to statistical physics aimed at understanding the collective behavior of systems with a large number of variables that interact with each other.

Since the end of the 1960s, research into critical phenomena and scale invariance benefited from another very fruitful connection: the Ising model. The latter is a mathematical model of ferromagnetism used to study phase transitions and critical points. This model is considered to be the simplest description of a system with a critical point; it played a central role in the development of research into critical phenomena, and it occupies a place of importance in the mind of econophysicists. Briefly, the Ising model consists of discrete variables that represent magnetic moments of atomic spins that can take one of two states, +1 ("up") or −1 ("down"), the two states referring to the direction taken by the spins. The concept of spin characterizes the circular movement of particles (electrons, positrons, protons, etc.), implying that they have a specific rotation as shown in figure 3.3.

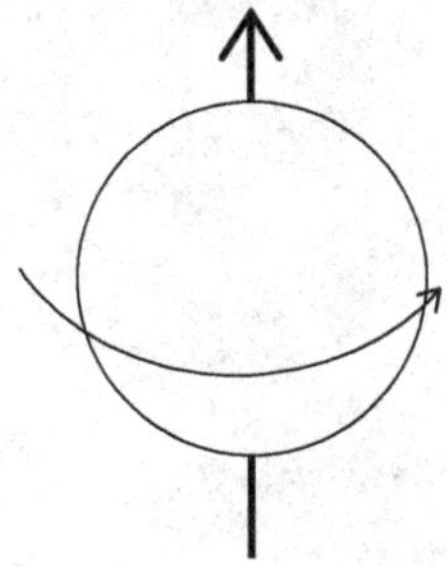

Figure 3.3 Schematization of a particle's spin

There is no way to speed up or slow down the spin of an electron, but its direction can be changed, as modeled by the Ising model. The interesting element is that the direction of one spin directly influences the direction of its neighbor spins (figure 3.4).

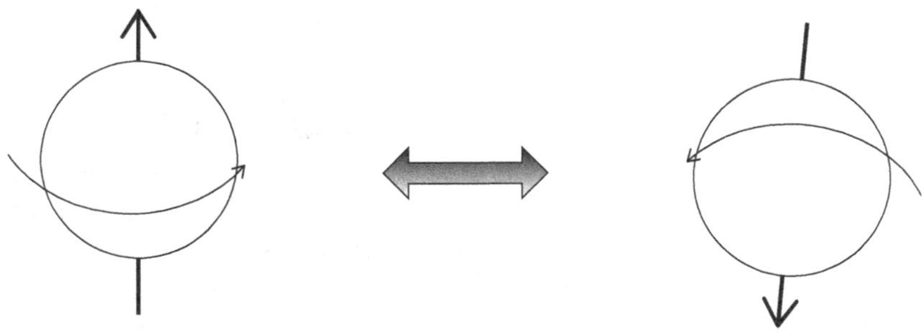

Figure 3.4 Schematization of the interaction between particles' spins

This influence can be by captured through a function of correlation that measures to what extent the behaviors of spins are correlated. The major idea of the Ising model is to describe this interaction between particles' spins. In this perspective, the spins are arranged in a graph, usually a lattice, in which each spin exerts an influence on its neighbors. This influence is measured by the distance over which the direction of one spin affects the direction of its neighbor spins. This distance is called the correlation length; it has an important function in the identification of critical phenomena. Indeed, the correlation length measures the distance over which the behavior of one microscopic variable is influenced by the behavior of another. Away from the critical point (at low temperatures), the spins point in the same direction. In such as situation, the thermal energy is too low to play a role; the direction of each spin depends only on its immediate neighbors, making the correlation length finite (figure 3.5).

Figure 3.5 Two-dimensional Ising model at low temperature
Source: Binney et al. 1992, 19. Reproduced by permission of Oxford University Press.

But at the critical point, when the temperature has been increased to reach the critical point, the situation is completely different. The spins no longer point in the same direction because thermal energy influences the whole system, and the magnetization spin-spin vanishes. In this critical situation, spins point in no specific direction and follow a stochastic distribution.

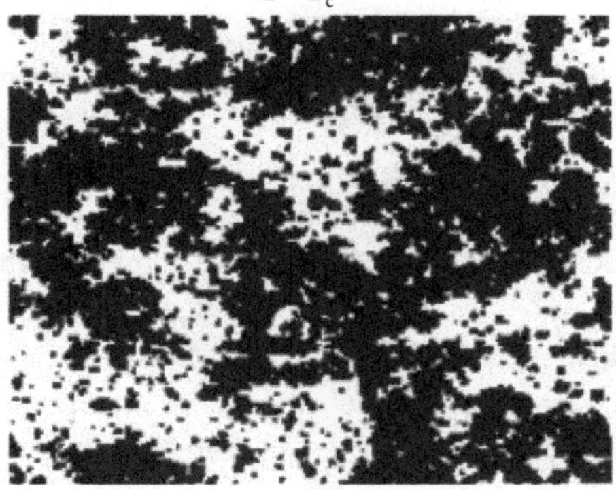

Figure 3.6 Two-dimensional Ising model at the critical temperature.
Source: Binney et al. 1992, 19. Reproduced by permission of Oxford University Press.

As we can see in figure 3.6, there are regions of spin up (black areas) and regions of spin down (white areas), but all these regions are speckled with smaller regions of the opposite type, and so on. In fact, at the critical point, each spin is influenced by all other spins (not only a particle's neighbors) whatever their distance. This situation is a particular configuration in which the correlation length[13] is very important (it is considered to be infinite). At this critical state, the whole system appears to be in a homogeneous configuration characterized by an infinite correlation length between spins, making the system scale invariant. Consequently, the spin system has the same physical properties whatever the scale length considered. The renormalization group method can then be applied, and by performing successive transformations of scales on the original system, one can reduce the number of interacting spins and therefore determine a solution from a finite cluster of spins.

Beyond the ability to describe the spins' movement, there is another point of interest in the Ising model. Because of its very simple structure, it is not confined to the study of ferromagnetism. In fact, "Proposed as a model of ferromagnetism, it 'possesses no ferromagnetic properties'" (Hughes 1999, 104)! Its abstract and general structure has enabled its use to be extended to the study of many other problems or phenomena:

> The Ising model is employed in a variety of ways in the study of critical point phenomena. To recapitulate, Ising proposed it . . . as a model of ferromagnetism; subsequently it has been used to model, for example, liquid-vapour transitions and the behaviour of binary alloys. Each of these interpretations of the model is in terms of a specific example of critical point behaviour. . . . [T]he model also casts light on critical point behaviour in general. Likewise, the pictures generated by computer simulation of the model's behaviour illustrate . . . the whole field of scale-invariant properties. (Hughes 1999, 124–25)

For these reasons, statistical physicists consider the Ising model the perfect illustration of the simplest unifying mathematical model. Their looking for such models is rooted in the scientific view of physicists, for whom "the assault on a problem of interest traditionally begins (and sometimes ends) with an attempt to identify and understand the simplest model exhibiting the same essential features as the physical problem in question" (Alastair and Wallace 1989, 237). The Ising model meets this requirement perfectly. Its use is not restricted to statistical physics because "the specification of the model has no specific physical content" (Hughes 1999, 99); its content is mathematical. Therefore, this model is independent of the underlying phenomenon studied, and it can be used to analyze any empirical data that share the same characteristics.

With these new theoretical developments, statistical physicists had powerful mathematical models and methods that could solve crucial problems in physics. They were able to establish the behavior of systems at their macroscopic level from hypotheses about their microscopic level, but without analyzing this microscopic level. The combination of the renormalization theory and the Ising model offers statistical physicists a unified mathematical framework that can analogically be used for the study of phenomena characterized by a large number of interacting microcomponents.

3.1.2. The Temptation to Apply the Methods of Statistical Physics outside Physics

Encouraged by the results obtained in the 1970s, certain physicists began investigating correspondences with collective behaviors of any kind of phenomena that appear critical, including social phenomena. For statistical physicists, as we will see now, this temptation to extend their models and methods outside physics seemed relevant.

First, we have to be aware of some features of physicists' scientific viewpoint. As we have just seen, physicists are very concerned by the identification of a simple unifying mathematical model. The Ising model, which is primarily a mathematical entity even if it has been developed for solving various types of problems in physics, is a perfect example of such a model. It can be used to solve a *universality class* of problems. This concept of universality class is used in physics to describe a category of phenomena that have the same behaviors regarding the dynamics of their critical states (even though they refer to very different realities). A common example of such a class is the association between the occurrence of earthquakes and financial crashes, the laws describing these events having the same statistical characteristics (we will detail this point in section 3.2.3). Research on critical phenomena offered statistical physicists the possibility of identifying *universality classes* of critical phenomena that share the same statistical behavior at their critical point. In this case, systems that are different microscopically have identical macroscopic behavior. Here again, the bedrock of universality classes is looking for the simplest unifying mathematical model. To understand this point, recall that the dynamics of critical points are characterized by a power law. Physicists associate each power law with a mathematical model describing the statistical features of a large variety of phenomena that have the same critical exponent. In other words, the idea of "universality" refers here to the fact that these phenomena can be studied with the same mathematical model independently of the context.

The use of critical phenomena analysis and its extension to social sciences suggest changes in scientific methodology that developed in the twentieth century. Giorgio Israel (1996) identifies a major change in the way of doing science through "mathematical analogies." These are based on the existence of unifying mathematical simple models that are not dedicated to the phenomena studied. Mathematical modeling then uses mathematical analogies by means of which the same mathematical formalism is able to account for heterogeneous phenomena. The latter are "only interconnected by an analogy that is expressed in the form of a common mathematical description" (Israel 1996, 41). The model then is an effective reproduction of reality without ontology, one that may provide an explanation of phenomena. The Ising model is a perfect illustration of these simple unifying mathematical models. Israel (1996) stressed that such mathematical analogies strongly contribute to the increasing mathematization of reality.

Mathematical analogies illustrate the origin of the temptation for statistical physicists to extend their models to analyzing critical phenomena beyond physics. First, they looked for phenomena with large numbers of interacting units whose microscopic behaviors would not be observed directly but which can generate observable macroscopic results. These results are consistent with the microscopic motions defined by a set of mathematical assumptions (which characterize random motion).[14] Therefore, modelers can look for statistical regularities often characterized by power laws:

> Since economic systems are in fact comprised of a large number of interacting units having the potential of displaying power-law behaviour, it is perhaps not unreasonable to examine economic phenomena within the conceptual framework of scaling and universality. (Stanley and Plerou 2001, 563)

This search led some statistical physicists to create new fields that were called "sociophysics" or "econophysics" depending on the topics to which their methods and models were applied.

A first movement, sociophysics,[15] emerged in the 1980s. One of the reasons that physicists attempt to explain social phenomena stems from the mathematical power of the new models borrowed from statistical physics:

> During my research, I started to advocate the use of modern theory phase transitions to describe social, psychological, political and economical phenomena. My claim was motivated by an analysis of some epistemological contradictions within physics. On the one hand, the power of concepts and tools of statistical physics [was] enormous, and on the other hand, I was expecting that physics would soon reach the limits of investigating inert matter. (Galam 2004, 50)

In the 1990s statistical physicists turned their attention to economic phenomena, and particularly finance, giving rise to econophysics. As two of its leading authors, Stanley and Mantegna, put it, econophysics is "a quantitative approach using ideas, models, conceptual and computational methods of statistical physics" (2000, 2). As mentioned above, these models and methods allow the study of macroscopic behaviors of any kind whose components behave randomly. This point is interesting because it echoes the efficient-market hypothesis (the cornerstone of financial economics, as explained in chapter 1), in particular Fama's 1970 formulation based on the assumption of a representative agent. This version of the efficient-market hypothesis is perfectly compatible with the statistical-physics approach that makes no hypothesis about specific behaviors of investors. Moreover, the renormalization group method seems to be an appropriate answer to finance, because it makes it possible to move from the microscopic level (i.e., agents whose behaviors are reduced to mathematical hypotheses) to the macroscopic level (i.e., the evolution of the financial prices empirically observed). Thus, by analogy, statistical physicists could consider the evolution of financial markets as the statistical and macroscopic results of a very large number of interactions at the microscopic level. The application of statistical physics to economics is not limited to finance; it touches on a number of other economic subjects.[16] However, an analysis of the articles published by econophysicists indicates that research conducted in this field mainly concerns the study of financial markets, marginalizing other fields. It is no accident, then, that econophysics is often associated with themes dealing with financial data (Rickles 2007, 4).

3.1.3. The Computerization of Science

The temptation to apply statistical physics to economic phenomena has had support from an important ally: the increasing use of computers in science and the acceleration of the computerization of scientific activities. In chapter 1 we mentioned the importance of computers in the development of financial economics. However, their role in econophysics is even greater, for two reasons at least. First, econophysicists are data driven (chapter 4). Second, the main statistical tool used, power laws, need an enormous quantity of data to be identified due to their asymptotic properties (i.e., the properties of power laws are verified for extremely large samples, ideally infinite). Thus, although partially independent of the theoretical developments that occurred in statistical physics, the increasing use of computers has enabled two major features: (1) the collection and the exploitation of very large databases; (2) the development of a new scientific approach supported by the extension of statistical physics outside its original borders.

As one can observe nowadays, computers have become a physical and intellectual extension in the process of providing data about the world. Computerization has provided an increasing quantity of data in a large number of fields, particularly fields related to social phenomena. Financial markets occupy a very specific place in this movement, because the financial databases are the largest bases for social phenomena. Indeed, since the end of the 1970s, all the major financial markets have been progressively automated thanks to computers,[17] making Fischer Black's wish (1971a, 1971b) for fully automated stock exchanges come true. In addition, some markets, like the foreign exchange market, became active 24 hours a day with electronic trading. Automation has allowed all transactions and all prices quoted to be recorded, leading to storage of a huge amount of financial data. Moreover, since the 1990s, use of computers has enabled the development of high-frequency transactions, and therefore the creation of high-frequency data (also called "intraday" data).[18] Previously, statistical data on financial markets were generally made up of a single value per day obtained by the average price or the last quotation of the day (chapter 2). In other words, the "daily" data were based on averages, which, by construction, dilute the intraday volatility, as figure 3.7 shows.

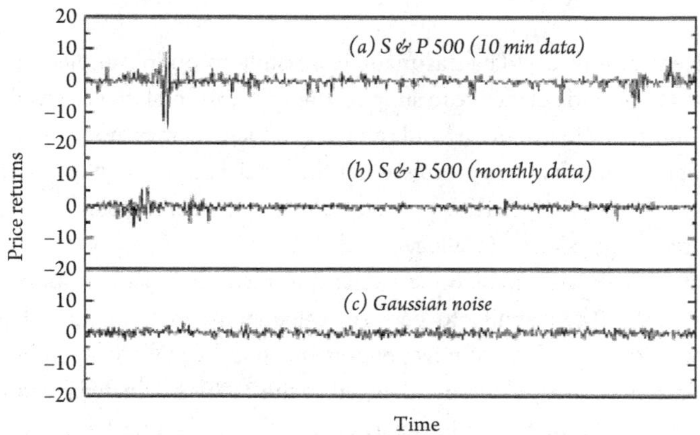

Figure 3.7 Intraday and monthly price return volatility
Source: Gopikrishnan et al. 1999, 5306. Reproduced by permission of the authors.

While the first time series shows the evolution of 10 minutes of data, the second one describes the evolution of the same data but recorded on a monthly interval. These graphs show that larger time intervals reduce the volatility of data, making them appear to more closely match the Gaussian framework (simulated in the third time series). Nowadays, with the recording of "intraday data," all prices quoted and tens of thousands of transactions are conserved every single day (Engle and Russell 2004).

The increasing quantity of data and the computerization of financial markets led to notable changes in techniques for detecting new phenomena. Intraday data brought to light new phenomena that could not be detected or did not exist with monthly or daily data. Among these are strategic behaviors that influence price variations.[19] More importantly, the new data have exhibited values more extreme than could be detected before. Indeed, monthly or daily prices recorded were generally the last prices quoted during a month or a day, or a mean of the prices quoted during a period, and therefore extreme values in these data are generally smaller and less frequent than in intraday data. As the figure 3.7 suggests, intraday data have increased interest in research on extreme values. They have brought new challenges in the analysis of stock price variations that have required the creation of new statistical tools to characterize them.

The increased quantity of statistical data on financial markets favors the growing interest in extending the methods and models of statistical physics into finance. Indeed, as previously mentioned, most of the results obtained in statistical physics are based on huge amounts of data, which makes this question crucial:

> Economics systems differ from often-studied physical systems in that the number of subunits is considerably smaller in contrast to macroscopic samples in physical systems that contain a huge number of interacting subunits, as many as Avogadro's number, 6×10^{23}. In contrast, in an economic system, one initial work was limited to analysing time series comprising of order of magnitude 10^3 terms, and nowadays with high-frequency data the standard, one may have 10^8 terms. (Stanley and Plerou 2001, 563–64)

The advent of intraday data has made it possible to build samples that are sufficiently broad to provide evidence to support the application of power-law distribution analysis to the evolution of prices and returns on financial markets. This explosion of financial data—which has no equivalent in other social sciences fields—comes closer to the standards to which statistical physicists generally work, making market finance "a natural area for physicists" (Gallegati et al. 2006, 1).

Computers have also transformed scientific research on distributions of stock market variations. Their ability to perform calculations more rapidly than humans paved the way for an analysis of new phenomena and the study of old phenomena in new ways. In this context, old issues debated in the 1970s by financial economics can be updated and re-evaluated. This is particularly true for stable Lévy processes.[20] As explained in chapter 2, in general there are no closed-form formulas for Lévy α-stable distributions—except for Gaussian, Pareto, and Cauchy distributions—which made their use in finance difficult in the 1970s. This point is still true today: to work on such distributions and the associated processes, one has to calculate the value of the parameters, and such complex calculations require numerous data. Of course, such calculus cannot be done by hand. However, computer simulations have changed the situation because they allow research when no analytic solution actually exists. Moreover, they make it possible to chart step-by-step the evolution of a system whose dynamics are governed by nonintegrable differential equations (i.e., there is no analytic solution). They have also provided a more precise visual analysis of empirical data and of the results obtained by mathematical tools. By allowing simulations with the different parameters of the Lévy α-stable distributions, they have facilitated work with these distributions, making possible visual research that could have appeared vague before (Mardia and Jupp 2000). Statistical and mathematical programs have been developed to compute stable densities, cumulative distribution functions, and quantiles, resolving most computational difficulties in using stable Lévy distributions in practical problems. In conclusion, then, the increasing use of computers created a context for reconsidering the use of stable Lévy distributions (and their power laws) in finance. The following section will detail this point.

3.2. A NEW TOOL FOR ANALYZING EXTREME VALUES: POWER-LAW DISTRIBUTIONS

One of the legacies of the theoretical results obtained in statistical physics since the end of the 1970s and the new computer techniques is extensive research into power laws. Generally, any work in econophysics advances empirical results to demonstrate that the phenomena studied are ruled by a distribution of variables or observables following a power law (Newman 2005).[21] This statistical approach can be considered one of the major characteristics of these studies. Its origin is rooted in the theoretical and methodological background of econophysicists clarified in the previous section. Power laws have attracted particular attention for, on the one hand, their interesting mathematical and theoretical properties, directly linked with critical phenomena, and, on the other hand, for empirical observations suggesting that their distribution fits with observations of a very large variety of natural and man-made phenomena. Given the place of power laws in econophysics, they can be considered the key tool of the econophysics approach.

This section will clarify the reasons that a vast majority of econophysics works are based on power laws. Afterward, we will study the links that can be made with finance in order to explain the use of such laws in financial economics.

3.2.1. The Key Role of Power Laws in Statistical Physics

As explained in the previous sections, power laws, in statistical physics, are closely linked with critical phenomena.[22] This link means that, from the viewpoint of statistical physicists, power laws are synonymous with complex systems, which makes their study particularly stimulating:

> Why do physicists care about power laws so much? . . . The reason . . . is that we're conditioned to think they're a sign of something interesting and complicated happening. The first step is to convince ourselves that in boring situations, we don't see power laws.[23]

Bouchaud (2001, 105) expresses a similar idea:

> Physicists are often fascinated by power laws. The reason for this is that complex, collective phenomena give rise to power laws which are *universal*, that is, to a large degree independent of the microscopic details of the phenomenon. These power laws emerge from collective action and transcend individual specificities. As such, they are unforgeable signatures of a collective mechanism.

These remarks underline the fascination of power laws for econophysicists and explain the numerous empirical studies of power laws (this point will be detailed in section 3.2.3). As previously mentioned, the link between power laws and critical phenomena occurs at three levels: correlation lengths, scale invariance, and universality classes.

The first level is correlation lengths. Section 3.1.1 presented the Ising model by introducing the concept of correlation length between spins (or interacting components) of a system. In this context, critical phenomena evolve into a fragile configuration of critical states in which the large correlation lengths that exist in the system at the critical point are distributed like a power law. Traditionally, physicists have characterized the correlations between the constituents of the system they analyze (at a given temperature T) as decaying like an exponential law $e^{\frac{-r}{\xi(T)}}$ (i.e., the correlation function), where r is the distance between two components and $\xi(T)$ is the correlation length.[24] With the purpose of characterizing the divergence observed at the critical point, physicists added to the exponential law a power law, taking the following for $r^{-\alpha}e^{\frac{-r}{\xi(T)}}$. At the critical point, as the previous section explained, correlations are infinite, making the exponential, $e^{\frac{-r}{\xi(T)}}$, equal to zero. This situation means that the correlation function is only distributed according to a power law,[25] $r^{-\alpha}$. In other words, away from the critical point, the correlation length between two constituents, x and y, decays exponentially,[26] $e^{\frac{-|x-y|}{\xi(T)}}$. But as the critical point is approached, the correlation length increases, and right *at* the critical point, the correlation length goes to infinity and decays in accordance with the power of the distance, $|x-y|^{-\alpha}$. As Shalizi explains intuitively in his notes, far from the critical point the microscopic dynamics mean that the central-limit theorem can be applied. In this case, the fluctuations are approximately Gaussian. As one approaches the critical point, however, giant, correlated fluctuations begin to appear. In this case, the fluctuations can deliver a non-Gaussian stationary distribution.[27]

The second level of influence between power laws and critical phenomena is scale invariance. At their critical point, the phenomena become independent of the scale; there is, therefore, a scaling invariance. The lack of a characteristic scale implies that the microscopic details do not have to be considered in the analysis. Scaling invariance is the footprint of critical phenomena; and, statistically speaking, power-law distribution is the sole distribution that has a scale-invariance property.[28] Indeed, consider the definition of scale invariance—no matter how closely you look, you see the same thing. Thus, one must have the same probability distribution for price variations on the interval $[110, 121]$ when the price quoted is 110 as for price variations on the interval $[100, 110]$ when the price quoted is 100. Mathematically speaking,[29] we have

$$\Pr[Y \geq x|X] = \Pr\left[Y \geq \frac{x}{X}\right], \quad \text{with} \quad x > X. \tag{3.1}$$

$$\Leftrightarrow F\left(\frac{x_1}{x_2}\right) = \frac{F(x_1)}{F(x_2)}. \tag{3.2}$$

If $F(x)$ is a power law, $F = X^a$, then

$$\left(\frac{x_1}{x_2}\right)^{\alpha} = \frac{x_1^{\alpha}}{x_2^{\alpha}}. \tag{3.3}$$

As one can see, a power-law distribution respects the scale-invariance property: what is true for the combination $\frac{X_1}{X_2}$ is true for the elements $(X_{1,} X_2)$ composing this combination. A power law is the sole statistical framework to that respects this property. In other words, at the critical point, if there is scaling, "The observable quantities in the system should adopt a power-law distribution" (Newman 2005, 35). This means that the shape of the phenomenon's size distribution curve does not depend on the observation scale, implying that the results are exactly the same for the micro and the macro levels. For this reason, power laws are sometimes called scaling laws.

The third association between power laws and critical phenomena is the existence of "universality classes." In statistical physics, a universality class refers to a collection of events likely to be described with mathematical models sharing the same statistical features through the same scaling function. The characteristic exponent of a power law directly determines its statistical characteristics. In this perspective, all phenomena whose dynamics can be described through the same power law belong to a specific category of phenomena sharing common statistical features. In other words, the identification of the critical exponent for a power law allows modelers to regroup all phenomena characterized by this particular power law in the same universality class. Again, the "universal aspect" mainly refers to the recurrence of the statistical characteristics whose measures appear to be the same whatever the context in which they have been observed. These parameters can therefore provide information about the behavior of these phenomena at their critical points.

Having explained the theoretical origins of the use of power laws by statistical physicists, we can now express these relations from a mathematical viewpoint. This mathematical formulation will be used in the next section in order to express the connections with finance. A finite sequence $y = (y_1, y_2, \ldots, y_n)$ of real numbers, assumed without loss of generality always to be ordered such that $y_1 \geq y_2 \geq \ldots \geq y_n$, is said to follow a power law if

$$k = c\, y_k^{-\alpha}, \tag{3.4}$$

where k is (by definition) the rank of y_k, c is a fixed constant, and a is called the critical exponent or the scaling parameter.[30] In the case of a power-law distribution, the tails decay asymptotically according to a—the smaller the value of a, the slower the decay and the heavier the tails. A more common use of power laws occurs in the context of random variables and their distributions. That is, assuming an underlying probability model P for a nonnegative random variable X, let $F(x) = P[X \leq x]$ for $x \geq 0$ denote the (cumulative) distribution function of X, and let $\bar{F}(x) = 1 - F(x)$ denote the complementary cumulative distribution function. In this stochastic context, a random variable X or its corresponding distribution function F is said to follow a power law or is scaling with index $\alpha > 0$ if, as $x \to \infty$,

$$P[X > x] = 1 - F(x) \approx cx^{-\alpha} \tag{3.5}$$

for some constant $0 < c < \infty$ and a tail index $\alpha > 0$. For $1 < \alpha < 2$, F has infinite variance but finite mean, and for $0 < \alpha \leq 1$, F has infinite variance and infinite mean. In general, all moments of F of order $\beta \geq \alpha$ are infinite.

3.2.2. Power Laws and Their Links with Financial Economics

From the mathematical definition of a power law proposed above, we can now express three connections with finance.

The first connection is that power laws are easily deduced from the financial definition of returns. Considering the price of a given stock, p_t, the (log-) stock return r_t is the change of the logarithm of the stock price in a given time interval Δt,

$$r_t = \ln p_t - \ln p_{t-\Delta t}. \tag{3.6}$$

Therefore, the probability of having a return r higher than the return x, $P[r > x]$, can be written as $\ln P[r > x] = -\alpha \ln x + c$, which can be rewritten as a power-law expression by using the exponential of both sides of the equation, $P[r > x] = c\, x^{-\alpha}$. This way of interpreting financial returns shows that power laws are an appropriate tool with which to characterize the evolution of financial prices.

The second connection is that power laws are easily linked with stochastic processes used in financial economics, which describe the evolution of a variable X (price, return, volume, etc.) over time (t). Knowing that a power law is a specific relationship between two variables that requires no particular statistical assumption, we may associate the evolution between the variables X and t with a power law. In this case, this evolution is said to be a stable Lévy process when

$$P(x) \sim \frac{C}{|x|^{1+\mu}} \quad (\text{for } x \to \pm\infty), \tag{3.7}$$

where C is a positive constant called the tail or scale parameter and the exponent μ is between 0 and 2 ($0 < \mu \leq 2$). It is worth mentioning that among Lévy processes, only stable Lévy processes can be associated with power laws[31] because the stability property is a statistical interpretation of the scaling property. As explained in chapter 2, the stability of a random variable implies that there exists a linear combination of two independent copies of that variable with the same statistical properties (distribution form and location parameters—i.e., mean, variance). This property is very useful in finance because a monthly distribution can be seen as a linear combination of a weekly or daily distribution, for example, meaning that statistical characteristics can easily be estimated for every time horizon. While stochastic processes used in financial economics are based on the Gaussian framework, as Mandelbrot (1963), Pagan (1996), and Sornette (2006, 97) explained, taking a Brownian random walk (i.e., Gaussian process) as a starting point, a no-normal diffusion law can be obtained by keeping the independence and the stationarity of increments but by characterizing their distribution through a distribution exhibiting fat tails. A telling example of such a law is a power law whose exponent μ will be between 0 and 2.

The third and final connection between power laws and financial economics refers to the work of Mandelbrot since the 1960s, which we discussed in chapter 2. The link between power laws and Lévy processes allows econophysicists to anchor their work in that of Mandelbrot, who tried to improve the first canonical models of financial economics. Econophysicists have in a sense concretized Mandelbrot's project (and they refer systematically to his work). However, while Mandelbrot and econophysicists arrive at the same result—modeling stock price variations using Lévy stable processes—they do not take the same path to get there. Mandelbrot starts his analysis from the stability of stochastic process. His suggestion was to generalize Gaussian processes by using Lévy stable distributions. For doing this, Mandelbrot singled out the Gaussian framework for its properties of stability. He considered stability the most important hypothesis for a process because without it we cannot use certain mathematical results (such as the central-limit theorem) to produce new interesting results in finance:

> It is widely believed that price series are not stationary, in the sense that the mechanism that generates them does not remain the same during successive time periods. . . . Statisticians tend to be unaware of the gravity of this conclusion. Indeed, so little is known of nonstationary time series, that accepting nonstationarity amounts to giving up any hope of performing a worthwhile statistical analysis. (Mandelbrot 1966b, 2)

Mandelbrot's path was to use the generalized central-limit theorem, which is compatible with Lévy stable distributions. In contrast, econophysicists' starting point is critical phenomena and the results obtained from renormalization group methods that can demonstrate stability for non-Gaussian stable processes. More precisely, the property of being distributed according to a power law is conserved under addition, multiplication, and polynomial transformation. When we combine two power-law variables, the one with the fatter-tailed distribution (that is, the one with the smaller exponent) dominates. The new distribution is the minimum of the tail exponents of the two combined distributions. Renormalization group methods focus on the scaling property of the process. According to Lesne and Laguës, such an approach led to the creation of a new mathematical approach. In this case, the attractor[32] is no longer the Lévy stable distribution—as it was in Mandelbrot's approach—but the critical point. The latter is the attractor in the sense of the scaling invariance.

> Scaling laws are a new type of statistical law on the same level as the law of large numbers and the central-limit theorem. As such they go far beyond the scope of physics and can be found in other domains such as finance, traffic control and biology. They apply to global, macroscopic properties of systems containing a large number of elementary microscopic units. (Lesne and Laguës 2011, 63)

This difference between Mandelbrot and econophysicists explains why the latter start systematically from power-law distributions, while Mandelbrot starts systematically from a stable Lévy distribution. The stable Lévy distribution is a specific case of the power-law distribution, since stable Lévy distribution is associated with a power law whose increments are independent. However, we must remember that when Mandelbrot began his research on the extension of physical methods and models to nonphysical phenomena, results from renormalization group theory had not yet been established. While this connection between Mandelbrot and econophysics seems to be an ad hoc creation, it does suggests that the roots of econophysics lie in an active research movement that emerged with the creation of financial economics (chapter 1).

3.2.3. Power-Law Distribution as a Phenomenological Law

The key role that power laws have played in developments in statistical physics since the end of the 1970s gave impetus to empirical research into power-law distributions. Since the critical exponent is deduced from the power-law distribution that is obtained empirically, econophysicists have provided a huge number of empirical results on power-law distributions. As Stanley and Plerou (2001, 563) explained, research was first focused on finding which phenomena display scaling invariance, and then on identifying empirical values of the exponent a. Proceeding in this way, statistical physicists have identified which phenomena have the same exponents and hence belong to the same universality class—even if none of these empirical researches explained in detail the reasons for this association between power laws and universality class. This first step has led to a large number of empirical investigations that have stressed the phenomenological universality of power-law distributions.

As mentioned, econophysics literature places strong emphasis on the statistical description of empirical observations. From their observations, econophysicists aim to identify a distribution or a mathematical model that they consider universal and that comes from physics.[33] This identification is the signal that they can apply their models and methods to the study of the underlying phenomenon. This is why most of the studies in econophysics exhibit empirical results to demonstrate that the phenomena studied are ruled by a power-law distribution.

First at all, we must mention that empirical investigations into phenomena distributed according to power laws (also often referred to as fat-tail distributions, Pareto distributions, Zipfian distributions, etc.) are nothing new. They date back to Pareto (1897) and have been regularly observed and studied for numerous phenomena since. Statistical physicists thus joined a larger movement, which has reinforced their perception that power laws and critical phenomena constitute important tools for analyzing empirical phenomena. Recently, authors have provided historical perspectives on the use of power laws and log-normal distributions in sciences.[34] We will not present here all phenomena that may be analyzed by means of power laws—they are extremely numerous. Instead, with the aim of understanding the emergence and the foundations of econophysics, we will point out some of the most important empirical results from a historical perspective. This will provide a general overview of the diversity and the precedence of these empirical observations.

In order to identify whether a phenomenon is distributed according to a power law, authors have traditionally used a visual analysis based on a double logarithmic axes histogram. Indeed, as mentioned previously, by taking the logarithm of both sides of equation (3.6), we see that the power-law distribution obeys $\ln P[r > x] = -a \ln x + c$, implying a straight line on a double-logarithmic plot whose slope is given by the scaling parameter a. Therefore, for any critical phenomenon, we expect to find the plot whose form directly depends on the value of the a (figure 3.8).

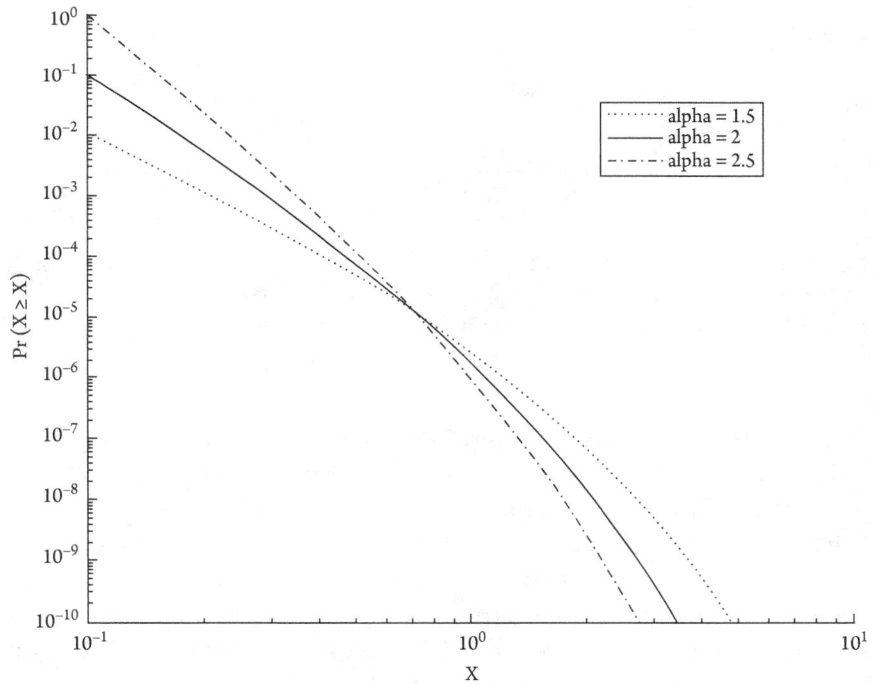

Figure 3.8 The slope of the graph (log-log axis) characterizing a power-law directly depends on the characteristic exponent

A potential infinity of power laws exists. Therefore, the common way of identifying power-law behavior consists in checking visually on a histogram whether the frequency distribution approximately falls on a straight line, which therefore provides an indication that the distribution may follow a power law (with a scaling parameter a

given by the absolute slope of the straight line).[35] To illustrate this visual test, one can consider, for instance, Gabaix et al. (2006). These authors combined on the same histogram the graph of a power law with ones describing empirical data from the Nikkei, the Hang Seng Index. and the S&P 500 index (figure 3.9).

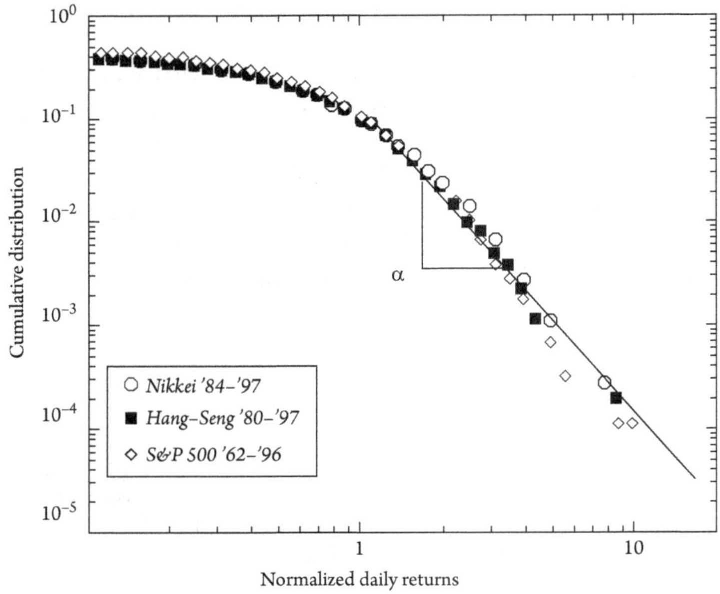

Figure 3.9 Empirical cumulative distribution function of the absolute value of the daily returns of the Nikkei (1984–97), the Hang-Seng (1980–97) and the S&P 500 (1962–96)
Source: Gopikrishnan et al. 1999, 5311. Reproduced by permission of the authors.

In their identification of the power law, Gabaix and al. (2006) varied the scaling parameter *a* of the power laws until they obtained the best fit between the graph of the power law and the ones describing the empirical data. In so doing, they approximately estimate the critical exponent. After having observed that the distributions of returns for three different country indices were similar, the authors concluded that the equation given by their power law, whose critical exponent has been estimated to 3, appears to hold for the data studied independently from the context. Finally, it is worth mentioning that due to the asymptotic dimension of power laws, these laws make sense only for a very large quantity of data.

This type of visual investigation has guided econophysicists' empirical research on power-law distribution. As mentioned above, this kind of approximation is nothing new, since Pareto (1897) was the first author to identify such empirical linearity for income distribution in the population—where many people seemed to have low incomes while very few seemed to have high incomes. Since then, this linearity has been observed in a wide variety of phenomena. The physicist Felix Auerbach (1913) pointed out that city sizes are also distributed according to a power law—there are many towns, fewer large cities, and very few metropolises.[36] The linguist Zipf (1949) refined this observation, hence the term "Zipf's Law" frequently used to refer to the idea that city sizes follow a Pareto distribution as a function of their rank. Interestingly, Auerbach suggested that this law of city sizes was "only a special case of a much more general law which can be applied to the most diverse problems in the natural sciences, geography, statistics, economics, etc." (Auerbach 1913, 76, in Rybski 2013, 1267).[37] In the same the vein, Estoup (1916), and some years later Condon (1928) and then Zipf (1935), observed this linear relationship in the occurrence of words in the vast majority of texts, regardless of the language.[38] In 1922, Willis and Yule (1922) discovered that the frequency of the sizes of biological genera collected by Willis (1922) satisfies a power-law distribution. Yule (1925) explained that the distribution of species among genera of plants also follows a power law. Lotka (1926) observed this distribution for the frequency of publications by scientists. Kleiber (1932) and Brody (1945) found that the mass-specific metabolic rate of various animals is a linear function of their body mass.

We can find many other authors who have made similar observations in a variety of fields—including earthquakes, DNA, and human memory retrieval. The number of these observations has considerably increased with the spread of computerized databases.[39] Power laws have become more and more popular in science, as Clauset explains:

> In the mid-1990s, when large data sets on social, biological and technological systems were first being put together and analyzed, power-law distributions seemed to be everywhere . . . . There were dozens, possibly hundreds of quantities, that all seemed to follow the same pattern: a power-law distribution. (2011, 7)

The result of this evolution was such that some "scientists are calling them more normal than normal [distribution; therefore,] the presence of power-law distributions in data . . . should be considered as the norm rather than the exception" (Willinger, cited in Mitchell 2009, 269).

This kind of relationship was also observed in financial and economic phenomena, in addition to Pareto's observations on income distribution.[40] As explained in chapter 2, Mandelbrot was the first to identify this linear relationship in stock price variations. This observation led him to apply the stable Lévy process to stock price movements in the early 1960s. Although financial economists did not follow Mandelbrot's research due to mathematical difficulties (chapter 2), economists have always used power laws as a descriptive framework to characterize certain economic phenomena. The relationship between the size of firms, cities, and organizations and one of their characteristics (number of employees, inhabitants, growth, profits, etc.) is an example. Recently, financial economists have shown a new interest in this distribution. For instance, Gabaix (2009) showed that the returns of the largest companies on the New York Stock Exchange exhibit the same visual linearity (figure 3.10).

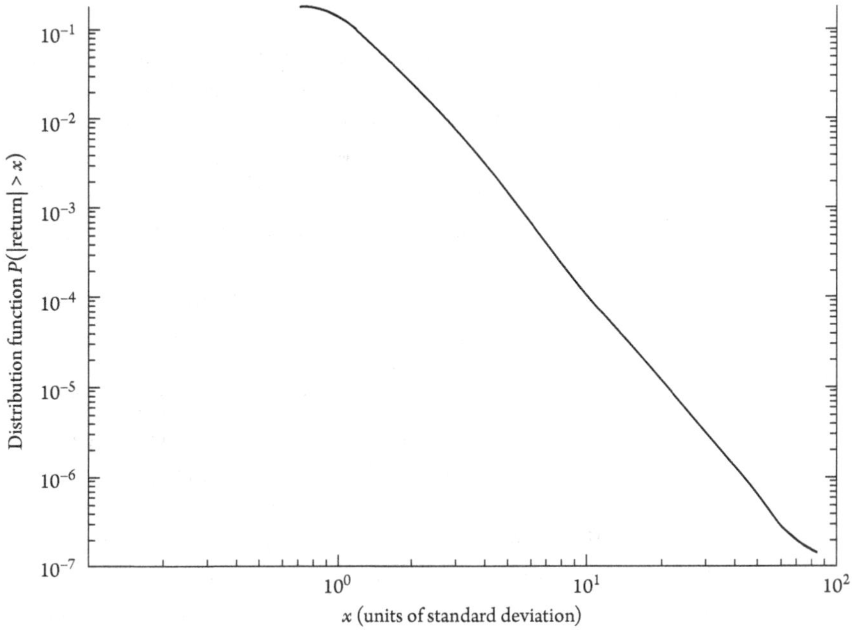

Figure 3.10 Empirical cumulative distribution of the absolute values of the normalized 15-minute returns of the 1,000 largest companies in the Trades and Quotes database for the two-year period 1994–95 (12 million observations)
Source: Gabaix et al. 2003, 268. Reproduced by permission of the authors.

These observations of statistical distributions have led to an emphasis on the phenomenological universality of power laws. These observations have in addition supported the idea that methods and models from statistical physics can be applied outside physics. However, we must stress that the association of these empirical regularities with a power law is not free of presuppositions directly inherited from physics. Indeed, associating empirical observations with a power law implies a specific theoretical reading,[41] since the search for a straight line on this kind of graph refers to the idea that the scaling property is appropriate for describing the studied phenomenon. However, it is worth mentioning that a perfect straight line on a log-log plot graph is rarely observed. In contrast, data rather imply convex or concave lines, suggesting the development of analytical techniques to deal with the inflection points. This situation is indirectly due to the asymptotic character of power laws, whose emergence requires a very large (theoretically infinite) amount of data. For a finite sample, the linear aspect of power laws often has to be corrected by specific techniques.[42]

3.3. HOW PHYSICISTS MADE POWER LAWS PHYSICALLY PLAUSIBLE

Because they see power laws as a key element, statistical physicists have prioritized statistical processes that can integrate these laws into the statistical characterization of physical systems. However, while they are interested in power laws for the statistical description of large fluctuations, some physicists, and particularly econophysicists (Koponen 1995; Mantegna 1991; Mantegna and Stanley 1994) have emphasized empirical difficulties in using these processes. They have pointed out oppositions between the mathematical properties of these processes and their physical applications. With the objective of resolving these oppositions, these authors have developed truncated techniques that have proved necessary for using power laws and associated stochastic processes.

3.3.1. The Necessary Truncation of Power Law

The necessity to truncate power laws comes from one of their mathematical properties, namely their asymptotic behavior. Non-Gaussian stable Lévy processes, whose evolution of variables follows an asymptotic power law, have infinite variance. Because of their asymptotic dimension, power laws make sense only for a very large quantities of data (we could say an "infinite amount" of data). The greater the amount of data, the greater the assurance that power-law behavior is correctly identified. Unfortunately, empirical samples are always finite. Moreover, real phenomena have neither infinite parameters nor asymptotic behavior. Thus, although these processes make it possible to keep scale invariance, which is a key theme in physics, their infinite variance is empirically never observed and therefore is not physically plausible. In this regard, some physicists have asserted that these processes are inapplicable, claiming that they have "mathematical properties that discourage a physical approach" (Gupta and Campanha 1999, 32). Specifically,

> Stochastic processes with infinite variance, although well-defined mathematically, are extremely difficult to use and, moreover, raise fundamental questions when applied to real systems. For example, in physical systems, the second moment is often related to the system temperature, so infinite variance implies an infinite temperature. (Mantegna and Stanley 2000, 4)

Consequently, at the end of the 1980s physicists were faced with a contradiction: while power laws (stable Lévy processes) appeared to be supported by visual analysis of empirical data, their major statistical feature (infinite variance) did not fit with a phenomenological description of physical systems, which all exhibit strictly finite measures.

Van der Vaart (2000) explained that two conceptual problems can emerge when an asymptotic regime is used to describe behaviors of finite systems: first, the number of empirical data is always finite, and second, the theoretical properties associated with an asymptotic regime are in opposition with data observed, which necessarily have finite variance due to the finitude of the sample. To solve these problems, statisticians have suggested truncation techniques. These techniques allow an adaptation of the asymptotic regime to empirical finite samples. Therefore, they have made power laws physically plausible.

The first reason for truncation is the need to fill the gap between the finiteness of every empirical sample of empirical data and the asymptotic framework defining the power-law regime. The truncation of a distribution is a statistical technique allowing modelers to transform an asymptotic and theoretical distribution into a finite and empirical one.[43] In other words, truncation is a conceptual bridge between empirical data and asymptotic results. This idea of truncation is nothing new in physics,[44] but research into this topic has accelerated during the past two decades. During this period, econophysicists have developed sophisticated statistical tools (truncation techniques) to escape the asymptotic regime and retain power laws to describe empirical data. Again, this need to hold onto power laws derives from their theoretical link with scaling invariance, exposed in the previous section.

The second reason for truncating power laws associated with non-Gaussian stable Lévy processes involves the need to transform these laws into a "physically plausible description" of reality. As we know, physical systems refer to real phenomena that can have neither asymptotic behavior nor an infinite parameter. Thus, using non-Gaussian stable Lévy processes to describe a finite sample with finite parameters, although they are based on an asymptotic regime generating an infinite variance, seems complicated. Truncation techniques allow modelers to transform an asymptotic regime into a finite sample by cutting off the asymptotic part of the distribution, thus providing finite variance. We will illustrate this process in the following sections.

3.3.2. Truncation Techniques

While truncation makes the use of power laws physically plausible, we have to point out that all truncations resulting from the finite dimension of physical systems necessarily imply a gap between asymptotical results and empirical data. In statistical terms, the finiteness of samples means that the number of data suddenly reaches a limit, implying an abrupt truncation of the distribution describing them.[45] However, very few physical phenomena come to an abrupt end. In this respect, the manner of truncating power laws must also make sense for physicists, leading them to develop progressively different truncations in order to make them physically plausible and theoretically justified. The development of truncation techniques is closely bound up with the emergence of econophysics[46] in the early 1990s, when statistical physics initiated research in order to solve the theoretical problem related to the infiniteness of variance.

In order to fit their statistical tools to financial distributions, econophysicists have to solve two theoretical problems: on the one hand, they look for finite variance, and on the other hand, they want to work in a nonasymptotic framework. Implicitly, the truncation of distribution has existed for a long time, because we have always worked with the finite asymptotical regime. By developing theoretical solutions for truncated distributions and by defining a function that allows a switch from one to the other, econophysicists provided a first theory of this changeover. Therefore, physicists applied asymptotical properties without misrepresenting them since they provided a specific formulation of the gap between these properties and empirical results. In this way, physicists clarified the bridge between the asymptotic and nonasymptotic regimes by making the switch physically plausible and theoretically justified.

Econophysicists resolved the challenge of obtaining stable Lévy processes with finite variance by using a "cutoff." The first truncation technique was established by Mantegna (1991), who developed his solution using financial data. He justified his choice to use financial data because they offer time series that take into account the occurrence of extreme variations. Later, Mantegna and Stanley (1994) generalized this approach with a truncated stable Lévy distribution with a cutoff at which the distribution begins to deviate from the asymptotic region. This deviation can take different forms, as shown in the equations below. With small amounts of data, that is, for a small value of x, $P(x)$ takes a value very close to what one would expect for a truncated stable Lévy process. But for large values of observations, n, $P(x)$ tends to the value predicted for a nontruncated stable Lévy process. In this framework, the probability of taking a step of size (x) at any time is defined by

$$P(x)=L(x)g(x), \tag{3.8}$$

where $L(x)$ is a stable distribution and $g(x)$ a truncation function. In the simplest case (abrupt truncation), the truncation function $g(x)$ is equal to a constant k and the abrupt truncation process can be characterized by

$$g(x)\begin{Bmatrix} kL(x) & \text{if}\,|x|\leq I \\ 0 & \text{if}\,|x|>I \end{Bmatrix}, \tag{3.9}$$

where I is the value from which the distribution is truncated. If x is not large enough (the physically plausible regime), a Lévy distribution behaves very much like a truncated stable Lévy distribution since most values expected for x fall in the Lévy-like region. When x is beyond the crossover value, we are in the nontruncated regime to which the generalized central-limit theorem (i.e., asymptotic regime) can be applied.

The goal is to reduce the fat tails of the non-Gaussian stable Lévy distribution without deforming the central part of the distribution in order to decompose it into a truncated stable part dedicated to the short and medium term and a nontruncated part dedicated to the long term.[47] This temporal decomposition is required because in the (very) long term, we necessarily have an asymptotic regime. Therefore, thanks to the truncation, in the short and medium term, we can leave the asymptotic regime. In other words, the truncation makes it possible to decompose the stable distribution into a physically plausible regime (truncated part) and an asymptotic one (nontruncated part) (figure 3.11).

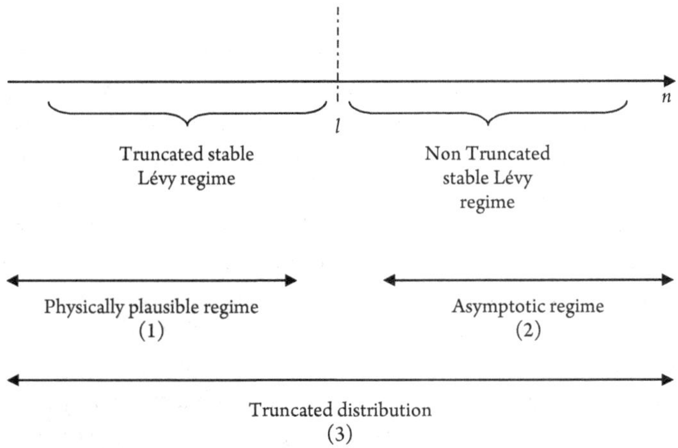

Figure 3.11 The idea of truncation for stable Lévy processes, where l is the selected cutoff and n the number of data

Thanks to the truncated non-Gaussian stable Lévy process, physicists can have a finite variance and hence a more physically plausible description of empirical systems. The idea is to avoid the statistical properties that are in opposition to empirical observation (example: an infinite variance) by keeping those that are perceived as useful (example: stability). It is worth mentioning that a truncated Lévy distribution taken as a whole is no longer stable since it is characterized by a statistical switch of regimes (the third arrow in figure 3.11). However, the truncated part of the distribution (first arrow in figure 3.11) keeps the statistical property of stability by offering a finite variance (Nakao 2000).

This first truncation technique based on a "cutoff" parameter provides a solution to the problem of infinite variance. However, this specific technique produces a distribution that truncates abruptly. Some physicists have claimed that this kind of truncation is not physically plausible enough because the physical system rarely changes abruptly:[48] "In general, the probability of taking a step [a variation] should decrease gradually and not abruptly, in a complex way with step size due to limited physical capacity" (Gupta and Campanha 1999, 232). This generalized empirical principle has led physicists to go beyond abruptly truncated stable Lévy processes, which do not have a sufficient physical basis (Mantegna and Stanley 2000). With this purpose, physicists have developed statistical techniques to solve this constraint related to the physically plausible dimension of the truncation technique.

Among them were Gupta and Campanha (1999), who considered the truncation with a cutoff that is a decreasing exponential function[49] (also called an exponential cutoff). The idea was to switch from a physically plausible regime to an asymptotic one through a gradual or an exponential cutoff after a certain step size, which may be due to the limited physical capacity of the systems under study. We can express the exponential truncation function[50] by using equation (3.10):

$$g(x)=\begin{cases} 1 & \text{if } |x|\leq I \\ \exp\left\{-\left(\dfrac{|x|-I}{k}\right)^{\beta}\right\} & \text{if } |x|>I \end{cases} \tag{3.10}$$

where I is the cutoff parameter at which the distribution begins to deviate from the Lévy distribution, $\exp\left\{-\left(\frac{|x|-I}{k}\right)^{\beta}\right\}$ is a decreasing function, and k and β are constants related to truncation.[51] Using this truncation function, Gupta and Campanha (1999) defined the probability of taking a step of size (x) at any time as being given by

$$P(x)=\begin{cases} k\,\mathrm{L}(x) & \text{if } |x|\leq \mathrm{I} \\ k\,L(x)\exp\left\{-\left(\frac{|x|-I}{k}\right)^{\beta}\right\} & \text{if } |x|\leq \mathrm{I} \end{cases}. \tag{3.11}$$

Like abruptly truncated Lévy distributions, exponentially (or gradually) truncated Lévy distributions have a finite variance,[52] but they offer a more physically plausible framework for describing finite systems (Gupta and Campanha 2002).[53]

3.4. CONCLUSION

The major contribution of chapter is to present the theoretical and methodological foundations of econophysics. The chapter explained the theoretical origins of the power law used in econophysics models. This objective is valuable simply because these foundations are usually not explicitly exposed in the literature. It is worth reminding ourselves that our analysis is based on a financial economist's viewpoint.

As detailed, the roots of econophysics come from the research on critical phenomena and from the scientific changes observed in the 1970s statistical physics. The major key themes of this discipline were presented: the renormalization group theory, the Ising model and scaling properties. We also discussed scale invariance, which is at the heart of these three themes. With the purpose of understanding econophysics, we explained the connections between power laws, scale invariance, and financial economics. Power laws make sense in relation to the definition of financial returns; they can also describe the evolution of financial fluctuations through stable Lévy processes. This is where stable Lévy processes play a key role for econophysicists. Readers were reminded that power laws are not new in financial economics, since Mandelbrot—for different reasons—introduced them into finance in the 1960s.

As this chapter showed, power laws are not perfectly adapted to describe physical (finite) systems, because they theoretically generate an infinite variance. To solve this problem, physicists have developed truncation techniques. Econophysicists are thereby able to obtain a finite variance while keeping the notion of scale invariance. As mentioned, these truncation techniques are closely associated with the emergence of econophysics.

The following chapter will define econophysics and explain how this discipline is related to financial economics.

4

THE DISCIPLINARY POSITION OF ECONOPHYSICS
NEW OPPORTUNITIES FOR FINANCIAL INNOVATIONS

The previous chapter traced the origins of econophysics in statistical-physics. It explained econophysicists' method for modeling extreme values. Since the 1990s, the introduction of intraday data combined with a series of financial crises has shed light on the issue of extreme values. One of the most telling examples is the collapse of Long-Term Capital Management (LTCM) in 1998. This fund was founded by two key authors of finance (Merton and Scholes), implying risk management based on the core models of financial economics. However, it appears that "fund managers at LTCM lacked a method for assessing the likelihood of more extreme risks in the long term" (Buchanan 2004, 6). Models and results provided by econophysicists could offer an interesting opportunity to reconsider the models used in financial economics. However, the dialogue between the two communities has almost been nonexistent since the birth of econophysics. How have we ended up with such situation? How can we explain this lack of dialogue?

The aim of this chapter is to identify the reasons for this lack of dialogue between financial economists and econophysicists. In this perspective, the way both communities produce their specific scientific ideas will be investigated. This chapter will set out the progressive institutionalization of econophysics in terms of the organization and diffusion of knowledge. It will show that although econophysics still lies outside financial economics, this discipline has progressively developed its autonomy from physics. This specific position of econophysics in the disciplinary space explains why, despite the fact that financial economists and econophysicists share the same research topics, dialogue between them is fraught with difficulty. Moreover, this chapter will investigate two kinds of consequences of this institutional position. A first direct consequence is that econophysicists have difficulty getting their research published in financial-economics journals. Another interesting consequence is that being outside financial economics, econophysicists have not been constrained by the former discipline's theoretical and methodological framework. As section 4.2 will detail, this situation has allowed econophysics to introduce some scientific innovations that have not been developed within financial economics.

4.1. THE EMERGENCE OF ECONOPHYSICS

The first part of this chapter deals with the birth and the institutionalization of econophysics. After having presented some contextual elements that favored the creation of this field, we will investigate the way econophysics has progressively been crystallized. With this purpose, a bibliometric analysis will be offered in order to clarify the disciplinary position of this new area of knowledge.

4.1.1. The Official Birth

As mentioned in the general introduction, the term *econophysics* generally refers to the extension of statistical physics to the study of problems commonly considered to fall within the sphere of economics, and particularly problems in finance. From a financial economist's viewpoint, econophysics aims to provide models that reproduce the statistical behaviors of stock price or return variations, including their extreme values, and then to apply these models to the study of financial products and strategies, such as options pricing. The movement's official birth announcement came in a 1996 article by Stanley et al. (1996), which coined the term *econophysics*.[1] However, following Kutner and Grech (2008), we can trace the informal birth of the movement to a paper published by Mantegna (1991) that studied the evolution of financial in terms of stable Lévy processes. As detailed in chapter 3, this birth finds some of its origins in the changes that have occurred since the 1970s in statistical physics and on financial markets.

The growing interest of physicists in economics and finance that led to the appearance of econophysics coincided with what Kaiser (2012) called the "second bubble of Physics Ph.D.s" observed in the 1980s. This situation was enhanced by defense policy under the Reagan administration combined with increasing fears of economic competition with Japan, triggering greater spending in biotech, engineering, and physical sciences. This second bubble clearly appears when one considers the number of physics PhDs defended during the twentieth century (figure 4.1). Moreover, this bubble is directly linked with the "golden age" of physics mentioned in chapter 3.

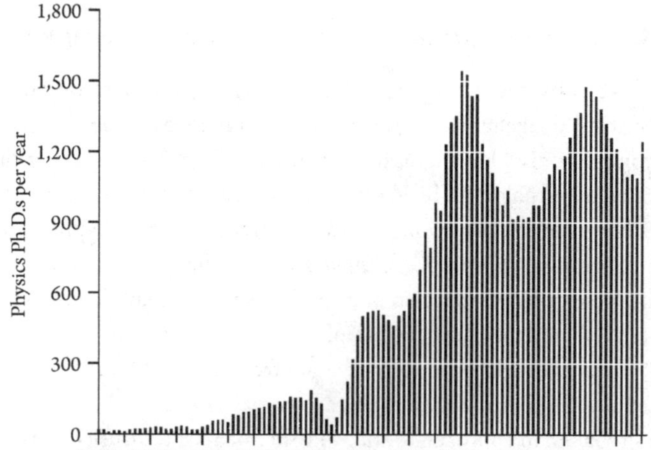

Figure 4.1 Number of physics PhDs granted by US institutions, 1900–2005.
Source: Kaiser 2012, 299. Reproduced by permission of the author.

The rapid rise in the public funding in the 1980s for young physicists generated a form of "déjà vu" since it resembled the first bubble observed during the "Sputnik era" of the 1960s (also visible in figure 4.1).[2] The second bubble was mainly favorable to physicists involved in condensed-matter physics because this area of knowledge benefited from the significant theoretical results obtained in the 1970s (chapter 3). Moreover, "[In this] field of research the line between fundamental physics and its practical applications was so close that it was often blurred" (Cassidy 2011, 131). This rhetoric was directly in line with the political community's expectations in the 1990s, leading to a higher number of public-funding opportunities for projects developed in this area of knowledge. This trend was strengthened in the 1990s with the second bubble, when this field became the first choice for new PhD students in physics to choose condensed-matter physics, generating the second bubble evoked above. In 2000, for instance, 41 percent of doctorates in physics were in condensed-matter physics (Cassidy 2011).

A point must be clarified here. In the previous chapter, we associated the foundations of econophysics with statistical physics. It is worth mentioning that statistical physics refers to a set of theoretical tools that can be applied to different physical systems, while condensed matter is the branch of physics dealing with the physical properties of matter phases. In other terms, condensed-matter physicists investigate the behavior of matter and how it can evolve toward different phases. In their study of matter, these physicists often use statistical methods (i.e., statistical physics). This context explains that several fathers of econophysics (e.g., McCauley and Stanley) and the vast majority of research centers providing PhD opportunities in this field are associated with condensed-matter physics. Telling examples are the Center for Polymer Studies in Boston and the Santa Fe Institute, which have been important actors in the organization and the diffusion of econophysics.

The following section will analyze the disciplinary position of econophysics in this particular context. Did econophysicists produce their knowledge in physics or financial economics (or both)? Did they publish their works in financial economics journals? These are the kind of questions we will investigate hereafter.

4.1.2. The Institutionalization of the New Discipline

While the 1990s saw the emergence of econophysics, the next decade witnessed a growing institutionalization of the field. To gain recognition for their field of research, econophysicists have adopted various strategies for spreading their knowledge. Specialized journals have been created, symposia have been organized and specific courses have been set up by physics departments in order to promote scientific recognition of the new approach. All these strategies have played a part not only in disseminating econophysics but also in creating a shared scientific culture, which is a key element in the creation of a new discipline (Nadeau 1995).

The first publications in econophysics date from the 1990s. The founding article by Stanley et al. (1996) strongly influenced physicists and mathematicians who developed a non-Gaussian approach to the study of financial returns (Kutner and Grech 2008). The proportion of articles devoted to econophysics has since grown steadily.

This trend appears clearly in the journal *Physica A* (figure 4.2), one of the three journals that publish the great majority of articles on the subject (we will return to this point in the next section).

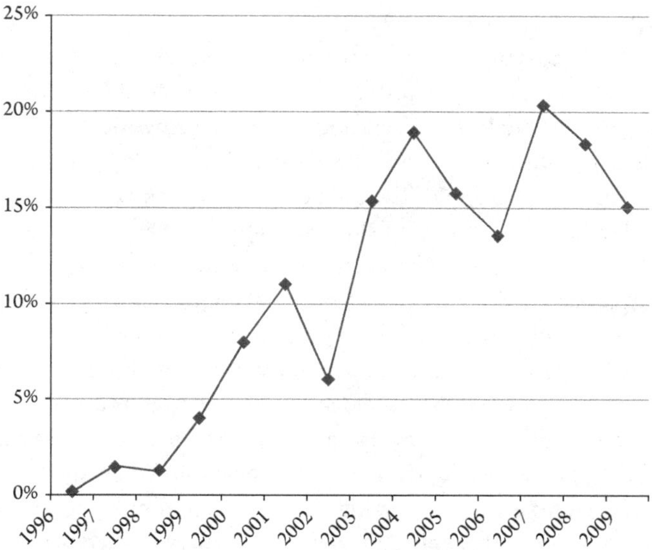

Figure 4.2 Number of articles on econophysics published in *Physica A* between 1996 and 2010
Source: Web of Science.

It is worth mentioning that the nonlinearity of the trend shown in figure 4.2 is mainly due to regularly published special issues devoted to econophysics. The trend observed for *Physica A* is also found in the three other major journals that have published articles in econophysics (*International Journal of Modern Physics C, Physical Review E,* and the *European Journal of Physics B*). This sustained growth in the number of articles published each year earned econophysics official recognition as a discipline by the Physics and Astrophysics Classification Scheme (PACS) in 2003—10 years after the first articles.

The emerging editorial activity in econophysics has followed a relatively clear line: at the beginning, econophysicists preferred to publish and gain acceptance in journals devoted to a preexisting theoretical field in physics (statistical physics) rather than create new journals outside a preexisting scientific space and structure. Moreover, these journals are among the most prestigious in physics. This editorial orientation results from the methodology used by econophysicists (derived from statistical physics, as was mentioned in the previous section) but also from the new community's hope, on the one hand, to quickly gain recognition from the existing scientific community and, on the other hand, to reach a larger audience. Next, econophysicists created journals with a title directly associated with economics or financial economics. One can consider, for instance, *Quantitative Finance,* created in 2001, a journal essentially devoted to questions of econophysics. The *Journal of Economic Interaction and*

Coordination (*JEIC*), which started in 2006, is open to econophysics although its main focus, the concept of interaction, is not a key theme in econophysics. Econophysicists have also increased their influence in economic journals that already existed. Among these is the *Journal of Economic Dynamics and Control*, created in 1979, which has been open to papers related to econophysics since the publication in 2008 of a special issue devoted to this theme.

The 1990s, then, stand as the decade in which econophysics emerged thanks to growth in the number of publications. Textbooks on econophysics were not far behind. The first textbook, *Introduction to Econophysics* by Mantegna and Stanley, was published in 2000. Several more have appeared since—by Roehner (2002) and McCauley (2004), for example. The publication of textbooks is a very important step in the development of a new field. They do not have the same status as articles or collections of articles. The latter are frequently aimed at spreading knowledge in an approach to the subject matter that remains exploratory and not unified. Textbooks, on the other hand, are more grounded in a unified analysis. Their contents therefore require a period of homogenization of the discipline, which is why they represent an additional step in the institutionalization process. They "contain highly elaborate models of linguistic forms for students to follow" (Bazerman 1988, 155). Textbooks play a sociological and educational role for neophytes by defining the patterns of learning and formulating statements appropriate to the community they wish to join. Given that collections of articles are published before textbooks, the interval between the publication of the former and that of the latter gives an indication of the discipline's evolution (Jovanovic 2008): econophysics appears, therefore, as a theoretical approach that is evolving relatively rapidly. Barely a decade was required to see the appearance of the first textbooks presenting econophysics as a unified and coherent field. The swiftness of the development of this discipline can be gauged by noting that it took twice as long, that is, two decades, for the first textbooks devoted to another recent specialty in finance, behavioral finance, to appear (Schinckus 2009).

Another way to spread knowledge related to a new field is to organize workshops and colloquiums. The first conference devoted to econophysics took place at the University of Budapest in 1997 and was organized by the Department of Physics. Two years later, the European Association of Physicists officially endorsed the first conference on applications, Applications of Physics in Financial Analysis (APFA), which was held in Dublin. The APFA colloquium was entirely dedicated to econophysics and was held annually until 2007. Today, several annual conferences dedicated to econophysics exist, such as the Nikkei Econophysics Research Workshop and Symposium and the Econophysics Colloquium. Combined with publications of papers and textbooks, these events contribute to the stabilization and spread of a common scientific culture among econophysicists.

Another important component of a truly institutionalized research field is the creation of academic courses and BA, MA, and PhD programs devoted solely to that field. Here again, physics has served as the institutional basis. Courses in econophysics have been offered exclusively in physics departments since 2002 (the universities of Ulm in

Sweden, Fribourg in Switzerland, Munster in Germany, Silesia and Wroclaw in Poland, and Dublin in Ireland). Most of the time, these courses are framed for physicists and focus on statistical physics applied to finance. An additional step in the institutionalization of econophysics has been the creation of full academic programs totally dedicated to this field. The first universities to introduce complete degree programs were Polish (Miskiewicz 2010). Indeed, since 2001, the University of Silesia has offered a bachelor's program in this field, and a master's program was created in 2009. Six other Polish universities also offer programs in econophysics, for example, Warsaw with a bachelor's program and Wroclaw with a master's. In 2006, the University of Houston in the United States was the first to coordinate a PhD in econophysics,[3] while a great number of physics departments offer a PhD with a major in econophysics.[4] In order to familiarize students with the reality of finance, these programs provide some courses on the financial *reality*, but they do not familiarize students with the *theoretical* basis of financial economics.

Finally, this process of institutionalization was reinforced because of econophysicists' ability to connect with other research themes. In 2006, the Society for Economic Science with Heterogeneous Interacting Agents (ESHIA) was created to promote interdisciplinary research combining economics, physics, and computer science (essentially artificial intelligence). Of course, this project does not directly focus on econophysics, since the analysis of the heterogeneity and interaction of agents is an approach that covers a wider field, including experimental psychology and artificial intelligence. However, ESHIA aims at promoting an interdisciplinary approach, which is precisely one of the major characteristics of econophysics. Besides, the society's new journal (*Journal of Economic Interaction and Coordination*) has been inviting authors to submit papers devoted to econophysics. A further sign of the growing influence of econophysics is the International Conference on Econophysics, a platform for the presentation of interdisciplinary ideas coming from different communities, especially economics, finance, and physics. Finally, let us mention the existence of an international forum dedicated to econophysics where scholars can share their opinions about the evolution of the field.[5] This forum is a way of diffusing knowledge; it also lists all available academic positions related to econophysics.

4.2. THE POSITION OF ECONOPHYSICS IN THE DISCIPLINARY SPACE

While econophysics was officially recognized as a new discipline in 2003,[6] it is crucial to situate it in the disciplinary space and to understand its connections with financial economics. An analysis of econophysics' position in the disciplinary space gives relevant information for understanding how it has developed its own models and methodology for studying finance. The current investigation is based on a bibliometric analysis (Gingras and Schinckus 2012). To analyze the position of econophysics in the disciplinary space, the most influential authors in econophysics were identified. Then their papers in the literature were tracked by using the Web of Science database of Thomson-Reuters.[7] The period studied—from 1980 to 2008—allows an analysis of the evolution of the field since the changes that occurred in its prehistory period and makes it possible to measure the impact of its birth (in 1996). The objective of the following section is to trace the birth and the beginning of econophysics in order to understand the context in which the field emerged. From this perspective, we will investigate the early period of econophysics between 1996 and 2008. Another reason for focusing our attention on this period refers of the fact that econophysics in its infancy was clearly defined (statistical physics applied to financial economics). As Chakraborti et al. (2011a, 2011b) and Schinckus (2012, 2017) showed, the econophysics literature has become more and more scattered since 2009–10.

4.2.1. In the Shadow of Physics

Let us consider first the disciplines in which the source papers have been published. More than 70 percent of the key papers that have been published since 1996 appear in physics journals, while only 21.6 percent have found their place in economics or finance journals (table 4.1). During the previous period (1980–95) there were very few papers written in journals of physics. They were mainly written in finance and economics journals and were not really based on an approach originating in physics.[8]

Table 4.1 Disciplines in which the source papers have been published

Discipline	*1980–95*	*%*	*1996–2008*	*%*	*Total*	*%*
Physics	8	32.0%	153	70.5%	161	66.5%
Economics and finance	13	52.0%	47	21.6%	60	24.2%
Mathematics	0	0.0%	9	4.1%	9	3.7%
Other fields	1	16.0%	3	3.8%	4	5%
Total	**25**	**100%**	**217**	**100%**	**242**	**100%**

Source: Web of Science.

These observations suggest that, although finance and economics journals did publish articles on econophysics, the field did not hold a large place in financial economics. In contrast, econophysics became more and more important in the discipline of physics. This observation corroborates the fact that all academic programs dedicated to econophysics have developed outside economics.

The centrality of physics for econophysics (between 1996 and 2008) is clearly visible in figure 4.3, which maps the network of co-citations between journals cited in papers citing our 242 source papers in econophysics. The dense core of the network is composed of physics journals, while economics and finance journals are peripheral (northwest of the map) and *Quantitative Finance* is in between.

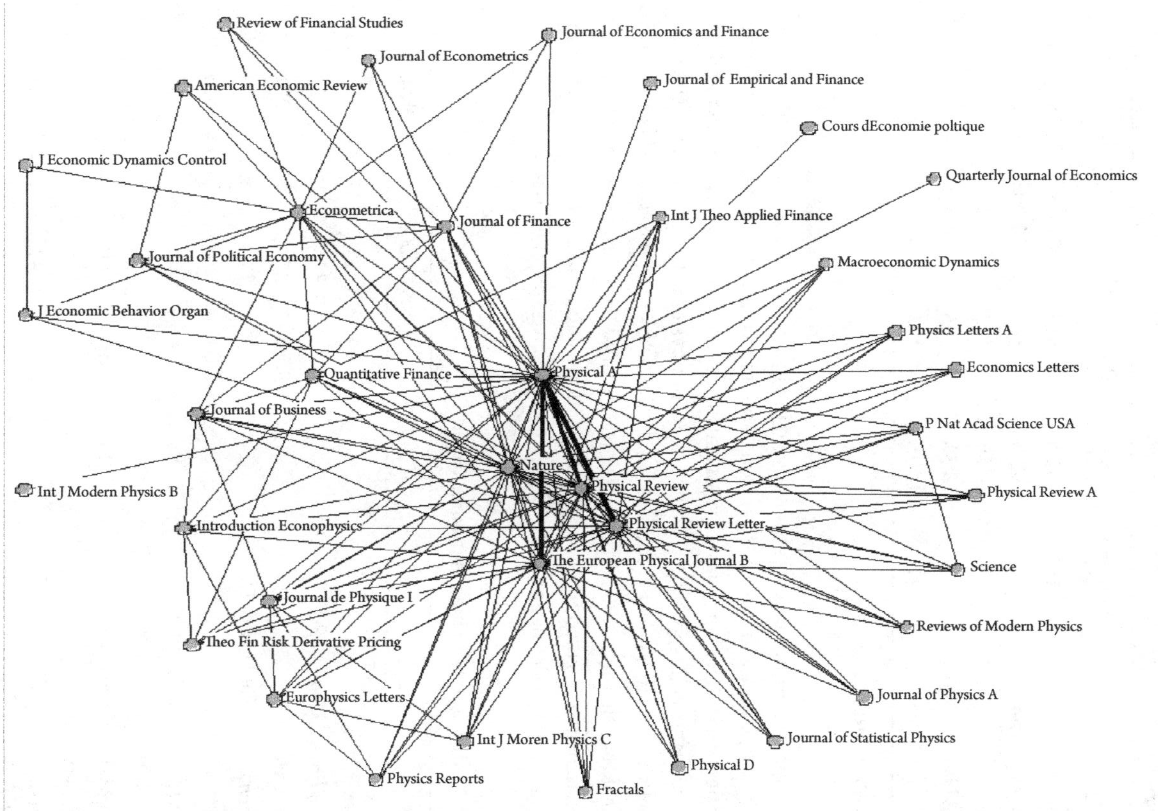

Figure 4.3 Most co-cited journals (and manuals) in papers citing our 242 source articles in econophysics (100 co-citations +)
Source: Gingras and Schinckus (2012). Reproduced by permission of the authors.

Another way to look at the centrality of physics journals is provided in table 4.2, which shows that between 1996 and 2008 only 12 percent of the citations of the source papers came from economics or finance journals. Interestingly, this trend was similar in the previous period (1980–95), even though more than half of the papers had been published in economics and finance journals.

Table 4.2 Disciplines citing the source papers

Discipline	*1980–95*	*%*	*1996–2008*	*%*	*Total*
Physics	16	76.2%	2489	76.1%	2505
Economics and finance	2	9.5%	399	12.2%	401
Mathematics	1	4.8%	112	3.4%	113
Other fields	1	9.5%	63	8.3%	64
Total	**21**	**100%**	**3272**	**100%**	**3293**

Source: Web of Science.

Econophysics is thus essentially discussed in physics journals, a result confirmed by table 4.3, which shows that, for both periods, about three-quarters of the citations come from papers published in physics journals usually devoted to condensed matter and statistical mechanics. The growing presence of econophysics in the pages of physics journals explains the official recognition of the discipline by the Physics and Astrophysics Classification Scheme in 2003. This concentration inside physics, together with the fact that the audience targeted by econophysics is increasingly made up of physicists, suggests that econophysics has been developed by physicists for physicists.

Table 4.3 Main journals citing the source papers

Journals	*1980–95*	*%*	*1996–2008*	*%*	*Total*	*%*
Physica A	3	14.3%	1213	37.1%	1216	36.9%
European Physical Journal B	0	0.0%	326	10.0%	326	9.9%
Physical Review E	2	9.5%	279	8.5%	281	8.5%
International Journal of Modern Physics C	1	4.8%	143	4.4%	144	4.4%
Quantitative Finance	0	0.0%	110	3.4%	110	3.3%
Journal of Economic Dynamics and Control	0	0.0%	68	2.1%	68	2.1%
Journal of Economic Behavior and Organization	1	4.8%	60	1.8%	61	1.9%
Acta Physica Polonica B	0	0.0%	42	1.3%	42	1.3%
Physical Review Letters	1	4.8%	36	1.1%	37	1.1%
Chaos Solitons and Fractals	0	0.0%	35	1.1%	35	1.1%

Journals	*1980–95*	*%*	*1996–2008*	*%*	*Total*	*%*
Journal of Physics A: Mathematical and General	1	4.8%	33	1.0%	34	1.0%
Macroeconomic Dynamics	0	0.0%	33	1.0%	33	1.0%
Journal of the Korean Physical Society	0	0.0%	30	0.9%	30	0.9%
Europhysics Letters	0	0.0%	29	0.9%	29	0.9%
Proceedings of the National Academy of Sciences of the United States of America	0	0.0%	25	0.8%	25	0.8%
Advances in Complex Systems	0	0.0%	24	0.7%	24	0.7%
Physics Reports—review section of *Physics Letters*	0	0.0%	24	0.7%	24	0.7%
Computer Physics Communications	0	0.0%	20	0.6%	20	0.6%
EPL	0	0.0%	20	0.6%	20	0.6%
International Journal of Bifurcation and Chaos	0	0.0%	20	0.6%	20	0.6%
Reports on Progress in Physics	0	0.0%	19	0.6%	19	0.6%
International Journal of Modern Physics B	0	0.0%	18	0.6%	18	0.5%
Journal of Statistical Mechanics: Theory and Experiment	0	0.0%	15	0.5%	15	0.5%

Source: Web of Science.

A more precise investigation of the bibliometric data shows that econophysics has not merely grown in the shadow of physics: it has progressively developed as an autonomous subfield in the discipline. Indeed, although most of the publications citing the source papers have appeared in journals of physics since 1996, we note that they are concentrated in only two journals: *Physica A* (devoted to "statistical mechanics and its applications") and *European Physical Journal B* (devoted to condensed matter and complex systems). Together these two journals account for 47.1 percent of the publications (table 4.3). In addition, table 4.4 shows that *Physica A* published by far the largest number of econophysics papers, with 41.5 percent of the total in the second period (1996–2008). It has thus become the leading journal of this new field. In second place is another physics journal, *European Physical Journal B*. This observation must be compared to the relative unimportance of *Physica A* in the first period: only 4 percent of the key papers were published in this journal between 1980 and 1996. With the *European Physical Journal B, Physica A* published 53.9 percent of the key papers between 1996 and 2008. In addition to the two journals already identified as the core publishing venues for econophysics, we find *Physical Review E,* the major American physics journal devoted to research on "statistical, nonlinear and soft-matter physics."

Table 4.4 Journals where the source papers have been published

Journals	*1980–95*	*%*	*1996–2008*	*%*	*Total*	*%*
Physica A	1	4.0%	90	41.5%	91	37.6%
European Physical Journal B	0	0.0%	27	12.4%	27	11.2%
Journal of Economic Behavior and Organization	2	8.0%	9	4.1%	11	4.5%
Quantitative Finance	0	0.0%	10	4.6%	10	4.1%
Physical Review E	0	0.0%	8	3.7%	8	3.3%

Source: Web of Science.

This concentration in physics journals, and the fact that econophysicists have a strong tendency to refer essentially to each other (Pieters and Hans 2002), suggest that econophysics has now established its autonomy within physics.

4.2.2. Outside Financial Economics

While econophysics has grown in the shadow of physics, its situation vis-à-vis financial economics is also singular. Until 1996, econophysicists published mainly in finance and economics journals, but since then econophysics has developed outside financial economics (table 4.1). The only economics-related journals citing econophysics are *Quantitative Finance*, the *Journal of Economic Dynamics and Control*, the *Journal of Economic Behavior and Organization*, and *Macroeconomic Dynamics* (table 4.3). Since the appointment of J. B. Rosser[9] as editor-in-chief in 2002, the *Journal of Economic Behavior and Organization* has begun publishing regular articles on the issue of complexity in economics, allowing econophysicists to publish their work in that journal. *Quantitative Finance*, a relatively new journal created in 2001, appears to be the main economics journal to publish papers devoted to econophysics (table 4.4). It can be considered one of the first nonphysics journals specifically devoted to the new field: its editorial board includes many econophysicists, and the editors are two econophysicists (Jean-Philippe Bouchaud and Doyne Farmer) and a mathematician (Michael Dempster). Another journal, the *Journal of Economic Interaction and Coordination*, was created in 2006 to promote research combining economics, physics, and computer science. This publication is mainly directed by physicists, and its editorial team features a substantial number of physicists and artificial intelligence specialists. Interestingly, in 2008 the most cited journal in this publication was *Physica A*, followed by *Quantitative Finance* itself, the *Journal of Economic Dynamics and Control*, and then by two physics journals (*European Physical Journal B* and *Physical Review E*).[10]

Lastly, a 2008 special issue of the *Journal of Economic Dynamics and Control* deserves mention: "Applications of Statistical Physics in Economics and Finance" explicitly proposed to "overcome the lack of communication between economists and econophysicists" (Farmer and Lux 2008, 3). Doyne Farmer and Thomas Lux[11] were the guest editors for this special issue, and its 12 articles devoted to econophysics were written by financial economists and physicists. We should emphasize that the economics-related journals citing econophysics cannot really be considered mainstream economics journals, but rather as what Backhouse (2004, 265) called "orthodox dissenter" journals, that is, journals that while rooted in mainstream theory are open to other approaches.[12] All this suggests that econophysics has found its place outside the major journals in financial economics. The complete absence of top-tier economic journals from table 4.4 again confirms that, between 1996 and 2008, econophysics developed beyond the margins of financial economics.

Since 2009, the term *econophysics* has been used more and more in the literature (Chakraborti et al. 2011a, 2011b; Schinckus 2012, 2017). However, the meaning of this label has been extended by articles that implement ARCH-type models (Anagnostidis and Emmanouilides 2015; Queiros and Tsallis 2005) or classical agent-based modeling (Abergel et al. 2014) and claim to be related to econophysics. This increasing fragmentation of the literature makes a bibliometric analysis difficult. Moreover, the professional climate has also opened doors for potential (sometimes not well-defined) collaboration between financial economists and econophysicists. In this perspective, it is worth mentioning that the online journal *Economics* has (since 2009) a specific section dedicated to econophysics, while the *International Review of Financial Analysis* appointed a topic editor devoted to econophysics. Let us also mention that this journal has published two special issues dedicated to this field in the last seven years (Li and Chen 2012; McCauley et al. 2016 [forthcoming]). This recent evolution shows that potential collaborations can be found between financial economics and econophysics. However, with the purpose of understanding the disciplinary position of the latter, this section has aimed at studying the period during which econophysics was progressively been crystallized—this target led us to focus on the years between 1996 and 2008.

Despite this growth in the field, table 4.5 shows that developments in economics and finance were still matters of concern for econophysicists, since nearly half the citations (46.5 percent) were to journals from these disciplines. Physics remains an important reference, with about a third of the citations going to papers published in physics journals, followed by mathematics journals (about 7 percent) and a tail of many different science journals (13 percent). During the first period (1980–95) more than 56 percent of the references cited were to economics or finance journals. We thus observe a decreasing dependence of econophysics on the economics literature and a growing presence of physics journals as a source of knowledge for econophysics, up from 19.2 percent to 32.6 percent.

Table 4.5 Disciplines cited in the source papers (two citations or more)

Discipline	*1980–95*	*%*	*1996–2008*	*%*	*Total*	*%*
Economics and finance	168	56.8%	2721	46.5%	2889	47.3%
Physics	56	19.2%	1943	33.3%	1999	32.6%
Mathematics	21	7.2%	419	7.2%	440	7.2%
Other fields	47	15.9%	752	13%	799	12.9%
Total	292	100%	5835	100%	6127	100%

Source: Web of Science.

This trend can also be observed in table 4.6, which lists the main journals cited in the source papers. While economics journals (e.g., *American Economic Review*) were often cited in the key papers written between 1980 and 1995, physics journals became the main source of knowledge for the papers published after 1996. As the table shows, between 1996 and 2008, among the first 10 journals listed, physics journals represent 22.6 percent, while economics and finance journals represent 10.7 percent of papers published.

Table 4.6 Main journals cited in the source papers (two citations or more)

Journals	*1980–95*	*%*	*1996–2008*	*%*	*Total*	*%*
Physica A	3	1.0%	551	9.4%	554	9.0%
European Physical Journal B	0	0.0%	260	4.5%	260	4.2%
Physical Review E	0	0.0%	196	3.4%	196	3.2%
Quantitative Finance	0	0.0%	179	3.1%	179	2.9%
Physical Review Letters	5	1.7%	162	2.8%	167	2.7%
Nature	2	0.7%	147	2.5%	149	2.4%
Journal of Finance	2	0.7%	128	2.2%	130	2.1%
American Economic Review	18	6.2%	107	1.8%	125	2.0%
International Journal of Theoretical and Applied Finance	0	0.0%	113	1.9%	113	1.8%
Econometrica	7	2.4%	101	1.7%	108	1.8%
International Journal of Modern Physics C	0	0.0%	107	1.8%	107	1.7%
Journal de Physique I	2	0.7%	93	1.6%	95	1.6%
Journal of Business	6	2.1%	85	1.5%	91	1.5%
Journal of Economic Behavior and Organization	5	1.7%	84	1.4%	89	1.5%
Journal of Political Economy	5	1.7%	73	1.3%	78	1.3%
Quarterly Journal of Economics	10	3.4%	62	1.1%	72	1.2%
Economic Journal	10	3.4%	58	1.0%	68	1.1%

Source: Web of Science.

Taken together, these data confirm that econophysics has developed on the existing institutional structures of physics, rather than attempting to impose itself inside the existing field of financial economics. As we have already pointed out, econophysics is being promoted by "outsiders" to financial economics.

4.3. ADVANTAGES AND DISADVANTAGES OF THIS INSTITUTIONAL POSITION

This singular institutional position—outside financial economics and in the shadow of physics—has structured exchanges between econophysicists and financial economists. While it is not hard to understand that this disciplinary structure makes dialogue difficult, it has provided a surprisingly fruitful context for scientific innovations. This section will analyze this fertility by investigating to what extent their position as outsiders has allowed econophysicists to innovate and to contribute to the understanding of financial markets.

4.3.1. The Difficult Dialogue between Financial Economists and Econophysicists

As the previous section showed, papers dedicated to econophysics are mainly published in physics journals, and their vocabulary, method, and models are those used in physics. Now, although scientific papers appear contextless, they are social constructions referring to a disciplinary culture whose knowledge is founded on the production, reception, and use of texts. In their organization, these texts share a highly stylized and formal system of presentation that aims to convince readers, who will expect to find this specific system (Knorr-Cetina 1981, chap. 5; Gilbert and Mulkay 1984; Bazerman 1988). Consequently, it has been easier for econophysicists to present their work to physics journals as examples of modeling exercises analogous to those found in physics than to try to get past the gatekeepers of financial-economics journals. This situation was compounded by the fact, already mentioned, that the conceptual foundations behind the mathematical techniques are very different from those found in financial economics. Beyond this mathematical difference, the position of econophysics in the disciplinary space also results from four other major obstacles to dialogue between the two communities. These obstacles, or difficulties, concern the vocabulary used, the publishing process, the use of data, and the methodology employed.

The first difficulty concerns the vocabulary used. Although econophysics and financial economics study the same topics (stock price variations), they differ in the way they define their mathematical concepts. Econophysics' distinctive feature is the use of power laws and stable Lévy processes for modeling stock price variations. However, the term commonly used in the econophysics literature is simply Lévy processes (omitting the qualifier "stable"). This vocabulary is confusing because financial economists also use Lévy processes in their conditional description of financial data (chapter 2).[13] However, the two communities do not associate the same statistical treatment with the label "Lévy processes": while financial economists use this term to characterize a conditional implementation (i.e., capturing the variability of a major trend) of Lévy processes, econophysicists associate the term with an unconditional use (i.e., describing the whole distribution) of stable Lévy processes (we will explain this opposition in detail in the following chapter). This confusion in nomenclature also generates debates on the real contributions of econophysics simply because many economists tend to consider this field as a pale copy of what Mandelbrot and Fama tried to do in the 1960s (chapter 2). In this context, the novelties in the econophysics approach are not always clear.

The second obstacle to dialogue is the different practices in the publication of knowledge. While economists usually wait several months (sometimes several years!) for the finalization of the editorial process, physicists consider that, once accepted for publication, a paper must be published quickly because its analysis and data are significant only in the period immediately following completion of the research, and not several months or years later.[14] For physicists, the excessively long editorial process of economics journals acts as a disincentive to submitting a paper. On the other hand, financial economists have to face to an amazing number of publications in which it is not easy to find the information they are looking for. Indeed, financial economists and econophysicists use different stylistic conventions that make reading laborious for the other community: both communities use their own classification scheme[15] and their own reference style.[16] Beyond the different stylistic conventions, Bazerman (1988) noted that financial economists and physicists tend to present their scientific writing differently. A common practice in financial economics is to write a substantial literature review "demonstrating the incrementalism of this literature" (Bazerman 1988, 274) in order to emphasize the accumulation of knowledge and the ability of authors to contribute to a preexisting codified knowledge. In complete contrast, physicists focus on the practical implications of their articles, mentioning only references that deal with potential applications.

These dissimilarities between publishing standards used in financial economics and in physics have helped to keep econophysics publications out of financial economic journals. This is consistent with Whitley's observation that "research which ignores current priorities and approaches and challenges current standards and ideals is unlikely to be published in academic journals of the discipline" (1986b, 192). A reliable measure of rejected submissions is difficult to obtain, but an informal survey shows that the major actors of econophysics did try to publish in those mainstream economics journals with little success. We sent a questionnaire to 27 leading econophysicists (included as the key authors mentioned in the bibliometric analysis presented in the previous section) about the degree of closure of economic journals to econophysicists. To the question "Have you submitted a paper to a ranked journal in economics," a large majority of authors replied yes. However, as we saw previously, very few papers are now published in economic journals. Thus, when authors were asked to give the main reasons for the rejection of their paper, they replied that referees in economic journals often have difficulties with the topic or/and the method used in their paper.[17] Although based on a small sample, these results strongly suggest that economic journals are reluctant to publish papers devoted to econophysics. It appears, therefore, that this resistance is what prompted econophysicists to exclude themselves and move toward journals more open to the econophysics perspective.

The third obstacle to dialogue is that financial economists and econophysicists diverge markedly on the way they use empirical data. Econophysicists claim that their approach is more neutral (i.e., not based on an a priori model). They explicitly demonstrate a willingness to develop models that are, on the one hand, more coherent from a physics point of view, and on the other hand based on "raw observations" of economic systems (Stanley, Gabaix, and Plerou 2008). By "raw observations," econophysicists mean nonnormalized data. Financial economics (and financial econometrics) is mainly based on the Gaussian framework, and when financial economists (financial econometricians) observe abnormal data (by abnormal data, we mean statistically unusual from a Gaussian point of view), they normalize these data. They use data mining in order to consider that all abnormal data have an expected mean equal to zero. In other words, financial economists implicitly assume that price changes obey the log-normal probability distribution implying that massive fluctuations have a small probability. According to econophysicists, that perspective leads them to underestimate the occurrence of financial crashes (Mandelbrot and Hudson 2004, 25). In marked contrast, econophysicists claim to work directly with observed data, in which there are no "abnormal data" since, from a physical point of view, extreme events are a specific configuration of the system (Schinckus 2010b, 2010c). Therefore, econophysicists consider any normalization as a priori reasoning about the economic phenomena that they study.

Therefore, although the "empirical data" are the same for financial economists and for econophysicists (financial quotations in the form of temporal series), the latter are quick to point to their "direct use of raw data," criticizing the statistical transformations performed by financial economists to "normalize" data. Here is Mandelbrot on this point:

> The Gaussian framework being a statistician's best friend, often, when he must process data that are obviously not normal, he begins by "normalizing" them . . . in the same way, it has been very seriously suggested to me that I normalize price changes. (1997, 142)

McCauley also discusses the normalizing practice used by financial economists, explaining,

> We [econophysicists] do not "massage" the data. Data massaging is both dangerous and misleading. (2006, 8)

This methodological position is widespread among econophysicists, who work in the spirit of experimental physics. An empirical perspective is also justified, in their view, by the evolution of financial reality. The computerization of financial markets has led to better quantification of financial data, which should be studied as an "empirical science" (McCauley 2004; Bouchaud 2002). However, this radical viewpoint, espoused by some econophysicists, has an element of naiveté. No way of collecting data can ever be totally neutral, in that all data are implicitly or explicitly the result of a selective process (Schinckus 2010a; Fayyad 1996; Hastie et al. 2005; Hand 1998). In a sense, any sampling method is embedded in a theory. By developing only physically plausible frameworks, econophysicists also appear to have some a priori beliefs about the world (Schinckus 2013). Although econophysicists and economists may study the same epistemological concept of "empirical realism," they do not agree about the definition of this criterion. In line with the confusion about the term "Lévy processes" evoked in the previous section, the two communities use the same words but seem to live in a different "conceptual matrix": while economists use data in the last step of their research process as an empirical justification of their theoretical argument, econophysicists use data as an epistemic starting point—suggesting the selection of an existing theoretical framework. Because data are not perceived, used, and presented in the same way in econophysics and financial economics, they can be a point of contention between the two communities.

The fourth and last obstacle to dialogue between the two communities concerns methodology. In this domain, financial economists and econophysicists do not share the same assumptions about readers' expectations. Although the empirical dimension is emphasized in both communities, financial economists take an apriorist approach (axiomatically justified argumentation), while econophysicists develop an a posteriori perspective (phenomenological data-driven models). These methodological divergences are responsible for two main shortcomings of econophysics: a lack of theoretical explanation and a lack of quantitative tests.

Although econophysicists have obtained numerous empirical observations (chapter 3), there are no theoretical explanations to support them (Mitzenmacher 2005). Now, from the statistical physics viewpoint, one can consider that there is a theoretical justification of sorts: the proof that the phenomenon studied is a critical phenomenon, which justifies the use of the specific models and approach coming from statistical physics. However, leaving this theoretical argument aside, econophysicists have produced no theoretical justification to explain why the economic phenomena studied are governed by a power law.[18] The economist Steven Durlauf pointed this out in 2005:

> The empirical literature on scaling laws [i.e. power laws] is difficult to interpret because of the absence of a compelling set of theoretical models to explain how the laws might come about. This is very much the case if one examines the efforts by physicists to explain findings of scaling laws in socioeconomic contexts. (Durlauf 2005, F235)

Consequently,

> The econophysics approach to economic theory has generally failed to produce models that are economically insightful." (Durlauf 2005, F236)

The lack of theoretical explanation constitutes a strong limitation on using econophysics' methods and models in financial economics. Indeed, financial economists largely base—one could even say almost exclusively base—their work on models *with* theoretical explanations.

Simulations of real phenomena without theory are considered weak results.[19] The Koopmans-Vining debate at the end the 1940s, which pitted the National Bureau of Economic Research against the Cowles Commission over the lack of theoretical explanations and the need to link measurement with theory, underlines the importance of this point.[20] More recently, the vector autoregressions (VARs) modeling and the real business cycle (RBC) models have faced the same criticism.[21] Some works focusing on the theoretical foundations of power laws have been initiated over the past few years. Chapter 5 will analyze them in detail. However, these attempts were marginal or not sufficiently general to be adopted by all. Some econophysicists today have a greater awareness of this dearth of theory:

> One [problem with the efforts to explain all power laws using the things statistical physicists know] is that (to mangle Kipling) there turn out to be nine and sixty ways of constructing power laws, and *every single one of them is right,* in that it does indeed produce a power law. Power laws turn out to result from a kind of central limit theorem for multiplicative growth processes, an observation which apparently dates back to Herbert Simon, and which has been rediscovered by a number of physicists (for instance, Sornette). Reed and Hughes have established an even more deflating explanation. . . . Now, just because these simple mechanisms exist, doesn't mean they explain any particular case, but it *does* mean that you can't legitimately argue "My favorite mechanism produces a power law; there is a power law here; it is very unlikely there would be a power law if my mechanism were not at work; therefore, it is reasonable to believe my mechanism is at work here." (Deborah Mayo would say that finding a power law does not constitute a severe test of your hypothesis.) You need to do "differential diagnosis," by identifying other, *non*-power-law consequences of your mechanism, which other possible explanations don't share. This, we hardly ever do.[22]

In addition to this lack of theoretical interpretation, there exists another issue related to techniques of validating statistical analysis. Chapter 3 explained that econophysicists base their empirical results on a visual technique for identifying a fit between a phenomenon and a power law. As the next chapter will explain, until recently there was no quantitative test on the power-law hypothesis. However, this visual approach can be considered qualitative testing, and it is extremely problematic for financial economists, who are strong defenders of quantitative tests. Durlauf pointed out the insufficiency of such qualitative tests:

> Literature on power and scaling laws has yet to move beyond the development of statistical measures to the analyses of model comparison and evaluation. In other words, many of the empirical claims in this literature concerning the presence of a particular law in some data set fail to address the standard statistical issues of identification and statistical power adequately. Hence, it is difficult to conclude that the findings in this literature can allow one to infer that some economic environment is complex. (Durlauf 2005, F232)

In aiming to understand such criticism, we must bear in mind that financial economists systematically use econometrics for testing their models. Moreover, econometric tests are a criterion of scientific acceptability on which financial economics was built (chapter 1). Section 4.3.3 will come back to this point: suffice it to say here that, at the time financial economists created their own discipline, they strongly rejected the visual approach used by the chartists and defended quantitative tests.[23] Quantitative tests were a crucial point in financial economists' argument that their approach was based on scientific criteria, while chartism was presented as a practice with no scientific foundation. Considering this methodological position, the visual tests used by econophysicists are considered to lack credibility, and even scientific foundation. The lack of quantitative tests makes econophysics literature unacceptable to financial economists:

> The power law/scaling literature has yet to develop formal statistical methodologies for model comparison exercises; until such methods are developed, findings in the econophysics literature are unlikely to persuade economists that scaling laws are empirically important. (Durlauf 2005, F234)

An important criticism of the visual test used in econophysics was formulated by LeBaron (2001), who latter showed that simple stochastic volatility models can produce behaviors similar to those obtained by econophysicists with power laws. Like econophysicists, LeBaron based his argument on a visual approach. His paper makes clear that visual inspections of log/log probability plots to uncover power laws can lead to misleading inferences.[24] Indeed, a significant disadvantage of the visual approach is that linearity is not a sufficient condition for having a power-law distribution, because power laws can visually be close to so-called exponential laws (Clauset, Shalizi, and Newman 2009; Newman 2005). Only a large volume of data make it possible to distinguish between the two types of law (Mitzenmacher 2004).[25] The problems created by the visual approach are also shared by other scientific communities—computer science, for instance (Mitzenmacher 2004)—and are acknowledged by some econophysicists:

> Well-founded methods for analyzing power-law data have not yet taken root in all, or even most, of these areas and in many cases hypothesised distributions are not tested rigorously against the data. This naturally leaves open the possibility that apparent power-law behavior is, in some cases at least, the result of wishful thinking . . . [T]he common practice of identifying and quantifying power-law distributions by the approximately straight-line behavior of a histogram on a doubly logarithmic plot should not be trusted: such straight-line behavior is a necessary but by no means sufficient condition for true power-law behavior. (Clauset, Shalizi, and Newman 2009, 691)

In fact, many of the power laws econophysicists been trying to explain are not power laws at all (Clauset, Shalizi, and Newman 2009). The next chapter will return to this crucial assertion in detail.

4.3.2. An Opportunity for Scientific Innovations

Although the position of econophysics in the disciplinary space creates a difficult dialogue between the two communities, one should not underestimate the impulses this seam gives to new ideas. It is well known that scientific disciplines are "reputationally controlled systems of knowledge production" that include specific behaviors, in particular vis-à-vis new ideas (Whitley 1986b, 190).

> The dominant characteristic of the modern Western sciences as particular kinds of social organisation which generate new knowledge is their combination of novelty with conformity. They reward intellectual innovation—only new knowledge is publishable—and yet contributions have to conform to collective standards and priorities if they are to be regarded as competent and scientific. Scientific fields can therefore be regarded as conservative novelty-producing systems. (Whitley 1986b, 186–87)

To publish new ideas, authors have to share the criteria, standards, and objectives of the scientific community of the specific field. Consequently, new ideas that are not plainly compatible with the scientific framework will be more frequently developed outside the field. This is particularly true in economics and physics, which are the most controlled disciplines and in which scientists share a strong awareness of the boundaries of their own discipline (Whitley 1986b, 193). Financial economics is an institutionalized discipline with a strong control over its theoretical goals and models. In this context, all new contributions have to conform to the *criteria of conventional acceptance*—postulates, beliefs, standards, priorities, and so on—shared by financial economists (Whitley 1986a, 1986b), and, consequently, there is a danger that novelties will be kept in the periphery of the discipline. In addition, like economics, financial economics "has a strong hierarchy of journals, so that researchers seeking the highest reputations have to adhere to the standards and contribute to the goals of those controlling the most prestigious outlets. . . . Because of this hierarchy, deviant economists publishing in new journals can be ignored as not meeting the highest standards of the discipline" (Whitley 1986b, 192–93). Because econophysics appears precisely to be a theoretical innovation that is not in line with the ideals, goals, and standards of financial economics, its position in the shadow of physics and outside financial economics has allowed econophysics to develop scientific innovations that would have very little chance of being developed inside financial economics.

Being outside financial economics, econophysicists can ignore the theoretical constraints imposed by the foundations of financial economics. The institutional situation of econophysics provides a significant advantage for easing scientific innovations. A telling example is option pricing. Econophysics models of option pricing generally ignore one of the most important strengths of the Black-Scholes-Merton model: the replicating portfolio reasoning.[26] Basically, this notion refers to the possibility of replicating (in terms of cash flows) the payoff of an option with a portfolio that is constituted by a combination of the risk-free asset and the underlying asset. The idea of replicating portfolio is very important in finance since it leads, by arbitrage reasoning, to obtaining only one price for the option (Cont and Tankov 2004). The practical usefulness of this approach is well known in finance (Derman 2009; Gaussel and Legras 1999).[27] Because econophysicists developed their knowledge outside of financial economics, they proposed option-pricing models partially independent of arbitrage reasoning. Moreover, the option-pricing models based on stable Lévy processes pose serious problems for obtaining a replicating portfolio, because in this case the market is incomplete (Ivancevic 2010; Takayasu 2006; Cont and Tankov 2004; Miyahara 2012; Zhang and Han 2013). The use of these processes is therefore problematic for financial economics since they are in conflict with the discipline's probabilistic framework, as defined in the work of Harrison, Kreps, and Pliska (chapters 1 and 2). This divergence helps to explain the marginal use of these processes in financial economics. It is no coincidence that financial economists and financial mathematicians have developed few models based on stable Lévy processes since the 1990s (although there exist some generalized Lévy processes in finance, as mentioned in chapter 2). One must conclude that it is precisely because econophysicists have developed their work outside the theoretical framework of financial economics that they can apply such processes more freely. This liberty paved the way to potential new developments, as we will illustrate in chapter 6.

Equilibrium is another example. There is a fundamental difference between financial economics and econophysics concerning financial market equilibrium. Equilibrium is a key concept in financial economics. While financial economics provides a less restrictive condition (a no-arbitrage condition) than the traditional economic equilibrium, econophysicists have developed a technical framework without having given any consideration to this aspect of nonarbitrage or to the theoretical assumptions that could bring the market to its equilibrium. Actually, these notions do not play a key role in econophysics; they instead appear for econophysicists as a priori beliefs[28] that provide a "standardised approach and a standardised language in which to explain each conclusion" (Farmer and Geanakoplos 2009, 17). Specifically, econophysicists do not reject the concept of equilibrium, but they do not assume a convergence toward such a state. In addition, equilibrium is considered merely a *potential* state of the system because "there is no empirical evidence for equilibrium" seen as a final state of the system (McCauley 2004, 6). Similarly, while they do not reject the condition of no arbitrage, they are indifferent to this restriction. Such a position is possible because econophysicists do not have to deal with the scientific framework that rules financial economics.

A last illustration refers to the way econophysicists handle empirical data, leading them to introduce models with power laws in order to deal with extreme values in finance. The vast majority of contributions from econophysicists take a phenomenological approach based on a determination of the probability distribution from stock prices, which are directly observed (chapter 3). In other words, their models are derived from empirical data. This approach, econophysicists believe, guarantees the scientificity of their work by ensuring that the model obtained is as close as possible to empirical data. From this perspective, econophysicists often present their discipline as a data-driven field, echoing a naive form of empiricism in which "rough data" would constitute the only empirical basis of science. This approach implicitly promotes a "passivist theory of knowledge" (Lakatos 1978, 20) according to which scientists merely have to describe phenomena as they appear to them. However, working with rough data does not prevent one's disciplinary background from influencing how phenomena are perceived. In the case of econophysics, given that power laws are a key framework in statistical physics (chapter 3), it is not surprising that econophysicists systematically identify power laws in their visual analysis of data. Indeed, while econophysicists rarely say so, they are expressly looking for a power law, on the basis that the phenomenon studied is complex and therefore ruled by such a law. This postulate emerges clearly when one considers the visual tests econophysicists use to validate observations with a power law (chapter 3). The power law is postulated first (chapter 5 will analyze this test in greater depth). In other words, it appears that, despite their phenomenological claims, econophysicists turn the empirical world into their theoretical world in accordance with a "conservative activism" (Lakatos 1978, 20).

In this regard, the major objective of econophysics studies is not to "reveal" the true statistical distribution that describes the rough data, but rather to determine the value of the critical exponent of the (expected) power law by calibrating the parameters of the law required to fit the data. Such an approach is, therefore, phenomenological in a very specific way: the implicit disciplinary assumption that econophysicists have regarding the identification of statistical laws comes from the hypothesis of the universality of power laws. To put it in other words, econophysics inductively expects to identify a power law. Figure 4.4 summarizes this approach based on an observational postulate.

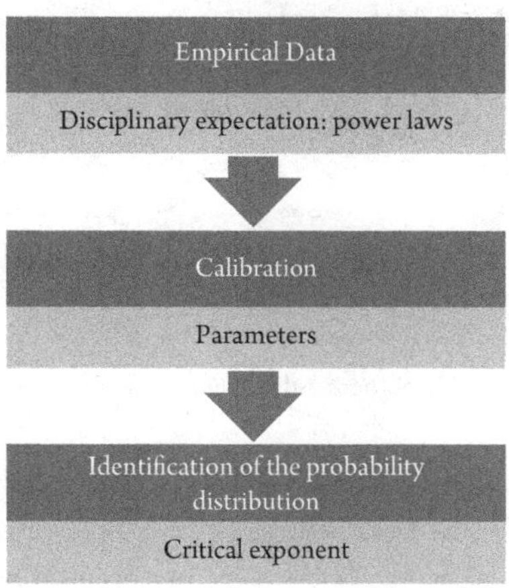

Figure 4.4 Econophysicists' phenomenological approach

The first step of this approach is the disciplinary expectation (observational postulate) of a power law that would govern the empirical data. The second step is to calibrate the parameters of this power law in order to fit the empirical data. Finally, the third step is to identify the critical exponent of the power law that best allows econophysicists to specify the category of models they can use to describe the data. This identification is based on visual tests, as explained in chapter 3.

This approach draws little attention in financial economics simply because the results do not respect two of the major scientific criteria in financial economics: on the one hand, the postulate that stock prices are not predictable or at least not predictable enough to make a profit; and, on the other hand, the fact that empirical works must be based on hypotheses that can be assessed by statistical tests. Because of these postulates, financial economists proceed in a very different way than econophysicists. Their first step is to postulate that financial markets are competitive, agents are rational, and prices result from market information. These postulates lead economists to formulate testable hypotheses. The best-known is the efficient-market hypothesis, according to which, when a market is competitive, prices reflect all available (and relevant) information and there is no arbitrage opportunity. The third step is to test this hypothesis with statistical tests. Thus, financial economists will follow a hypothetico-deductive method: they proceed by formulating a hypothesis from experiences. This hypothesis can then be found to be valid or invalid by a statistical test on observable data.[29] In other words, in the hypothetico-deductive method, models are derived/deduced from theory (figure 4.5).

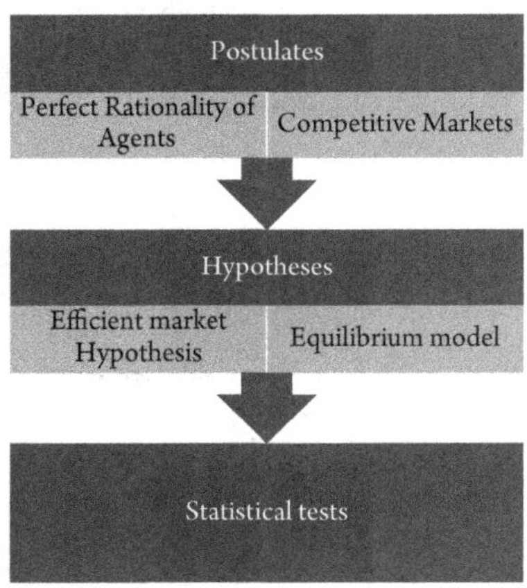

Figure 4.5 Financial economists' hypothetico-deductive method

This deductive approach is often criticized by econophysicists (Sornette 2014; McCauley 2006). They decry it as "top-down" because it is driven not by data but by a priori theoretical interpretations of the market. The main criticism is the Gaussian distribution that econophysicists strictly associate with the efficient-market hypothesis. However, chapter 1 explained that this hypothesis has to be separated from the Gaussian distribution. In addition, chapter 2 clarified that statistical tests have forced financial economists to keep the Gaussian framework until now. Finally, it is worth mentioning that the problem is not the phenomenological approach. Indeed, some work in financial economics also follows a phenomenological approach that seems quite similar to the one used in econophysics. In this category of work, one could mention the very popular ARCH-type modeling (chapter 2).[30] However, in this case, financial economists have to deal with their scientific constraints, which are different from those ruling econophysics. Specifically, the hypothetico-deductive method influences the phenomenological approach in financial economics. The ARCH-type models propose a corrective technique (conditional distribution) combined with a classical Gaussian description (unconditional distribution) in order to capture the occurrence of extreme values. On the one hand, ARCH-type models are methodologically associated with the efficient-market hypothesis, because they were developed for testing the correlations in stock market returns/prices (and consequently their predictability). On the other hand, the statistical tests used by financial economists are the classic ones developed in the Gaussian framework based on asymptotic reasoning (the central-limit theorem). Consequently, these empirical works, which, at first sight, adopt a phenomenological approach, are implicitly built in order to be compatible with the Gaussian framework. Figure 4.6 summarizes the so-called phenomenological approach associated with ARCH-type models.

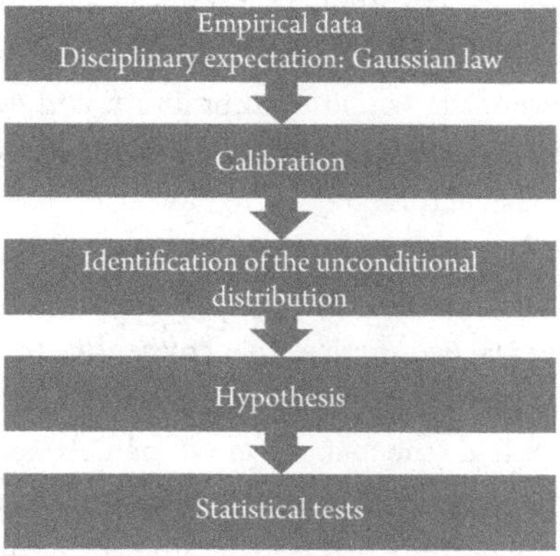

Figure 4.6 Financial economists' phenomenological approach

The five steps portrayed in figure 4.6 describe the whole phenomenological approach observed in the implementation of certain models in financial economics. When financial economists try to describe the occurrence of extreme values in empirical data, they combine an empirical analysis of these data based on the existence of a main Gaussian trend with more phenomenological techniques relying on ARCH-type models to capture the high volatility of this main trend. This technique is usually associated with a conditional distribution whose calibration allows financial economists to identify clearly the models (GARCH, EGARCH, etc.) they will implement. The identification of this conditional distribution remains compatible with the Gaussian framework, making it possible to save the classical foundations of financial economics. This conceptual machinery is finally validated through statistical tests.

A comparison between the two phenomenological approaches underlines a major difference between the two fields. Because of the scientific constraints ruling each discipline, when financial economists adopt a phenomenological approach, their modeling differs from that in econophysics. Being outside of financial economics, econophysicists were not theoretically constrained by the conceptual framework developed by financial economists. In this open context, they implemented a phenomenological approach based on their own disciplinary matrix by focusing on the use of power laws to characterize the dynamics of financial markets. Because the use of such tools was abandoned in financial economics in the 1970s (chapter 2), their reintroduction in finance is doubtless the major contribution of econophysics. Consequently, econophysicists can freely investigate financial markets to innovate and develop a new way of describing financial return/price fluctuations. The introduction of power laws is the direct result of this lack of constraints that rule financial economics.

In our view, the position of econophysics in the disciplinary space explains why econophysicists positioned themselves in theoretical a niche that mathematicians and economists have barely investigated, or not investigated at all, because of their theoretical constraints. The three previous examples provide a telling illustration of this specific situation for introducing scientific innovations. As Kuhn (1989) put it, a scientific framework provides a cognitive foundation for a specific community. That shared way of thinking defines theoretical constraints without which organized research would not be possible. An absence of theory would lead to a chaotic situation that would undermine the confidence of the scientific community, and possibly lead to its disintegration. In other words, the conceptual framework shared by a specific community allows the development of structured research. However, that framework also defines the conceptual horizons for that community. Because econophysics emerged in the shadow of physics, it did not have to deal with the theoretical constraints that determine the structure of financial economics. That conceptual freedom favored scientific innovation by paving the way for the development of a new perspective shaping financial knowledge from outside the mainstream (Chen, Anderson, and Barker 2008). This strategy of positioning itself in theoretical niches is not specific to econophysicists. It was exactly the one used by financial economists to introduce innovations in finance when they created their field in the 1960s and the 1970s, during the period of high theory of finance.

4.3.3. A Strategy Already Used by Financial Economics to Innovate

The parallelism between the creation of financial economics and the birth of econophysics provides an interesting framework for analyzing the relation between the two disciplines and their potential contribution. Although econophysics was created more than 30 years later than financial economics, the actors involved in the emergence of these two fields used the same strategies to promote their works and to find a place in the disciplinary space: in both cases, a recognized discipline expanded toward a new field of research whose study had hitherto been dominated by another framework. In the 1960s, economics expanded to the study of financial markets, which at the time was dominated by the chartism; in the 1990s, statistical physics expanded to the study of financial markets, which at the time were dominated by current financial economics. In both cases, the new community was made up of scientists trained outside the discipline, and hence outside the mainstream. A particular colonization of finance has occurred.

The beginning of this colonization can be detected in the new arrivals' publication strategy. In the 1960s, the newcomers took control of the two main journals specializing in finance at the time, the *Journal of Business* and the *Journal of Finance*. The aim was to modify the content of published articles by imposing a more strongly mathematical content and by using a particular structure: presenting the mathematical model and then empirical tests. To reinforce the new orientation, these two journals also published several special issues. Once control over these journals had been established, the newcomers developed their own journals, such as the *Journal of Financial and Quantitative Analysis*, created in 1965. Similarly, econophysicists chose to publish and gain acceptance in journals devoted to an existing theoretical field in physics (statistical physics) rather than create new journals outside an existing scientific space and hence structure. As explained in section 4.1, they took control of editorial boards (as in the case of *Physica A* and the *European Journal of Physics B*). Once control over these journals had been established, econophysicists developed their own journals, such as *Quantitative Finance* and the *Journal of Economic Dynamics and Control*. This "colonization strategy" allowed the adepts of the new approach to bypass the partisans of the dominant paradigm (and hence of the so-called mainstream journals), who rejected these new theoretical developments in which they were not yet proficient. Gradual recognition of the new discipline subsequently allowed new specialist journals to be created, making it possible to reach a wider readership (especially in economics).

In aiming to colonize finance, the partisans of the two disciplines used the same discourse to justify the scientificity of the new approach. In each case, outsiders challenged the traditional approach by asking its adepts to prove that it was scientific. This "confrontational" attitude is founded upon the challengers' contention that the empirical studies, the new mathematics and methodology they use guarantee a scientificity (i.e., a way of doing science) absent from the traditional approach.[31] The challengers maintain that the scientificity of a theory or a model should determine whether it is adopted or rejected. During the 1960s and 1970s, financial economists underlined the importance of the empirical dimension of their research from their very first publications (Lorie 1965, 3). They saw the testability of their models and theories as a guarantee of scientificity (Jovanovic 2008). Consider Fama's three articles (Fama 1965a, 1965b, 1970). All used the same structure: the first part dealt with theoretical implications of the random-walk model and its links with the efficient-market hypothesis, while the second part presented empirical results that validate the model. This sequence—theory, then empirical results—is today familiar in financial economics. It constitutes the hypothetico-deductive method, the scientific method that has been defended in economics since the middle of the twentieth century. Indeed, in the 1960s, financial economists criticized the chartists for their inability to present their works with "scientific" arguments, accusing them of using a pure rhetorical justification rather than a strong theoretical demonstration of their findings.[32] Financial economists then developed a confrontational approach in their opposition to the chartists. As an example, James Lorie (1965, 17) taxed the chartists with not taking into account the tools used in a scientific discipline such as economics. In this debate, financial economists argued that their approach was based on scientific criteria, while chartism was based on folklore and had no scientific foundation.[33] Consequently, financial economics should supplant previous "folkloric" practices, judged to be groundless.

Econophysicists have proceeded in like fashion. In their work, they belittle the methodological framework of financial economics, using a familiar vocabulary. They describe the theoretical developments of financial economics as "inconsistent . . . and appalling" (Stanley et al. 1999, 288). Despite being an economist,[34] Keen (2003, 108–9) discredits financial economics by highlighting the "superficially appealing" character of its key concepts and by comparing it to a "tapestry of beliefs." Marsili and Zhang (1998, 51) describe financial economics as "anti-empirical," while McCauley (2006, 17) does not shrink from comparing the scientific value of the models of financial economics to that of cartoons. The vocabulary used is designed to leave the reader in no doubt: "scientific," "folklore," "deplorable," "superficial," "sceptical," "superstition," "mystic," "challenge." All these wrangling words serve to dramatize a situation in which actors simply hold divergent positions.

Another feature of this colonization strategy is the use of new mathematical tools combined with the creation of new statistical data, both being considered as a guarantee of scientificity. Chapters 1 and 3 showed that the development of modern probability theory, on the one hand, and the evolution of financial markets, which are increasingly quantitative (or digitized), on the other, contributed to the emergence of financial economics and of econophysics. In each case these two factors triggered the emergence of an alternative approach. In the 1960s, some financial economists took up random processes at a time when mathematical developments had become newly accessible to nonmathematicians (chapter 1). The use or nonuse of these new tools—modern probability theory and work on statistical data—constituted the main element setting the "new approach" against the "traditional approach" of the time.[35] This mathematical evolution went hand in hand with technological developments as the use of computers became widespread. Computers made it possible to perform tests on empirical data to assess the methods proposed for earning money on financial markets, particularly chartist analysis.[36] The creation of empirical databases stimulated the application of mathematical models taken from modern probability theory and research into stock market variations.

The development of probability theory and finer quantification of financial markets (thanks to developments in computing) were also triggering factors in the emergence of econophysics. Indeed, since the 1990s, electronic markets have ruled the financial sphere, while the use of information technologies has grown consistently in companies. Computerization allowed the use of "high-frequency data" offering a more accurate study of the evolution of real-time data (chapter 3). Accumulated data are then stored in the form of time series. While this type of data has been studied by economists for several decades, the automation of markets has enabled "intraday" data to provide "three orders of magnitude more data" to be recorded (Stanley et al. 2000, 339). The quantity of data is an important factor at a statistical level because the larger the sample, the more reliable the identification of probabilistic patterns. In other words, the development of computers, both in the 1960s and in the 1990s, created two favorable decades for the development of probability theory, and chapter 3 introduced the evolution of this theory in the 1990s (with the development of truncation techniques). Quantified information and statistical data possess this property of readily moving disciplinary boundaries and show the role of quantification in the construction of an objective knowledge for an emerging field. Actors involved in the development of financial economics and those who developed econophysics made use of technological evolution to remain up-to-date with computational possibilities.

This parallel between these two disciplines is particularly interesting because this institutional strategy occurred during the years of high theory of financial economics (chapter 1). In both cases, discriminating against existing practices, challengers attempted to introduce scientific innovations that could not be developed in the discipline because they were incompatible with the existing theoretical framework.

4.4. CONCLUSION

This chapter showed that econophysics is nowadays a fully-fledged scientific field with its own journals, conferences, and education, which standardize and promote the key concepts associated with this new approach. Econophysics emerged in the shadow of physics and, until recently, has stayed outside financial economics. Two general consequences of this disciplinary position were studied. First, this background generates a difficult dialogue between econophysicists and financial economists. Second, being outside financial economics, econophysicists have been able to develop scientific innovations that have not been explored by financial economists. We consider that this issue of innovation is crucial for a future dialogue between the two areas of knowledge. This chapter pointed out that financial economists followed the same path, introducing new ideas and models, when they were outside the mainstream of finance in the 1960s—these innovations led to the creation of modern finance theory. This similarity in the evolution of the two fields suggests that the outsider position of econophysics might lead to the introduction of their innovations in financial economics. This chapter emphasized that some scientific innovations are directly related to the phenomenological approach (implemented in both econophysics and financial economics). However, the comparison between the techniques of modeling implemented in the two fields showed that the current phenomenological approach (bottom-up) provided by econophysicists is quite similar to the one implemented by financial economists in the 1960s. We suggested that econophysics could evolve toward a more deductive (top-down) method like the one financial economists use. We can therefore expect that stable Lévy processes and other contributions pushed by econophysicists will be integrated into a framework common to financial economics and econophysics. This is the path we will explore in the two last chapters.

5

MAJOR CONTRIBUTIONS OF ECONOPHYSICS TO FINANCIAL ECONOMICS

As explained in the two previous chapters, econophysics made a useful contribution in the understanding of stock price and return variations. As detailed in chapter 3, this contribution is mainly based on the use of power-law distributions to characterize the occurrence of extreme values.[1] While fat-tailed distributions in finance are supported by a large number of observations, chapter 2 pointed out that power laws pose problems for financial economics because they invalidate the traditional measurement of risk given by variance, which is used in all pricing models.

In this challenging context, this chapter scrutinizes the possible contributions of econophysics to finance by stressing the financial point of view. Our approach differs from that generally used in the literature dedicated to econophysics, which usually starts from the viewpoint of econophysics or complexity. Precisely, we aim to go beyond the disciplinary boundaries. This chapter will discuss four potential uses of econophysics' results by emphasizing to what extent this field can be useful in trading rooms and for traders/financiers. Afterward, this chapter will focus on the contributions of econophysics seen from the viewpoint of financial economists. This analysis will show the surprising proximity between the two fields. In this context, the conditions of a potential emergence of a common conceptual scheme will be discussed. For this purpose, recent advances in all key concepts of econophysics (power laws, self-criticality, etc.) are analyzed by clarifying what remains to be done to produce integrated models and a theoretical framework common to econophysics and financial economics.

5.1. THE USE OF ECONOPHYSICS IN TRADING ROOMS

Econophysics literature devoted to financial economics contains numerous heterogeneous observations, showing that power laws appear to fit most of the relevant financial data. Among others, Bassler et al. (2007) demonstrated that the euro-dollar exchange rate can be fitted to such distribution in time; with respect to foreign-exchange markets, Seemann et al. (2011) showed that the mean square fluctuation of increments can be fitted to power-law scaling in time. Gopikrishnan et al. (2000) described the volume of individual transactions on the NYSE with a power-law distribution, while Mandelbrot (1997) and Lillo and Mantegna (2004) showed that the cumulative sum of negative returns following a crash can also be approximated with such a distribution. In the same vein, Lillo and Mantegna (2004) identified a power-law-like relationship between financial prices and market capitalization, whereas Kaizoji and Kaizoji (2004) used the same relation to describe the occurrence of calm-time intervals in price changes. Mike and Farmer (2008) described the liquidity and the volatility derived from empirical regularities in trading order flow by using a power law. Financial autocorrelations have also been analyzed through the lens of this distribution. Studies have shown that autocorrelations of order volume (Farmer and Lillo 2004), of signs of trading orders (Bouchaud, Mezard, and Potters 2002; Potters and Bouchaud 2003; Ivanov et al. 2004; Farmer et al. 2005), and of liquidity at the best bid and ask prices (Farmer and Lillo 2004) can all also be modeled with this pattern. One could extend the list to many other publications. Basically, the point that all these empirical works have in common is the conceptual role played by power laws, which appears to be universally associated with different phenomena independently of their microscopic details. The empirical studies have highlighted statistical properties related to financial data that financial economists traditionally do not take into account in their work. As shown in chapter 4, economics and physics use different methods of producing scientific knowledge and results. We must bear in mind that for statistical physicists, working on empirical data is the first step in scientific methodology, the second step being the construction of a theoretical framework.[2] This phenomenological approach used by econophysicists is, per se, a first significant contribution of econophysics to finance because it has identified statistical patterns in raw financial data. This approach should not be considered separately from the fact that the mathematics and statistics on which econophysics models are based are relatively recent and are still in development.[3] In this context, "Rather than investigating the underlying forces responsible for the universal scaling laws of financial markets, a relatively large part of the econophysics literature mainly adapts physics tools of analysis to more practical issues in finance. This line of research is the academic counterpart to the work of 'quants' in the financial industry who mostly have a physics background and are occupied in large numbers for developing quantitative tools for forecasting, trading and risk management" (Lux 2009, 14). Moreover, one has to consider that the impact of econophysics on financial practices is potentially substantial because it involves the statistical description of financial distributions and thus the statistical characterization of financial uncertainty. However, this potential impact must be considered by taking into account several drawbacks that we will discuss in this section.

To date, one can consider five major practical contributions of econophysics to finance: practical implementations; identification of the common critical exponent; volatility considered as a whole; uses in a long-term perspective; and prediction of financial crashes and their possible management.

5.1.1. Practical Implications

The practical implications of econophysics and its models for the financial industry can roughly be associated with three observed trends, (1) hedging, (2) trading and portfolio management, and (3) software, and with one potential issue related to the future of risk management.

The first issue deals with option pricing and hedging. It is well known that the statistical description of financial distribution is the major information on which portfolio managers can base their decisions. Two different statistical descriptions will necessarily generate two different decision schemas. A non-Gaussian framing of financial distributions will produce a pricing different from one typically proposed by classical Gaussian descriptions (McCauley 2004; Dionisio, Menezes, and Mendes 2006), and consequently a different hedging strategy (Mantegna and Stanley 2000). While early works in econophysics showed that an optimal hedging strategy appears impossible in a non-Gaussian framework (Aurell et al. 1997; Bouchaud and Sornette 1994), more recent articles have defined mathematical conditions for optimal hedging, in line with what financial economists mean by "optimal hedging" (McCauley, Gunaratne, and Bassler 2007; Bucsa et al. 2014). We will illustrate this point in the next chapter.

Although a hedging solution based on econophysics is in its infancy, the pricing issue has already generated high interest among practitioners, and econophysics-based portfolio management leaves room for a theoretical integration of a potential financial crisis. The use of distributions in which extreme values can occur leads portfolio managers to consider more appropriate track records in the case of large variations. This probably explains why some banks and investment firms (BNP Paribas, Morningstar Investment, Ibbotson Associates, etc.) have successfully used models from econophysics (Casey 2013).[4] Moreover, some econophysicists have created their own investment companies that propose econophysics-based management.[5] Although these firms do not reveal which models they use, physics-based management is clearly part of their strategy and advertising. For example, Capital Fund Management's website states,

> Research in the statistical properties of financial instruments and the development of systematic trading strategies are carried out at CFM by a team of Ph.D.'s, most of them former physicists from prestigious international institutions.[6]

The third practical implementation concerns software whose algorithms are based on models related to econophysics. Among these are *ModEco*,[7] developed by a retired academic physicist, and *Rmetrics*,[8] developed by the Econophysics Group at the University of Zurich—ETH Zurich. It is worth mentioning that the latter is directly used in university modules developed by this group.[9] Better-known statistical and mathematical software is gradually integrating key econophysics concepts. *Mathematica*, for example, has proposed a "stable distributions package" for 2005 (see Rimmer and Nolan 2005). Aoyama et al. (2011) showed that the statistical software *Stata* and *SAS* can also be used for an econophysical analysis of economic data. We can also mention Alstott et al. (2014), or the script provided by Aaron Clauset on his web page,[10] to be used with *Matlab*. The development of computerized solutions based on econophysics will contribute to widespread use of econophysics models (although customers usually use these computerized solutions as "black boxes") in financial practices.

The last practical implementation concerns risk management. The most recent financial crisis questioned the ability of risk managers to predict and limit financial catastrophes. In this challenging context, calls emerged for a new conceptual framework for risk management. The objective of risk managers, portfolio managers, and regulators is to limit the potential damage resulting from crises. Their ability to limit damage depends directly on their understanding of financial uncertainty. By providing a different statistical characterization of empirical distributions, econophysicists offer a new perspective on modeling financial uncertainty. From this perspective, econophysics could raise questions about the models used in financial regulation, which are mainly based on the concept of value-at-risk (VaR—introduced by JPMorgan in 1992). VaR, the most widely used measure of market risk, "refers to the maximum potential loss over a given period at a certain confidence level" (Bormetti et al. 2007). This measure is very well known to practitioners since it can also be used to estimate the risk of individual assets or portfolios. In practice, VaR models are easy to use since they refer to a high quartile of the loss distribution of a portfolio over a certain time horizon. Therefore, calculating VaR implies knowledge of the tail behavior of distribution returns. To promote the diffusion of its variance model, JPMorgan developed a computer program, *RiskMetrics*, that is widely used in the financial industry. Some econophysicists (Wang, Wang, and Si 2012; Bormetti et al. 2007) proposed an empirical comparison between results produced by RiskMetrics and a VaR model based on non-Gaussian distributions (such as Lévy processes for instance), concluding that the latter provide better forecasting of extreme variations in financial prices.[11] Although in their infancy, these reflections on non-Gaussian descriptions of financial distributions could have a direct impact on the use of VaR (and consequently on the statistical models used) in financial regulations and the prudent supervision of financial institutions.

These practices and practical reflections have been implemented at the same time that academicians have provided practical results in four major domains, which we will set out in the four next sections.

5.1.2. Identification of a Common Critical Exponent

The first practical result one can find in the literature of econophysics is the identification of a common critical exponent. This critical exponent enables modelers to identify a specific (stable Lévy) stochastic regime for distributions. When the evolution of a random variable can be characterized by a power law whose critical exponent is lower than 2, the process is said to be stable, implying that all statistical features of this process are the same whatever the level of study. As mentioned in chapter 2, statistical characterization can be very useful in finance, where scale refers to differ investment periods (day, week, month, etc.). Regarding this exponent, Rama Cont et al. (1997) identified a critical exponent for characterizing the power-law behaviors of financial assets whose evolution can be described with a stable process. Currently, the identification of a common critical exponent can be associated with the identification of a category of phenomena (universality class) for which a unifying mathematical model could be used. In other terms, phenomena whose dynamics can be described through a power law are assumed to have the same statistical features. According to Stanley and Plerou (2001, 563), the identification of a universality class for financial data was "vital" in experimental research into critical phenomena in finance, because in this phenomenological perspective, identifying a critical exponent will provide a model that can be tested (see chapter 4).

Nowadays, a consensus has emerged in econophysics literature on the value of the critical exponent, since stock price variations follow a power law with an exponent close to 3 (Stanley, Gabaix, and Plerou 2008; Plerou and Stanley 2008; Gopikrishnan et al. 1999; Malevergne, Sornette, and Pisarenko 2005; Plerou et al. 1999). This result also concerns options, commodities, currencies, and interest rates (Bouchaud and Challet 2014). Figure 5.1 illustrates this result for US stocks, for the "at the money" volatility of the corresponding options, and for credit default swaps on these same stocks.

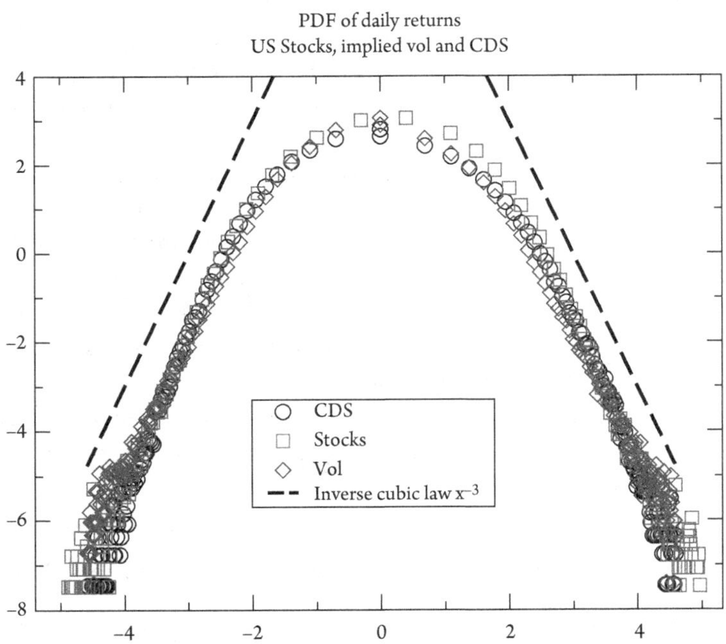

Figure 5.1 Distribution for daily returns
Source: Bonart cited from Bouchaud and Challet 2014. Reproduced by permission of the author.

This is a major practical contribution of econophysics to finance. Indeed, having this parameter fixed, it is much easier to implement financial economics models based on econophysics results. It also facilitates the creation of statistical tests, as we will explain in the next chapter.

5.1.3. Volatility Considered as a Whole

The second practical result concerns volatility, which is closely linked with distribution. Broadly speaking, econophysicists use power laws to describe the evolution of financial prices in two ways. A first category of studies focuses on modeling volatility distribution (only the tail part of a distribution is considered in this case) with a specific (conditional) distribution. A second category of studies use power laws to characterize the entire distribution of financial prices/returns.

Econophysicists who use power laws to describe the evolution of volatility (i.e., description of fat tails only), implement the same methodology as financial economists with the ARCH class of models, which are nowadays the principal econometric used in financial economics to model financial returns. The key idea behind these models is that the most recent volatility influences current volatility. As chapter 2 explained, the ARCH class of models assumes that financial returns follow the Gaussian distribution (called unconditional distribution in the ARCH class of models) but characterize the dynamics of the volatility with another distribution, which is not necessarily Gaussian. The distribution describing the evolution of volatility is called "conditional distribution." It is worth mentioning that the conditional and unconditional dimensions are defined in reference to the way we consider the history of the data. An unconditional study will consider that all past data have the same influence on the current evolution of the variable; data are considered in their entirety, and no specific weight is assigned to the various past fluctuations. In contrast, a conditional treatment will consider recent fluctuations to have a stronger influence on the current evolution of the variable, and so more weight will be given to recent fluctuations. These time-dependent dynamics can be modeled through various potential statistical processes (Kim et al. 2008), and this variety has generated a huge literature.[12] To characterize the occurrence of extreme values, financial economists use a conditional distribution with the Gaussian distribution, in which large variations are associated with another distribution that can take the form of a power law. In this situation, power laws are considered a corrective tool for modeling important fluctuations that the Gaussian framework does not capture: the Gaussian (unconditional) distribution can therefore be combined with a power law (characterizing the conditional distribution) in order to obtain a better fit with empirical results. The major advantage of a conditional approach is to capture the time-dependent dynamics observed in the variability of financial prices. However, this advantage is weakened by the assumed Gaussian dimension of unconditional distribution, which underestimates risk even when associated with a power law for describing the (conditional) evolution of volatility, as explained by Farmer and Geanakoplos. However, when the model is matched with real data, the tail exponent is much too large, that is, "The tails of an ARCH process are too thin to explain the fat tails of prices" (Farmer and Geanakoplos 2009, 17).

Unlike this first category of works, the great majority of studies by econophysicists do not break down statistical analysis into conditional and unconditional dimensions; instead, they use power laws to characterize the entire distribution. However, keeping the previous vocabulary, we can say that they mainly work on unconditional distributions by considering the empirical time series as a whole. Econophysicists often underline the advantage of dealing with historical distributions by claiming that financial distributions must be described as they appeared in the past and not as they should be according to a preexisting theoretical framework (McCauley 2004).[13] Beyond this positivist justification, the major advantage of focusing on unconditional distributions is that they do not require conditional parameterization (i.e., a definition of time-dependent dynamics), which can generate a particular "subjectivism" (Matei, Rovira, and Agell 2012, 95) because "conditional evidence is unobserved and there is no natural and intuitive way to model the conditional heteroskedasticity, so that each model will try to capture features considered important by the author" (Matei, Rovira, and Agell 2012, 95). The parameterization of conditional distribution can open the door to an "adhocity" of statistical treatments whose outcome could result from a high level of parameterization (McCauley 2006). This argument provides justification for the unconditional approach embraced by econophysicists; and, as Farmer and Geneakoplos (2009, 18) explained,

> The practical value of the power law for risk control is that it results in more efficient risk estimates than extrapolation methods [...] [W]hen used to extrapolate risk levels that are not contained in the sample [i.e., the use of unconditional distribution], they will consistently underestimate risk. The power law, in contrast, is more parsimonious, and so is more efficient with limited data. This can result in less biased estimates.

However, it is worth mentioning that what econophysicists view as an advantage is seen as a drawback by financial economists: although working with an unconditional approach enables econophysicists to avoid the "ad hoc perspective," the unconditional perspective cannot capture short-term, time-varying volatility. This static disadvantage of an unconditional approach justifies the use of the ARCH class of models in financial economics.

As another practical contribution of econophysics, we would point out that the opportunity to consider volatility in its entirety also offers very interesting practical results since it simplifies the statistical treatment of investment periods. A new framework based on the statistical property of stability could significantly influence financial practices. By emphasizing the importance of unconditional distributions, econophysicists have influenced the way that this level of statistical description of financial fluctuations is modeled: Broda et al. (2013), for example, have tried to overcome the drawbacks evoked in this section by using an ARCH framework within the unconditional distribution characterized by a power law.

5.1.4. Uses in a Long-Term Perspective

The third practical result still concerns volatility, which is a key concept in finance because it measures risk. Statistical characterization of volatility has generated much debate, especially regarding what we call "volatility clustering." The "clustering" of volatility is a stylized fact referring to an observed empirical pattern in the amplitude (volatility) of financial fluctuations whose strong correlation suggests that a big move in a given time period is likely to be followed by another big move in the next time period (although the sign of this move, positive or negative, remains unpredictable). The biggest hurdle in this time dependence involves the appropriate horizon on which we can observe statistical dependence.

Some authors (Bollerslev 1986; Engle 1982; Rachev et al. 2011) have claimed that current financial prices are more sensitive to recent fluctuations of the market. In other words, statistical description of financial returns should take into account this short-term influence by proposing a conditional level assigning autocorrelations on the second moment of the distribution that attribute a greater weight to more recent returns (Bollerslev 1986). Current volatility is assumed to be more closely correlated to its more recent variations than to its older ones. From this perspective, ARCH models are particularly well suited to describing the evolution of short-run dynamics of volatility since, because of their definition, these models assign more weight to the influence of recent fluctuations in describing current volatility. This short-term perspective on financial stocks makes ARCH models useful for traders, whose investment window is often shorter than three months. In this context, traders often characterize the dynamics of variation through ARCH models by adjusting a three-month volatility to the daily volatility of assets. Moreover, the fact that traders rarely work on a sample older than four years does not favor the use of power laws in trading rooms.[14]

However, in some specific situations, financial management has to focus on long-term issues. Stress tests, for example, are a well-known analysis to determine the extent to which a financial instrument (an institution or a portfolio) can deal with an economic crisis or the occurrence of extreme situations that could generate a critical loss. By generating a computerized simulation based on historical distributions, this methodology gauges how robust a financial asset (institution, portfolio) is in a crisis situation. In this situation, a long-term approach is usually implemented since a longer sample will provide a better estimation of large fluctuations without diminishing the magnitude of the maximum variation (Matei, Rovira, and Agell 2012). Large disruptive events are not frequent, but they can be captured and approximated through a long-term historical (unconditional) analysis (Buchanan 2004). Because extreme variations involve the vulnerability of financial assets to a crisis situation, the statistical characterization of fat tails is very important. In that perspective, power laws are the most appropriate statistical framework for extreme value management, whose key theory (extreme-value theory) can be seen as "a theoretical background for power law behavior" (Alfarano and Lux 2010, 2).

The pertinence of power laws for estimating long-term risk was highlighted by the dramatic case of Long-Term Capital Management (LTCM).[15] Buchanan (2004, 5) argued that the collapse of this hedge fund was partly due to inadequate estimation of long-term risk, whose historical (unconditional) form took the form of a power law. In Buchanan's view,

> Fund managers at LTCM were sophisticated enough to be aware that their bell-curve estimates were probably low, yet they lacked methods for assessing the likelihood of more extreme risks [in the long term]. In September of 1998, "unexpected" volatility in the markets, set off by a default in Russia's sovereign debt, led LTCM to lose more than 90 percent of its value. . . . A power law is much better than the bell curve at establishing this long term risk. It is also better at helping managers avoid the painful consequences of "unexpected" fluctuations." (Buchanan 2004, 5)

Although LTCM managers knew their unconditional distributions were not normally distributed, they applied a mainstream way of managing the fund (Bernstein 2007) for which "they just add a large fudge factor at the end [as proposed by ARCH class of models]. It would be more appropriate for the empirical reality of market fluctuations—as captured by the power law—to be incorporated in the analysis of risk" (Buchanan 2004, 6).

In the same vein, Buchanan (2004) also mentioned the importance of unconditional power laws for estimating financial risk for pension funds and the insurance industry. The first have to provide stable growth over the long term in order to ensure periodic payments related to pensions. That financial objective makes pension funds particularly sensitive to liquidity risk, leading them to deal with a long-term horizon to predict the worst loss possible and avoid "liquidity black holes" (Franzen 2010). The insurance industry is faced with the challenge of integrating extreme variations into their portfolio management, especially insurance companies involved in contracts related to natural disasters. "The bell curve does the job with automobile insurance but it fails miserably when assessing large catastrophic losses due to hurricanes and earthquakes" (Buchanan 2004, 6).

Moreover, there is empirical evidence supporting the existence of a long-memory process in the volatility of prices, meaning that there is persistent temporal dependence between observations widely separated in time. That long-memory property is well known and well documented in specialized literature (Ding, Enlge, and Granger 1993; Andersen and Bollerslev 1997; Breidt, Crato, and de Lima 1998). The origin of the long-memory process lies in the work of Hurst (1951), a hydrologist commissioned by the British government to study changes in the level of the Nile. More specifically, he was in charge of designing dams to manage water reserves guarding against risk of drought. This task required a deep understanding of Nile floods, which Hurst described with a temporal series characterizing the changes in water levels. In his research, he observed that the optimal storage capacity for water tanks divided by the standard deviation of the river floods was proportional by following a power law with an exponent of between 0.5 and 1.0. Moreover, Hurst noticed that the evolution of water levels was not independent in time: a major recent flood would influence a great number of future floods, which implies a long-memory process.

Several long-memory processes have been observed in finance: volatility for stocks (Ding, Enlge, and Granger 1993), exchange rates (Lu and Guegan 2011), and trading volume (Lillo and Mantegna 2004).[16] Financial economists acknowledge the existence of long-memory processes, which they have usually captured through a myriad of ARCH-type models (IGARCH, EGARCH, GARCH, NGARCH, etc.) gradually moving away from the use of power laws (Lux 2006). However, although ARCH models provide a good approximation for short-time dependence, they fail to capture this long-memory property (Ding, Enlge, and Granger 1993) and, contrary to models that explicitly take long memory into account, an ARCH model that fits on one timescale does not work well on a different timescale (Farmer and Geanakoplos 2009, 19). The necessity of capturing long-memory properties from time series, such as long-term volatility clustering or management mainly based on the long term, should encourage the use of power laws in finance.

In order to pinpoint the differences between the ways in which financial economists and econophysicists deal with fat-tailed distributions, table 5.1 summarizes the main methodological differences between them.

Table 5.1 Statistical treatment of fat-tailed distributions in financial economics and econophysics

	Financial economists	*Econophysicists*
Statistical tool	ARCH models	Power laws
Analysis	Broken down into two levels: unconditional (Gaussian) distribution and conditional distribution	One level of analysis: unconditional distribution based on historical data
Unconditional distribution	Gaussian	Often associated with a power law, but this is not a necessary condition
Application	To characterize the fat tails of the distribution	To describe the whole of the distribution or to characterize the fat tails of the distribution
Conditional distribution	A variety of distribution depending on the type of ARCH model	Often associated with a power law, but this is not a necessary condition
Methodology	Corrective	Descriptive
Necessary condition	Existence of second statistical moment (because volatility is associated with this parameter)	None
Time dependence	Short-memory property (volatility clustering)	Long-memory property (Hurst exponent)
Time horizon	Short term	Long term

5.1.5. Prediction of Financial Crashes and Their Possible Management

The fourth practical result concerns the prediction of financial crashes and, consequently, their possible management. Some econophysicists have applied their models to forecast financial crashes, and more specifically to predicting financial-market downturns or "changes of regime" (Sornette and Cauwels 2015; Ausloos, Ivanova, and Vandewalle 2002; Johansen and Sornette 2000; Pandey and Stauffer 2000). This kind of application calls on the theoretical framework of econophysics regarding critical phenomena (we discussed in chapter 3). In this perspective, financial markets are characterized by transformations associated with the usual phase transitions observed in critical phenomena. In this way of conceptualizing crashes, all large transformations detected on the financial market are looked on as a passage from one phase to another. This evolution can be statistically characterized by a power law. In so doing, econophysicists use one property of the scaling hypothesis according to which there "is a sort of data collapse, where under appropriate axis normalization, diverse data 'collapse' onto a single curve called a scaling function" (Preis and Stanley 2010, 4). Sornette and Woodard (2010, 119) explained that

> according to this "critical" point of view, the specific manner by which prices collapsed is not the most important problem: a crash occurs because the market has entered an unstable phase and any small disturbance or process may reveal the existence of the instability. . . . The collapse is fundamentally due to the unstable position; the instantaneous cause of the collapse is secondary. In the same vein, the growth of the sensitivity and the growing instability of the market close to such a critical point might explain why attempts to unravel the proximal origin of the crash have been so diverse. Essentially, anything would work once the system is ripe.

In this perspective, econophysics describes the occurrence of a financial crash as the apparition of a critical point/state of a complex system. This approach paves the way for new practical tools to detect and manage financial-market instabilities. A telling example of this application is the Log-Periodic Power Law (LPPL),[17] which is a log-periodic oscillation model for describing the characteristic behavior of a speculative bubble (and thus for predicting its subsequent crash). This model was originally proposed by Sornette, Johansen, and Bouchaud (1995), Sornette and Johansen (1997, 2001), and Feigenbaum and Freund (1996, 1998). In its simplest form, this model states that the asset price, p, before a crash evolves according to

$$ln[p(t)] = A + B(t_c - t)^{\beta}\{1 + C cos[\omega ln(t_c - t) + \phi]\}, \tag{5.1}$$

where $p(t)$ is the price index at time t, t_c is most probable time of crash (i.e., the critical time) and quantifies the power-law acceleration of prices, β is the exponent of the power-law growth, ω is the frequency of the fluctuations during the bubble, and the remaining variables carry no structural interpretation (A, B, C, and ϕ).[18]

The LPPL model echoes two concepts well known in financial economics: noise traders (Black 1986; Grossman 1976; Dow and Gorton 2008; Shleifer and Summers 1990; Kyle 1985) and mimetic/herding behaviors (Orléan 1989; Keynes 1936, chap. 12; Orléan 1995; Banerjee 1993; Welch 1992).[19] Indeed, according to this LPPL model, two categories of agents trade on financial markets: rational traders (who share the same characteristics/preferences) and noise traders (who mimic their network of friends). In this context, the decisions of the latter depend on the behavior of traders within their network. Financial crashes occur when mimetic behaviors between noise traders become self-reinforcing, leading to a large proportion of noise traders to share the same position. In this situation the market becomes extremely sensitive to small global disturbances and a crash can occur. As mentioned by Johansen et al. (1999, 7), "If the tendency for traders to 'imitate' their 'friends' increases up to a certain point called the 'critical' point, many traders may place the same order (sell) at the same time, thus causing a crash." This collective phenomenon takes place when the market is close to its critical point. This situation can be detectable through the size of the fluctuations: the closer the market is its critical point, the greater the price fluctuations (see chapter 3 for the analogy with critical phenomena in statistical physics).

LPPL-type modeling has already provided some successful predictions, such as the fall of the Japan Nikkei index in 1999, the 2007 crash, and some others (Jiang et al. 2010). The Financial Crisis Observatory (FCO), which was created by the Econophysics Group at the University of Zurich, has developed an indicator of this type with the aim of monitoring the risk of crises.

5.2. THE CONTRIBUTIONS OF ECONOPHYSICS SEEN FROM FINANCIAL ECONOMISTS' VIEWPOINT

As we have seen, some financial practitioners are using econophysics models, even if these models are currently less used than those of financial economics. We will turn now our attention to the theoretical contributions of econophysics models to financial economics. This section will also underline the major puzzles currently associated with econophysics, which have to be solved before the development of a potential common framework between the two fields.

First, let us recall an important finding from the previous chapter: econophysics has innovated and could provide a useful contribution to the understanding of stock price and return variations, because it has sprung up outside financial economics. The outsider position of econophysicists is also fueled by the fact that "econophysics . . . rarely postulates new economic or financial theories, or finds contradictory evidence to existing theories" (2004, 175). Chapter 4 mentioned the remark by the economist Blake LeBaron (2001), who showed that a number of simple stochastic volatility models can visually produce power laws and long-memory effects similar to those that have been reported in econophysics literature. LeBaron did not call for rejecting econophysics' results, on the contrary: "It does not say that power-law results are wrong. It is only that they should be viewed as less conclusive than they often are, since there may be many explanations beyond those related to critical phenomena" (2001, 629). He added that "The search for reliable scaling laws in economics and finance should continue. . . . The visual indication of a straight line going through some points should not be taken on its own as a 'test for complexity,' or critical behavior. . . . It would be best not to abandon these concepts, but to improve statistical understanding of both the empirical tests and the theoretical models under consideration" (2001, 630). In the same vein, the economist Steven Durlauf (2005), who is one of the defenders of complexity in economics,[20] asks econophysicists to consider the results from economics. Precisely, numerous econophysicists ignore the literature of financial economics and present their results as completely new when they are not:

> One often finds [in the literature of econophysics] a scolding of the carefully maintained straw man image of traditional finance. In particular, ignoring decades of work in dozens of finance journals, it is often claimed that "economists believe that the probability distribution of stock returns is Gaussian," a claim that can easily be refuted by a random consultation of any of the learned journals of this field. In fact, while the (erroneous) juxtaposition of scaling (physics!) via Normality (economics!) might be interpreted as an exaggeration for marketing purposes, some of the early econophysics papers even

gave the impression that what they attempted was a first quantitative analysis of financial time series ever. If this was, then, performed on a level of rigor way below established standards in economics (a revealing example is the analysis of supposed day-of-the-week effects in high-frequency returns in Zhang, 1999) it clearly undermined the standing of econophysicists in the economics community. (Lux 2009, 15)

These remarks corroborate results detailed in chapter 4: up to now, models developed by econophysicists have mainly stayed within the boundaries of statistical physics. It is important to emphasize that these quotations are more a call for collaboration than a critique of econophysicists.[21] The problem is not econophysics concepts, per se, but rather the lack of links with the existing knowledge in financial economics. Indeed, as illustrated in chapter 4, the majority of econophysicists apply concepts and models of physics as they exist today, ignoring features of financial economics, particularly the need for quantitative tests validating the power laws and the need to have generative models that explain the emergence of such patterns.

One must admit that, for a long time, research into power laws has suffered from these two major weaknesses. On the one hand, there were no statistical tests, the only tests being based on a visual comparison method (chapter 3). On the other hand, no generative models existed for explaining the emergence of power laws. These two absences are crucial for financial economists because, as chapter 1 explained, statistical tests and theoretical explanations are the twin foundations of their discipline. Indeed, from the most common viewpoint in financial economics, a scientific model must not only reproduce reality but also be validated by econometric tests and by a theoretical explanation that is compatible with the recognized theoretical framework. Some econophysicists do not feel especially concerned by these two conditions because, as explained in chapters 3 and 4, from their scientific perspective, they do not need to meet these conditions in order to propose a model. By contrast, these two conditions have largely contributed to the maintenance of the Gaussian framework by financial economists even when they describe the occurrence of extreme variations (chapter 2). Consequently, this methodological gap has strongly supported the misgivings of financial economists about the potential contribution of econophysics to their field. Up to now, these contributions are still difficult to value in light of the theoretical mainstream in financial economics.

The gap evoked above is not only due to the methodological dissimilarities between the two communities. It also results from the current lack of knowledge about the statistical treatment of power laws. These misgivings were given strong expression in 2005 by Michael Mitzenmacher, a professor of computer science. In a seminal paper on power laws, he asserted that the characterization of empirical distributions by power laws is only a part of the challenge that faces researchers involved in explaining the causes and roles of these laws. More precisely, he pointed out the need for theoretical models that could explain them:

While numerous models that yield power law behavior have been suggested and, in fact, the number of such models continues to grow rapidly, no general mechanisms or approaches have been suggested that allow one to validate that a suggested model is appropriate. . . . [W]e have beautiful frameworks, theory, and models—indeed, we have perhaps far too many

> models—but we have been hesitant in moving to the next steps, which could transform this promising beginning into a truly remarkable new area of science. (Mitzenmacher 2005, 526)

Mitzenmacher (2005, 526) suggests a sequence of five steps for studies on power laws:

1. Observe: Gather data on the behavior of a system and demonstrate that a power-law distribution appears to fit the relevant data.
2. Interpret: Explain the significance of the power-law behavior to the system.
3. Model: Propose an underlying model that explains the power-law behavior.
4. Validate: Find data to validate, and if necessary specialize or modify, the model.
5. Control: Use the understanding from the model to control, modify, and improve the system behavior.

Mitzenmacher's disclaimer was relevant for econophysics. Like other fields (geography, biology, etc.) using power laws in their research, econophysics had not really been able to go beyond the third step when Mitzenmacher published his article in 2005. Mitzenmacher's argument is important because, on the one hand, it underlines that the claims made by economists have an echo in other fields dealing with power laws; and on the other hand, it paves the way for a potential research agenda that would ease the collaboration between econophysics and financial economists.

This situation indicates that the approach used by econophysicists is not unknown to financial economists. Indeed, the models of the ARCH class and of econophysics deal with data in the same way: both make a calibration in order to estimate the parameters of the models (chapters 2 and 4). This similarity helps to explain why the lack of interest in econophysics models is not fully comprehensible to econophysicists, and by contrast why it is so comprehensible to financial economists. From a financial economics' viewpoint there are two nuances in these phenomenological approaches—although these might appear very tenuous. First, the ARCH class of models use statistical tests, while econophysics models use visual tests. Financial economists are skeptical about such visual tests because they provide no results about the statistical behavior of the quantities estimated. Second, the ARCH class of models is based on the Gaussian framework and is associated with the efficient-market hypothesis by testing the predictability of stock price/return variations, both of which are founding hypotheses of financial economics (chapter 1). Therefore, most financial economists using the ARCH class of models consider their models to have foundations from a theoretical point of view (and not merely from a statistical one).

The next section will show that the situation concerning statistical tests for power laws has changed very recently; this section will give some details concerning the theoretical foundations of the ARCH class of models. It seems that there is a misunderstanding of the theoretical importance of the Gaussian framework: many econophysics studies have associated the Gaussian random character of stock market prices/returns with the efficient-market hypothesis, believing that it has been theoretically demonstrated, as financial economics' literature suggests. However, as explained in chapters 1 and 2, this association is not theoretically demonstrated: efficient markets and the random walk or the martingale hypothesis are two distinct ideas. A random walk or a martingale is neither necessary nor sufficient for an efficient market; in addition, the efficient-market hypothesis implies no particular stochastic process. Therefore, it must be admitted that the methodology used with the ARCH class of models is similar to that used in econophysics modeling: a purely statistical modeling approach without theoretical interpretations.[22] In addition, it must be clarified that ARCH models "do not provide an avenue towards an *explanation* of the empirical regularities" (Lux 2006, 8). In fact, "Few [economic] models are capable of generating the type of ARCH [class of models] one sees in the data" (Pagan 1996, 92), leading Adrian Pagan to conclude his survey on the econometrics of financial markets with the following remarks:

> One cannot help but feel that these statistical approaches to the modeling of financial series have possibly reached the limits of their usefulness. . . . Ultimately one must pay more attention to whether . . . it is possible to construct economic models that might be useful in explaining what is observed. . . . For many economists . . . it is desirable to be able to understand the phenomena one is witnessing, and this is generally best done through theoretical models. Of course this desire does not mean that the search for statistical models which fit the data should be abandoned. . . . It is this interplay between statistics and theoretical work in economics which needs to become dominant in financial econometrics in the next decade. (Pagan 1996, 92)

Since 1996, very little progress has been made toward a higher interplay. As one can see, the approaches defended in econophysics and in financial econometrics are very close: they both describe financial data without explaining the emergence of the observed patterns.[23] Methodologically speaking, it appears the two fields are using the same kind of phenomenological approach, leading us to complete our analysis initiated in the previous chapter. Indeed, chapter 4 showed that econophysicists follow the same three first steps as does the hypothetico-deductive approach used by financial economists. The two last steps (formulation of hypotheses and validation with statistical tests) do not really appear (yet) in econophysics literature (figure 5.2).

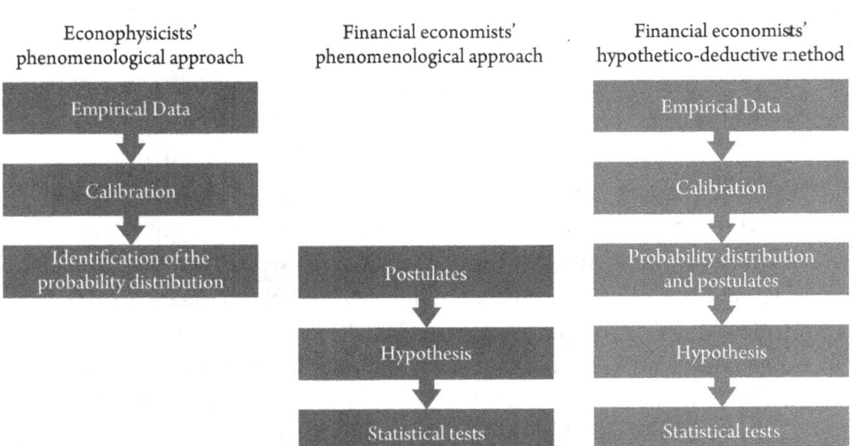

Figure 5.2 Comparison of the three approaches

However, regarding the evolution of financial economics (chapters 1 and 2), econophysics appears to be at the same stage as financial economics was in the 1960s. At that time, financial economists tried to identify the most appropriate statistical description in accordance with the data available at the time and their disciplinary expectations (i.e., the existence of a Gaussian trend—see chapter 1). In the same vein, since the 1990s, econophysicists have focused on statistical characterization of empirical data through the data available and their disciplinary expectations (i.e., the existence of a power law). After calibrating their statistical description, econophysicists can identify the class of models likely to explain the occurrence of extreme values (McCauley 2006). When econophysicists identify such a class of models, they can provide, on the one hand, a potential explanation for the emergence of power laws and, on the other hand, statistical tests to validate their use in finance. Chapters 6 will study this agenda. In this analysis, econophysics could take the form of a hypothetico-deductive approach: testing the class of models identified from empirical data (figure 5.3).

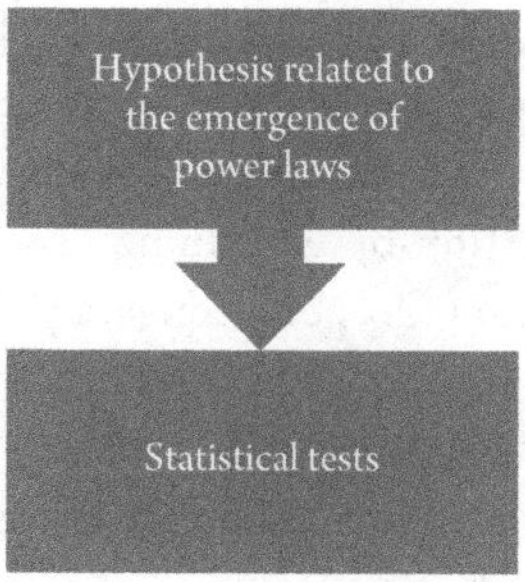

Figure 5.3 Toward a potential hypothetico-deductive approach in econophysics

What econophysicists will suggest to explain the emergence of power laws will act as future hypotheses, which will have to be tested and validated through statistical tests. Such an evolution could methodologically ease the development of future collaborations between this field and financial economics.

Such a rapprochement between the two fields could be supported by general developments we observe in the sciences. Sciences are not static; over the past few decades disciplinary borders have been changing, and new fields have emerged that are not monodisciplinary. If disciplinarity implies a monodiscipline describing a specialized scientific field, multidisciplinarity (or pluridisciplinarity), interdisciplinarity, and transdisciplinarity imply a variety of disciplines.[24] "Researchers from different fields not only work closely together on a common problem over an extended period but also create a shared conceptual model of the problem that integrates and transcends each of their separate disciplinary perspectives" (Rosenfield 1992, 55). All participants then have common roles and try to offer a holistic scheme that subordinates disciplines. The ecology of today can be looked on as an illustration of these changes. Max-Neef (2005) explained that *growth* and *environment* were frequently identified as opposites in conventional economics because they were mainly based on anthropocentric reasoning. By taking into account different fields (economics, demography, biophysics, etc.), a more biocentric ecology has recently been developed. This ecology has proposed a new framework in order to solve the traditional opposition between *environment* and *growth*. In this perspective, these opposite concepts can now be seen as complementary in a unified *development*.

The emergence of econophysics is a clear illustration of this recent evolution. But, as we have observed, to date no common conceptual scheme integrating and transcending financial economics and econophysics has emerged. By staying within their traditional boundaries, (econo)physicists and financial economists do not facilitate the creation of a common scientific literature that could be shared by the two disciplines and could allow the creation of new models or knowledge. Morin (1994) explained that "the big problem is to find the difficult path of the inter-relationship (*l'entre-articulation*) between sciences that have not only their own language, but basic concepts that cannot move from one language to another." Although an integrated approach requires that disciplines share common features, and in particular a common conceptual scheme, the problem of language (concordances) must be also considered. As Klein (1994) explained, "A 'pidgin' is an interim tongue, based [on] partial agreement on the meaning of shared terms. . . . [An integrated approach] will begin with a pidgin, with interim agreement on basic concepts and their meanings." The concept of a pidgin was introduced by Galison (1997), who called Kuhnian incommensurability into question by explaining how people from different social groups can communicate.[25] From this perspective, a pidgin can be seen as a means of communication between two (or more) groups that do not have a shared language.[26] Galison (1997, 783) used the metaphor of "trading zone" (because in situations of trade, groups speak languages other than that of their home country) to characterize this process of communication between people who do not share the same language. More specifically, "Two groups can agree on rules of exchange even if they ascribe utterly different significance to the objects being exchanged" (Galison 1997, 783). As Chrisman (1999) pointed out, the emergence of a pidgin requires specific conditions: regular contact between the language communities involved, the need to communicate between these communities, and, last, the absence of a widespread interlanguage.

All the conditions seem to be met for the emergence of a new pidgin in the case of econophysics and financial economics. Some theoretical continuities exist between these two disciplines because Gaussian processes are a particular case of Lévy processes. These continuities do not imply a common language, but they do encourage the potential emergence of a common conceptual scheme based on a new axiomatic, which would make sense for financial economists and econophysicists as well. In accordance with the analysis of Morin and Klein, a more integrated approach must take into account the constraints that both original disciplines have to face: for econophysicists the need for statistical processes to be physically plausible (i.e., in line with the properties of physical systems) combined with the fit between model and empirical data; for financial economists, the existence of reliable statistical tests for distribution describing data on the one hand, and the compatibility between the model and theoretical framework on the other. In other words, this potential language implying a common conceptual scheme must result from a double movement: models from physics must incorporate the theoretical framework from financial economics and, at the same time, theories and concepts from financial economics must be modified so that they encompass richer models from physics.

This double movement is a necessary step toward a more integrative approach in econophysics. This adaptation implies the integration of theoretical constraints observed in each discipline in such a way that the new shared conceptual framework will make sense in each discipline. As Chrisman (1999, 5) has pointed out, the emergence of a pidgin can be seen as a new integrated jargon between two disciplines, as opposed to a multidisciplinary approach that relies on what Chrisman called "boundary objects," which imply an agreement and an "awareness" between the groups involved through which each can understand that the other may not see things in the same way. The following section will present recent developments that could pave the way to a progressive integration of econophysics models into financial economics.

5.3. RECENT DEVELOPMENTS: TOWARD POSSIBLE INTEGRATION

In recent years, substantial steps toward a common conceptual scheme and the emergence of a new pidgin have been made: econophysicists have developed a number of collaborations with economists (Gabaix et al. 2000; Farmer and Lux 2008; Farmer and Foley 2009; Ausloos, Jovanovic, and Schinckus 2016; McCauley et al. 2016 [forthcoming]), economists have provided a conceptual reflection on econophysics (Keen 2003; Rosser 2010, 2008),[27] and financial economists have been taking power laws into account in their ARCH family models (Broda et al. 2013). In addition, since Mitzenmacher's disclaimer in 2005, several authors have done significant work on providing statistical tests for power laws, and generative models to explain the power-law behaviors of financial-asset prices/returns.

5.3.1. New Generative Models

The first crucial step in very recent contributions by econophysicists concerns generative models in order to explain power-law behavior in financial data. As previously mentioned, such models are vital from the perspective of financial economics, because they shed light on the potential reasons that power laws emerge. In this section, we present the four main categories of generative models that explain the power-law behavior of financial data and could pave the way to a potential collaboration between the two communities. According to these models, power laws would come from

1. A statistical effect (more precisely, from specific conditions on random growth);
2. The heterogeneity of investor sizes;
3. A specific organization (microstructure) of the market;
4. Self-organized criticality.

The first two categories of models find the origin of power laws in the time series, while the last two associate these macro laws with an emerging property resulting from a statistical expression of a large number of microinteractions. It is worth mentioning that the majority of these works (except the first category) have been developed by theoreticians involved in econophysics. While the first category emerged from strictly statistical development, the second category refers to a theory proposed by a financier trained in mathematics (Xavier Gabaix) in collaboration with econophysicists (particularly Eugene Stanley). In the same vein, the third category of models combines works proposed by economists with models provided by econophysicists. However, this category is a direct application of the renormalization group theory developed in physics, presented in chapter 3. The last set of models refers to a strictly physical perspective on power laws, since it is founded on what physicists call the self-organized criticality that we introduced in chapter 3.

5.3.1.1. Random Growth and Power Laws

The first generative model for explaining the distribution of phenomena according to a power law dates back to Yule (1925), who claimed that the distribution of species among genera of plants followed a power law; he then proposed a stochastic process based on proportional random growth, allowing this specific distribution to be generated. This notion was introduced into economics by Champernowne (1953) and Simon (1955) and studied in detail by Kesten (1973) to explain the distribution of city populations. Later, Gabaix (1999) clarified the idea by showing that an approximate power law might emerge from Gibrat's Law: in this context, the assumption is that the expected rate of growth of a city and its variance are independent of its size. Economists have progressively been using models of this kind, for example Gabaix (1999, 2009) and Krugman (1991, 1996a, 1996b).[28] Although Champernowne (1953), Simon (1955), and Kesten (1973) did not directly deal with financial data in their models, they left room for a specific explanation of the rise of power laws in finance, as explained below.

Roughly speaking, the model proposed by Champernowne (1953) refers to a population P_t^i of the city i at time t for which a normalized population size is defined as $S_t^i = \frac{P_t^i}{P_t}$, where P_t is the average population and where S_t^i is assumed to grow at a rate of γ_{t+1}^i from time t to $t+1$, so that we can write,

$$S_{t+1}^i = S_t^i + \gamma_{t+1}^i. \tag{5.2}$$

Using the seminal model proposed by Yule (1925), Kesten (1973) showed that this basic equation can generate a power law when the growth rate itself follows a power law. More precisely, Kesten (1973) associated the probability at time $t+1$ to observe a population S^i higher than a specific size x with the distribution function $D_{t+1}(x)$, which he formalized as follows:

$$D_{t+1}(x) = P(S_{t+1}^i > x)$$

$$= P(S_t^i + \gamma_{t+1}^i > x)$$

$$= P\left(S_t^i > \frac{x}{\gamma_{t+1}^i}\right). \tag{5.5}$$

If growth rates in time are assumed to be i.i.d. random variables with a density $f(\gamma)$, the previous equation can be rewritten as

$$D_{t+1}(x) = \int_0^{\infty} D_t\left(\frac{x}{\gamma}\right) f(\gamma) d\gamma, \tag{5.6}$$

which can be reformulated in terms of city size (S),

$$D(S) = \int_0^{\infty} D\left(\frac{S}{\gamma}\right) f(\gamma) d\gamma. \tag{5.7}$$

Yule's model (1925), extended in economics by Champernowne (1953) and Kesten (1973), defines the condition for which this equation can generate a power law: the growth rate (γ) must itself follow a power law. In other words, the expected value of the growth rate must be equal to 1, which can be expressed as

$$E\left[\gamma^{a}\right] = 1. \tag{5.8}$$

Reed and Hughes (2002) sustained this statistical analysis later and showed that a power-law distribution can be obtained when things grow exponentially at random times. The formalization presented here shows that the condition for which D_t describes a power law results from a technical constraint in the statistical description of economic data. In other words, the origin of power laws is not in the observed phenomenon but rather in its statistical characterization independently of the disciplinary context in which this statistical investigation is made. However, a more economic explanation of why the equation above generates a power law can be derived from Gibrat (1931), who claimed that frictions preventing cities (or firms) from becoming too small must be built into the model. Gibrat explained that, in the presence of frictions, the pure random growth process modeled by Yule (1925) will follow not a power law but the Gaussian law. In this perspective, the condition under which the above equation generates a power law requires the addition of a disturbing factor (a positive cost) characterizing the existence of frictions. As Gabaix (2009) explained, this technical point developed by Gibrat (1931) paved the way (which was not followed) for an economic explanation for the emergence of power laws, since this idea of friction can easily take the form of a positive probability of death or a high cost of expansion that prevents cities (or firms) from growing.

Gabaix (2009) also explained that the statistical constraint identified by Yule (1925) opened the door to another unexpected potential explanation for the emergence of power laws: they could result from a specific parameterization of ARCH-type models since they imply random growth. And indeed, in line with what we mentioned above, ARCH models can generate a power law if they are parameterized with a random growth rate that follows a power law. Let us illustrate this idea with a classical application of an ARCH model taking the form

$$\sigma_t^2 = \alpha\sigma_{t-1}^2\varepsilon_t^2 + \beta, \tag{5.9}$$

where $\varepsilon_t^2\,\sigma_{t-1}^2$ is the return, with ε_t independent of σ_t. Therefore, in line with the Yule-Kesten model, it is possible to reformulate this ARCH model using $S_t = \sigma_t^2$, $\gamma_t = \alpha\varepsilon_t^2$, and the β as a constant. From this perspective, ARCH models are consistent with the random-growth model presented previously, which will generate a power law under either of the following two conditions:

- A situation in which $\beta = 0$, implying a classical model of a random-growth process that will generate a power law when the rate $\gamma_t(\alpha\varepsilon_t^2)$ follows a power law
- A situation in which β (or $E(\beta)$) >0, meaning that this parameter characterizes some frictions in the growth preventing the process from converging toward a Gaussian distribution

This ARCH origin of power laws is conceptually troubling: ARCH models are supposed to describe the evolution of financial returns through an improved Gaussian description whose parameterization can generate a power law! While econophysicists see a power law "in the observations," financial economists create it through statistical treatment of data. Indeed, this statistically generated power law appears to be a simulacrum aimed at capturing the occurrence of extreme variations in line with the methodological framework (based on the importance of the Gaussian unconditional distribution) used in finance. This first category of models generating power laws does not really explain the origin of the macro laws, since they appear to result from another power law characterizing the evolution of the growth rate. As strange as this might be, we will find this kind of explanation again in the following section.

5.3.1.2. Heterogeneity of Investor Sizes and Power Laws

In their model, Gabaix et al. (2003) demonstrated that an institutional reason can explain power-law behaviors. These authors detailed their model in a second paper (Gabaix et al. 2006) directly inspired by existing literature on the behavior of institutional investors. Specifically, they showed that institutional investors' trades have an impact on the evolution of financial prices. In this analysis, the volatility of financial prices is derived from the distribution of the trading volume:

> The fat-tailed distribution of investor sizes generates a fat-tailed distribution of volumes and returns. When we derive the optimal trading behavior of large institutions, we are able to replicate the specific values for the power law exponents found in stylized fact (i) [the

> observation of a power-law distribution for trading volume] and (ii) [the observation of a power law for the financial returns]. (Gabaix et al. 2006, 463)

The model's starting point is observation of the distribution related to the investors' size, which takes the form of a power law.[29] The fat-tailed distribution means that we can observe a big difference between large and small trading institutions, implying an important heterogeneity of actors (in terms of size). This diversity results in a dispersal of trading power in which only bigger institutions will have a real impact on the market.[30] Starting from this conceptual framework, Gabaix et al. (2003, 2006) used three initial empirical observations. First, the distribution of the size of investors (in the United States) can be characterized through a power law (with an exponent of 1). Second, the distribution of the trading value follows a power law (with an exponent equal to 1.5). Third, the distribution of financial returns can be described with a power law (whose exponent is equal to 3).

Given these observations, Gabaix et al. demonstrated that optimal trading behavior of large institutions (considering that they are the only elements influencing market prices) can generate a power law in the distribution of trading volume and financial returns. Gabaix et al. (2003, 2006) proposed a model describing a single risky security with a fixed supply and with the price at time t denoted $p(t)$. At time t, a large fund gets a signal M about a mispricing ($M < 0$ is associated with a selling signal, while $M > 0$ is a buying one). That signal leads the fund to negotiate with a market supplier a potential buy on the market. Of course, there is a lag between the negotiation, the transaction, and the impact on the market price. Basically, at $t = 1 - 2\varepsilon$ (ε is a small positive number), the fund buys a quantity V of shares at price $p + r$, where r is the price concession (or the full price). Afterward, at $t = 1 - \varepsilon$, the transaction is announced on the market. Consequently, the price jumps, at $t = 1$, to $p(1) = p + \pi(V)$, where $\pi(V)$ is called the permanent impact, while the difference ($\varphi = r - \pi$) is the temporary price impact. In this modeling, the generalized evolution of price will take the form

$$p(t) = p + \pi(V) + \sigma[B(t)], \tag{5.10}$$

where B is a standard Brownian motion with $B(1) = 0$. By using this generalized evolution of price, Gabaix et al. (2006) showed that a power law describing the evolution of financial returns can result from an optimizing behavior in line with a classical methodology used in financial economics. Specifically, the liquidity supplier and the large fund will try to maximize their utility function formalized as

$$U = E[w] - \lambda[Var(w)]^{\delta/2}, \tag{5.11}$$

where λ is a positive factor describing the aversion to risk, and δ is the δth order of risk aversion. $W(r)$ is the money earned during the trade, which directly depends on the expected return $E[r]$ generated by the transaction. In other words, the optimizing process implies a maximization of the expected value of total return given by the trade (r). This return must take into account a potential uncertainty (denoted C) on the mispricing signal M. When the mispricing signal results only from noise, this uncertainty parameter is equal to zero $(C = 0)$; otherwise, C is positive when the mispricing is real. If the fund is assumed to spend S dollars in assets that it buys for a volume of V_t in a transaction in which it pays a price concession equal to $R(V_t)$, the total return of the fund's portfolio can be summarized through the equation

$$r_t = \frac{V_t\left(CM_t - R(V_t) + u_t\right)}{S}, \tag{5.12}$$

where u_t is the mean zero noise. By simulating data with this model, Gabaix et al. (2003, 2006) were able to replicate the power law observed for financial returns. More formally, their model showed that the evolution of financial returns can generate a power law when the trading volume is used as an explanative variable. To put it in another way, a classical model maximizing a utility function based on wealth can generate a power law related to the trade volume under the condition that the size distribution of traders follows a power law, $r \sim kV^{\alpha}$, k being a positive parameter. In this theory, power laws in the financial sphere would result from another power law characterizing the heterogeneity of investors' size. The origin of power laws in financial data would be due to another (unexplained) power law observed in the size distribution of investors. We find here the same kind of argument as that used in the previous section. Although this theory incorporates some key optimizing elements used in the financial mainstream, it must be explained "by a more complete theory of the economy along with the distribution of firm sizes [investors]" (Lux 2009, 8). Moreover, the theoretical framework proposed by Gabaix et al. (2003, 2006) appears to be incompatible with the observation made by Aoki and Yoshikawa (2007) that financial and foreign exchange markets are disconnected from their underlying economic fundamentals, since the first usually demonstrate power-law behavior, while the latter are characterized by an exponential distribution.[31]

5.3.1.3. Power Laws and Microstructure of the Market

According to the third category of underlying models, the source of power laws in finance can be found in the organization of the market. More precisely, authors involved in this area of knowledge design their models by integrating specific microstructure features of the markets (i.e., bid-ask spread, double auction, etc.) related to the exchange mechanism, which they sometimes combine with certain behavioral biases (mimetism, over- or underestimation, etc.) observed in the financial markets in order to replicate the power laws associated with the evolution of financial returns. In this context, this category of models sheds new light on the trading conditions in which power laws can emerge.

First of all, we must remember that the microstructural behaviors of financial markets have been investigated in financial economics in theoretical frameworks other than the one set out in chapters 1 and 2. In the 1980s there emerged two alternative theoretical approaches that took as their starting point a questioning of empirical anomalies[32] and of the main hypotheses of the dominant framework: behavioral finance and financial market microstructure. Both directly called upon the informational efficiency theory, which, as we have seen, was a crucial element in the birth of financial economics. Although the theory of financial market microstructure has been developing since the 1980s,[33] the first works appeared closer to 1970 with an article by Demsetz (1968), which looked at how to match up buyers and sellers to find a price when orders do not arrive synchronously. In 1971, Jack Treynor, editor-in-chief of *Financial Analysts Journal* from 1969 to 1981, published a short article under the pseudonym of Walter Bagehot, "The Only Game in Town," in which he analyzed the consequences when traders have different motivations for trading. Maureen O'Hara, one of the leading authors of this theoretical trend, defined market microstructure as "the study of the process and outcomes of exchanging assets under a specific set of rules" (1995). Financial market microstructure focuses on how specific trading mechanisms and how strategic behaviors affect the priceformation process. This field deals with issues of market structure and design, price formation and price discovery, transaction and timing cost, information and disclosure, and market-maker and investor behavior. A central idea in the theory of market microstructure is that asset prices do not fully reflect all available information even if all participants are rational. Indeed, information may be unequally distributed between, and differently interpreted by, market participants. This hypothesis stands in total contradiction to the efficient-market hypothesis defended by the dominant paradigm.[34]

The second alternative approach is behavioral finance. In 1985 Werner F. M. De Bondt and Richard Thaler published "Does the Stock Market Overreact?," effectively marking the start of what has become known as behavioral finance. Behavioral finance studies the influence of psychology on the behavior of financial practitioners and the subsequent effect on markets.[35] Its theoretical framework is drawn mainly from behavioral economics. Behavioral economics uses social, cognitive, and emotional factors to understand the economic decisions of economic agents performing economic functions, and their effects on market prices and resource allocation. It is primarily concerned with the bounds of rationality in economic agents. The first important article came from Kahneman[36] and Tversky (1979), who used cognitive psychology to explain various divergences of economic decision-making from neoclassical theory. There exists as yet no unified theory of behavioral finance.[37] According to Schinckus (2009b), however, it is possible to characterize this new school of thought on the basis of three hypotheses common to all the literature: (1) the existence of behavioral biases affecting investor behavior; (2) the existence of bias in investors' perception of the environment that affects their decisions; 3) the existence of systematic errors in the processing of information by individuals, which affects the market's informational efficiency. The markets are therefore presumed to be informationally inefficient.

The third category of underlying models from econophysics for explaining power-law behaviors of financial data is close to the microstructure behaviors that we find in financial economics. The approach defended in this category of models can methodologically be broken down into two steps: (1) designing the model by defining specific rules governing agents' interactions; (2) simulating the market in order to replicate (hopefully) the data initially recorded on the financial markets. This methodology provides a microsimulation of economic phenomena. It was initiated by Stigler (1964) and was mainly expanded in the 1990s with the development of what is known as agent-based modeling.

Initiated by the Santa Fe Institute in the 1980s, agent-based modeling was gradually developed in the 1990s and has now become one of the most widely used tools to describe dynamic (adaptive) economic systems (Arthur 2005). The methodology designs sets of abstract algorithms intended to describe the "fundamental behavior" of agents, formulating it in a computerized language in which agents' behavioral characteristics are inputs, while outputs are associated with the macro level resulting from the computerized iterated microinteractions. The microscopic level is characterized by hypotheses about agents' behaviors. Agent-based modeling is also widely used in economics literature, with authors using it to model many economic phenomena: the opinion transmission mechanism (Amblard and Deffuant 2004; Guillaume 2004); the development of industrial networks and the relationship between suppliers and customers (Epstein 2006; Gilbert 2007; Brenner 2001) the addiction of consumers to a brand (Janssen and Jager 1999); the description of secondhand (car) markets (Izquierdo and Izquierdo 2007), and so on.[38] In this section, we mention only agent-based models used in finance, and, more specifically, we focus on models in which a large number of computerized iterations can generate power laws describing the evolution of financial returns.[39]

Lux and Marchesi (1999, 2000) proposed a model simulating an "artificial financial market" in which fat tails characterizing large fluctuations (described through a power law) would result from speculative periods leading to the emergence of a common opinion among agents, who regularly tend to over and underestimate financial assets. This agent-based approach integrating the over/underestimation bias as a major interaction rule has been confirmed by Kou et al. (2008) and Kaizoji (2006). In the same vein, Chen, Lux, and Marchesi (2001) and Lévy et al. (1995, 2000) proposed a model in which traders can switch between a fundamentalist and a chartist strategy. In this framework, the authors showed that financial returns follow a power law only when financial prices differed significantly from the evolution of economic fundamentals (in contrast with the efficient-market paradigm). Alfarano and Lux (2005) proposed an agent-based model in which power laws emerged from interactions between fundamentalists and chartists whose adaptive behaviors are based on a variant of the herding mechanism. By using only elements from the microstructure, Wyart et al. (2008) proposed a model in which a power law can result from a specific relationship between the bid-ask spread and the volatility. More specifically, their model generates a power law when these variables are directly related through the following form:

$$\frac{Ask - Bid}{Price} = k\frac{\sigma}{\sqrt{N}}, \tag{5.13}$$

where σ is the daily volatility of the stock, N is the average number of trades for the stock, and k is a constant. Bouchaud, Mezard, and Potters (2002) and Bouchaud, Farmer, and Lillo (2009) also defined some conditions in the trade process that can generate a power law in the evolution of financial returns.

Unlike the models presented in the previous section, these models do not associate the emergence of power laws in finance with the existence of another unexplained power law. However, there are gaps in the explanation proposed by these models. Although they provide particular conditions under which financial distributions can take the form of a power law, they do not really explain how these conditions might come about. Models referring to behavioral biases do not explain why the selected bias would primarily shape the market, while models defining specific conditions in terms of the relationship between variables involved in the exchange do not explain why these conditions would exist. It is worth mentioning that the feedback effects between micro and macro levels lead to complex behaviors that cannot be analytically studied in terms of renormalization group theory (Sornette 2014).

Although work in this category avoids the argument consisting in justifying the emergence of a power law through the existence of another power law, it raises another curiosity, since power laws appear as an emergent macroproperty resulting from a large number of computerized iterations characterizing microinteractions (Lux 2009). By identifying the trading conditions in which a power law can emerge, this category of models sheds new light on the occurrence of such laws. However, this idea of a power law as an emergent property still generates debate, since its "microfoundations remain unclear" (Gabaix 2009, 281). Theoreticians involved in self-organized criticality models, which are presented in the following section, have also used this reference to an emerging mechanism.

5.3.1.4. Self-Organized Criticality

The fourth type of generative models is based on "self-organized criticality." Such models are another direct application in finance of the theoretical framework of statistical physics that we studied in chapter 3. They are based on the idea that the phenomena studied by their very nature maintain themselves continuously at their critical point.

As explained in chapter 3, aggregate physical phenomena can appear that show macroproperties distinct from the properties associated with their microcomponents. When this perspective is imported into economics, agents can be considered to be interacting particles whose adaptive behaviors create different structures (such as molecules, cells, crystals, etc.). These studies are methodologically in line with the class of models presented in the previous section, since the calibration of microinteractions requires assumptions concerning individual behaviors, which can generate an (unexpected) emerging macro order. Unlike the studies discussed in the previous section, these works implement an agent-based modeling combined with noneconomic assumptions to calibrate microinteractions, as explained below.

There is a growing literature combining econophysics and agent-based modeling. Bak et al. (1997) used a reaction diffusion model to describe the dynamics of orders. In this model, orders were particles moving along a price line, whose random collisions were seen as transactions (see also Farmer et al. 2005 for the same kind of model). Maslov (2000) tried to make the model developed by Bak et al. (1997) more realistic by adding specific features related to the microstructure (organization) of the market. In the same vein, Challet and Stinchcombe (2001) improved Maslov's (2000) model by considering two particles (ask and bid) that can be characterized through three potential states: deposition (limit order), annihilation (market order), and evaporation (cancellation). Slanina (2001) also proposed a new version of Maslov's model in which individual position (order) is not taken into account but rather substituted by a mean-field approximation. Some authors used an agent-based approach to characterize the emergence of nontrivial behavior such as herding: Eguiluz et al. (2000), Stauffer et al. (1999), and Wang et al. (2005), for example, associate the information-dissemination process with a percolation model among traders whose interactions randomly connected their demand through clusters.[40]

These works can be methodologically characterized by a noneconomic agent-based approach since noneconomic assumptions are initially made or used for the calibration of microinteractions. In this perspective, econophysicists define algorithmic rules (generating microinteractions) that are calibrated in terms of physically plausible events. Therefore, agents and their interactions are defined in terms usually applied to physical systems such as potential states (deposition, cancellation, annihilation, etc.), thermal features (heat release rate, ignition point, etc.), or magnetic dimensions (magnetic permeability, excitation). In line with the comment made for the previous category of models, the computerized technique used by econophysicists to generate a power law implies the idea that these macro-laws are an emergent property. Although this emerging mechanism appears strange at first sight, it is not new, given the development of the self-criticality theory introduced, in physics, by Bak et al. (1987) and applied in finance by Bak et al. (1988).[41] According to Bak, the linearity visually identified in the histogram related to the occurrence of a phenomenon can be interpreted as the expression of the phenomenon's complexity (Bak 1994, 478). Although this theory was developed to describe the emergence of power laws characterizing the evolution of physical systems, its theoretical justification is often used by econophysicists to defend the existence of similar macro laws in the finance area. Concerning the visual linearity observed in a log-log scale graph, Bak explained:

> This is an example [plot with occurrences of earthquakes] of a scale-free phenomenon: there is no answer to the question "how large is a typical earthquake?" Similar behaviour has been observed elsewhere in Nature. . . . The fact that large catastrophic events appear at the tails of regular power-law distributions indicates that there is "nothing special" about those events, and that no external cataclysmic mechanism is needed to produce them. (Bak 1994, 478)

The author associated "self-organized criticality" with "slowly driven dynamic systems, with many degrees of freedom, [that] naturally self-organize into a critical state obeying power-law statistics" (Bak 1994, 480). More specifically, some physical systems appear to be ruled by a single macroscopic power law describing the frequency at which phase transitions occur (Newman 2005). Chapter 3 already introduced this idea when the foundations of statistical physics were presented. The particularity of the self-organized criticality refers to the assumption that certain phenomena maintain themselves near a critical state. An illustration of such a situation is a stable heap of sand to which the addition of one grain generates miniavalanches. At some point, these minicascades stop, meaning that the heap has integrated the effect of this additional grain. The sand heap is said to have reached its self-organized critical state (because the addition of a new grain of sand would generate the same process). Physicists talk about a "critical state" because the system organizes itself into a fragile configuration resting on a knife-edge (where the addition of a single sand grain would be enough to modify the sand heap).

This self-organized criticality has been extended in economics by Bak et al. (1993), who proposed a model in which a shock in the supply chain (which acts as an additional grain in the sand heap) generates economy-wide fluctuations (like miniavalanches in the sand) until the economy self-organizes critically (i.e., at a fragile state that could easily be modified by an additional small shock). In their model, the authors showed that the occurrence of large fluctuations in the economy can statistically be described through a power law. This conceptual framework can also be applied in finance. Ponzi and Aizawa (2000), Bartolozzi et al. (2004), and Dupoyet et al. (2011) proposed models describing financial markets as self-organized critical systems in which actors would tend to drive the market to a stable state. Once the market is close to this stable level, profits become lower and lower until negative variations (returns) are generated. These variations act as the extra grain of sand, leading to a cascade of losses, putting some agents out of the market until a situation in which profit for the remaining actors becomes possible again. In this context, new agents, attracted by the profit, re-enter the market, which therefore will tend toward a stable state, and so on. In this perspective, power laws are presented as fluctuations around the market stable state, which is looked on as a critical state perennially set on a razor's edge.

The idea that the phenomenon is always at its critical point allows physicists to give a meaning to the emergence of power laws in their field. Indeed, for a large number of self-organized critical systems, Bak et al. (1987) showed that many extreme variations (i.e., critical modifications of the system) follow a power-law distribution.

In contrast with the first two categories of models, which were based on a dynamical mechanism for producing power laws that are stochastic processes and in which noise was supplied by an external source,

> Under appropriate conditions it is . . . possible to generate power laws from deterministic dynamics. This occurs when the dynamics has a critical point. This can happen [with] self-organized criticality, which keep a system close to a critical point for a range of parameters. Critical points can amplify noise provided by an external source, but the amplification is

> potentially infinite, so that even an infinitesimal noise source is amplified to macroscopic proportions. In this case the properties of the resulting noise are independent of the noise source, and are purely properties of the dynamics. (Farmer and Geanakoplos 2008, 43)

In other words, the emergence of power laws results from the evolution of microconfigurations of the system itself and not from an external factor such as the existence of another power law or frictions in the growth rate.

However, as with the previous category of works, the self-organized criticality theory is silent on how the power laws would emerge. This framework associates power laws with an emergent statistical macro result. Econophysicists have justified the existence of power laws in finance through two arguments: (1) microscopically, the market can be seen as a self-organized critical system (i.e., sand heap) and (2) macroscopically, the statistical characterization of the fluctuations in such a self-organized system appears to be "universally" associated with power laws since "there are many situations, both in dynamical systems theory and in statistical mechanics, in which many of the properties of the dynamics around critical points are independent of the details of the underlying dynamical system" (Farmer and Geanakoplos 2008, 45–46).

Although the four categories of works presented in this section do not really explain the reasons why power laws emerge on the financial markets, they open conceptual doors for a potential economic interpretation of these macro laws. The following section will deal with the second crucial step for the potential development of an integrative collaboration between econophysicists and economics: the creation of statistical tests validating the power laws.

5.3.2. New Quantitative Tests

As chapter 3 explained, the existence of a power law is commonly tested by econophysicists through a visual inspection: the authors plot the data in a double logarithmic scale and attempt to fit a line to part of it. This procedure dates back to Pareto's work at the end of the nineteenth century. Unfortunately, this method generates significant systematic errors by wrongly attributing power-law behaviors to phenomena[42] (Clauset, Shalizi, and Newman 2009, Stumpf and Porter 2012, Gillespie 2014). From a financial-economics viewpoint, such visual tests have two major drawbacks. First, they provide no objective criterion for determining what a "good fit" is. Second, as already explained in chapters 1 and 4, financial economists consider only statistical tests scientific. Therefore, empirical investigations from the literature of econophysics tend to be regarded with suspicion by financial economists. However, it is worth mentioning that financial economists are not alone in noting the weaknesses of visual inspection; some econophysicists have also pointed out that "better and more careful testing is needed, and that too much of data analysis in this area relies on visual inspection alone" (Farmer and Geanakoplos 2008, 24).

The difficulty of implementing statistical tests dedicated to power laws is not unrelated to the fact that historically the vast majority of statistical tools have been developed in the Gaussian framework (due to the asymptotic properties of the central-limit theorem), which is not suitable for testing power laws. In other words, satisfactory statistical tools and methods for testing power laws do not yet exist. This is a big challenge, and one that very few authors have been working on. Moreover, from the perspective of financial economics, there are several obstacles to the development of statistical tests dedicated to power laws. For instance, Broda et al. (2013) explain that the computation of stable Paretian distribution density is complex. While with modern computing power parameter estimation is no longer a hindrance, "There still appears to be no existing method which is both fast and delivers the high accuracy required for likelihood optimization" (2013, 293). In addition, these authors point out that "the real problem with the use of the stable-Paretian, or any skewed, fat-tailed distribution for modelling the unconditional distribution of asset returns, is that they cannot capture the time-varying volatility so strongly evident in daily and higher frequency returns data" (Broda et al. 2013). Last, according to these authors, the stability property of the stable distribution and the definition of log returns imply that "the tail index of the return distribution should remain the same at any frequency, i.e., intraday, daily, weekly, monthly, etc. However, it is well known that this is usually not the case, with, say, daily returns exhibiting a tail index considerably lower than two, but monthly data exhibiting nearly normal behavior. This occurs because, for such series, the returns are not *i.i.d.* stable Paretian, but rather have a distribution such that, via a central-limit theorem, their sums approach normality" (Broda et al. 2013).

Although no appropriate statistical tools exist to date, the use by econophysicists of stable Lévy processes based on power-law distribution has implicitly generated a need for statistical tools to test the power-law behaviors of data. In recent years significant results have emerged from the rapid expansion of statistical studies on this topic. The literature has taken two different paths: in one, authors have used a rank-size rule; in the other, authors have focused on the size-frequency relation.

The rank-size approach starts by transforming the size frequency of the power-law distribution, $P\,[X > x] = c\,x^{-a}$, by ordering the observations according to rank size:

$$x_{(1)} \geq x_{(2)} \geq \cdots \geq x_{(r)} \geq \cdots \geq x_{(n-1)} \geq x_{(n)}. \tag{5.15}$$

Thus, the rank of the observation r is given by $r \approx n * P\,[X > x_{(r)}] \approx n * [c\,x_{(r)}^{-a}]$. Considering the logarithms—that is, $\log(r) = \log(n + c) - \alpha \log(x_r)$ which can take the following form, $\log(\text{Rank}) = c - \alpha \log(\text{Size})$, where c is a constant—the critical exponent a is determined by running the OLS on the log-log rank-size regression. Gabaix and Ibragimov (2011) pointed out that the previous OLS log-log rank-size regression is strongly biased for small samples; they demonstrated that this bias can be reduced by using $\log(\text{Rank} - 1/2)$ rather than $\log(\text{Rank})$—that is, $\log(\text{Rank} - 1/2) = c - \alpha \log(\text{Size})$.

Authors who have focused on size frequency have built statistical tests for the purpose of comparing the power law with other distributions that are very close, mainly the log-normal distribution (Eeckhout 2004; Clauset, Shalizi, and Newman 2009; Fujimoto et al. 2011; Malevergne, Pisarenko, and Sornette 2011; Rozenfeld et al. 2011; Goerlich 2013).[43] Among these works, the most significant research is probably by Clauset, Shalizi, and Newman (2009), wherein they presented a set of statistical techniques that allow the validation of power laws and calculation of their parameters. "Properly applied, these techniques can provide objective evidence for or against the claim that a particular distribution follows a power law" (Clauset, Shalizi, and Newman 2009, 692). As explained hereafter, their test follows three steps.

The first step aims to estimate the two parameters of the power law by using the method of maximum likelihood: the lower bound to the power law,[44] x_{min}, and the critical exponent, α. The necessity for estimating the lower bound comes from the fact that, in practice, few empirical phenomena obey a power law for all values of x. More often the power law applies only for values greater than some minimum x_{min}, leading to the use of truncated distributions (as explained in chapter 3) for capturing statistical characteristics associated with values $< x_{min}$. These authors suggest the following maximum likelihood estimator:

$$\hat{\alpha} \cong 1 + n\left[\sum_{i=1}^{n} \ln \frac{x_i}{x_{\min} - \frac{1}{2}}\right]^{-1}. \tag{5.16}$$

The maximum likelihood estimators are only guaranteed to be unbiased in the asymptotic limit of large sample size, $n \to \infty$. For finite data sets, biases are present, but decay with the number of observations for any choice of x_{min}. In order to estimate the critical exponent, α, they provide a method that estimates x_{min} by minimizing the "distance" between the power-law model and the empirical data using the Kolmogorov-Smirnov statistic, which is simply the maximum distance between the cumulative distribution functions of the data and the fitted model. This first step makes it possible to fit a power-law distribution to a given data set and to provide an estimation of the parameters x_{min} and α.

The second step aims to determine whether the power law is a plausible fit to the data. Clauset, Shalizi, and Newman propose a goodness-of-fit test, which generates a p-value that quantifies this plausibility. Such tests are based on the Kolmogorov-Smirnov statistic previously obtained, which enables measurement of the "distance" between the distribution of the empirical data and those of the hypothesized model. The p-value is defined as a fraction of the synthetic distances that are larger than the empirical distance. If the resulting p-value is greater than 0.1, the power law is a plausible hypothesis for the data; otherwise it is rejected.

The third and last step aims to compare the power law with alternative hypotheses via a likelihood-ratio test. Even if a power law fits the data well, it is still possible that another distribution, such as an exponential or a log-normal distribution, might give as good a fit or better. To eliminate this possibility, Clauset, Shalizi, and Newman suggest using a goodness-of-fit test again, calculating a p-value for a fit to the competing distribution and comparing it with the p-value for the power law. For each alternative, if the calculated likelihood ratio is significantly different from zero, then its sign indicates whether the alternative is favored over the power-law model or not.

Goerlich (2013) extended the article by Clauset et al. (2009) by proposing another kind of test derived from the Lagrange multiplier principle. He showed that the statistical power of the Lagrange multiplier test is higher than the bootstrapped Kolmogorov-Smirnov test and needs less computational time. However, according to Gillespie (2014), Clauset, Shalizi and Newman's method has three main drawbacks: "First, by fitting x_{min} we are discarding all data below that cut-off. Second, it is unclear how to compare distributions where each distribution has a different x_{min}. Third, making future predictions based on the fitted model is not possible since values less than x_{min} have not been directly modelled."

These two kinds of tests provide an important contribution to the creation of an approach more integrated between financial economics and econophysics, because they pave the way for testing explicative theoretical models based on the power-law behavior of financial prices/returns. However, it is worth emphasizing that the development of such tests could directly contribute to the development of an integrative approach between econophysicists and financial economists: this kind of test can establish the scientific justification for using power laws while paving the way for an appropriate comparison between these statistical laws and patterns usually used in finance. This statistical approach is very recent and is not widely disseminated among econophysicists. Moreover, it is worth mentioning that, to date, statistical tests of power laws have not yet been used with financial data. (They have been used for wealth, income, city sizes and firm sizes). Despite their drawbacks and the fact that further investigation is needed, we can consider that these tests have opened the door to some research into statistical tests. We can add that while visual tests are the most common in the econophysics' literature for testing the power-law distribution, some econophysicists use statistical tests. Among other works we may mention Redelico et al. (2009) and Gligor and Ausloos (2007), who used Student's *t*-test; Clippe and Ausloos (2012) and Mir et al. (2014), who used a chi-square test; and Queiros (2005), Zanin et al. (2012), Theiler et al. (1992), Morales et al. (2013).

5.4. CONCLUSION

This chapter analyzed the potential uses of econophysics models by financial economists. Although econophysics offers a set of practical solutions, its theoretical developments remain outside of financial economics. In this challenging context, the question of theoretical integration is crucial. First of all, this chapter studied how econophysics can be useful in trading rooms and also the drawbacks in its broader use. Beyond these practical implementations, the theoretical contributions of econophysics were also investigated from the viewpoint of financial economists. The similarities between the phenomenological approach used by financial economists and the one implemented by econophysicists have been presented. Afterward, we discussed to what extent this methodological situation can play a key role in a potential future rapprochement between the two fields. In this context, we also explained how econophysics' contributions can become effective. Two conditions have then been highlighted: (1) the elaboration of models explaining the emergence of power laws and (2) the creation of statistical tests validating (or not) these macro laws. As explained, the latter calls for further research in statistics.

6

TOWARD A COMMON FRAMEWORK

The two previous chapters identified what remains to be done (from an economist's point of view) for econophysicists to contribute significantly to financial economics (and finance) and to develop a fruitful collaboration between these two fields. Chapter 5 showed that recent developments in mathematics and statistics have created an opportunity for an integration of results from econophysics and financial economics. It pointed out that three paths are still waiting to be investigated: (1) development of a common framework/vocabulary in order to better compare and integrate the two approaches; (2) creation of statistical tests to identify and to test power laws or, at least, to provide statistical tests to compare results from econophysics models with those produced by financial models; and, finally, (3) work on generative models for giving a theoretical explanation of the emergence of power laws. These three axes of research could be considered as a possible research program to be developed in the coming years by those who would like to contribute to financial theory by developing "bridges" between econophysics and financial economics.

Of the three paths mentioned above, the creation of statistical tests is the most crucial step from the point of view of attracting the attention of financial economists and practitioners. As explained in the previous chapters, financial economists have founded the scientific dimension of their discipline on the use of statistical tests for the characterization of empirical data. Consequently, such tests are a necessary condition for doing research in financial economics. Although several problems still present obstacles to the development of statistical tests dedicated to power laws, significant results have emerged in recent years (chapter 5). Moreover, because of the rapid expansion of statistical studies on this topic, new research may develop in the near future. Developing such tests is a research program on its own and cannot be undertaken here without leading us very far from the initial objectives of this book. However, from our point of view, research of this kind is an important first step in the search for a common theoretical framework between financial economics and econophysics. If one wants to create statistical tests for comparing results produced by models from the two fields, the first question is to know what is to be compared. Although econophysics is a vibrant research field that has given rise to an increasing number of models that describe the evolution of financial returns, the vast majority focus on a specific statistical sample without offering a generic description of the phenomenon. The lack of a homogeneous perspective creates obvious difficulties related to the criteria for choosing one model rather than another in a comparison with key models of financial economics. Consequently, the existing literature offers a broad catalog of models but no unified conceptual framework. The standardization of knowledge through such a common framework is a necessary condition if econophysics is to become a strong discipline (Kuhn 1962).

This chapter will propose the foundations of a unified framework for the major models published in econophysics. To this end, it will provide a generalized formula describing the evolution of financial returns. This formula will be derived from a meta-analysis of models commonly used in econophysics. By proposing a generic formula characterizing the statistical distributions usually used by econophysicists (Lévy, truncated Lévy, or nonstable Lévy distributions), we are seeking to pave the way toward a more unified framework for econophysics. This formula will be used to propose an econophysics option-pricing model compatible with the basic concepts used in the classical Black and Scholes framework.

6.1. PROPOSITIONS FOR A COMMON FRAMEWORK

6.1.1. The Issues for a Common Framework

The literature of econophysics proposes a wide variety of models to describe the probability distribution of stock market price variations, each using various types of probability functions. Broadly speaking, and in line with what was mentioned in chapter 4, every econophysicist has his or her own model. To date, none of these models is supported by statistical tests acceptable according to the scientific criteria used in financial economics (chapter 5). In addition, while the number of such models continues to grow, no comparison between them has been proposed in order to identify a general common mechanism. Another question has to be considered: while models in econophysics seem to provide significant empirical results, until now there has been no "crucial experiment or test" to demonstrate that they successfully predict occurrences that financial economics models do not. By that measure, there is no theoretical basis for preferring econophysics models, and their use rather than those from financial economics appears to be a choice more ideological than scientific.

Most conceptual comparisons between econophysics and financial economics support this conclusion about the force of ideology, since they suggest that the results and methodology of the two disciplines are not directly comparable. A recent article by Sornette (2014) illustrates the point. Adopting a physicists' viewpoint, Sornette provided a stimulating review and an interesting discussion of the slow cross-fertilization between physics and financial economics. But despite its well-documented argument, the article perpetuates a widespread misunderstanding that keeps the window of controversy between econophysicists and financial economists wide open. This misunderstanding is rooted in the crucial differences, explained by Sornette, between the modeling methodology used by economists and that used by physicists, which is broadly summarized by the "*difference between empirically founded science and normative science*" (Sornette 2014, 3). Sornette added:

> The difference between [the model for the best estimate of the fundamental price from physics] and [the model for the best estimate of the fundamental price from financial economics, i.e. efficient-market theory] is at the core of the difference in the modelling strategies of economists, [which] can be called top-down (or from rational expectations and efficient markets), compared with the bottom-up or microscopic approach of physicists. (7)

The distinction is frequently found in econophysics literature.[1] From the elements discussed in the previous chapters, we can claim that this distinction between the two modeling "strategies" is false and that the authors who rely on it are confusing two levels of analysis—the methodological aspect and the modeling dimension. More importantly, this confusion provides a good illustration of the nature of the differences between financial economics and econophysics by highlighting a difficulty in comparing them. Let us explore this point.

In the literature of econophysics, it is commonly asserted that the "modelling strategies of economists can be called top-down" because a "financial modeller builds a model or a class of models based on a pillar of standard economic thinking, such as efficient markets, rational expectations, representative agents" in order to draw "some prediction that is then tested statistically, often using linear regressions on empirical data" (Sornette 2014, 5). In this context, rational expectations and the idea that markets are efficient are assumed. So it appears from this formulation that, methodologically, economists usually start their analysis with assumptions that they implement in modeling and from which they deduce conclusions; "top-down" modeling appears therefore to be associated with the deductive approach mainly used in economics. Econophysics is, in contrast, presented as a data-driven field founded on descriptive models resulting from observations. First of all, it is worth mentioning that the belief in "*no* a priori" is in itself an a priori since it refers to a form of positivism. Second, in such a comparison, this inductive approach is implicitly considered to be a "bottom-up" methodology because it starts with data related to a phenomenon rather than assumptions about it. In this case then, the terms "top-down" and "bottom-up" refer to methodological strategies rather than to modeling methods.

Although the difference between the two dimensions seems subtle, it is important: methodology refers to the conceptual way of dealing with phenomena (i.e., quantitatively vs. qualitatively; empirically vs. theoretically, etc.), while modeling methods concern the kind of computation (and data) used by scientists. Actually, by contrasting the two fields in this way, authors focus on a very specific way of doing econophysics and economics (i.e., on a very specific part of the literature related to these two areas of knowledge). On the one hand, although a part of economics is well known for its representative-agent hypothesis, there are works in financial economics that do not necessarily implement top-down modeling. Agent-based modeling, which has become a common practice in (financial) economics, is directly founded on a micro-oriented modeling from which an aggregate (bottom-up) result is derived. On the other hand, a large part of the literature of econophysics is dedicated to the phenomenological macrodescription of the evolution of financial prices, making these studies ineligible for consideration as "bottom-up" modeling.

As mentioned in chapters 4 and 5, a number of economists have pointed out this confused way of contrasting econophysics and economics and stressed the limitations of doing so. In the words of Lux (2009, 230) we have quoted previously,

> One often finds [in the literature of econophysics] a scolding of the carefully maintained straw man image of traditional finance. In particular, ignoring decades of work in dozens of finance journals, it is often claimed that "economists believe that the probability distribution of stock returns is Gaussian," a claim that can easily be refuted by a random consultation of any of the learned journals of this field.

In addition, while econophysicists use models based on statistical physics in an attempt to reproduce stylized facts, they also use the fact that the Gaussian law is a foundation of financial economics to argue that economists ignore empirical and stylized fact. However, in doing so, econophysicists skillfully ignore the fact that economists identified stylized facts on stock price extreme variations and their leptokurticity several decades before the emergence of econophysics (chapter 2).

The misunderstanding between the two communities is often due to a comparison between two different conceptual levels: it is very common for econophysicists to compare the results of their statistical models with the theoretical framework of financial economics. When authors explain that econophysics employs a microscopic approach, they are implicitly referring to the way of dealing with data (experimental level), contrasting this with the efficient-market hypothesis, which involves assumptions usually made in economics (theoretical level). In this context, it is a truism to claim that the experimental level is closer to reality than the theoretical one (whatever the field). Econophysicists seem to consider that economic reality is a given, while financial economists directly contribute to the determination of the reality they are supposed to be studying. Physicists are aware that they have an influence on the *measurement* of physical phenomena, but they do not influence the *nature* of the physical phenomena they study. Financial economics is a little different, since financial reality is a social reality that must be built using a conceptual framework. Consequently, the efficient-market hypothesis can be seen as an idealized framework that has been used theoretically in the development (computerization of financial markets, elaboration of a legal framework, etc.) of financial spheres (Schinckus 2008). This clarification is important because an interdisciplinary comparison makes sense only if one compares the same conceptual levels.

If one wishes to compare the experimental levels and statistical models used in the two disciplines, the comparison should be between econophysicists' models and the ARCH class of models empirically implemented by financial economists. Surprisingly, and as chapter 5 explained, despite the fact that econophysicists and financial economists in general do not use the same methodology (the former's is data-driven, while the latter's starts with assumptions), such a comparison shows that they proceed in the same way in the implementation of their models: both start with an empirical calibration of their models in order to simulate features (price variations). The sole difference lies in the way of modeling extreme values: econophysicists consider these values part of the system, whereas financial economists associate these extreme values with a statistical distribution characterizing the error terms of a major trend. In other words, financial economists break down stylized facts into two elements, a general trend (assumed to be governed by a Brownian uncertainty) and a statistical error term that follows a conditional distribution for which a calibration is required. For these conditional distributions, it goes without saying that data-driven calibrations (i.e., without theoretical justification) are common in financial economics. As explained in chapter 5, the major difference between the two fields appears in how they calibrate their models: calibration in econophysics mainly results from data, whereas most financial economists consider their models to have theoretical foundations from a financial (and not merely from a statistical) point of view.[2]

In conclusion then, econophysicists and financial economists model in the same way (calibrating models to fit data), but the latter combine the calibration step with a specific theoretical framework,[3] while the former claim to be more data-driven. Rather than focusing on the differences, we see in these similarities a need to develop statistical tools in order to compare the two ways of modeling and then to create a common framework. However, before talking about a possible comparison, it is important to know what has to be compared. While the key models of finance are clearly defined in the literature, there is no agreement on what would be the core models in econophysics. The following section will propose a unified framework, generalizing several important models identified in the literature of econophysics.

6.1.2. A Generic Model for Econophysics' Price-Return Models

For the purpose of providing a framework to unify econophysics models, this section will propose a generic formula for econophysics models dedicated to the analysis of extreme values. This formula will open the door to potential comparisons between econophysics and key models of the financial mainstream. Such comparisons will also pave the way for the development of a common framework between the two fields.

Our generic formula results from a meta-analysis of econophysics literature dealing with the statistical description of financial returns, integrating more than 20 of the key models. In our meta-analysis, we focused on the manner of describing the evolution of financial returns from stocks, and specifically on the treatment of extreme values, since this aspect is a defining element of econophysics. Our selection of models refers to a specific statistical methodology: they all provide an unconditional description of the evolution of returns. Tables 6.1 to 6.5, given in the appendix to this chapter, list the main econophysics articles dedicated to distribution of price returns. From our statistical analysis of these articles (see tables 6.1 and 6.2 for detailed comments on each article), we propose the following generalized formula for the probability distribution function:

$$P(x) = Cf(x)e^{-g[h(x)]+d}, \qquad (6.1)$$

where C and d are constants that might have temporal variation. The analytical form of $f(x)$ is not always known for all the values of x, but it has a power law variation in the limit of large x ($x \to \infty$):

$$f(x) \sim \frac{1}{x^{b_1 + a_1 \alpha}} \quad \text{for} \quad |x| \to \infty. \tag{6.2}$$

The parameters a_1 and b_1 (usually equal to 1) define the shape of the distribution at large x, and a is the principal exponent of the power law. The function $g(x)$ introduced in equation (6.1) has the form

$$g(x) = (a_2 h(x) + b_2)^{c_2} \tag{6.3}$$

with two possible forms for $h(x)$: x or $\log(x)$. As mentioned in chapter 1, the use of the log-normal law in finance was introduced by Osborne (1959) in order to avoid the theoretical possibility of negative prices. Moreover, this use is also based on the assumption that rates of return (rather than price changes) are independent random variables. In equation (6.3), a_2, b_2, and c_2 are parameters that differ from one model to another, defining the final shape of the distribution function. Finally, our generic probability distribution function can be expressed as

$$P(x) \sim C \frac{1}{x^{b_1 + a_1 \alpha}} e^{-(a_2 x + b_2)^{c_2} + d}. \tag{6.4}$$

This metaformula makes it possible to rewrite and to compare the probability distribution function of price changes used in the main econophysics models identified in the literature that deal with the statistical description of financial returns. Actually, these models can be classified in three groups depending on the distribution used: stable Lévy distribution, truncated stable Lévy distribution, and nonstable Lévy distribution.

As previous chapters explained, stable Lévy distributions were first proposed by Mandelbrot (1962) and afterward used by the pioneers of econophysics to describe the tail of the distribution of financial data. Most importantly, for large x values, stable Lévy distributions are well approximated by a power law as described in equation (6.2), with the exponent a having values between 1 and 2, generally around 1.5. Regarding the equation (6.4), most authors[4] use $a_1 = b_1 = 1$, with one special case where $a_1 = -1$ and $b_1 = 1$ (Weron, Mercik, and Weron 1999). The parameter a_2 is nonzero only in three cases (Cont and Bouchaud 2000; Gupta and Campanha 2002; Louzoun and Solomon 2001), and Louzoun and Solomon (2001) set $c_2 = -1$. The other parameters of equation (6.4) are taken to be zero in three cases out of 20 models studied in our meta-analysis. The observed nonzero a_2 involves the presence of an exponential term in the distribution function $P(x)$, which is derived by using models to explain the empirical data—for example, the generalized Lotka-Voltera model (Louzoun and Solomon 2001) and the Percolation model (Cont and Bouchaud 2000; Gupta and Campanha 2002). But most often the authors focus on calculating the power-law exponent of the distribution tail in some specific situations.

As explained in chapter 3, the main drawback of stable Lévy distributions is that they have infinite variance, a situation that in physics cannot be accepted (because physically plausible measures cannot be infinite). Remember that econophysicists developed truncated Lévy distributions in order to solve the problem of infinite variance. This is the second category of models covered by equation (6.4). For these models, stable Lévy distributions are used with the specific condition that there is a cutoff length for the price variations above which the distribution function is set to zero, in the simplest case (Mariani and Liu, 2007), or decreases exponentially (Gupta and Campanha 2002, 52–55). Using our generic formula, we obtain truncated distributions when $a_1 = b_1 = 1$ and at least a_2 and c_2 are nonzero—we should mention that b_2 is nonzero in some articles (Gupta and Campanha 1999; Michael and Johnson 2003; Gabaix et al. 2007). Only Gunaratne and McCauley (2005) give a distribution function with the d constant nonzero. For the simply truncated distribution proposed by Mariani and Liu (2007) one can consider a_2 very large (going to ∞) beyond the cutoff length. Concerning truncated stable distribution, one has nonzero a_2 and b_2 parameters that ensure the stability of the distributions and the finiteness of the variance.

Finally, the last category of models covered by our equation (6.4) is those based on nonstable Lévy distributions, whose use is motivated by several reasons. For instance, because some empirical studies of financial markets suggested that stable Lévy distributions could overestimate the presence of large price variations even though they fit the data better than the Gaussian distribution (Gabaix et al. 2007), some authors have developed a power-law variation of $P(x)$ for large x but with the values of the characteristic exponent greater than 2. The parameters of equation (6.4) are in this case $a_1 = b_1 = 1$ (Lux 1996; Gopikrishnan et al. 1999; Mantegna and Stanley 1994; Alejandro-Quiñones et al. 2006) and $a_2 = b_2 = c_2 = 0$—except for the paper by Clementi, Di Matteo, and Gallegati (2006), where $a_1 = -1$, $b_1 = 1$, a_2 is nonzero, and $c_2 = 1$. In this last case, one can use the Focker Planck equation for anomalous diffusion to derive the probability function.[5] A nonstable Lévy distribution is also obtained as a special case of a Tsallis distribution derived by McCauley and Gunaratne (2003). One should also note that for large x, a Student distribution, such as used by McCauley (2003), approaches Lévy distributions. Finally, some authors have proposed exponential distribution functions in terms of logarithmic price differences for the intraday trading of bonds and foreign exchange (Gallegati et al. 2006; McCauley 2003; McCauley and Gunaratne 2003). In terms of price differences, such a distribution would be a power law as described in equation (6.2) (thus in this case $h(x) = \log(x)$).

When dealing with nonstable distributions, econophysicists consider that a_2 and b_2 are always zero. A telling example of this category of models was developed by Gopikrishnan et al. (1999, 2000) and Stanley et al. (2008), who showed that the characteristic exponent (α) exhibited in equation (6.4) would be approximately equal to 3 for financial markets. These authors studied the distribution of the fluctuations in an index (S&P 500) between 1984 and 1996, but also price fluctuations for financial stocks (from 1926 to 1996); they concluded that in both cases these distributions can be described with a power law in line with our equation (6.4), whose characteristic exponent is asymptotically equal to 3—meaning that the greater the volume of data, the higher the probability of approximating 3. In a such context, our generalized probability distribution function could be simplified as follows:

$$P(x) \sim C\frac{1}{x^{1+3}} \sim C\frac{1}{x^4}. \quad (6.5)$$

In their publications, Gopikrishnan et al. (1999, 2000) explained that this asymptotic observation (i.e., the exponent = 3 for a greater volume of data) could not be captured by classical financial models such as GARCH, because they deal only with short-term investment horizons; note that what is presented as a drawback for econophysicists is often seen as an advantage for financial economists, who focus on short-term investment strategies (see chapter 5).

6.1.3. Perspectives on the Generic Model

Our generic formula offers a general equation whose domain of applicability is wider than the particular models studied in our meta-analysis. From this perspective, our formula can be seen as a "conceptual generalization" (i.e., an abstract generalization coming from an inductive meta-analysis of existing models [Tsang and Williams 2012]). This kind of generalization makes sense only because all models studied in our meta-analysis can be described as a specific case of our generic formula. The development of such a unified framework raises methodological questions: first, beyond the idea of associating several models, a generalized formula provides a unified conceptual way of thinking about the evolution of financial returns. By identifying the key parameters appearing in every model, this generalization paves the way to a better (re)estimation of the weight of each variable. In other words, this generalized formula can also contribute to new potential adjustments in the statistical understanding of financial returns by opening the door to the development of new tests, for example. As mentioned in chapter 5 and detailed in the following section, this aspect is a key issue in the future evolution of econophysics and its potential for recognition by financial economists.

By covering the key models developed in econophysics, our generalized formula points out the coherent progress that has taken place in this field in recent years, but it also opens up the possibility of a search for common variables between econophysics and financial economics. As explained in chapter 2, the vast majority of models used by the financial mainstream are developed in the Gaussian framework. Now, the Gaussian framework can be seen as a specific case of our generalized framework. Specifically, the Gaussian distribution, which is simplest case of equation (5.4), can also be obtained for the following specific parameters:

$$c = \frac{1}{\sqrt{2\pi\sigma^2}},\ a_1 = b_1 = 0,\ b_2 = d = 0,\ c_2 = 2 \text{ and } a_2 = \frac{1}{\sqrt{2\sigma^2}}.$$

In this situation, equation (6.4) can be expressed as the Gaussian distribution:

$$P(x) = \frac{1}{\sqrt{2\pi\sigma^2}} e^{-x^2/(2\sigma^2)}. \tag{6.6}$$

This point is important for two reasons: first, this generalization shows that a conceptual bridge between econophysics and financial economics is possible, implying the need to develop new non-Gaussian statistical tests; second, it opens the door to the identification of potential statistical similarities that would go beyond the disciplinary perspectives. In other words, our meta-analysis proposes a unified equation that can make statistical sense for both economists and econophysicists. This methodological implication is in line with the "transdisciplinary analysis" proposed in our previous work (Jovanovic and Schinckus 2013) in which we suggested that an integrated conceptual framework could transcend the disciplinary perspectives as summarized in figure 6.1.

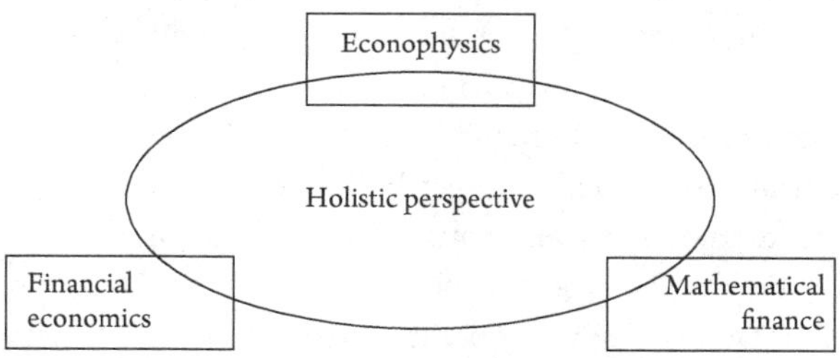

Figure 6.1 Transdisciplinarity (cooperation with integrative collaboration)

This transdisciplinary approach to econophysics is possible only if the scientists involved in this field (economists and physicists) can develop integrative research. Although some collaborations exist,[6] integrative research of this kind has not yet appeared in the literature. However, in considering that the statistical description can be similar in financial economics and physics, we implicitly assume an analogical generalization whose role is to propose a conceptual framework for unifying a field that has not yet been investigated. In this perspective, our generalized equation can be seen as a preliminary condition for the development of more integrative research between economists and physicists.

6.2. APPLICATION TO OPTION PRICING

A first application of our generic formula is to develop an option-pricing model based on the econophysics approach that is compatible with the framework of financial economics. The model proposed here must be considered a basic and preliminary application, because it does not have stochastic volatility (which is generally present in contemporary modeling of option pricing in financial economics). Nevertheless, it shows that a theoretical bridge between econophysics and the original Black and Scholes model (the nonstochastic volatility model) is possible. Our model shows that, from a theoretical point of view, an unconditional use of a stable Lévy framework (as enhanced by econophysicists) can make sense in the financial mainstream.

The key element in the Black and Scholes model was the application of the "arbitrage argument," which is an extension of the economic law of one price in perfect capital markets.[7] This law was popularized by Modigliani and Miller (1958)[8] and is used as the foundation of equilibrium in financial economics. In financial economics' option-pricing model, the arbitrage argument ensures that the replicating portfolio has a unique price. In econophysics' models, this concern does not exist,[9] something completely unacceptable according to the fundamental intuitions of financial economics, in which this arbitrage argument is a necessary condition for the uniqueness of the solution for any option-pricing methods.

The model presented in this section must be considered a first attempt to work within an integrated framework between econophysics and financial economics. More specifically, we will use our generic formula originating in econophysics to describe the evolution of underlying returns by showing that this statistical description is also compatible with the necessary condition for the use of an arbitrage argument (so important in financial economics). As explained below, we will use our generic formula in its truncated form in order to avoid the problem of infinite variance (discussed in chapter 3). Some authors have worked on this issue: Matacz (2000) and Boyarchenko and Levendorskii (2002, 2000) offered interesting option-pricing models based on an exponential truncated stable Lévy distribution. However, although these authors gave a procedure for minimizing an estimated risk, they did not define the conditions for a potential optimal risk hedge. In contrast, McCauley et al. (2007b), for example, showed that a non-Gaussian option-pricing model can provide optimal risk hedging; but their model focused on general conditions without defining an individual cutoff. Significantly, this existing literature does not directly address the implications of truncated exponential Lévy models for the optimal option-hedge ratio problem. However, this is of interest in an econophysics context as the result of various contributions stretching back to studies by Mantegna and Stanley in the mid-1990s that employed truncation to deal with statistical limitations of "infinite variance."

Our model aims to define the minimal condition required for an optimal risk hedging for a particular cutoff based on an exponentially truncated stable Lévy distribution. In other words, our contribution is to show that a (nonconditional) exponential stable Lévy description of a financial distribution (i.e., description of the whole distribution, as usually proposed by econophysicists) is compatible with an admissible hedging strategy in the sense defined by Harrison and Kreps (1979) and Harrison and Pliska (1981), who showed that the existence of an equivalent martingale measure is a necessary condition for optimal hedging (see Carr and Madan 2005 for further details on this theme). It is worth bearing in mind that this probabilistic framework defined by Harrison, Kreps, and Pliska has progressively become the mainstream in financial economics (chapter 2).

Section 6.2.1 presents our generalized model in line with the Black and Scholes framework (based on a martingale measure), and section 6.2.2 defines a specific risk measure for a truncated stable Lévy version of this model that will be presented in section 6.2.3. In line with McCauley et al. (2007a), we use an exponentially truncated stable Lévy distribution whose statistical conditions are defined to make this model viable (meeting the necessary condition) in the sense suggested by Harrison and Kreps (1979).

6.2.1. An Econophysics Model Compatible with the Financial Economics Framework

Let us consider a portfolio made up of a (call) option and a short position on ϕ stocks. At time $t = 0$, the value of this portfolio V is $V = C - \phi S$, where C is the price of the call option (with strike price K and expiration T); S is the stock price, and ϕ is the quantity of the stock. The product $\phi S = \sum \phi_i S_i$ is to be seen as a scalar product with S_i the price for each stock. Initially the stock price is considered to be S_0, and the portfolio is considered to be self-financing. In other words, the value of the portfolio only changes with changes in the stock price. In this situation the variation of the portfolio between time $t = 0$ and T is given by $\Delta V = \Delta C - \phi \Delta S$. The variation of the portfolio due to the call option is, when continuously discounted at the risk-free rate r,

$$e^{-rT} \Delta V = e^{-rT} \max(S - K, 0) - e^{-r0} C(S_0, K, T) - e^{-rT} \phi \Delta S, \tag{6.7}$$

where the first term is the value of the option at time T and the second term is the premium paid for the option at time $t = 0$. Assuming that one is operating in a no-arbitrage market, the discounted stochastic price process must be a martingale (Harrison and Kreps 1979). The option price is

$$C(S_0, K, T) = e^{-rT} E[\max(S - K, 0)] = e^{-rT} \int_K^{\infty} (S - K) f(S) dS. \tag{6.8}$$

Due to the stochastic nature of the price process, risk is inherent in the financial evaluation of options and stocks. Black and Scholes (1973) showed that for the log-normal distribution, this risk can be hedged by using an appropriate hedging condition (the so-called ϕ hedging) for the financing strategy. But for nonnormal models, the Black and Scholes procedure for hedging risk no longer works.[10] A measure of risk that was also used in Bouchaud and Sornette (1994) and Aurell et al. (1997) is the variance of the value of the portfolio $V = C - \phi S$. We make the supposition here that this variance is finite.[11] Thus:

$$R = E[\Delta V^2] = E[(\max(S - K, 0) - C(S_0, K, T) - \phi \Delta S)^2]. \tag{6.9}$$

First of all, note that for uncorrelated assets, one has the following expression: $E[(\phi \Delta S)^2] = \phi^2 \sigma^2 = \sum \phi_i^2 \sigma_i^2$, where σ_i is the volatility. However, when there exists a correlation between the assets, one can write $E[(\phi \Delta S)^2] = \sum \phi_i^2 \sigma_i^2 = 2 \sum_{i,j} \phi_i \phi_j \sigma_{ij}$, where σ_{ij} is the covariance matrix. In a sense, our conceptual model defined in equation (6.9) is in line with the generalized call-option pricing formula defined by Tan (2005), in which S is observed for non-Gaussian distributions. This approach is well known in finance and requires a minimization of the risk with respect to the trading strategy:

$$\phi^* = \frac{1}{\sigma^2} E[(S_0 - S) \max(S - K, 0)] = \frac{1}{\sigma^2} \int_K^{\infty} (S_0 - S)(S - K) f(S) dS. \tag{6.10}$$

This equation is valid for a martingale process S with $E[\Delta S]=0$, ensuring the necessary condition for an optimal hedging solution. If there is more than one uncorrelated asset (stock), the above equation should be applied for each stock individually in order to obtain the total optimal hedging strategy. The optimal strategy for the ith asset would be written like the above equation with index i on all variables. For many correlated assets using $E[(\phi\Delta S)^2]=\sum\phi_i^2\sigma_i^2=2\sum_{i,j}\phi_i\phi_j\sigma_{ij}$, one finds

$$\phi_i^* = \frac{1}{\sigma_i^2}\left[\int_K^{\infty}(S_{i0}-S_i)(S_i-K)f(S_i)dS_i-\sum_j\phi_j\sigma_{ij}\right], \tag{6.11}$$

It is straightforward to observe that in the simplest case of the Gaussian distribution with log-returns, the optimal hedging strategy given in equation (6.10) is the same as the hedging strategy from the Black and Scholes model, that is, $\left(\frac{dC}{dS}\right)$. The minimal risk R corresponding to the optimal hedging strategy is obtained from equation (6.9): $R^*=R_C-\phi^{*2}\sigma^2$ for one stock. Note that R_C is a risk term not dependent on the investment strategy, defined as $R_C=\int_K^{\infty}(S-K)^2f(S)dS-\left(\int_K^{\infty}(S-K)f(S)dS\right)^2$. In general cases with many correlated assets, minimal risk is obtained by taking $E[(\phi\Delta S)^2]=\phi^2\sigma^2=\sum\phi_i^2\sigma_i^2$ into account. Bouchaud and Sornette (1994) showed that R^* vanishes when a log-normal density is used. In other words, equation (6.10) provides a martingale-based risk measure, which must be minimized in an incomplete market structure.

6.2.2. Hedging Strategy with Exponentially Truncated Lévy Stable Distribution

As previously mentioned, a stable Lévy framework generates infinite variance, and hence a noncomputable risk, leading authors to search for a solution. To solve this problem, this section focuses on a particular cutoff based on an exponentially truncated stable Lévy process for option pricing by determining conditions for which the risk measure defined in the previous section could be viable in a hedging framework developed by Harrison and Kreps (1979) (i.e., the risk measure for our model is based on a martingale). We start our reasoning with our generalized formula for the probability distribution function (6.4) we defined earlier:

$$P(x)\sim C\frac{1}{x^{b_1+a_1\alpha}}e^{-(a_2x+b_2)^{c_2}+d}. \tag{6.4}$$

In line with the central-limit theorem, a stable Lévy regime will converge[12] toward a Gaussian asymptotic distribution after a very high number of variables x. In other words, there is a cross-value l after which the stable Lévy process is assumed to switch into the asymptotic (Gaussian) regime. That particular evolution implies a Gaussian asymptotic regime for $x > l$ and a truncated stable regime for $x < l$. The former can also be seen as a specific case of the generic formula (6.4) with the following parameters, $C = \frac{1}{\sqrt{2\pi\sigma^2}}$, $a_1 = b_1 = 0$, $b_2 = d = 0$, $c_2 = 2$, and $a_2 = \frac{1}{\sqrt{2\sigma^2}}$; the latter can be described through the following specific case where distribution density function for the log returns of underlying options can take the form

$$f(x) = \bar{C}\frac{e^{-\gamma|x|}}{|x|^{\alpha+1}}, \tag{6.12}$$

where $x = \log(S/S_0)$, $\bar{C} > 0$, $\gamma \geq 0$, and $0 < a < 2$, which is the necessary condition for a stable Lévy distribution. $\bar{C}$ can be seen as a measure of the level of activity in a case where all other parameters are constant (i.e., a parameter of scale). The parameter γ is the speed at which arrival rates decline with the size of the move (i.e., rate of exponential decay). This model accords with studies dealing with exponential truncation exposed in chapter 3, and the formula is a symmetric version of the so-called CGMY model (named after the authors of Carr, Geman, Madan, and Yor 2002) and a generalization of the exponentially truncated Lévy stable models proposed by Koponen (1995) and by Boyarchenko and Levendorskii (2002, 2000). However, while Carr et al. (2002) applied this model in a time-changed framework, Koponen (1995) did not apply his model to option pricing, while Boyarchenko and Levendorskii (2002, 2000) did not seek conditions for a potential risk hedge. Our objective here is to show that a stable Lévy regime (with no time-changed distribution) is theoretically compatible with a key assumption of the financial mainstream. Consequently, the rest of this chapter will focus only on the stable Lévy regime.

Because stable Lévy processes generate infinite variance, we use an exponential truncation implying an exponential decay of the distribution. This restriction means that the truncated distribution generates finite variations, making possible the estimation of the variance (in the stable Lévy regime), which is given by the following equation:

$$\sigma^2 = 2\bar{C}\gamma^{\alpha-2}\Gamma(2-\alpha) \text{ with } \Gamma(z) = \int_0^l e^{-t}t^{z-1}dt. \tag{6.13}$$

Using the general equation (6.6), we calculate the option price for this model for the chosen portfolio, by considering the density distribution of stock returns:

$$C = e^{-rT}\int_{\ln(K/S_0)}^{\infty}(S_0e^{-x} - K)\bar{C}\frac{e^{-\gamma x}}{x^{\alpha+1}}dx. \tag{6.14}$$

Using the result $\int_{x}^{\infty}\frac{e^{-u}}{u^{n}}du=\frac{E_{n}(x)}{x^{n-1}}$ with $E_{n}(x)=\int_{1}^{\infty}\frac{e^{-xt}}{t^{n}}dt$ in equation (6.14), and expressing $\bar{C}$ as a function of squared volatility, yields:

$$C=\frac{\sigma^{2}e^{-rT}}{2\gamma^{\alpha-2}\Gamma(2-\alpha)}\left[\ln\left(\frac{K}{S_{0}}\right)\right]^{-\alpha}\left\{S_{0}E_{\alpha+1}\left[(\gamma-1)\ln\left(\frac{K}{S_{0}}\right)\right]-KE_{\alpha+1}\left[\gamma\ln\left(\frac{K}{S_{0}}\right)\right]\right\}. \tag{6.15}$$

Given this result, we can estimate the hedging strategy that minimizes risk by using equation (6.10):

$$\phi^{*}=\frac{\bar{C}}{\sigma^{2}}\int_{\ln(K/S_{0})}^{\infty}(S_{0}-S_{0}e^{x})(S_{0}e^{x}-K)\frac{e^{-\gamma x}}{x^{\alpha+1}}dx. \tag{6.16}$$

However, this optimal hedging can be implemented in the nonasymptotic regime, implying that the variance (equation (6.13)) is finite only for $x < l$. By integrating $\Gamma(2-\alpha)=\int_{0}^{l}e^{-t}t^{z-1}dt$, we can detail equation (6.16) as

$$\phi^{*}=\frac{1}{2\gamma^{\alpha-2}l^{1-\alpha}(e^{-l}-1)}*\left[\ln\left(\frac{K}{S_{0}}\right)\right]\left\{\begin{array}{l}(S_{0}K+S_{0}^{2})E_{\alpha+1}\left[(\gamma-1)\ln\left(\frac{K}{S_{0}}\right)\right]\\ -S_{0}^{2}E_{\alpha+1}\left[(\gamma-2)\ln\left(\frac{K}{S_{0}}\right)\right]-S_{0}KE_{\alpha+1}\left[\gamma\ln\left(\frac{K}{S_{0}}\right)\right]\end{array}\right\}.$$

Although Tan (2005) did not deal with infinite variance processes, we came to the same conclusions as he did about non-Gaussian densities, ϕ^{*}, which explicitly depend on (1) higher partial derivatives of the call-option pricing function toward the price of the underlying asset; and (2) the value of the cumulants (as they are used in the logarithm of the characteristic function). Although equation (6.14) could then be further generalized as proposed by McCauley et al. (2007b) and Tan (2005), generalization would require specific statistical conditions (defined in this chapter) in order to offer a viable hedging solution in a stable Lévy framework. Our objective here is to show the theoretical compatibility between an exponentially truncated stable Lévy framework and the necessary condition for an optimal hedging in the Harrison, Kreps, and Pliska theoretical framework.

6.3. CONCLUSION

The objective of this final chapter was to develop a unified framework generalizing major models found in econophysics literature. The identification of such a framework allowed us to work on the minimal condition under which it could be compatible with the financial mainstream. This task suggests that a potential fruitful future collaboration between econophysicists and financial economists is possible.

The first step in the elaboration of a conceptual bridge between the two fields was to show that, in the diversified econophysics literature dealing with extreme values in econophysics, it was possible to deduce a unified technical framework. We proposed such a unification in the first section of this chapter by showing that econophysics models can be seen as a specific derivation of a generalized equation. The second step was to show that the generalized equation elaborated to describe the key models developed in econophysics could be compatible with a strictly Gaussian approach. That was the aim of our second section. Equations (6.4) and (6.6) showed that the Gaussian framework can be expressed as a specific case of the generalized equation. This point is important, since it facilitates the potential development of a common vocabulary between the two communities. While equation (6.4) highlighted the statistical parameters common both to models used in econophysics and to those used in finance, the next step will be to give them an economic/financial meaning. In a sense, proposing a generalized equation is a preliminary condition for this kind of theoretical investigation, which requires a combination of theoretical and technical knowledge of the key assumptions used by econophysicists and economists, because the interpretation of the statistical parameters must make sense for both communities. After defining such a unified equation, we presented it in the light of the financial mainstream. We used our generic formula originating in econophysics to describe the evolution of underlying returns by showing that this statistical description is also compatible with the necessary condition for the use of an arbitrage argument. The model proposed here must be considered a basic and preliminary application whose objective is to stress the feasibility of a conceptual framework common to econophysics and financial economics. Hopefully, this first attempt will generate further research on the topic.

APPENDICES: MODELS STUDIED IN OUR SURVEY

Table 6.1 Lévy stable – Gaussian distributions

Reference	*Author formula*	*Generic formula*
1. Bachelier (1900) The first model for the stochastic process of returns	$P(x)=\frac{1}{\sqrt{2\pi\sigma^2}}e^{-x^2/(2\sigma^2)}$	$P(x)\sim C\frac{1}{x^{b_1+a_1\alpha}}e^{-(a_2x+b_2)^{c_2}+d}$ *for* $x\to\infty$ $C=\frac{}{\sqrt{2}}$ $, h(x)=x$ $a_1=0, b_1=0, a_2=1/(2\sigma^2)^{0.5}, b_2=0, c_2=2, d=0$
2. Black and Scholes (1973) An option pricing technique – the Gaussian distribution is one of the principal assumptions	$P(x)=\frac{1}{x}\frac{1}{\sqrt{2\pi\sigma^2}}e^{\left[\log(x/x_0)-(\mu-\sigma^2/2)\right]^2/(2\sigma^2)}$	$P(x)\sim C\frac{1}{x^{b_1+a_1\alpha}}e^{-(a_2x+b_2)^{c_2}+d}$ *for* $x\to\infty$ $C=\frac{1}{\sqrt{2\pi\sigma^2}}, h(x)=log(x)$ $a_1=0, b_1=0, a_2=1/(2\sigma^2)^{0.5}, b_2=0, c_2=2, d=0$
3. Clark (1973) Mixture of Gaussian distributions	$P(x)=\frac{1}{\sqrt{2\pi\sigma^2}}e^{-x^2/(2\sigma^2)}$	$P(x)\sim C\frac{1}{x^{b_1+a_1\alpha}}e^{-(a_2x+b_2)^{c_2}+d}$ *for* $x\to\infty$ $C=\frac{1}{\sqrt{2\pi\sigma^2}}, h(x)=x$ $a_1=0, b_1=0, a_2=1/(2\sigma^2)^{0.5}, b_2=0, c_2=2, d=0$
4. Martin Schaden (2002)	$P(s',t_f;s,t_i)=(4\pi\sigma^2Ts's)^{-1}\exp\left[\frac{(\log(s'/s)+BT)^2}{2\sigma^2T}\right]$ s' – price at time t_f; s – price at time t; $T=t_f-t_i$	$P(x)\sim C\frac{1}{x^{b_1+a_1\alpha}}e^{-(a_2\log(x)+b_2)^{c_2}+d}$ *for* $x\to\infty$ $h(x)=\log(x)$ $a_1=0, b_1=-1, a_2=1/(2\sigma^2\mathrm{T})^{0.5}$, $b_2=[\mathrm{BT}\text{-}\log(\mathrm{s})]/(2\sigma^2\mathrm{T})^{0.5}, c_2=2, d=0$

Table 6.2 Lévy stable – Paretian distributions

Reference	*Author formula*	*Generic formula*
5. Weron *et al.* (1999) They use the conditionally exponential decay model Power-law distribution Apply this distribution function for modelling daily returns of the DJIA and S&P500 financial indices as well as returns of the USD/DEM exchange rate	$f(r)=\begin{cases} C_1(\lambda r)^{\alpha-1}, 0\le \lambda r \le 1 \\ C_2(\lambda r)^{-(\alpha/k)-1}, \lambda r \ge 1 \end{cases}$ $\alpha \cong 1.09$ C_1, C_2 depend upon parameters α, λ and k	$P(x) \sim C\frac{1}{x^{b_1+a_1\alpha}}e^{-(a_2x+b_2)^{c_2}+d}\ for\, x \to \infty$ $a_1 = -1, b_1 = 1, a_2 = b_2 = c_2 = 0$ $\alpha \cong 1.09$ $h(x) = x, d = 0$
6. Louzoun and Solomon (2001) They use the Generalized Lotka Voltera (GLV) model to explain power law distributions in individual wealth (Pareto laws) and in financial market returns	$P(x_i) = x_i^{-1-\alpha}e^{-2a/(Dx_i)}$ $\alpha = 1.5$	$P(x) \sim C\frac{1}{x^{b_1+a_1\alpha}}e^{-(a_2x+b_2)^{c_2}+d}\ for\, x \to \infty$ $a_1 = 1, b_1 = 1, a_2 = 2a/D, b_2 = 0, c_2 = -1$ $\alpha \cong 1.5$ $h(x) = x, d = 0$
7. Blanck and Solomon (2000) They model the distribution of population in cities and that of the wealth Power law with $\alpha \approx 1.4$	$P(w) \propto w^{-1-\alpha}$ $\alpha \approx 1.4$	$P(x) \sim C\frac{1}{x^{b_1+a_1\alpha}}e^{-(a_2x+b_2)^{c_2}+d}\ for\, x \to \infty$ $a_1 = 1, b_1 = 1, a_2 = b_2 = c_2 = 0$ $h(x) = x, d = 0$ $\alpha \cong 1.4$

(continued)

Table 6.2 (Continued)

Reference	*Author formula*	*Generic formula*
8. Malcai, Biham et al. (1999) Power law with $\alpha = 1.5$	Power law α=1.5 Idem to article 7 above. Obs. Articles 6, 7, 8 are connected	$P(x) \sim C\frac{1}{x^{b_1+a_1\alpha}}e^{-(a_2x+b_2)^{c_2}+d}\ for\, x \to \infty$ $a_1 = 1, b_1 = 1, a_2 = b_2 = c_2 = 0$ $\mathrm{h}(x) = x, d = 0$ $\alpha \cong 1.5$
9. Scalas and Kim (2007) Lévy α stable distribution Ex: $\alpha = 1.57, \beta = 0.159, \gamma = 6.76 \times 10^{-3}, \delta = 3.5 \times 10^{-4}$ General forms for Lévy distributions The paper illustrates a procedure for fitting financial data with Lévy α-stable distributions	The characteristic function for symmetric distributions: $L_\alpha(k) = \exp\left(-a\lvert k\rvert^\alpha\right)$ $L_\alpha(x) \sim \frac{1}{\lvert x\rvert^{1+\alpha}}\ for\, x \to \infty$	$P(x) \sim C\frac{1}{x^{b_1+a_1\alpha}}e^{-(a_2x+b_2)^{c_2}+d}\ for\, x \to \infty$ $a_1 = 1, b_1 = 1, a_2 = b_2 = c_2 = 0$ $\mathrm{h}(x) = x, d = 0$ $\alpha \cong 1.4$
10. Mandelbrot (1963b) Application of Lévy distributions for cotton price changes (rather log differences) in USA (1800 – 1958)	$L_\alpha(k) = \exp\left(-a\lvert k\rvert^\alpha\right)$ $L_\alpha(x) \sim \frac{1}{\lvert x\rvert^{1+\alpha}}\ for\, \lvert x\rvert \to \infty$	$P(x) \sim C\frac{1}{x^{b_1+a_1\alpha}}e^{-(a_2x+b_2)^{c_2}+d}\quad for\ x \to \infty$ $a_1 = 1, b_1 = 1, a_2 = b_2 = c_2 = 0$ $\mathrm{h}(x) = x, d = 0$ $\alpha = 1.7, \beta = 0, \delta = 0$

11. Skjeltorp (2000) Analyse variations on the Norwegian and USA stock markets Measure the local Hurst exponent H (related to α; $\alpha = 1/H$) Reach the conclusion that Lévy stable distributions describe empirical data much better than Gaussian. H is obtained from log-log plot of $P(D_t)$ when $D_x = 0$	Lévy stable - $\alpha = 1.64$	$P(x) \sim C\frac{1}{x^{b_1+a_1\alpha}}e^{-(a_2x+b_2)^{c_2}+d}$ $for\ x \to \infty$ $a_1 = 1, b_1 = 1, a_2 = b_2 = c_2 = 0$ $h(x) = x, d = 0$ $\alpha \cong 1.64$
12. Cont and Bouchaud (2000) Percolation theory—one gets the distribution for the cluster (of financial operators) size—identic to the distribution of price changes according to percolation theory The probability that financial operators interact between them is c/N; N is the total number of operators	$P(S) \sim \frac{1}{S^{5/2}}\exp\left(-\varepsilon^2 S\right)$ S—cluster size; $\varepsilon = 1-c$ for $c = 1$, one has a pure power law, Lévy symmetrical, distribution with $\alpha = 3/2$.	$P(x) \sim C\frac{1}{x^{b_1+a_1\alpha}}e^{-(a_2x+b_2)^{c_2}+d}$ $for\ x \to \infty$ $a_1 = 1, b_1 = 1, a_2 = \varepsilon^2, b_2 = 0, c_2 = 1$ $\alpha \cong 1.5$ $h(x) = x, d = 0$ $\varepsilon = 1-c$ $h(x) = x, d = 0$
13. Bouchaud (2002)	$P(S) \sim \frac{1}{S^{5/2}}\exp\left(-\varepsilon^2 S\right)$ $\alpha = 3/2$	$P(x) \sim C\frac{1}{x^{b_1+a_1\alpha}}e^{-(a_2x+b_2)^{c_2}+d}$ $for\ x \to \infty$ $a_1 = 1, b_1 = 1, a_2 = \varepsilon^2, b_2 = 0, c_2 = 1$ $h(x) = x, d = 0$ $\alpha \cong 1.5$

Table 6.3 Lévy non-stable distributions

Reference	*Author formula*	*Generic formula*
14. Gopikrishnan, Mayer, Amaral, Stanley (1998) Power law (asymptotic) distribution $\alpha = 3$	$P(g_i(t) > g) \propto g^{-\alpha}$ $\alpha \approx 3$	$P(x) \sim C \frac{1}{x^{b_1+a_1\alpha}} e^{-(a_2x+b_2)^{c_2}+d}$ *for* $x \to \infty$ $a_1 = 1, b_1 = 1, a_2 = b_2 = c_2 = 0$ $\mathrm{h}(x) = x, d = 0$ $\alpha \cong 3$
15. Lux (1996) Examination of German stocks with stable Lévy distributions A detailed analysis leads to conclusion that Lévy stable is not such a good fit – it is assumed that the real distribution is not stable	See comments - Power law – Lévy non-stable	$P(x) \sim C \frac{1}{x^{b_1+a_1\alpha}} e^{-(a_2x+b_2)^{c_2}+d}$ *for* $x \to \infty$ $a_1 = 1, b_1 = 1, a_2 = b_2 = c_2 = 0$ $\mathrm{h}(x) = x, d = 0$ $\alpha > 2$
16. Gopikrishnan, Plerou, Amaral, Meyer, Stanley (1999) They analyse the values of the S&P500 index	$P(g > x) \propto \frac{1}{x^{\alpha}}$ g is a normalized return : $g = \frac{G - \langle G \rangle_T}{v}$ $v^2 = \langle G^2 \rangle_T - \langle G \rangle_T^2$ volatility $\alpha \approx 3$ for $3 < g < 50$ $\alpha \approx 1.6$ for $3 < g < 50$	$P(x) \sim C \frac{1}{x^{b_1+a_1\alpha}} e^{-(a_2x+b_2)^{c_2}+d}$ *for* $x \to \infty$ $a_1 = 1, b_1 = 1, a_2 = b_2 = c_2 = 0$ $\mathrm{h}(x) = x, d = 0$ $\alpha \cong 3$

17. Alejandro-Quinones, Bassler, Field, McCauley, Nicol et al. (2006) Theoretical model that uses Focker Plank equation (describes anomalous diffusion) to derive the probability function Non constant diffusion coefficient One approaches a power law for high u and a quadratic variation for D	$F(u)=C\exp\left(\frac{-\lvert u\rvert}{D_0\varepsilon}\right)(\varepsilon\lvert u\rvert+1)^{\alpha-1}$ for $D=D_0(1+\varepsilon\lvert u\rvert)$, $u=\frac{x}{\sqrt{t}}$ x price return $F(u)=\frac{C}{(1+\varepsilon u^2)^{1+\beta}}, D=D_0(1+\varepsilon u^2)$	$P(x)\sim C\frac{1}{x^{b_1+a_1\alpha}}e^{-(a_2x+b_2)^{c_2}+d}$ *for* $x\rightarrow\infty$ $a_1=-1, b_1=1, a_2=1/(D_0\varepsilon), b_2=0, c_2=1$ $h(x)=x, d=0$
18. Clementi, Di Matteo and Gallegati (2006) They estimate the power law tail exponent (α) using Hill estimator, for the personal income in Australia and Italy	$P(i>x)\propto\frac{1}{x^{\alpha}}$ $\alpha\sim 2.3$ – Australia $\alpha\sim 2.5$ – Italy	$P(x)\sim C\frac{1}{x^{b_1+a_1\alpha}}e^{-(a_2x+b_2)^{c_2}+d}$ *for* $x\rightarrow\infty$ $a_1=1, b_1=1, a_2=b_2=c_2=0$ $h(x)=x, d=0$ $\alpha\cong 2.5$

Table 6.4 Lévy truncated distributions

Reference	*Author formula*	*Generic formula*
19. Mantegna and Stanley (1994). Truncated Lévy distribution, α=1.5 Lévy distribution normalized by a constant. Not stable, has finite variance.	$P(x)=\begin{cases}0, & x>l\\ cP_l(x), & -l<x<l,\\ 0, & x<l\end{cases}$ $P_1(x)$ – Lévy function	$P(x)\sim C\frac{1}{x^{b_1+a_1\alpha}}e^{-(a_2x+b_2)^{c_2}+d}\quad for\ x\to\infty$ $a_1=1, b_1=1, a_2=b_2=c_2=0$ $\alpha\cong 1.5$ for $-l<x<l$. $h(x)=x, d=0$ $P(x)=0$ for all other values of x, $a_2\sim\infty$
20. Mariani and Liu (2007). Study of market indices from Brazil, Mexico, Argentine Exponentially truncated Lévy distribution α <2	They use the characteristic function in simulations - Probably same kind of equation as at number 21	$P(x)\sim C\frac{1}{x^{b_1+a_1\alpha}}e^{-(a_2x+b_2)^{c_2}+d}\quad for\ x\to\infty$ $a_1=1, b_1=1, a_2=1/k, b_2=-1/k, c_2=1$ $h(x)=x, d=0$ $\alpha<2$ for $\|x\|>1$
21. Gupta and Campanha (1999) They propose a gradually truncated Lévy distribution.	$P(x)=\begin{cases}cL_\alpha(x,\Delta t), -l_C\le x\le l_C\\ CL_\alpha(x,\Delta t)\exp\left\{-\left(\frac{\|x\|-l_C}{k}\right)^\beta\right\}, \|x\|\rangle l_C\end{cases}$ k, β are constants $\alpha\cong 1.2$, $\beta\approx 0.6$ pour S&P500	$P(x)\sim C\frac{1}{x^{b_1+a_1\alpha}}e^{-(a_2x+b_2)^{c_2}+d}\quad for\ x\to\infty$ $a_1=1, b_1=1, a_2=1/k, b_2=-1/k, c_2=\beta\sim 0.6$ $h(x)=x, d=0$ $\alpha=1.2$ for $\|x\|>1$

22. Cont and Bouchaud (2000). Percolation theory – one gets the distribution for the cluster (of financial operators) size – identic to the distribution of price changes The probability that operators interact between them is c/N; N is the total number of operators	$P(S) \sim \frac{1}{S^{5/2}} \exp\left(-\varepsilon^2 S\right)$ S – cluster size; $\varepsilon = 1-c$ for $c < 1$, one has an exponentially truncated Lévy distribution	$P(x) \sim C \frac{1}{x^{b_1+a_1\alpha}} e^{-(a_2x+b_2)^{c_2}+d} \quad for\ x \to \infty$ $a_1 = 1, b_1 = 1, a_2 = -\varepsilon^2, b_2 = 0, c_2 = 1$ $h(x) = x, d = 0$ $\alpha \cong 1.5$ $\varepsilon = 1-c$
23. Bouchaud (2002) See discussion of results of number 22	$P(S) \sim \frac{1}{S^{5/2}} \exp\left(-\varepsilon^2 S\right)$	$P(x) \sim C \frac{1}{x^{b_1+a_1\alpha}} e^{-(a_2x+b_2)^{c_2}+d} \quad for\ x \to \infty$ $a_1 = 1, b_1 = 1, a_2 = -\varepsilon^2, b_2 = c_2 = 0$ $h(x) = x, d = 0$ $\alpha \cong 1.5$

Table 6.5 Other Distributions

Reference	*Author formula*	*Generic formula*
24. Michael and Johnson (2003) Tsalis power law distribution The value of q smaller than 5/3 allows a finite variance Can be classified as Lévy stable	$P(x,t) = \frac{1}{Z(t)}\left\{1+\beta(t)(q-1)\left[x-\bar{x}(t)\right]^2\right\}^{\frac{1}{1-q}}$ $P(x,t) = x^{\frac{-2}{q-1}} = x^{-(\alpha+1)}$ for x large q Tsallis parameter, (1.64 for S&P500) –good fit on the empirical data for q = 5/3 one gets Gaussian; for 1 < q ≤ 5/3 – Lévy non stable; for 5/3 < q < 3 – Lévy stable.	$P(x) \sim C\frac{1}{x^{b_1+a_1\alpha}}e^{-(a_2x+b_2)^{c_2}+d}$ *for* $x \to \infty$ $a_1 = 1, b_1 = 1, a_2 = b_2 = c_2 = 0$ $h(x) = x, d = 0$ $\alpha \sim 2.15$
25. Blattberg and Gonedes (1974) Student-t-distribution	$St_\alpha(x) = \frac{C(\alpha)}{(A^2+x^2)^{(1+\alpha)/2}}$ $St_\alpha(x) \sim x^{-(1+\alpha)}$ *for* $x \to \infty$ behaves like Lévy distribution for large x	$P(x) \sim C\frac{1}{x^{b_1+a_1\alpha}}e^{-(a_2x+b_2)^{c_2}+d}$ *for* $x \to \infty$ $a_1 = 1, b_1 = 1, a_2 = b_2 = c_2 = 0$ $h(x) = x, d = 0$ α - parameter
26. Richmond (2001) Power law distribution	$P(\phi) = \frac{1}{Z\lvert\phi\rvert^{1-\frac{J}{D}}}\exp\left\{\left(2b\phi - c\phi^2\right)/D\right\}$ ϕ is related to price return b, c, D, J parameters	$P(x) \sim C\frac{1}{x^{b_1+a_1\alpha}}e^{-(a_2x+b_2)^{c_2}+d}$ *for* $x \to \infty$ $h(x) = x, d = -b^2/(cD)$ $a_2 = c^{1/2}, h_2 = -b/c^{1/2}, c_2 = 2, a_1, b_1$, and α - parameters

27. McCauley and Gunaratne (2005) Empirical Exponential Distribution function for intraday trading of bonds and foreign exchange, written in terms of returns $x = \ln(p(t)/p(t_0))$.	$f(x,t) = \frac{\nu^2}{\gamma+\nu} e^{-\nu(x-R\Delta t)}, x > R\Delta t$ $f(x,t) = \frac{\gamma^2}{\gamma+\nu} e^{\gamma(x-R\Delta t)}, x < R\Delta t$ $\nu, \gamma \propto \Delta t$	$P(x) \sim C \frac{1}{x^{b_1+a_1\alpha}} e^{-(a_2x+b_2)^{c_2}+d} \quad for\ x \to \infty$ $a_1 \neq 0, b_1 = 0, a_2 = 0, b_2 = 0, c_2 = 0$ $h(x) = \log(x), d = 0$
28. McCauley (2003) Empirical Exponential Distribution function for intraday trading of bonds and foreign exchange, written in terms of returns $x = \ln(p(t) / p(t_0))$.	$f(x,t) = \frac{\nu^2}{\gamma+\nu} e^{-\nu(x-R\Delta t)}, x > R\Delta t$ $f(x,t) = \frac{\gamma^2}{\gamma+\nu} e^{\gamma(x-R\Delta t)}, x < R\Delta t$ $\nu, \gamma \propto \Delta t$	$P(x) \sim C \frac{1}{x^{b_1+a_1\alpha}} e^{-(a_2x+b_2)^{c_2}+d} \quad for\ x \to \infty$ $a_1 \neq 0, b_1 = 0, a_2 = 0, b_2 = 0, c_2 = 0$ $h(x) = \log(x), d = 0$
29. Gunaratne and McCauley (2005) Empirical Exponential Distribution function for intraday trading of bonds and foreign exchange, written in terms of returns $x = \ln(p(t) / p(t_0))$.	$f(x,t) = \frac{\nu^2}{\gamma+\nu} e^{-\nu(x-R\Delta t)}, x > R\Delta t$ $f(x,t) = \frac{\gamma^2}{\gamma+\nu} e^{\gamma(x-R\Delta t)}, x < R\Delta t$ $\nu, \gamma \propto \Delta t$	$P(x) \sim C \frac{1}{x^{b_1+a_1\alpha}} e^{-(a_2x+b_2)^{c_2}+d} \quad for\ x \to \infty$ $a_1 \neq 0, b_1 = 0, a_2 = 0, b_2 = 0, c_2 = 0$ $h(x) = \log(x), d = 0$

CONCLUSION
WHAT KIND OF FUTURE LIES IN STORE FOR ECONOPHYSICS?

This book has investigated the development of econophysics and its potential implications for financial economics. Our project was to analyze the issues and contributions of these two disciplines, focusing mainly on extreme values on stock prices/returns and a common vocabulary and perspective. As we have explained, in the context of the difficult dialogue between the two communities, there is now a pressing need to adopt a homogenous presentation. This opens a door to a real comparison between the contributions of the two disciplines; it paves the way for a profitable dialogue between the two fields; and it also offers conceptual tools to surmount barriers that currently limit potential collaborations between the two communities. For the purpose of providing a homogenous perspective, we have identified the disciplinary constraints ruling each discipline and then suggested some paths for econophysicists and financial economists to overcome the current limitations of their collaboration.

Throughout the book, we have studied econophysics' contributions in the light of the evolution of financial economics. In addition, all our analyses have taken the standpoint of financial economics. In so doing, we have expressed the dissimilarities in terms of vocabulary and methods of modeling between the two fields in a common terminology. We have sought to provide financial economists with a clear introduction to econophysics, its current issues, its major challenges, and its possible future developments in relation to financial economics. We have shown that econophysics literature holds a twofold interest for financial economists: first, this discipline provides alternative tools for analytical characterization of financial uncertainty (through a specific statistical treatment of long-term samples). Second, by defending a strict phenomenological method, econophysics renews the analysis of empirical data and practical implications. Beyond the interest for financial economists, this book also concerns econophysicists. Indeed, it gives an opportunity on the one hand to understand the reasons why financial economists have been unable to use econophysics models in their current form; and on the other hand, to identify the current challenges econophysics has to solve in order to be accepted in financial economics and to provide more efficient models for analyzing financial markets.

In taking stock of the current situation of econophysics and in identifying potential paths for further investigation, this book is a first step toward more integrative research between econophysics and financial economics. Collaborative research will not be easy: after two decades, econophysics is a well-established and recognized scientific field analyzing numerous topics in finance. However, it still lacks recognition among financial economists. In this challenging context, this book has clearly identified a future research agenda for improving collaboration between financial economists and econophysicists. As we have shown, three research axes are still waiting to be investigated: (1) the development of a common framework/vocabulary in order to better compare and integrate the two approaches; (2) the creation of statistical tests to measure results from econophysics models with those produced by financial models; and finally (3) the elaboration of generative models to provide a theoretical explanation for the emergence of power laws. This research agenda can be considered the key challenge that econophysics has to face in the future; more generally, it can be seen as what Lakatos (1978, 135) called a "positive heuristic," "a set of suggestions or hints on how to change, develop the 'variants' of the research programme." In other words, such a research agenda, which is a body of beliefs, suggests revising modeling methods without abandoning the core assumptions that have developed in both disciplines. In accordance with this idea, it is crucial for econophysicists to show to what extent their works improve the statistical description used by financial economists, since the Gaussian framework is a specific case of power laws.

We have illustrated this possible extension by proposing a first unified econophysics framework to characterize the evolution of financial prices while keeping the key characteristics of the Gaussian approach. This unified framework can be seen as the first step in building conceptual bridges between the two fields. Given the diversified literature dealing with extreme values in econophysics, our analysis has led us to put forward a unified technical nomenclature for characterizing econophysics models. In our opinion, this is an important contribution of this book. First, our generalized econophysics framework describes the evolution of financial prices in a way that is compatible with financial economics, easing the potential development of a common vocabulary that makes sense to both communities. Second, it facilitates future comparisons between models developed in financial economics and those used in econophysics in a common framework. Third, it constitutes a first step through the development of statistical tests applicable to both sets of models. It is worth mentioning that the need for statistical tests is crucial for financial economists, but also for econophysicists: as Ausloos has claimed, "The econophysics approach should be taken with caution, indeed. The robustness and soundness of models are fundamental questions. Models should be predictive, and should be tested" (2013, 109).

We believe that the creation of statistical tests is the most crucial step for attracting the attention of financial economists and practitioners. From a theoretical perspective, statistical tests will allow systematic comparison of the models used by econophysicists with those used by financial economists. From a practical perspective, statistical tests will make it possible to measure the efficiency of each category of models and to improve them. Statistical comparison between models from the two fields is relevant because the two areas of knowledge deal with the same financial phenomena, both using a frequentist approach[1]. More specifically, key models in financial economics and in econophysics usually consider empirical data as a random sample from a hypothetical infinite population in which frequencies are associated with probabilities. In this perspective, the question of comparison becomes inevitable, but econophysicists and financial economists work in different statistical frameworks, and at present there are no uniform statistical tests allowing one to choose between a model from a strictly non-Gaussian framework and one developed in the Gaussian framework.

Given the current situation, two future research areas can be investigated: on the one hand, development of Bayesian tests in order to compare Gaussian-based models with non-Gaussian ones and, on the other hand, development of (frequentist) statistical tests for identifying power laws. A Bayesian approach uses the Bayes factor for comparing two models using the ratio of the marginal likelihood of data used by the models. The advantage of this testing approach lies in the fact that it is independent of the statistical distribution of data. In other words, it offers a statistical framework for comparing Gaussian and non-Gaussian models. Conversely, the second possible area of investigation involves developing a new frequentist testing approach implying the possibility of comparing non-Gaussian models with the Gaussian one.

One of our reasons for developing a generalized formula was precisely to create room for the development of statistical tests. Indeed, in proposing a generalized formula, we have solved the problem of the lack of unified non-Gaussian statistical description of financial returns, thus justifying the need to develop non-Gaussian statistical tests. Moreover, our formula shows that econophysics models, though varied, are technically compatible and can be presented through a unified and coherent framework. This can then be used as a theoretical benchmark for a comparison with traditional Gaussian descriptions (GARCH-type models) used in financial economics. Statistically speaking, the fact that the Gaussian framework can be expressed as a specific case of the generalized equation shows that a comparison between econophysics models and financial ones makes sense. In our opinion, a Bayesian comparison could provide an interesting conceptual tool in order to go beyond the differences in terms of modeling since it would compare models based on a conditional distribution (GARCH approach) and models based on an unconditional description of return (econophysics perspective).

The last point on the research agenda is the development of generative econophysics models to explain the emergence of power laws in financial data. The main idea of these models is to go beyond the mere statistical description given by current power-laws model. As we saw, Gabaix et al. (2003) showed that institutional investors' trades have an impact on the emergence of a power law in the evolution of financial prices. Although some technical models explaining the emergence of a power law in statistical data exist, this area of investigation is still in its infancy concerning the economic interpretation of these factors. Future collaboration between econophysics and financial economics must pay more attention to this question.

To conclude, although the suggested agenda raises a number of questions and challenges, it creates many research opportunities by improving collaboration between financial economists and econophysicists.

NOTES

Introduction

1. The literature has expanded greatly since the early 2000s (Bouchaud, Mezard, and Potters 2002; Potters and Bouchaud 2003; McCauley 2009; Gabaix 2009; Lux 2009; McCauley, Gunaratne, and Bassler 2007; Sornette 2014; Bouchaud 2002; McCauley 2006; Stanley and Plerou 2001; Durlauf 2005, 2012; Keen 2003; Chen and Li 2012; Ausloos 2001; Chakrabarti and Chakraborti 2010; Farmer and Lux 2008; Carbone, Kaniadakis, and Scarfone 2007; Ausloos 2013; Jovanovic and Schinckus 2016; Schinckus 2010a, 2010b).
2. Those who are interested in such presentations can refer to the literature (Bouchaud and Potters 2000; Cai, Lax, and Xu 2006; Chakrabarti, Chakraborti, and Chatterjee 2006; Malevergne and Sornette 2005; Mantegna and Stanley 2000; Roehner 2002; Savoiu 2013; Sornette 2003, 2006; Voit 2005; Bouchaud and Potters 2003; McCauley 2004; Richmond, Mimkes, and Hutzler 2013; Takayasu 2002; Slanina 2014; Takayasu, Watanabe, and Takayasu 2010; Paul and Baschnagel 2013).

Chapter 1

1. In this book, we use the term "stock market variations" to cover fluctuations in both the prices and the returns of securities.
2. It is worth mentioning that this statement is true for any science. Physics, for instance, is based on Euclidean geometry (or since the beginning of the twentieth century, non-Euclidian geometrics, such as quantic physics). Euclidean geometry is founded on five axioms or postulates, that is, five propositions that are accepted without proof. One of these postulates, for example, states that a straight line segment can be drawn joining any two points. By changing these postulates, it has been possible to create non-Euclidean geometries, which enable the creation of other mathematics.
3. Jules Regnault (1834–1894) came from modest beginnings but died a millionaire, a fact probably not unconnected with the model he proposed for determining stock market variations. A biography of Regnault can be found in Jovanovic 2004, 2006a, 2016. His work is analyzed by Jovanovic (2006a, 2000, 2002, 2016) and by Jovanovic and Le Gall (2001).
4. On Quételet, see Hankins 1908; Porter 1986; or Donnelly 2015.
5. Regnault never explicitly named the normal law: the term only appeared in 1877 with Wilhelm Lexis (Armatte 1991).
6. The central-limit theorem, along with the law of large numbers, is one of the most important results of probability theory. This theorem is crucial because it states that the sum of many independent random variables with finite variance will tend to the normal distribution. This phenomenon was first observed by Gauss. Proof of the theorem was provided by de

Moivre and Laplace and published in 1738 in the second edition of *The Doctrine of Chances* by Abraham de Moivre. It was subsequently generalized by Gnedenko and Kolmogorov in 1954. Let us remind readers that the central-limit theorem states that the average of many independent and identically distributed random variables with finite variance tends toward a normal distribution irrespective of the distribution followed by the original random variables.

7. The term "random" first appeared in its statistical meaning in 1898 (Frankfurter and McGoun 1999, 166–67), and the term "random walk" was first used in 1905 by Karl Pearson (1905a, 1905b).
8. This term is explicitly used by Regnault (1863, 40).
9. Mathematically, his model is of the following type: $P_{t+1} = P_t + \varepsilon_{t+1}$, where $\varepsilon = \{\varepsilon_t, t \in N\}$ is white noise and P_{t+1} the price of the bond at time *t*. As a result, the expectation of profit between two periods is nil, $E(P_{t+1} - P_t) = 0$.
10. These recordings were a way for the French government to control government bond prices. France looks like an exception, because in other countries, official price data recording started later (Preda 2007, 48). For instance, "The *Wall Street Journal* began publishing closing quotations only in 1868. The NYSE got an official quotation list on February 28, 1872. 'Official' did not mean, however, that the NYSE guaranteed price data. In the 1860s in London, only the published quotations of consols were closing prices" (Preda 2006, 760). By contrast, continuous data began to be organized with the introduction in 1923 of the Trans-Lux Movie Ticker (Preda 2006). Of course, technology was not available for recording these continuous flows of data.
11. It is worth mentioning that Regnault's ideas were diffused and used both during his lifetime and also after (Jovanovic 2016).
12. Bachelier's research program and his work are presented by Courtault et al. (2002), Jovanovic (2000, 2012), Davis and Etheridge (2006), and Ben-El-Mechaiekh and Dimand (2006, 2008).
13. Here we preserve Bachelier's notation, which we have reproduced in contemporary language.
14. We should point out that equation 1.2 is not, strictly speaking, the law of probability of a Brownian movement, but that of a Brownian movement multiplied by the standard deviation, σ, which here is equal to $\sqrt{2\pi k}$.
15. "Primes" (i.e., premiums) are derivative contracts similar to options but with some differences, particularly in the evolution of their prices (Courtadon 1982; Cuoco and Barone 1989; Jovanovic 2016). A "prime" is a conditional forward contract that allows the holder to buy (or sell) an underlying asset at the strike price at the liquidation date of the primes. To buy this contract, traders had to pay a fixed forfeit called "prime" (i.e. premium). The expression "dont" served to indicate the amount to be forfeited. One traded *Primes* from France to Central Europe (Weber 2009, 455).
16. Note that Bachelier did not evoke this second type of derivative contract, which did not exist on the French stock market at the time. For this second type of contract, his calculations were purely theoretical mathematical explorations with no empirical basis.
17. See Cramer 1983 for a presentation of the context and contributions of this period.
18. In 1906 Andrei Markov introduced Markov chains for the purpose of generalizing the law of large numbers for a series of interdependent experiments.
19. Smoluchowski (1906) described Brownian motion as a limit of random walks.

20. Wiener (1923) carried out the first rigorous mathematical study of Brownian motion and proved its existence.
21. One of the difficulties in reading Bachelier stemmed from the language he used, which was not that of pure mathematics but that of mathematical physics: "In fact, the mathematicians of the 30s who read Bachelier felt that his proofs are not rigorous and they are right, because he uses the language of a physicist who shows the way and provides formulas. But again, there is a difference between using that language and making mistakes. Bachelier's arguments and formulas are correct and often display extreme originality and mathematical richness" (Taqqu 2001, 23).
22. One of the major contributions of Kolmogorov's 1931 article was to make rigorous the move from discrete to continuous schemes, a development that is a direct continuation of Bachelier's work. Moreover, Bachelier also influenced Khinchine (1933), with whom Kolmogorov worked.
23. The two main schools studying probability theory prior to the 1940s were the French and the Russian. From the 1940s onward, a number of important papers were developed in Japan, influenced by Kiyosi Itô's work in particular. On Japanese contributions, see Watanabe 2009.
24. On the Cowles Commission and its links with financial econometrics, see Morgan 1990; Mirowski 2002; Christ 1994; and Dimand 2009. See also Hendry and Morgan 1995 on the foundations of econometric analysis.
25. Working was professor of economics and statistics at Stanford University's Food Research Institute. He was never a member of the Cowles Commission, but took part in its summer conferences.
26. A Tippett table is "random number table," used to produce series of random numbers. There are several such tables, the first being created by the English statistician Leonard Henry Caleb Tippett in 1927. It is made up of 10,400 four-digit numbers extracted from nineteenth-century British census records.
27. Slutsky published his 1927 article in Russian; it was translated into English in 1937.
    Barnett (2011) provides a detailed presentation of Slutsky's contributions from the perspective of the history of economics.
28. For example, Brown, Goetzmann, and Kumar (1998) redid Cowles's calculations, disregarding these ambiguous forecasts, and obtained the opposite result: William Peter Hamilton's recommendations made it possible to achieve a better performance than the market. For further details on this point, see also Dimand 2009 and Dimand and Veloce 2010.
29. Note that Cowles and Jones (1937) compared the observed distribution of stock prices with the normal distribution to determine the possibility of making a profit.
30. In his article, Roberts used the same graphical methodology as Slutsky and Working to demonstrate the random character of stock price variations. He did not analyze the distribution of prices.
31. The work of Regnault and Bronzin seems unknown to American writers, and almost none of the American writers working in financial econometrics prior to 1955 were aware of the work of Bachelier. Two exceptions were Samuelson, who in the 1930s learned of Bachelier's work, and Arne Fisher, who in 1922 suggested applying Bachelier's formulas to securities (Jovanovic 2012).
32. On the emergence of financial economics see Jovanovic 2008, 2009a, 2009b; MacKenzie 2006; and Whitley 1986a.

33. For a retrospective on Markowitz, see Rubinstein 2002 and Markowitz 1999. On Roy's contribution, see Sullivan 2011.
34. As previously mentioned, diversification strategy was already used at the end of the nineteenth century (Edlinger and Parent 2014; Rutterford and Sotiropoulos 2015). Moreover, the relationship between risk and return had already been emphasized by Williams (1938), although he did not provide an operational definition of this link.
35. This theorem can actually be thought of as an extension of the "separation theorem" originally developed by Irving Fisher (1930). For an introduction to the work of Fisher, see Dimand and Geanakoplos 2005. For a retrospective look at the Modigliani and Miller model, see Miller 1988 and Rubinstein 2003.
36. Formally, these definitions take place in a probability space (Ω, F, P) with filtration $(\Phi_n)_{0\leq n\leq N}$. A filtration is an ascending—or descending—family of Φ_i tribes: $\Phi_1 \subset \Phi_2 \subset \Phi_3 \ldots \subset \Phi_{n-1} \subset \Phi_n$, a tribe being a family of parts, verifying stability hypotheses, of all states of nature, Ω. The Φ_t tribe is a list of the events of which one can say at date t whether they have occurred or not. It translates all information known on date t.
37. Note that if stock exchange prices follow a martingale, the expectation of profit, y, between two consecutive periods is nil, $E(y_{t+1}/\Phi_t)=0$, taking into account information Φ_t. In other words, this is a fair game, as is the random walk also. Following Samuelson's and Mandelbrot's articles, random movements of stock market prices were represented using martingales.
38. Markowitz (1952, 1955), for instance, was the first scholar to apply the expected-utility theory in financial (portfolio) management.
39. See Mackenzie 2006, 72–73; Whitley 1986a, 1986b; Fourcade and Khurana 2009; and Bernstein 1992.
40. The same issues were raised in training sessions given by Financial Analysts Seminar, one of the leading professional organizations connected with financial markets (Kennedy 1966).
41. It is worth mentioning that the CAPM is often presented as a logical extension of the portfolio theory, developed by Markowitz (1952), based on expected-utility theory.
42. See, for instance, Cohen and Pogue 1967.
43. As explained by Jovanovic (2008), this polarization of results largely stems from the theoretical frameworks propounded at MIT (Keynesian) and the Graduate School of Business at the University of Chicago (monetarist).
44. Cowles and Jones (1937) had obtained a statistical dependence on monthly or weekly averages of daily prices. Working (1960) explained that in this case it is possible to obtain a degree of dependency because statistical analyses based on average prices can introduce artificial correlations between consecutive variations.
45. In Fama's thesis, this equilibrium value is the fundamental—or intrinsic—value of a security. The signification of this value is unimportant: it may be the equilibrium value determined by a general equilibrium model, or a convention shared by "sophisticated traders" (Fama 1965a, 36 n. 3). Fama later dropped the reference to a convention.
46. This is the most commonly accepted definition of efficiency, which Fama proposed in his 1970 paper: "A market in which prices always 'fully reflect' available information is called 'efficient'" (1970, 383).
47. Fama acknowledged the difficulties involved in this joint test in a report on efficiency published in 1991 (Fama 1991, 1575–76).
48. Nearly all direct contributors to this hard core have received the Nobel Prize in Economics: Markowitz, Sharpe, and Miller were joint winners in 1990; Merton and Scholes

received the award jointly in 1997. Although the contributions of Black (1938–1995) were explicitly recognized, he was not a named recipient, as the prize cannot be awarded posthumously. Fama was awarded in 2013.

49. See Mehrling 2005 on Fischer Black, and MacKenzie 2006 on the influence of this model.
50. Merton (1973) would later show that use of the CAPM was unnecessary.
51. A security is said to be contingent if its realization depends on states of another factor (price of another asset, climatic conditions, etc.).
52. Elimination of risk is a misnomer, because there is always a modeling risk related to, among other things, the choice of the process or distribution to model stock market variations.
53. In an economy having *T* periods, the existence of a complete system of markets allows agents from the initial moment to make intertemporal choices for all present and future prices at determined prices that are known to all. The organization of such a system of markets appears very complicated, since it would require a market for every good at every period. Arrow (1953) showed that a complete system of markets can be replaced by a financial market through which the assets exchanged allow agents to transfer their revenue independently in each state (Arrow's equivalency theorem). Subsequently Ross (1976b) showed that options can complete incomplete markets and thus lend greater verisimilitude to Arrow-Debreu general equilibrium. Bayeux-Besnainou and Rochet (1996) extended Ross's work to a multiperiod model. However, it was the work of Harrison, Kreps, and Pliska that would provide the rigorous mathematical framework for this intuition.
54. John McQuown at Wells Fargo and Rex Sinquefield at American National Bank in Chicago established the first Standard and Poor's Composite Index Funds in 1973 (http://www.ifa.com).
55. These are the PriceWaterhouseCooper and BGI report (1998), *25 Years of Indexing*, and the PriceWaterhouseCooper and BDM Alliance report (1999), *Investment Style and Its Growing Role in Packaged Investment Products.*
56. This influence is also found in the Basel II Accords (Pillar 3 explicitly refers to efficiency).
57. Specifically, these authors demonstrate two fundamental theorems. Th. 1: A market is arbitrage-free (efficient) if there exists at least one martingale measure.

    This means that in a market free of arbitrage the stochastic price process for financial assets must have at least one martingale measure—under which the expected value of the stochastic price does not change in time. Th. 2: A market is complete if there is a unique martingale measure for the financial assets.

    This theorem gives the conditions for a market to be complete: the stochastic price must have the martingale property and there must be only one martingale measure. Thus in order to price a financial asset (such as options) one must find the unique martingale probability measure and then use the martingale property for the stochastic price.
58. In this case there is more than one probability measure that causes the stochastic price process to be a martingale, and, consequently, this is an arbitrage-free market.

    For an incomplete market it can be shown that the price of a contingent security in a market that does not allow arbitrage is found in an interval of values, $x_{\min} \leq E_Q[\beta_T X] \leq x_{\max}$, with X the contingent security and β the discount process $(\beta_T = e^{-rT})$. The existence of many possible prices is equivalent with the existence of a risk imbalance between the buyer and the seller of the option. In this case, to have a unique price for the options, we have to add a minimization procedure for the risk that leads to some mathematical conditions in the final option formula.

59. We might add that the continuity that characterizes Brownian motion is also a vital element of the Black and Scholes model.
60. http://post.nyssa.org/nyssa-news/2010/10/in-defense-of-the-quant-ii-the-ups-and-downs-of-the-normal-distribution.html.

Chapter 2

1. The expression is $P(x)=\frac{1}{\sqrt{2\pi\sigma^2}}\exp\left(-\frac{(x-x_0)^2}{2\sigma^2}\right)$, defined for $-\infty < x < +\infty$. Therefore, the deviations from the mean larger than a few standard deviations are rare for the Gaussian law, as one can see on figure 2.3.
2. Olivier pointed this out in his thesis (1926, 81), which was one of the first (if not the first) exhaustive analysis on time-series analysis applied to economic phenomena: "Regardless of the importance of the problem of the dispersion of prices and their distribution around their mean—and for my part I believe the problem to be fundamental—hitherto it has been only very insufficiently studied. This is explained by the very small number of prices tracked by financial and economic newspapers that publish price index numbers."
3. Cowles and Jones (1937) were the only authors to compare the distribution and cumulative frequency of observed series of stock price variations with those of the random series. They used them in order to determine the distribution of the expected net gain (Cowles and Jones 1937, 293).
4. Armatte (1995), Boumans (2007), Friedman (2009), Le Gall (1994, 2006), Morgan (1990, 2012), and Morgan and Klein (2001) provided careful analysis of this development. However, we should point out that index numbers did not exist before that time, because goods were not sufficiently standardized and quantifiable to guarantee reliable data.
5. Barometers being defined as "time-series representations of cyclical activity" (Morgan 1990, 57).
6. See, for instance, Friedman 2009 on this barometer. We can also mention Wesley Clair Mitchell at Columbia and Irving Fisher at Yale, who also promoted rigorous empirical approaches for understanding economic fluctuations.
7. Fisher (1911) published the first systematic research on the mathematical formula that can be applied to price indices calculus.
8. Mitchell (1915) can be considered as the first major study, because he provided a theoretical and a practical analysis of index numbers.
9. As we explained in chapter 1, Osborne made the same observation in 1959 and also suggested using the logarithm of the price: finding that the distribution of price changes was not normal, he suggested the use of logarithms of stock prices, which did exhibit the normal distribution. By proceeding in this way, these authors sought to return to the normal distribution so that they could apply the results from statistics and the probability theory that we know today.
10. The cotton price time series was the most complete, and daily quotations were available.
11. We can mention, for instance, Eugene Fama, Benjamin King, and Arnold Moore at Chicago; and Walter Barney, John Bauer, Sidney Levine, William Steiger, and Richard Kruizenga at MIT.
12. For instance, if X_1 and X_2 are independent random variables that are normally distributed with the respective parameters $(\mu_1+\sigma_1)$ and $(\mu_1+\sigma_2)$, then their sum, $X_1 + X_2$, is also a normal random variable with parameters $(\mu_1+\mu_2,\sqrt{\sigma_1^2+\sigma_2^2})$.
13. Since there is no closed-form formula for densities, a Lévy distribution is often described by its characteristic. See Nolan 2005 and Samorodnitsky and Taqqu 1994 for different equivalent definitions of stable Lévy distributions.

14. Only three parameters appear in equation (2.1) because the fourth one, δ, is included in the set $\mathfrak{R}$.
15. See Nolan 2009 for the demonstration.
16. Paretian law was the first statistical regularity associated with leptokurtic distribution used in science. Pareto used it in his *Cours d'économie politique* (1896–97) to characterize the distribution of income and wealth.
17. "Scale invariance," a term that Mandelbrot held dear, is in a sense the geometric translation of the stability of the distribution of a stochastic process in probability theory.
18. The general central-limit theorem claims that a sum of many independent and identically distributed random variables with power-law distributions decreasing through a Paretian law, as $\frac{1}{|x|^{\alpha+1}}$ where $0 < \alpha < 2$, will tend to be distributed according to a small attractor distribution (i.e., an asymptotic limit for statistical distribution). When $\alpha = 2$, we have the Gaussian case of central-limit theorem where the variance is finite and for which the attractor distribution is normal, whereas a $0 < \alpha < 2$ process converges instead toward stable Lévy distribution, as we will explain in this chapter. In other words, the sum of random variables according to a Lévy law, distributed independently and identically, converges toward a stable Lévy law having the same parameters.
19. This speculative approach is identical, for example, to that which led to the discovery of the Higgs boson, whose existence was first theoretically assumed (and demonstrated) before being empirically observed.
20. When $\alpha = 1$, there is no impact of an increasing diversification on the scale factor, and when $\alpha < 1$, the scale factor increases in case of increasing diversification (Fama 1965b, 412).
21. Student distribution arises when estimating the mean of a normally distributed population in situations where the sample size is small and population standard deviation is unknown. This distribution is symmetric and bell-shaped, like the normal distribution, but has heavier tails. It approaches the normal distribution when the number of degrees of freedom grows.
22. Obviously, stability concerns Gaussian processes too.
23. Fama and Roll (1971) showed that a stable nonnormal process cannot be obtained from a mixture of (stable) normal processes.
24. It is worth mentioning that these empirical series were based on relatively small samples in comparison with the data available nowadays in finance. This point is quite important because the length of price series can reduce the scope of the results. For instance, the occurrence of a power law only makes sense on very large samples and working with a small sample directly influences the statistical description that will emerge from the data.
25. Note that the technique used by Fama and Roll (1968) was generalized by McCulloch (1986), who provided an estimation for all four parameters with no restriction on the symmetry of distribution. Basically, McCulloch (1986) used the information given by the empirical distributions' quantiles, from which he computed the four parameters of the process.
26. The method based on iterated regressions developed by Press (1972) was generalized by Arad (1980) and Koutrouvelis (1980). Also worthy of mention is the Paulson-Holcomb-Leitch (1975) method, which minimizes the difference between the theoretical characteristic function and a polynomial extrapolation of the empirical characteristic function. For further information about these methods, see Embrechts, Klüppelberg, and Mikosch 1997b and Nolan 2009.
27. This relationship between risk and return was given shape in Markowitz's seminal portfolio theory (1952, 1959).
28. For instance, Blume (1968) and Officer (1972).

29. Since the only statistical condition for describing this jump is the provision of a finite mean in order to ensure the finiteness of variability (in line with the mean variance approach).
30. "The random-walk model, however, even in modified logarithmic form, has been found inadequate on the basis that the tails of the distribution of price changes (or their logarithms) appear to be too long, based on sample evidence, to be accounted for by the appropriate normal distribution. One effort at compensation engendered the variant of the random-walk model due to Cootner (1962), which added reflecting barriers to the Markov (random-walk) process. Mandelbrot (1962) proposed a model for the behaviour of security-price changes that generated keen interest in the finance area, in the mathematics of stable laws" (Press 1967, 318).
31. See Cont and Tankov 2004 for an overview of this literature.
32. "One-block reasoning" is not the only difference between the jump-diffusion processes presented above and pure-jump processes. Indeed, while the first can use stable Lévy processes to characterize the jump part of the model, the latter deal only with nonstable Lévy processes (i.e., with a characteristic exponent alpha > 2), allowing them to value all statistical moments.
33. See Cont and Tankov 2004 for further details on this literature.
34. This time-dependence dynamic is defined by the modeler.
35. See Francq and Zakoian 2010; Bauwens et al. 2006; Tim 2010; and Pagan 1996 for further details on these categories of models.

Chapter 3

1. We have borrowed the term from Le Gall (2002, 5), who provides an excellent introduction to the analysis of methodology transfer between physical sciences and economics.
2. Note that the explanations about statistical physics are borrowed from an article by Richard Fitzpatrick (2012) available on the Web (farside.ph.utexas.edu/teaching/sm1/statmech.pdf).
3. As Fitzpatrick (2012) noticed, to solve a system with 6×10^{23} particles exactly, we would have to write down 1,024 coupled equations of motion, with the same number of initial conditions, and then try to resolve the system.
4. In particular the central-limit theorem.
5. For instance, as Fitzpatrick (2012) commented, the familiar equation of state of an ideal gas, $PV = nRT$, is actually a statistical result. In other words, it relates the average pressure (P) and the average volume (V) to the average temperature (T) through the number (n) of particles in the gas. "Actually, it is virtually impossible to measure the pressure, volume, or temperature of a gas to such accuracy, so most people just forget about the fact that the above expression is a statistical result, and treat it as a law of physics interrelating the actual pressure, volume, and temperature of an ideal gas" (Fitzpatrick 2012, 6).
6. As Lesne and Laguës (2011, 3) point out, the study of critical phenomena was initiated by Cagnard de Latour in 1822 and then boosted with the work of Thomas Andrews from 1867 onward. In 1869 Andrews observed a spectacular opalescence near the critical point of carbon dioxide. However, "The 1960s saw the emergence of a new general approach to critical phenomena, with the postulation of the so-called scaling laws, algebraic relations holding between the critical exponents for a given system" (Hughes 1999, 111).
7. It is important to mention that the concept of equilibrium can be associated with the notion of phase in an "all other things being equal" analogy. Indeed, in the case of continuous variations of pressure/temperature, the phase is progressively moving toward a critical state, implying that it cannot be associated with a static equilibrium.

8. Lesne and Laguës (2011) and Lesne (1998) provide an extremely clear and exhaustive presentation of renormalization methods. These papers make a very good introduction to intuitions and formalisms. Stanley (1999) provides a short presentation. See also Wilson 1993; Jona-Lasinio 2001; Calvo et al. 2010; and Stanley 1971 for further details.
9. Sornette (2006, chap. 2) provides a detailed presentation of this method.
10. For more details, see Samorodnitsky and Taqqu 1994; and Lesne 1998.
11. For instance, it exists in the work of Euclid and Galileo.
12. To understand the importance of this approach, one has to keep in mind that the macroscopic level is directly observable—for instance, a table—but the microscopic level—the molecules that constitute the table—is not directly observable (one needs a tool, as a microscope).
13. It is worth mentioning that large variation correlation length appears to be ruled by a power law, as the next section will detail.
14. Proceeding by analogies is very common in sciences, and particularly in economics. For instance, Henri Lefevre used analogies with the human body to analyze financial markets (Jovanovic 2006). Cohen (1993) provides a good analysis of the use of analogy, homology, and metaphor in interactions between the natural sciences and the social sciences.
15. The physicist Serge Galam initiated this discipline in papers published between 1980 and 1983, and proposed the term sociophysics in 1982 (Chakrabarti, Chakraborti, and Chatterjee 2006; Stauffer 2005, 2007; Galam 2008). Săvoiu and Iorga-Simăn (2013) give some historical perspective on sociophysics.
16. For instance, corporate revenue (Okuyama, Takayasu, and Takayasu 1999), the emergence of money (Shinohara and Gunji 2001), and global demand (Donangelo and Sneppen 2000).
17. In 1977, the Toronto Stock Exchange became the first stock exchange to be fully automated. Then, the Paris Stock Exchange (now Euronext) imported Toronto's system and became fully automated at the end of the 1980s. These changes occurred for NASDAQ between 1994 and 2004, and later for the NYSE in 2006 with the introduction of the NYSE hybrid market. The Tokyo Stock Exchange switched to electronic trading for all transactions in 1999.
18. The term "high-frequency data" refers to the use of "intraday" data, meaning that price changes can be recorded at every transaction on the market.
19. Today there is a large literature on this subject, in particular with the theory of financial market microstructure, which focuses on how specific trading mechanisms and how strategic comportments affect prices. Maureen O'Hara (1995), one of the leading lights of this theoretical trend, provides a good introduction to this field.
20. As explained in chapter 2, a process is said to be a Lévy process when it has (1) independent increments; (2) stationary increments, and (3) a continuous probability function. Lévy processes include a large category of statistical distributions (Poisson, Gaussian, Gamma, etc.).
21. There are some exceptions, particularly in the most recent works (Nakao 2000). We will come back to these recent works in chapter 5.
22. Let us mention the so-called Kosterlitz-Thoules transition, which is an exception characterizing a transformation from a disordered vortex fluid state with equal number of vortices to an ordered molecular like state composed by pairs of vortices with different polarities. We thank Marcel Ausloos for this precision. For further details on this point, see Hadzibabic et al. 2006.
23. Shalizi's notebook, http://bactra.org/notebooks/power-laws.html.
24. Precisely, $\xi(T) \propto |T - Tc|^{-\upsilon}$.

25. Precisely, at the critical point $T = T_C$ the correlation length diverges. There is no typical size. Hence, at the critical point: $\xi(T) \to \infty$; $\frac{r}{\xi(T)} \to 0$; $e^{\frac{-r}{\xi(T)}} \to 1$; $\frac{1}{r^{\alpha}} e^{\frac{-r}{\xi(T)}} \to \frac{1}{r^{\alpha}}$.
26. The correlation length is finite. The exponential term "wins" over the power-law term, since it decreases more rapidly as the distance *r* increases. Hence the correlation function is described by an exponential function.
27. Shalizi's notebooks are available at http://bactra.org/notebooks/. One can also read Jona-Lasinio 2001 for further details.
28. The first studies on statistical scale invariance came from Kolmogorov (1942, 1941), who studied data related to phenomena associated with turbulence. His research on turbulence also led him to introduce power laws (and their scaling property) into physics at the same period. These concepts progressively became widespread in the discipline (Hughes 1999). In the 1960s, scholars such as Domb and Hunter (1965), Widom (1965a, 1965b), Fisher (1967), and Kadanoff (1966) established some of the most important theoretical results on scaling properties, which contributed to the crucial developments that have occurred in physics since the 1970s.
29. We use here the easiest case of scaling invariance (i.e., scaling factor = 1.1). For more information about more complex scaling properties, see Hartemink et al. 2001.
30. The negative sign is not really important, since it depends on the choice of axes for the histogram. We base our presentation on Li et al. 2005, which provides a clear mathematical presentation of power laws. Newman (2005) also provides a clear and exhaustive mathematical analysis (included the determination of the moments).
31. Stable Lévy processes can be characterized through a specific power law exhibiting an independence of increments (a defining element of Lévy processes). While all power laws with $0 < \mu \leq 2$ are said to be stable, only those with $0 < \mu < 2$ are associated with a distribution whose variance is infinite, since an exponent equal to 2 is a Gaussian distribution (and therefore a finite variance). In other words, a Gaussian process can be looked on as a specific case of stable Lévy processes or, to put it in another way, a Gaussian distribution can mathematically be expressed as a stable power law with an exponent equal to 2 (Nolan 2009). It is worth mentioning that independence of increments is not a required condition for power laws, which can also describe dependent increments (the reason that power laws are also used for characterizing long memory). In other words, statistical stability implies scaling properties, while the reverse is not true (Schoutens 2003).
32. By attractor, we mean an asymptotically approached set of points in phase space, which is invariant under dynamics.
33. Note that this phenomenological approach is much less common in economics. On the phenomenological approach in physics, see Cartwright 1983.
34. Mitzenmacher (2004) and Simkin and Roychowdhury (2011) are the best-documented articles.
35. In addition to the variation of the characteristic exponent (α), econophysicists also try to fit the data by adjusting the constant C in the equation $\ln P[r > x] = -\alpha \ln x$. The variation of this parameter C explains why the curves do not begin at the same point in the figure 3.7. It is worth mentioning that, because power laws are scale invariant, the positive constant C, associated with the scale of analysis, does not play a key role in the statistical characterization of data.
36. It is worth mentioning that Vitanov et al. (2014), like many others, showed that this is not always true.

37. According to Rybski (2013), Berry and Okulicz-Kozaryn (2012) distinguish three periods in research on city-size distributions. The first period was initiated by Auerbach's empirical discovery. Then Zipf's work (1949) was the starting point of the second period that gave rise to empirical studies for estimating the exponent for city distributions and cross-national analyses. During this second period, an article by Simon (1955) proposed a statistical process for explaining these observations. He suggested that the probability of a city growing by a unit is proportional to its size, which is known today as preferential attachment. Finally, the lack of an intuitive theoretical model led to the third phase. Despite a variety of early modeling approaches from various disciplines, Berry attributes the first economic theory addressing city-size distributions to Gabaix (1999).
38. In 2002 the journal *Glottometrics* dedicated a special issue edited by Gunther Altam to Zipf's work.
39. See Dubkov et al. (2008) for an astonishing list of stable Lévy-type phenomena in physical, biological, chemical, and social systems.
40. Lévy (2003) and Klass et al. (2006) confirmed Pareto's results by showing that wealth and income distribution can both statistically be characterized by a power law. Amaral et al. (1997) explained that annual growth rates of US manufacturing companies can also be described through a power law, while Axtell (2001), Luttmer (2007), and Gabaix and Landier (2008) claimed that this statistical framework can also be used to characterize the evolution of companies' size as a variable of their assets, market capitalization, or number of employees. These "size models" have since been applied for describing the evolution of cities' size (Cordoba 2008; Eeckhout 2004; Gabaix 1999; Krugman 1996). In the same vein, Lux (1996) and Gabaix et al. (2007) observed that the large fluctuations on the financial markets can be captured through a power law. We can also read Gabaix's (2009) survey on power laws in economics and finance.
41. The two next chapters will discuss this point and some limits of this approach.
42. See Ausloos 2014a for a detailed analysis of these analytical tools and Ausloos 2014b for an application of these techniques.
43. See Ding 1983 for further details on the use of asymptotic (theoretical) statistics for describing physical (empirical) systems.
44. This idea of truncation dated back to the 1700s, with the famous St. Petersburg paradox (Csorgor and Simons 1983). Indeed, many works have considered this idea as empirical evidence because all physical systems are finite.
45. The finite configuration of all samples implies that there is necessarily an upper bound rank making the statistical description of these samples possible. However, as previously mentioned, statistical physicists wanted to combine the asymptotic properties of power laws with the finite dimension of empirical samples. That is the reason why some physicists went beyond the use of ranks in the treatment of power laws (Mantegna 1991; Mantegna and Stanley 1994). On this point, see also Ausloos 2014a.
46. It is worth mentioning that Mandelbrot (1963) already mentioned the possibility of using truncation techniques in the 1960s at low rank scale.
47. See Figueiredo et al. 2007 for a statistical explanation of this slow convergence.
48. However, knowing that critical phenomena have a continuous and abrupt change, we can suppose that their choice is not independent of this consideration.
49. It is worth mentioning that the first exponentially truncation technique was introduced in physics by Koponen (1995). However, this author did not justify his paper using a physically

plausible argument, as was the case in the literature after the critique made by Gupta and Campanha (1999).

50. The truncation technique based on a gradual cutoff can be considered a specific case of the exponential technique (Matsushita, Rathie, and Da Silva 2003).
51. These constants are usually derived from physical theories (Gupta and Campanha 2002), thus offering a variety of potential definitions for the truncation function.
52. It is worth mentioning that a variety of exponential truncation functions have been developed in the specialized literature (Schinckus 2013). Two factors can explain the diversity of these functions: first, the collection of physical theories that can be used to define the form of the function; and second, the will to develop more data-driven truncations (Matsushita, Rathie, and Da Silva 2003).
53. These techniques have been presented as a potential solution for power laws based on high-frequency data. For low-frequency items (i.e., not financial data), some physicists implemented alternative solutions by using other statistical law (the Lavalette law, for instance). See Ausloos 2015; Cerqueti and Ausloos 2015; and Tripp and Feitelson 2001.

Chapter 4

1. Actually, Stanley was the first scholar to propose the term "econophysics" during a conference dedicated to "physics of economics" organized in Kolkata (India) in 1995 (Chakrabarti and Chakraborti 2010).
2. According to Standler (2009), the end of this kind of bubble can partly be explained by a generational shift in the administration: senior officers close to retirement who favored funding of specific scientific research are no longer able to insist on this generous financial support.
3. See http://phys.uh.edu/research/econophysics/index.php.
4. See http://www.tcd.ie/Physics/people/Peter.Richmond/Econophysics/Position.html and http://www.itp.phys.ethz.ch/research/comp/econophys for examples. For further information on these programs, see Kutner and Grech 2008 and the website of these universities.
5. http://www3.unifr.ch\econophysics.
6. It earned its official recognition in the Physics and Astrophysics Classification Scheme (PACS): since 2003, econophysics has been an official subcategory of physics under the code 89.65 Gh.
7. The sample is composed of Eugene Stanley, Rosario Mantegna, Joseph McCauley, Jean-Philippe Bouchaud, Mauro Gallegati, Benoît Mandelbrot, Didier Sornette, Thomas Lux, Bikas Chakrabarti, and Doyne Farmer. Moreover, given the usual practice of citations, other important authors have been retrieved through the analysis of the cited references in these papers as well as in the papers citing those source papers. A group of 242 source papers covering the domain of econophysics and the papers that cite them over the period 1980–2008 were identified in order to analyze the evolution of the field. Starting with these core papers, which construct the population of researchers, 1,817 other papers that cited the source articles have been identified.
8. These papers were mainly written by Thomas Lux and Mauro Gallegati and dealt with macroeconomics (Gallegati 1990; Lux 1992a, 1992b; Gallegati 1994) or the history of economics (Gallegati and Dardi 1992).
9. His research focuses partly on complexity in economics, a topic that may cause him to be more open to the approach proposed by econophysicists.

10. The data on the cited journals come from the "Journal of Citation Report 2008" published by Thomson Reuters and part of the Web of Knowledge.
11. The first is a physicist and the second an economist, and both were in our source authors.
12. Following Backhouse (2004, 265), we distinguish "orthodox dissenters" from "heterodox dissenters"; the latter reject the mainstream theory and aim at profoundly changing conventional ideas, while the former are critical but work within mainstream economics.
13. Chapter 2 explained that financial economists describe the occurrence of extreme values through the evolution of the Gaussian trend (unconditional distribution) corrected by a conditional capturing the large variations.
14. Eugene Stanley, who is often presented as the father of econophysics, told us privately that after more than six years (!) he decided to cancel his submission to the *American Economic Review*—although it is a top 10 journal in economics.
15. While economists use the *JEL* (*Journal of Economic Literature*) classification, physicists organize their knowledge through their PACS (Physics and Astrophysics Classification Scheme) under which econophysics has its own code (89.65 Gh).
16. Economists usually employ stylistic conventions defined by the University of Chicago Press or the Harvard citation style, where references are listed in alphabetical order, while physicists adopt the conventions used by the American Institute of Physics, where references are listed in the order in which they appear in the text.
17. They had to choose from five reasons for having been rejected and were invited to comment on their choices: (1) the topic of the paper; (2) the assumptions used in the paper; (3) the method used in the paper; (4) the results of the paper; or (5) another reason.
18. This situation is not specific to economics. It also existed in the other fields into which statistical physicists have extended their models and methods (Mitzenmacher 2005).
19. This is one of the main reasons for having the efficient-market theory depict its weak connection with the random character of stock price variations, as we saw in chapter 1.
20. Mirowski (1989) gives a good overview on this controversy.
21. The VAR approach has been developed by Christopher Sims (1980a, 1980b). VAR models are a set of related linear difference equations in which each variable is in turn explained by its own lagged values, plus current and past values of the remaining $n - 1$ variables (Christiano 2012; Stock and Watson 2001). Numerous economists have critiqued these models because they do not shed any light on the underlying structure of the phenomena or the economy studied (Chari, Kehoe, and McGrattan 2008, 2009; Christiano 2012). Similarly, the RBC approach is based on calibration. It has been developed by Finn E. Kydland and Edward C. Prescott (1982). These macroeconomic models study business cycle fluctuations as the result of exogenous shocks. Their model is based on a calibration approach, and it is validated if the simulations provided by the model fit with empirical observations. Numerous economists have critiqued this method (Eichenbaum 1996; Gregory and Smith 1995; Hansen and Heckman 1996; Hendry 1995; Hoover 1995; Quah 1995; Sims 1996; Wickens 1995). De Vroey and Malgrange (2007) offer a presentation of this model and its influence in macroeconomics literature.
22. Shalizi's notebook, http://bactra.org/notebooks/power-laws.html.
23. Chartism (also called "technical analysis") is a financial practice based on the observation of the historical evolution of assets' prices. More precisely, actors try to identify visual patterns that help them give a meaning to the financial reality.

24. Stanley and Plerou (2001) replied to LeBaron's critic. Although their reply provided a technical answer—particularly the limited number of data used by LeBaron—it underlines the difficulties in the expectations of the two communities.
25. Chapter 2 also emphasized that econophysicists can find this linearity by treating statistically the potential inflection points that could appear in the visual analysis of data.
26. We can mention Bouchaud and Sornette (1994) and Bouchaud and Potters (2003, 2000), who proposed a first approximation to the European call option formula that is equivalent to the option-pricing formula obtained in financial economics under the risk-neutral approach. However, their arguments are different from those used in financial economics.
27. It is worth mentioning that most practitioners have developed their own formulas that are far from Black-Scholes-Merton model (Haug and Taleb 2011).
28. When econophysicists deal with equilibrium, they rather use a "statistical equilibrium" coming from a statistical mechanism (i.e., a reconciliation between a mechanism and thermodynamics). See Bouchaud 2002.
    See Schinckus 2010a, 2010c for further information about the importance of equilibrium in econophysics.
29. It is worth mentioning that the hypothetico-deductive method is considered the major scientific method by many authors in philosophy of science (for instance, Popper 1959). When (financial) economics emerged as discipline, economists integrated hypothetico-deductive reasoning as a scientific foundation: the assumption of the perfectly rational agent allows economists to deduce implications in terms of individual behaviors, while the hypothesis of representative agent offers them the ability to generalize microbehaviors at a macroeconomic level. Even recent developments such as behavioral finance kept this deductive method by giving a generalization of the perfect rational agent (Schinckus 2009).
30. ARCH-type models include ARCH, GARCH, NGARCH, EGARCH, and similar models.
31. See, for instance, Lorie 1966, 107.
32. In epistemological terms, this opposition between early financial economists and chartists shaded the classical opposition between deduction (used by financial economists) and induction (used by chartists). See Jovanovic 2008 for further details on this opposition.
33. See, for instance, Cootner 1964, 1; Fama 1965b, 59; Fisher and Lorie 1964, 1–2; and Archer 1968, 231–32.
34. With Rosser (2006, 2008), Keen (2003) is one of the rare breed of economists who have engaged in a dialogue with econophysicists.
35. See, for instance, Weston 1967, 539.
36. In this respect, Rosenfeld (1957, 52) proved to be visionary when he suggested using computers for testing theories on a large sample.

Chapter 5

1. One should point out that, more recently, econophysics models have less frequently used power laws; this represents a new diversification of econophysics models that will be discussed in this chapter.
2. As detailed in chapter 3, theoretical investigation in econophysics is considered only after having observed patterns in the empirical results.
3. Mandelbrot (1962, 6) had already underlined the need for a phenomenological approach in his early works applied to finance. From this perspective Mandelbrot's agenda (building new mathematical models, new statistical tools, etc.) was very ambitious for the 1960s.

4. By "success," Casey (2013) meant that these models were able to detect an overestimation of the market (in the credit default swap bubble, for example).
5. Examples are Jean-Philippe Bouchaud and Mark Potters, who created Capital Fund Management, and Tobias Preis, who created Artemis Capital Asset Management.
6. https://www.cfm.fr/en/.
7. http://modeco-software.webs.com/econophysics.htm.
8. https://www.rmetrics.org/.
9. https://www.rmetrics.org/sites/default/files/2013-VorlesungSyllabus.pdf.
10. http://tuvalu.santafe.edu/~aaronc/powerlaws/.
11. Cornelis (2005) and Guégan and Zhao (2014) point out that extreme events lead to the failure of VaR.
12. Pagan (1996) offers a very clear and useful perspective on econometric models applied to financial markets. See also Bauwens et al. 2006 and Francq and Zakoian 2010 for further details on these categories of models.
13. Considering the time series as a whole is the most common approach in natural sciences and is associated with scaling laws.
14. We thank Nicolas Gaussel for helpful discussion on this topic.
15. LTCM was a hedge-fund management firm that utilized absolute-return trading strategies combined with high financial leverage. The firm was founded in 1994 and collapsed in 1998. Members of its board of directors included Myron S. Scholes and Robert C. Merton. Initially successful with extremely high annualized return in the first years (21 percent, 41 percent, and 43 percent after fees), in 1998 it lost $4.6 billion in less than four months following the Asian and the Russian financial crisis. See Dunbar 2000 and Lowenstein 2000.
16. Harrison (1998) showed that the characteristics of eighteenth-century financial-asset returns are the same as those of the twentieth century: "The distribution of price changes now and then both exhibit the same patterns or regularities. In particular, the distribution of price changes is leptokurtic, and fluctuations in variance are persistent" (1998, 55). In other words, these regularities are stable.
17. Fantazzini and Geraskin (2011) provide a clear presentation of LPPL models.
18. $A > 0$ is the value of $\ln p(t_c)$ at the critical time, $B < 0$ is the increase in $\ln p(t)$ over the time unit before the crash if C were to be close to zero, $C \neq 0$ is the proportional magnitude of the oscillations around the exponential growth, $0 < \beta < 1$ should be positive to ensure a finite price at the critical time, while $0 < \delta < 2\pi$ is a phase parameter.
19. The opinions of other participants influence each participant. It is the well-known beauty contest described by Keynes in chapter 12 of the *General Theory*, in which judges picked whom they thought other judges would pick, rather than whom they considered to be the most beautiful.
20. Durlauf set out his position more clearly in a later paper (2012, 14).
21. Let us mention, for instance, that Durlauf (Arthur, Durlauf, and Lane 1997; Blume and Durlauf 2006) was involved in the meetings organized by the Santa Fe Institute dedicated to the application of physics to economics, while Lux regularly published articles dealing with econophysics (Lux 2009).
22. In the same vein as Mitzenmacher, a theoretical interpretation is considered here in the sense of explaining the significance of a mathematical model.
23. However, as explained in chapter 2, the characterization of these statistical patterns is developed in different conceptual framework (i.e., the Gaussian framework for financial economists and the power-law perspective for econophysicists).

24. See Jovanovic and Schinckus 2013 for a detailed discussion of this point in connection with econophysics and financial economics.
25. Galison (1997) explained how engineers collaborated with physicists to develop particle detectors and radar.
26. A Creole (e.g., Chavacano in the Philippines, Krio in Sierra Leone, and Tok in Papua New Guinea) is often presented as an example of a pidgin because it results from a mix of regional languages; see Todd 1990.
27. Note also special issues of economic journals, such as the *Journal of Economic Dynamics and Control* dedicated to the "Application of Physics to Economics and Finance" published in 2008, and the issue of the *International Review of Financial Analysis* titled "Contributions of Econophysics to Finance," published in 2016.
28. Brakman et al. (1999) extended Krugman's (1991) model by introducing negative externalities.
29. In contrast, Farmer et al. (2004) have shown that large price changes in response to large orders are very rare. See also Chiarella, Iori, and Perello 2009 for a more recent model showing that large price changes are likely to be generated by the presence of large gaps in the book of orders.
30. It is worth mentioning that this hypothesis is similar to those of Fama (1965) when he defined and demonstrated the efficiency of financial markets for the first time.
31. From an economic perspective, the difference observed between the distributions characterizing the evolution of financial variables (returns, foreign exchange) and those describing economic fundamentals could result from the higher liquidity of the former. See Aoki and Yoshikawa 2007 for more information on this subject.
32. A number of empirical studies very soon contradicted the conclusions of the theoretical framework built during the 1960s and the 1970s (see chapter 1). These empirical studies gave birth to what is known as the "anomalies literature," which has become extensive and well organized since the 1980s. Schwert (2003) provides a fairly exhaustive review of anomalies.
33. The term "market microstructure" was coined by Mark Garman (1976), who studied order flux dynamics (the dealer must set a price so as to not run out of stock or cash). For a presentation of the discipline, see O'Hara 1995; Madhavan 2000; and Biais et al. 2005.
34. The first generation of market microstructure literature has shown that trades have both a transitory and a permanent impact on prices (Biais, Glosten, and Spatt 2005). For instance, Copeland and Galai (1983) showed that a dealer who cannot distinguish between informed and uninformed investors will always set a positive spread to compensate for the expected loss that he will incur if there is a positive probability of some investors being informed. Kyle (1985) suggests that informed dealers can develop strategic behavior to profit from their information by concealing their orders among those of noninformed dealers. While informed dealers thus maximize their own profits on the basis of the information they hold, their behavior restricts dissemination of the information. O'Hara (2003) presents another example of results that contradict the dominant paradigm. In this article, she shows that if information is asymmetrically distributed, and if those who do not have information know that others know more, contrary to the suggestions of the CAPM, we will not get an equilibrium where everyone holds the market portfolio.
35. See Schinckus 2009a, 2009b for a presentation of this school and its positioning vis-à-vis the dominant paradigm.
36. In 2002 Daniel Kahneman received the Nobel Prize in Economics for his work on the integration of psychology with economics.

37. Note that Shefrin (2002) made a first attempt to unify the theory.
38. Agent-based modeling is a computational method applied in so many fields (Epstein 2006) that it is not possible to number them in this chapter. The agent-based approach appeared in the 1990s as a new tool for empirical research in many fields, including economics (Axtell 1999), voting behavior (Asselain 1985), military tactics (Ilachinski 2000), organizational behavior (Prietula, Carley, and Gasse 1998), epidemics (Epstein and Axtell 1996), and traffic-congestion patterns (Rasmussen and Nagel, 1994). For a detailed literature review on the topic, see Epstein 2006 or more recently Cristelli 2014.
39. See LeBaron 2006 for details on agent-based modeling used in economics.
40. Note that this agent-based econophysics is not limited to financial issues, since Pickhardt and Seibold (2011), for example, explained that income-tax evasion dynamics can be modeled through an "agent-based econophysics model" based on the Ising model of ferromagnetism, while Donangelo and Sneppen (2000) and Shinohara and Gunji (2001) approached the emergence of money through studying the dynamics of exchange in a system composed of many interacting and learning agents. Focardi et al. (2002) and Chiarella and Iori (2002) also provided an Ising-type model with interactions between nearest neighbors.
41. Bak became an external member of the Santa Fe Institute, where he found the perfect environment to promote his theory of criticality, which gradually spread to several disciplinary contexts in the 1990s (Frigg 2003). The Santa Fe Institute was founded in 1984 to conduct theoretical research outside the traditional disciplinary boundaries by basing it on interdisciplinarity. Its original mission was to disseminate complexity theory (also called complex systems). This institute plays a key role in econophysics due to a fruitful collaboration between economists and physicists, among them some Nobel laureates such as Phil Anderson and Kenneth Arrow. For further details, see Schinckus 2016.
42. The visual tests make it difficult to distinguish between power-law, log-normal, and exponential distributions. See Clauset et al. 2009 for further details on this point.
43. The difficulty of distinguishing between log-normal and Pareto tails has been widely commented on in the literature (Embrechts, Klüppelberg, and Mikosch 1997; Bee, Riccaboni, and Schiavo 2011).
44. This bound comes from the size of the sample that leads the probability density to diverge when x tends toward zero.

Chapter 6

1. Stanley et al. 1999, 157; Challet, Marsili, and Cheng Zhang 2005, 14; Bouchaud and Potters 2003; McCauley 2004; Bouchaud and Challet 2014; McCauley 2006. See also Rickles 2008 and Schinckus 2010, who discussed this point.
2. Although econophysicists (McCauley 2006, Sornette 2014) criticize this theoretical dependence of the modeling step, it is worth mentioning that physics also provides telling examples in which a theoretical framework is accepted while the empirical results are wholly incompatible with this framework. One could mention the recent example of the Higgs boson. The conceptual existence of the Higgs boson predated its observation, meaning that its theoretical framework was assumed for a number of years without the particle being observed. In the same vein, string theory is an elegant mathematical framework, empirical/concrete evidence of which is still debated. These are not unique examples: "There are plenty of physicists who appear to be unperturbed about working in a manner detached

from experiment: quantum gravity, for example. Here, the characteristic scales are utterly inaccessible, there is no experimental basis, and yet the problem occupies the finest minds in physics" (Rickles 2008, 14).

3. By being derived from a theoretical framework setting up the initial calibration, the "model becomes an a priori hypothesis about real phenomena" (Haavelmo 1944, 8).
4. See, for instance, Mandelbrot 1963; Malcai, Biham, and Solomon 1999; Blanck and Solomon 2000; Skjeltorp 2000; Cont and Bouchaud 2000; Louzoun and Solomon 2001; Gupta and Campanha 2002; and Scalas and Kim 2007.
5. Derived distributions like that obtained by Clementi, Di Matteo, and Gallegati (2006) are in general not Lévy-like distributions, but they approach a Lévy distribution for a very large number of data.
6. Bouchaud, Mezard, and Potters 2002; Potters and Bouchaud 2003; McCauley 2009; Gabaix 2009; Lux 2009; McCauley, Gunaratne, and Bassler 2007b; Sornette 2014; Bouchaud 2002; McCauley 2006; Stanley and Plerou 2001; Durlauf 2005, 2012; Keen 2003; Chen and Li 2012; Ausloos 2001; Chakrabarti and Chakraborti 2010; Farmer and Lux 2008; Carbone, Kaniadakis, and Scarfone 2007; Ausloos 2013; Jovanovic and Schinckus 2016.
7. The law of one price suggests that the forces of competition will ensure that any given commodity will be sold at the same price.
8. Although Modigliani and Miller were not the first to apply the arbitrage proof in finance (Rubinstein 2003), their article led to its popularity for two reasons: (1) their article was one of the first to use modern probability theory to analyze a financial problem; and (2) the authors were members of strong academic departments (MIT and the University of Chicago).
9. Except in Bouchaud and Potters 1994. They reach a first approximation to the European call option formula that is quite equivalent with the option-pricing formula obtained in mathematical finance under the risk-neutral approach, but they use arguments that are somehow different from those used in mathematical finance.
10. The reason is due to the incompleteness of markets (Ivancevic 2010; Takayasu 2006; Cont and Tankov 2004; Miyahara 2012; Zhang and Han 2013). See also chapters 1 and 4.
11. Because we work unconditionally on the whole distribution (and not only on its fat-tail part), we need not define a short-term time dependence for the variance as is usually done in conditional methodology, such as ARCH-type models.
12. It is worth mentioning that this convergence of x to a Gaussian regime is extremely slow due to the stable property of the Lévy distribution (Mantegna and Stanley 1994). The crossover value N_c can be derived by using the Berry-Esseen theorem (Shlesinger 1995) or by using a method based on the probability of x returning to the origin (Mantegna and Stanley 1994)—both approaches provide a crossover value equal to $N_c \sim c^{-\alpha} l^{-\alpha}$, where c is the scale factor and l the cross-value at which the regime will switch from a stable Lévy to a Gaussian one.

Conclusion

1. Although the Bayesian framework is also implemented in finance, it is not the statistical approach used by the mainstream. For further details on this point, see Rachev et al. 2008.

REFERENCES

Abergel, Frédéric, Hideaki Aoyama, Bikas K. Chakrabarti, Anirban Chakraborti, and Asim Ghosh, eds. 2014. *Econophysics of Agent-Based Models*. Cham: Springer.

Alastair, Bruce, and David Wallace. 1989. "Critical phenomena: Universal physics at large length scales." In *The New Physics*, edited by Paul Davies, 109–52. Cambridge: Cambridge University Press.

Alejandro-Quiñones, Ángel L., Kevin E. Bassler, Michael Field, Joseph L. McCauley, Matthew Nicol, Ilya Timofeyev, Andrew Török, and Gemunu H. Gunaratne. 2006. "A theory of fluctuations in stock prices." *Physica A* 363 (2): 383–92.

Alexander, Sidney S. 1961. "Price movements in speculative markets: Trends or random walk." *Industrial Management Review* 2: 7–26.

Alfarano, Simone, and Thomas Lux. 2005. "A noise trader model as a generator of apparent financial power laws and long memory." *Macroeconomic Dynamics* 11: 80–101.

Alfarano, Simone, and Thomas Lux. 2010. "Extreme value theory as a theoretical background for power law behavior." MPRA Paper No. 24718. August 30.

Alstott, Jeff, Ed Bullmore, and Dietmar Plenz. 2014. "Powerlaw: A Python package for analysis of heavy-tailed distributions." *PloS One* 9 (1): e85777.

Altam, Gunther, ed. 2002. Special issue dedicated to Zipf law. *Glottometrics* 3.

Amaral, Luis A. Nunes, Sergey V. Buldyrev, Shlomo Havlin, Heiko Leschhorn, Philipp Maass, Michael A. Salinger, H. Eugene Stanley, and Michael H. R. Stanley. 1997. "Scaling behavior in economics: I. Empirical results for company growth." *Journal de Physique* 7: 621–33.

Amblard, Frédéric, and Guillaume Deffuant. 2004. "The role of network topology on extremism propagation with the relative agreement opinion dynamics." *Physica A* 343: 725–38.

Anagnostidis, Panagiotis, and Christos J. Emmanouilides. 2015. "Nonlinearity in high-frequency stock returns: Evidence from the Athens Stock Exchange." *Physica A: Statistical Mechanics and Its Applications* 421: 473–87.

Andersen, Torben G., and Tim Bollerslev. 1997. "Intraday Periodicity and Volatility Persistence in Financial Markets." *Journal of Empirical Finance* 4: 115–58.

Annaert, Jan, Frans Buelens, and Angelo Riva. 2015. "Financial history databases: Old data, new issues, new insights." Paper presented at Financial History Workshop, Judge Business School, Cambridge, July 23–24.

Aoki, Masanao, and Hiroshi Yoshikawa. 2007. *A Stochastic Approach to Macroeconomics and Financial Markets*. Cambridge: Cambridge University Press.

Aoyama, Hideaki, Yoshi Fujiwara, Yuichi Ikeda, Hiroshi Iyetomi, and Wataru Souma. 2011. *Econophysics and Companies: Statistical Life and Death in Complex Business Networks*. Cambridge: Cambridge University Press.

Arad, Ruth W. 1980. "Parameter estimation for symmetric stable distribution." *International Economic Review* 21 (1): 209–20.

Arbulu, Pedro. 1998. "La Bourse de Paris au XIXe siècle: L'exemple d'un marché émergent devenu efficient." *Revue d'Economie Financière* 49: 213–49.

Archer, Stephen H. 1968. "Introduction." *Journal of Financial and Quantitative Analysis* 3 (3): 231–33.

Armatte, Michel. 1991. "Théorie des erreurs, moyenne et loi 'normale.'" In *Moyenne, milieu, centre: Histoires et usages*, edited by Jacqueline Feldman, Gérard Lagneau, and Benjamin Matalon, 63–84. Paris: Editions EHESS.

Armatte, Michel. 1992. "Conjonctions, conjoncture, et conjecture: Les baromètres économiques (1885–1930)." *Histoire et Mesure* 7 (1–2): 99–149.

Armatte, Michel. 1995. "Histoire du modèle linéaire: Formes et usages en statistique et en econométrie jusqu'en 1945." Doctoral dissertation, EHESS.

Armatte, Michel. 2003. "Cycles and Barometers: Historical insights into the relationship between an object and its measurement." In *Papers and Proceedings of the Colloquium on the History of Business-Cycle Analysis*, edited by Dominique Ladiray, 45–74. Luxembourg: Office for Official Publication of the European Communities.

Arrow, Kenneth Joseph. 1953. *Le rôle des valeurs boursières pour la répartition la meilleure des risques: (The role of securities in the optimal allocation of risk bearing)*. Cowles Commission for Research in Economics. Chicago: University of Chicago.

Arrow, Kenneth Joseph, and Gérard Debreu. 1954. "Existence of an equilibrium for a competitive economy." *Econometrica* 22 (3): 265–90.

Arthur, W. Brian. 2005. "Out-of-equilibrium economics and agent-based modeling." Santa Fe Institute Working Paper No. 2005-09-03.

Arthur, W. Brian, Steven N. Durlauf, and David A. Lane, eds. 1997. *The Economy as an Evolving Complex System II*. Reading, MA: Addison-Wesley.

Asselain, Jean-Claude. 1985. *Histoire économique: De la révolution industrielle à la première guerre mondiale*. Paris: Presses de la Fondation Nationale des Sciences Politiques & Dalloz.

Auerbach, Felix. 1913. "Das Gesetz der Bevölkerungskonzentration." *Petermanns Geographische Mitteilungen* 59: 73–76.

Aurell, Erik, Jean-Philippe Bouchaud, Marc Potters, and Karol Zyczkowski. 1997. "Option pricing and hedging beyond Black and Scholes." *Journal de Physique IV* 3 (3): 2–11.

Ausloos, Marcel. 2001. "Editorial of the Special issue on econophysics." *European Physical Journal B* 20 (4): 471.

Ausloos, Marcel. 2013. "Econophysics: Comments on a few applications, successes, methods and models." *IIM Kozhikode Society & Management Review* 2 (2): 101–15.

Ausloos, Marcel. 2014a. "Toward fits to scaling-like data, but with inflection points and generalized Lavalette function." *Journal of Applied Quantitative Methods* 9 (2): 1.

Ausloos, Marcel. 2014b. "Two-exponent Lavalette function: A generalization for the case of adherents to a religious movement." *Physical Review E: Statistical, Nonlinear, and Soft Matter Physics* 89 (6): 062803.

Ausloos, Marcel. 2015. "France new regions planning? Better order or more disorder?" *Entropy* 17 (8): 5695–710.

Ausloos, Marcel, Kristinka Ivanova, and Nicolas Vandewalle. 2002. "Crashes: Symptoms, diagnoses and remedies." In *Empirical Sciences of Financial Fluctuations: The Advent of Econophysics*, edited by Hideki Takayasu, 62–76. Berlin: Springer Verlag.

Ausloos, Marcel, Franck Jovanovic, and Christophe Schinckus. 2016. On the "usual" misunderstanding between econophysics and finance: Some clarifications on modelling approaches and efficient market hypothesis. *International Review of Financial Analysis* 47: 7–14.

Axtell, Robert L. 1999. "The emergence of firms in a population of agents: Local increasing returns, unstable Nash equilibria, and power law size distributions." Santa Fe Institute Working Paper No. 99-03-019.

Axtell, Robert L. 2001. "Zipf distribution of U.S. firm sizes." *Science in Context* 293: 1818–20.

Bachelier, Louis. 1900. "Théorie de la spéculation." *Annales de l'Ecole Normale Supérieure*, 3rd ser. 17 (January): 21–86. Reprint, 1995, J. Gabay, Paris.

Bachelier, Louis. 1901. "Théorie mathématique du jeu." *Annales de l'Ecole Normale Supérieure*, 3rd ser. 18 (January): 77–119. Reprint, 1995, J. Gabay, Paris.

Bachelier, Louis. 1910. "Les probabilités à plusieurs variables." *Annales Scientifiques de l'École Normale Supérieure* 339–60.

Bachelier, Louis. 1912. *Calcul des probabilités*. Paris: Gauthier-Villars.

Backhouse, Roger E. 2004. "A suggestion for clarifying the study of dissent in economics." *Journal of the History of Economic Thought* 26 (2): 261–71.

Bagehot, Walter (pseudonym used by Jack Treynor). 1971. "The only game in town." *Financial Analysts Journal* 8: 31–53.

Bak, Per. 1994. "Introduction to self-criticality." In *Complexity: Metaphors, Models, and Reality*, edited by G. Cowan, D. Pines, and D. Meltzer, 476–82. Santa Fe: Santa Fe Institute.

Bak, Per, Kan Chen, José Sheinkman, and Michael Woodford. 1993. "Aggregate fluctuations from independent sectorial shocks: Self-organized criticality in a model of production and inventory dynamics." *Ricerche Economische* 47 (1): 3–30.

Bak, Per, Maya Paczuski, and Martin Shubik. 1997. "Price variations in a stock market with many agents." *Physica A* 246 (3–4): 430–53.

Bak, Per, Chao Tang, and Kurt Wiesenfeld. 1987. "Self-organized criticality: An explanation of 1/f noise." *Physical Review Letters* 59 (4): 381–84.

Bak, Per, Chao Tang, and Kurt Wiesenfeld. 1988. "Self-organized criticality." *Physical Review A* 38 (1): 364–74.

Banerjee, Abhijit V. 1993. "The economics of rumors." *Review of Economic Studies* 60 (2): 309–27.

Banz, Rolf W. 1981. "The relationship between return and market value of common stocks." *Journal of Financial Economics* 9 (1): 3–18.

Banzhaf, H. Spencer. 2001. "Quantifying the qualitative: Quality-adjusted price indexes in the United States, 1915–61." In *History of Political Economy*, annual supplement, *The Age of Economic Measurement*, edited by Judy L. Klein and Mary S. Morgan, 345–70. Durham, NC: Duke University Press.

Barbut, Marc. 2003. "Homme moyen ou homme extrême? De Vilfredo Pareto (1896) à Paul Lévy (1936) en passant par Maurice Fréchet et quelques autres." *Journal de la Société Française de la Statistique* 144 (1–2): 113–33.

Barnett, Vincent. 2011. *E. E. Slutsky as Economist and Mathematician: Crossing the Limits of Knowledge*. London: Routledge.

Bartolozzi, Marco, and Anthony William Thomas. 2004. "Stochastic cellular automata model for stock market dynamics." *Physical Review E* 4: 46–69.

Bassler, Kevin E., Joseph L. McCauley, and Gemunu H. Gunaratne. 2007. "Nonstationary increments, scaling distributions, and variable diffusion processes in financial markets." *Proceedings of the National Academy of Sciences of the United States of America* 104 (44): 17287–290. doi: 10.1073/pnas.0708664104.

Batterman, Robert W. 2002. *The Devil in the Details: Asymptotic Reasoning in Explanation, Reduction and Emergence*. New York: Oxford University Press.

Bauwens, Luc, Sébastien Laurent, and Jeroen V. K. Rombouts. 2006. "Multivariate Garch models: A survey." *Journal of Applied Econometrics* 21 (1): 79–109.

Bayeux-Besnainou, Isabelle, and Jean-Charles Rochet. 1996. "Dynamic Spanning: Are Options an Appropriate Instrument?" *Mathematical Finance*, 6 (1): 1–16.

Bazerman, Charles. 1988. *Shaping Written Knowledge: The Genre and Activity of the Experimental Articles in Science*. Madison: University of Wisconsin Press.

Bee, Marco, Massimo Riccaboni, and Stefano Schiavo. 2011. "Pareto versus lognormal: A maximum entropy test." *Physical Review E* 84 (2): 026104.

Ben-El-Mechaiekh, Hichem, and Robert W. Dimand. 2006. "Louis Bachelier." In *Pioneers of Financial Economics*, vol. 1: *Contributions Prior to Irving Fisher*, edited by Geoffrey Poitras, 225–37. Cheltenham: Edward Elgar.

Ben-El-Mechaiekh, Hichem, and Robert W. Dimand. 2008. "Louis Bachelier's 1938 volume on the calculus of speculation: Efficient markets and mathematical finance in Bachelier's later work." Working paper.

Bernstein, Peter L. 1992. *Capital Ideas: The Improbable Origins of Modern Wall Street*. New York: Free Press; Toronto: Maxwell Macmillan Canada.

Bernstein, Peter L. 2007. *Capital Ideas Evolving*. Hoboken, NJ: John Wiley & Sons.

Berry, Brian J. L., and Adam Okulicz-Kozaryn. 2012. "The city size distribution debate: Resolution for US urban regions and megalopolitan areas." *Cities* 29 (supplement 1): S17–S23.

Biais, Bruno, Larry Glosten, and Chester Spatt. 2005. "Market microstructure: A survey of microfoundations, empirical results, and policy implications." *Journal of Financial Markets* 8 (2): 217–64.

Binney, James, N. J. Dowrick, Andrew J. Fisher, and Mark E. J. Newman. 1992. *The Theory of Critical Phenomena: An Introduction to the Renormalization Group*. Oxford: Clarendon Press.

Black, Fischer. 1971a. "Toward a fully automated stock exchange (part 1)." *Financial Analysts Journal* 27 (4): 28–35, 44.

Black, Fischer. 1971b. "Toward a fully automated stock exchange (part 2)." *Financial Analysts Journal* 27 (6): 24–28, 86–87.

Black, Fischer. 1986. "Noise." *Journal of Finance* 41 (3): 529–43.

Black, Fischer, and Myron Scholes. 1973. "The pricing of options and corporate liabilities." *Journal of Political Economy* 81 (3): 637–54.

Blank, Aharon, and Sorin Solomon. 2000. "Power laws in cities population, financial markets and internet sites (scaling in systems with a variable number of components)." *Physica A* 287 (1–2): 279–88.

Blattberg, Robert, and Nicholas Gonedes. 1974. "A comparison of the stable and Student distributions as statistical models for stock prices: Reply." *Journal of Business* 47 (2): 244–80.

Blattberg, Robert, and Thomas Sargent. 1971. "Regression with non-Gaussian stable disturbances: Some sampling results." *Econometrica* 39 (3): 501–10.

Blume, Lawrence E., and Steven N. Durlauf, eds. 2006. *The Economy as an Evolving Complex System III: Current Perspectives and Future Directions*. New York: Oxford University Press.

Blume, Marshall. 1968. "The assessment of portfolio performance: An application of portfolio theory." Doctoral dissertation, University of Chicago.

Bollerslev, Tim. 1986. "Generalized autoregressive conditional heteroskedasticity." *Journal of Econometrics* 31: 307–27.

Bollerslev, Tim. 2010. "Glossary to ARCH (GARCH)." In *Volatility and Time Series Econometrics: Essays in Honour of Robert F. Engle*, edited by Tim Bollerslev, Jeffrey R. Russell, and Mark W. Watson, 137–64. New York: Oxford University Press.

Borak, Szymon, Wolfgang Hardle, and Rafal Weron. 2005. "Stable distributions." SFB Working Paper, Humboldt University Berlin.

Bormetti, Giacomo, Enrica Cisana, Guido Montagna, and Oreste Nicrosini. 2007. "A non-Gaussian approach to risk measures." *Physica A* 376: 532–42.

Bouchaud, Jean-Philippe. 2001. "Power laws in economics and finance: Some ideas from physics." *Quantitative Finance* 1 (1): 105–12.

Bouchaud, Jean-Philippe. 2002. "An Introduction to statistical finance." *Physica A* 313 (1): 238–51.

Bouchaud, Jean-Philippe, and Damien Challet. 2014. "Behavioral finance and financial markets: Arbitrage techniques, exuberant behaviors and volatility." *Opinion et débats* 7: 20–35.

Bouchaud, Jean-Philippe, Doyne Farmer, and Fabrizio Lillo. 2009. "How markets slowly digest changes in supply and demand." In *Handbook of Financial Markets: Dynamics and Evolution*, edited by Thorsten Hens and Klaus Reiner Schenk-Hoppe, 57–160. Amsterdam: North-Holland, Elsevier.

Bouchaud, Jean-Philippe, Marc Mezard, and Marc Potters. 2002. "Statistical properties of stock order books: Empirical results and models." *Quantitative Finance* 2: 251–56.

Bouchaud, Jean-Philippe, and Marc Potters. 2000. *Theory of Financial Risks: From Statistical Physics to Risk Management*. Cambridge: Cambridge University Press.

Bouchaud, Jean-Philippe, and Marc Potters. 2003. *Theory of Financial Risk and Derivate Pricing*. Cambridge: Cambridge University Press.

Bouchaud, Jean-Philippe, and Didier Sornette. 1994. "The Black-Scholes option pricing problem in mathematical finance: Generalisation and extension to a large class of stochastic processes." *Journal de Physique I* 4: 863–81.

Boumans, Marcel, ed. 2007. *Measurement in Economics: A Handbook*. London: Elsevier.

Bouzoubaa, Mohamed, and Adel Osseiran. 2010. *Exotic Options and Hybrids: A Guide to Structuring, Pricing and Trading*. London: John Wiley & Sons.

Bowley, Arthur Lyon. 1933. "The action of economic forces in producing frequency distributions of income, prices, and other phenomena: A suggestion for study." *Econometrica* 1 (4): 358–72.

Boyarchenko, Svetlana I., and Sergei Z. Levendorskiĭ. 2000. "Option pricing for truncated Lévy processes." *International Journal of Theoretical and Applied Finance* 3 (3): 549–52.

Boyarchenko, Svetlana I., and Sergei Z. Levendorskiĭ. 2002. "Barrier options and touch-and-out options under regular Lévy processes of exponential type." *Annals of Applied Probability* 12 (4): 1261–98.

Brada, Josef, Harry Ernst, and John van Tassel. 1966. "The distribution of stock price differences: Gaussian after all?" *Operations Research* 14 (2): 334–40.

Brakman, Steven, Harry Garretsen, Charles Van Marrewijk, and Marianne van den Berg. 1999. "The return of Zipf: Towards a further understanding of the rank-size distribution." *Journal of Regional Science* 39: 183–213.

Breidt, F. Jay, Nuno Crato, and Pedro de Lima. 1998. "On the detection and estimation of long memory in stochastic volatility." *Journal of Econometrics* 83: 325–48.

Brenner, Menachem. 1974. "On the stability of distribution of the market component in stock price changes." *Journal of Financial and Quantitative Analysis* 9: 945–61.

Brenner, Thomas. 2001. "Self-organisation, local symbiosis of firms and the life cycle of localised industrial clusters." Papers on Economics and Evolution, Max Planck Institute of Economics, Jena.

Breton, Yves. 1991. "Les économistes français et les questions de méthode." In *L'Economie Politique en France au XIXe Siècle*, edited by Yves Breton and Michel Lutfalla, 389–419. Paris: Economica.

Broda, Simon A., Markus Haas, Jochen Krause, Marc S. Paolella, and Sven C. Steude. 2013. "Stable mixture GARCH models." *Journal of Econometrics* 172 (2): 292–306.

Brody, Samuel. 1945. *Bioenergetics and Growth*. New York: Reinhold.

Bronzin, Vinzenz. 1908 "Theory of Premium Contracts." In *Vinzenz Bronzin's Option Pricing Models: Exposition and Appraisal*, edited by Wolfgang Hafner and Heinz Zimmermann. 2009. Berlin: Springer, 113–200.

Brown, Stephen J., William N. Goetzmann, and Alok Kumar. 1998. "The Dow theory: William Peter Hamilton's track record reconsidered." *Journal of Finance* 53 (4): 1311–33.

Buchanan, Mark. 2004. "Power law and the new science of complexity management." *Strategy + Business* 34: 104–7.

Bucsa, Gigel, Emmanuel Haven, Franck Jovanovic, and Christophe Schinckus. 2014. "The practical use of the general formula of the optimal hedge ratio in option pricing: An example of the generalized model of an exponentially truncated Levy stable distribution." *Theoretical Economics Letters* 4 (9): 760–66.

Cai, Wei, Melvin Lax, and Min Xu. 2006. *Random Processes in Physics and Finance*. Oxford: Oxford University Press.

Calvo, Iván, Juan C. Cuchí, José G. Esteve, and Fernando Falceto. 2010. "Generalized central limit theorem and renormalization group." *Journal of Statistical Physics* 141: 409–21.

Carbone, Anna, Giorgio Kaniadakis, and Antonio Maria Scarfone. 2007. "Where do we stand on econophysics." *Physica A* 382: 11–14.

Carr, Peter, Hélyette Geman, Dilip Madan, and Marc Yor. 2002. "The fine structure of asset returns: An empirical investigation." *Journal of Business* 75: 305–32.

Carr, Peter, and Dilip B. Madan. 2005. "A note on sufficient conditions for no arbitrage." *Finance Research Letters* 2 (3): 125–30.

Cartwright, Nancy. 1983. *How the Laws of Physics Lie*. Oxford: Oxford University Press.

Casey, Michael. 2013. "Move over economists, markets need physicists." *Market Watch Magazine*, July 10.

Cassidy, David. 2011. *A Short History of Physics in the American Century*. Cambridge: Harvard University Press.

Cerqueti, Roy, and Marcel Ausloos. 2015. "Evidence of economic regularities and disparities of Italian regions from aggregated tax income size data." *Physica A: Statistical Mechanics and Its Applications* 421: 187–207.

Chaigneau, Nicolas, and Philippe Le Gall. 1998. "The French connection: The pioneering econometrics of Marcel Lenoir (1913)." In *European Economists of the Early 20th Century*, vol. 1: *Studies of Neglected Thinkers of Belgium, France, the Netherlands and Scandinavia*, edited by Warren J. Samuels, 163–89. Cheltenham: Edward Elgar.

Chakrabarti, Bikas K., and Anirban Chakraborti. 2010. "Fifteen years of econophysics research." *Science and Culture* 76: 9–10.

Chakrabarti, Bikas K., Anirban Chakraborti, and Arnab Chatterjee. 2006. *Econophysics and Sociophysics: Trends and Perspectives*. Weinheim: Wiley-VCH.

Chakraborti, Anirban, Ioane Muni Toke, Marco Patriarca, and Frédéric Abergel. 2011a. "Econophysics review: I. Empirical facts." *Quantitative Finance* 11 (7): 991–1012.

Chakraborti, Anirban, Ioane Muni Toke, Marco Patriarca, and Frédéric Abergel. 2011b. "Econophysics review: II. Agent-based models." *Quantitative Finance* 11 (7): 1013–41.

Challet, Damien, Mateo Marsili, and Yi Cheng Zhang. 2005. *Minority Games: Interacting Agents in Financial Markets*. Oxford: Oxford University Press.

Challet, Damien, and Robin Stinchcombe. 2001. "Analyzing and modeling 1+1d markets." *Physica A* 300 (1–2): 285–99.

Champernowne, David Gawen. 1953. "A model of income distribution." *Economic Journal* 63: 318–51.

Chancelier, Éric. 2006a. "L'analyse des baromètres économiques de Persons et Wagemann: Instrument de prévision—instrument de théorisation, 1919–1932." *Revue d'Économie Politique* 116 (5): 613–32.

Chancelier, Éric. 2006b. "Les premiers baromètres économiques américains (1990–1919)." *Revue d'Histoire des Sciences Humaines* 15 (2): 135–55.

Chane-Alune, Elena. 2006. "Accounting standardization and governance structures." Working Paper No. 0609, University of Liège.

Chari, V. V., Patrick J. Kehoe, and Ellen R. McGrattan. 2008. "Are structural VARs with long-run restrictions useful in developing business cycle theory?" *Journal of Monetary Economics* 55 (8): 1337–52.

Chari, V. V., Patrick J. Kehoe, and Ellen R. McGrattan. 2009. "New Keynesian models: Not yet useful for policy analysis." *American Economic Journal: Macroeconomics* 1 (1): 242–66.

Chen, Shu-heng, and Sai-ping Li. 2012. "Econophysics: Bridges over a turbulent current." *International Review of Financial Analysis* 23: 1–10. doi: 10.1016/j.irfa.2011.07.001.

Chen, Shu-Heng, Thomas Lux, and Michele Marchesi. 2001. "Testing for non-linear structure in an artificial financial market." *Journal of Economic Behavior and Organization* 46 (3): 327–42.

Chen, X., H. Anderson, and P. Barker. 2008. "Kuhn's theory of scientific revolutions and cognitive psychology." *Philosophical Psychology* 11 (1): 5–28.

Chiarella, Carl, and Giulia Iori. 2002. "A Simulation analysis of the microstructure of double auction markets." *Quantitative Finance* 2 (5): 346–53.

Chiarella, Carl, Giulia Iori, and Josep Perello. 2009. "The impact of heterogeneous trading rules on the limit order book and order flows." *Journal of Economic Dynamics and Control* 33: 525–37.

Chrisman, Nicholas. 1999. "Trading Zones or Boundary Objects: Understanding Incomplete Translations of Technical Expertise." San Diego.

Christ, Carl F. 1994. "The Cowles Commission's contributions to econometrics at Chicago, 1939–1955." *Journal of Economic Literature* 32 (March): 30–59.

Christiano, Lawrence J. 2012. "Christopher A. Sims and vector autoregressions." *Scandinavian Journal of Economics* 114 (4): 1082–104.

Clark, Peter K. 1973. "A Subordinated stochastic process with finite variance for speculative prices." *Econometrica* 41 (1): 135–55.

Clauset, Aaron. 2011. *Inference, Models and Simulation for Complex Systems*. Lecture 3. in, Santa Fe, http://tuvalu.santafe.edu/~aaronc/courses/7000/csci7000-001_2011_L3.pdf

Clauset, Aaron, Cosma Rohilla Shalizi, and Mark Newman. 2009. "Power-law distributions in empirical data." *SIAM Review* 51 (4): 661–703.

Clementi, Fabio, Tiziana Di Matteo, and Mauro Gallegati. 2006. "The power-law tail exponent of income distributions." *Physica A* 370 (1): 49–53.

Clippe, Paulette, and Marcel Ausloos. 2012. "Benford's law and Theil transform of financial data." *Physica A: Statistical Mechanics and Its Applications* 391 (24): 6556.

Cohen, I. Bernard. 1993. "Analogy, homology and metaphor in the interactions between the natural sciences and the social sciences, especially economics." In *Non-natural Social Science: Reflecting on the Enterprise of "More Heat Than Light"*, edited by Neil De Marchi, 7–44. Durham, NC: Duke University Press.

Cohen, Kalman J., and Jerry A. Pogue. 1967. "An empirique evaluation of alternative portfolio-selection models." *Journal of Business* 40 (2): 166–93.

Condon, E. U. 1928. "Statistics of vocabulary." *Science* 67 (1733): 300.

Cont, Rama, and Jean-Philippe Bouchaud. 2000. "Herd behavior and aggregate fluctuations in financial markets." *Macroeconomic Dynamics* 4 (2): 170–96.

Cont, Rama, Marc Potters, and Jean-Philippe Bouchaud. 1997. "Scaling in stock market data: Stable laws and beyond." In *Scale Invariance and Beyond: Les Houches Workshop, March 10–14, 1997*, edited by B. Dubrulle, F. Graner, and D. Sornette, 75–85. New York: Springer.

Cont, Rama, and Peter Tankov. 2004a. *Financial Modelling with Jump Processes*. London: Chapman & Hall/CRC.

Cont, Rama, and Peter Tankov. 2004b. "Non-parametric calibration of jump-diffusion option pricing models." *Journal of Computational Finance* 7 (3): 1–49.

Cootner, Paul H. 1962. "Stock prices: Random vs. systematic changes." *Industrial Management Review* 3 (2): 24.

Cootner, Paul H. 1964. *The Random Character of Stock Market Prices*. Cambridge, MA: MIT Press.

Copeland, Thomas E., and Dan Galai. 1983. "Information effects and the bid-ask spread." *Journal of Finance* 38 (5): 1457–69.

Cordoba, J. 2008. "On the distribution of city sizes." *Journal of Urban Economics* 63: 177–97.

Cornelis, A. Los. 2005. "Why VAR fails: Long memory and extreme events in financial markets." *Journal of Financial Economics* 3 (3): 19–36.

Courtadon, Georges. 1982. "A note on the premium market of the Paris stock exchange." *Journal of Banking and Finance* 6 (4): 561–65.

Courtault, Jean-Michel, Youri Kabanov, Bernard Bru, Pierre Crépel, Isabelle Lebon, and Arnaud Le Marchand. 2002. "Louis Bachelier on the centenary of *Théorie de la spéculation*." In *Louis Bachelier: Aux origines de la finance mathématique*, edited by Jean-Michel Courtault and Youri Kabanov, 5–86. Besançon: Presses Universitaires Franc-Comtoises.

Cover, John H. 1937. "Some investigations in the Sampling and Distribution of Retail Prices." *Econometrica* 5 (3): 263–79.

Cowles, Alfred. 1933. "Can stock market forecasters forecast?" *Econometrica* 1 (3): 309–24.

Cowles, Alfred. 1944. "Stock market forecasting." *Econometrica* 12 (3/4): 206–14.

Cowles, Alfred. 1960. "A revision of previous conclusions regarding stock price behavior." *Econometrica* 28 (4): 909–15.

Cowles, Alfred, and Herbert E. Jones. 1937. "Some a posteriori probabilities in stock market action." *Econometrica* 5 (3): 280–94.

Cox, John C., and Stephen Ross. 1976. "The valuation of options for alternative stochastic processes." *Journal of Financial Economics* 3 (1-2): 145–66.

Cramer, Harald. 1983. "Probabilité mathématique et inférence statistique: Quelques souvenirs personnels sur une importante étape du progrès scientifique." *Revue de Statistique Appliquée* 31 (3): 5–15.

Cristelli, Matthieu. 2014. *Complexity in Financial Markets: Modeling Psychological Behavior in Agent-Based Models and Order Book Models*. Milan: Springer.

Csorgor, S., and G. Simons. 1983. "On the Steinhpaus's resolution of the St-Petersburg Paradox." *Probability and Mathematical Statistics* 14: 157–71.

Cuoco, Domenico, and Eugenio Barone. 1989. "The Italian market for 'premium' contracts: An application of option pricing theory." *Journal of Banking and Finance* 13 (4): 709–45.

Daemen, Job. 2010. "Ketchup economics: What is finance about?" Presented at the 14th Annual Conference of the European Society for the History of Economic Thought, Amsterdam, March.

Davis, Mark, and Alison Etheridge. 2006. *Louis Bachelier's Theory of Speculation*. Princeton, NJ: Princeton University Press.

De Bondt, Werner F. M., and Richard Thaler. 1985. "Does the stock market overreact?" *Journal of Finance* 40 (3): 793–805.

De Meyer, Bernard, and Hadiza Moussa Saley. 2003. "On the strategic origin of Brownian motion in finance." *International Journal of Game Theory* 31: 285–319.

De Vroey, Michel, and Pierre Malgrange. 2007. "Théorie et modélisation macro- économiques, d'hier à aujourd'hui." *Revue Française D'économie* 21 (3): 3–38.

Debreu, Gérard. 1959. *Theory of Value*. New Haven: Yale University Press.

Demsetz, Harold. 1968. "The cost of transacting." *Quarterly Journal of Economics* 82: 33–53.

Derman, Emanuel. 2001. "A guide for the perplexed quant." *Quantitative Finance* 1 (5): 476–80.

Derman, Emanuel. 2009. "Models." *Financial Analysts Journal* 65 (1): 28–33

Diewert, W. Erwin. 1993. "The early history of price index research." In *Essays in Index Number Theory*, vol. 1, edited by W. Erwin Diewert and Alice O. Nakamura, 33–65. Amsterdam: North Holland.

Dimand, Robert W. 2007. "Irving Fisher and financial economics: The equity premium puzzle, the predictability of stock prices, and intertemporal allocation under risk." *Journal of the History of Economic Thought* 29 (2): 153–66. doi: 10.1080/10427710701335885.

Dimand, Robert W. 2009. "The Cowles Commission and Foundation on the functioning of financial markets from Irving Fisher and Alfred Cowles to Harry Markowitz and James Tobin." *Revue d'Histoire des Sciences Humaines* 20: 109–30.

Dimand, Robert W., and John Geanakoplos, eds. 2005. *Celebrating Irving Fisher: The Legacy of a Great Economist*. Malden, MA: Blackwell.

Dimand, Robert W., and William Veloce. 2010. "Alfred Cowles and Robert Rhea on the predictability of stock prices." *Journal of Business Inquiry* 9 (1): 56–64.

Ding, E-Jiang. 1983. "Asymptotic properties of the Markovian master equations for multi-stationary systems." *Physica A* 119: 317–26.

Ding, Zhuanxin, Robert F. Enlge, and Clive W. J. Granger. 1993. "A long memory property of stock market returns and a new model." *Journal of Empirical Finance* 1 (1): 83–106.

Dionisio, Andreia, Rui Menezes, and Diana A. Mendes. 2006. "An econophysics approach to analyse uncertainty in financial markets: An application to the Portuguese stock market." *European Physical Journal B* 50 (1): 161–64.

Domb, Cyril, and D. Hunter. 1965. "On the critical behaviour of ferromagnets." *Proceedings of the Physical Society* 86: 1147.

Donangelo, Raul, and Kim Sneppen. 2000. "Self-organization of value and demand." *Physica A* 276: 572–80.

Donnelly, Kevin. 2015. *Adolphe Quetelet, Social Physics and the Average Men of Science, 1796–1874*. New York: Routledge.

Doob, Joseph L. 1953. *Stochastic Process*. New York: John Wiley & Sons.

Dow, James, and Gary Gorton. 2008. "Noise traders." In *The New Palgrave: A Dictionary of Economics*, 2nd ed., edited by Steven N. Durlauf and Lawrence E. Blume. New York: Palgrave Macmillan.

Dubkov, Alexander A., Bernardo Spagnolo, and Vladimir V. Uchaikin. 2008. "Lévy flight superdiffusion: An introduction." *International Journal of Bifurcation and Chaos* 18 (9): 2649–72.

Dunbar, Frederick C., and Dana Heller. 2006. "Fraud on the market meets behavioral finance." *Delaware Journal of Corporate Law* 31 (2): 455–532.

Dunbar, Nicholas. 2000. *Inventing Money: The Story of Long-Term Capital Management and the Legends behind It.* New York: Wiley.

Dupoyet, Brice, Rudolf H. Fiebig, and David P. Musrgrove. 2011. "Replicating financial market dynamics with a simple self-organized critical lattice model." *Physica A* 390: 3120–35.

Durlauf, Steven N. 2005. "Complexity and empirical economics." *Economic Journal* 115: F225–F243.

Durlauf, Steven N. 2012. "Complexity, economics, and public policy." *Politics Philosophy Economics* 11 (1): 45–75.

Eberlein, Ernst, and Ullrich Keller. 1995. "Hyperbolic distributions in finance." *Bernouilli* 1: 281–99.

Edlinger, Cécile, and Antoine Parent. 2014. "The beginnings of a 'common-sense' approach to portfolio theory by nineteenth-century French financial analysts Paul Leroy-Beaulieu and Alfred Neymarck." *Journal of the History of Economic Thought* 36 (1): 23–44.

Eeckhout, Jan. 2004. "Gibrat's law for (all) cities." *American Economic Review* 94 (1): 1429–51.

Eguíluz, Victor M., and Martin G. Zimmermann. 2000. "Transmission of information and herd behavior: An application to financial markets." *Physical Review Letters* 85 (26): 5659–62.

Eichenbaum, Martin. 1996. "Some comments on the role of econometrics in economic theory." *Economic Perspectives* 20 (1): 22.

Einstein, Albert. 1905. "Uber die von der molekularkinetischen Theorie der Wärme geforderte Bewegung von in ruhenden Flüssigkeiten suspendierten Teilchen." *Annalen der Physik* 17: 549–60.

Embrechts, Paul, Claudia Klüppelberg, and Thomas Mikosch. 1997a. *Modelling Extremal Events: For Insurance and Finance.* New York: Springer.

Embrechts, Paul, Claudia Klüppelberg, and Thomas Mikosch. 1997b. *Modelling Extreme Values.* Berlin: Springer.

Engle, Robert F., and Jeffrey R. Russell. 2004. "Analysis of high frequency financial data." In *Handbook of Financial Econometrics: Tools and Techniques*, edited by Yacine Ait-Sahalia and Lars Hansen, 383–426. Amsterdam: Elsevier.

Engle, Robert F. 1982. "Autoregressive conditional heteroskedasticity with estimates of the variance of United Kingdom inflation." *Econometrica* 50: 987–1007.

Epstein, Joshua M. 2006. *Generative Social Science: Studies in Agent-Based Computational Modeling.* Princeton, NJ: Princeton University Press.

Epstein, Joshua M., and Robert L. Axtell. 1996. *Growing Artificial Societies: Social Science from the Bottom Up.* Cambridge, MA: MIT Press.

Estoup, Jean-Baptiste. 1916. *Gammes sténographique.* Paris: Institut Sténographique.

Fama, Eugene F. 1963. "Mandelbrot and the stable Paretian hypothesis." *Journal of Business* 36 (4): 420–29.

Fama, Eugene F. 1965a. "The behavior of stock-market prices." *Journal of Business* 38 (1): 34–105.

Fama, Eugene F. 1965b. "Portfolio analysis in a stable Paretian market." *Management Science Series A: Sciences* 11 (3): 404–19.

Fama, Eugene F. 1965c. "Random walks in stock-market prices." *Financial Analysts Journal* 21 (5): 55–59.

Fama, Eugene F. 1970. "Efficient capital markets: A review of theory and empirical work." *Journal of Finance* 25 (2): 383–417.

Fama, Eugene F. 1976a. "Efficient capital markets: Reply." *Journal of Finance* 31 (1): 143–45.

Fama, Eugene F. 1976b. *Foundations of Finance: Portfolio Decisions and Securities Prices.* New York: Basic Books.

Fama, Eugene F. 1991. "Efficient capital markets: II." *Journal of Finance* 46 (5): 1575–617.

Fama, Eugene F. 2008. "Interview with Professor Eugene Fama by Professor Richard Roll." August 15.

Fama, Eugene F., Lawrence Fisher, Michael C. Jensen, and Richard Roll. 1969. "The Adjustment of Stock Prices to New Information." *International Economic Review* 10 (1): 1–21.

Fama, Eugene F., and Kenneth French. 2004. "Capital asset pricing model: Theory and evidence." *Journal of Economic Perspective* 18 (3): 25–36.

Fama, Eugene F., and Richard Roll. 1968. "Some properties of symmetric stable distributions." *Journal of the American Statistical Association* 63 (323): 817–36.

Fama, Eugene F., and Richard Roll. 1971. "Parameter estimates for symmetric stable distributions." *Journal of the American Statistical Association* 66 (334): 331–38.

Farmer, J. Doyne, and Duncan Foley. 2009. "The economy needs agent-based modelling." *Nature* 460: 685–86.

Farmer, J. Doyne, and John Geanakoplos. 2008. "Power laws in economics and elsewhere." Working paper.

Farmer, J. Doyne, and John Geanakoplos. 2009. "The Virtues and Vices of Equilibrium, and the Future of Financial Economics." Working paper, Cowles Foundation.

Farmer, J. Doyne, Laszlo Gillemot, Fabrizio Lillo, Szabols Mike, and Anindya Sen. 2004. "What really causes large price changes?" *Quantitative Finance* 4: 383–97.

Farmer, J. Doyne, and Fabrizio Lillo. 2004. "On the origin of power law tails in price fluctuations." *Quantitative Finance* 4 (1): 7–11.

Farmer, J. Doyne, and Thomas Lux. 2008. "Introduction to special issue on 'Applications of Statistical Physics in Economics and Finance.'" *Journal of Economic Dynamics and Control* 32 (1): 1–6.

Farmer, J. Doyne, Paolo Patelli, Ilija I. Zovko, and Kenneth J. Arrow. 2005. "The predictive power of zero intelligence in financial markets." *Proceedings of the National Academy of Sciences of the United States of America* 102 (6): 2254–59.

Fayyad, U. 1996. "Data mining and knowledge discovery: Making sense out of data." *Intelligent Systems* 11 (5): 20–25.

Feigenbaum, James A., and Peter G. O. Freund. 1996. "Discrete scale invariance in stock markets before crashes." *International Journal of Modern Physics B* 10 (27): 3737–45.

Feigenbaum, James A., and Peter G. O. Freund. 1998. "Discrete scale invariance and the 'second Black Monday.'" *Modern Physics Letters B* 12 (3): 57–60.

Feller, William. 1957. *An Introduction to Probability Theory and Its Applications.* Vol. 1. New York: Wiley.

Feller, William. 1971. *An Introduction to Probability Theory and Its Applications,* Vol. 2. New York: Wiley.

Figueiredo, Annibal, Raul Matsushita, Sergio Da Silva, Maurizio Serva, Ganghi Viswanathan, Cesar Nasciment, and Iram Gleria. 2007. "The Lévy sections theorem: An application to econophysics." *Physica A* 386 (2): 756–59.

Fisher, Irving. 1911. *The Purchasing Power of Money*. London: Macmillan.

Fisher, Irving. 1922. *The Making of Index Numbers: A Study of Their Varieties, Tests, and Reliability*. Boston: Houghton Mifflin.

Fisher, Irving. 1930. *The Theory of Interest as Determined by Impatience to Spend Income and Opportunity to Invest It*. New York: Macmillan.

Fisher, Lawrence, and James H. Lorie. 1964. "Rates of return on investments in common stocks." *Journal of Business* 37 (1): 1–21.

Fisher, Mark. 1967. "The theory of equilibrium critical phenomena." *Reports on Progress in Physics* 30: 615–730.

Fitzpatrick, Richard. 2012. "Thermodynamics and statistical mechanics: An intermediate level course."

Focardi, Sergio, Silvano Cincotti, and Michele Marchesi. 2002. "Self-organization and market crashes." *Journal of Economic Behavior and Organization* 49 (2): 241–67.

Fourcade, Marion, and Rakesh Khurana. 2009. "From social control to financial economics: The linked ecologies of economics and business in twentieth-century America." Presented to the Annual Meeting of the SASE, Paris.

Francq, Christian, and Jean-Michel Zakoian. 2010. *GARCH Models: Structure, Statistical Inference and Financial Applications*. London: Wiley.

Frankfurter, George M., and Elton G. McGoun. 1999. "Ideology and the theory of financial economics." *Journal of Economic Behavior and Organization* 39: 159–77.

Franzen, Dorothee. 2010. "Managing investment risk in defined benefit pension funds." OECD Working Papers on Insurance and Private Pensions.

Friedman, Walter A. 2009. "The Harvard Economic Service and the problems of forecasting." *History of Political Economy* 41 (1): 57–88.

Frigg, R. 2003. "Self-organised criticality: What it is and what it isn't." *Studies in the History and Philosophy of Science Part A* 34 (3): 613–32.

Fujimoto, Shouji, Atushi Ishikawa, Takayuki Mizuno, and Tsutomu Watanabe. 2011. "A new method for measuring tail exponents of firm size distributions." *Economics* 5 (2011–20): 1. doi: 10.5018/economics-ejournal.ja.2011-20.

Gabaix, Xavier. 1999. "Zipf's law for cities: An explanation." *Quarterly Journal of Economics* 114: 739–67.

Gabaix, Xavier. 2009. "Power laws in economics and finance." *Annual Review of Economics* 1: 255–93.

Gabaix, Xavier, Parameswaran Gopikrishnan, Vasiliki Plerou, and H. Eugene Stanley. 2000. "Statistical properties of share volume traded in financial markets." *Physical Review E* 62 (4): R4493–R4496.

Gabaix, Xavier, Parameswaran Gopikrishnan, Vasiliki Plerou, and H. Eugene Stanley. 2003. "A theory of power law distributions in financial market fluctuations." *Nature* 423: 267–70.

Gabaix, Xavier, Parameswaran Gopikrishnan, Vasiliki Plerou, and H. Eugene Stanley. 2006. "Institutional investors and stock market volatility." *Quarterly Journal of Economics* 121: 461–504.

Gabaix, Xavier, Parameswaran Gopikrishnan, Vasiliki Plerou, and H. Eugene Stanley. 2007. "A unified econophysics explanation for the power-law exponents of stock market activity." *Physica A* 382: 81–88.

Gabaix, Xavier, and Rustam Ibragimov. 2011. "Rank—1 / 2: A simple way to improve the OLS estimation of tail exponents." *Journal of Business and Economic Statistics* 29 (1): 24–39.

Gabaix, Xavier, and A. Landier. 2008. "Why has CEO pay increased so much?" *Quarterly Journal of Economics* 123: 49–100.

Galam, Serge. 2004. "Sociophysics: A personal testimony." *Physica A* 336 (2): 49–55.

Galam, Serge. 2008. "Sociophysics: A review of Galam models." arXiv:0803.1800v1.

Galam, Serge, Yuval Gefen, and Yonathan Shapir. 1982. "Sociophysics: A mean behavior model for the process of strike." *Journal of Mathematical Sociology* 9 (2): 1–13.

Galison, Peter. 1997. *Image and logic: A Material Culture of Microphysics*. Chicago: University of Chicago Press.

Gallais-Hamonno, Georges, ed. 2007. *Le marché financier français au XIXe siècle*. Vol. 2. Paris: Publications de la Sorbonne.

Gallegati, Mauro. 1990. "Financial instability, income distribution and the stock market." *Journal of Post Keynesian Economics* 12 (3): 356–74.

Gallegati, Mauro. 1994. "Composition effect and economic fluctuations." *Economics Letters* 44 (1–2): 123–26.

Gallegati, Mauro, and Marco Dardi. 1992. "Alfred Marshall on speculation." *History of Political Economy* 24 (3): 571–94.

Gallegati, Mauro, Steve Keen, Thomas Lux, and Paul Ormerod. 2006. "Worrying trends in econophysics." *Physica A* 370 (1): 1–6.

Garman, Mark. 1976. "Market microstructure." *Journal of Financial Economics* 3: 257–75.

Gaussel, Nicolas, and Jérôme Legras. 1999. "Black-Scholes ... what's next?" *Quants* 35: 1–33.

Geman, Hélyette. 2002. "Pure jump Lévy processes for asset price modelling." *Journal of Banking and Finance* 26 (7): 1297–316.

Geraskin, Petr, and Dean Fantazzini. 2011. "Everything you always wanted to know about log-periodic power laws for bubble modeling but were afraid to ask." *The European Journal of Finance* 19 (5): 1–26.

Gibrat, Robert. 1931. *Les inégalités économiques*. Paris: Librairie du Recueil.

Gilbert, G. Nigel. 2007. *Agent Based Models*. London: Sage.

Gilbert, G. Nigel, and Michael Mulkay. 1984. *Opening Pandora's Box*. New York: Cambridge University Press.

Gillespie, Colin S. 2014. "A complete data framework for fitting power law distributions." arXiv:1408.1554.

Gillet, Philippe. 1999. *L'efficience des marchés financiers*. Paris: Economica.

Gingras, Yves, and Christophe Schinckus. 2012. "Institutionalization of econophysics in the shadow of physics." *Journal of the History of Economic Thought* 34 (1): 109–30.

Gligor, Mircea, and Marcel Ausloos. 2007. "Cluster structure of EU-15 countries derived from the correlation matrix analysis of macroeconomic index fluctuations." *European Physical Journal B* 57 (2): 139–46.

Gnedenko, Boris Vladimirovich, and Andrei N. Kolmogorov. 1954. *Limit Distributions for Sums of Independent Random Variables*. Cambridge, MA: Addison-Wesley.

Godfrey, Michael D., Clive W. J. Granger, and Oskar Morgenstern. 1964. "The random-walk hypothesis of stock market behavior." *Kyklos* 17: 1–29.

Goerlich, Francisco J. 2013. "A simple and efficient test for the Pareto law." *Empirical Economics* 45 (3): 1367–81.

Gopikrishnan, Parameswaran, Martin Meyer, Luis A. Nunes Amaral, and H. Eugene Stanley. 1998. "Inverse cubic law for the probability distribution of stock price variations." *European Physical Journal B* 3: 139–40.

Gopikrishnan, Parameswaran, Vasiliki Plerou, Xavier Gabaix, and H. Eugene Stanley. 2000. "Statistical properties of share volume traded in financial markets." *Physical Review E* 62: 4493–96.

Gopikrishnan, Parameswaran, Vasiliki Plerou, Yanhui Liu, Luis A. Nunes Amaral, Xavier Gabaix, and H. Eugene Stanley. 2000. "Scaling and correlation in financial time series." *Physica A: Statistical Mechanics and its Applications* 287 (3): 362–73. doi: 10.1016/S0378-4371(00)00375-7.

Gopikrishnan, Parameswaran, Vasiliki Plerou, Luis A. Nunes Amaral, Martin Meyer, and H. Eugene Stanley. 1999. "Scaling of the distribution of fluctuations of financial market indices." *Physics Review E* 60 (5): 5305–16.

Granger, Clive W. J., and Oskar Morgenstern. 1963. "Spectral analysis of New York Stock Exchange prices." *Kyklos* 16: 1–27.

Gregory, Allan W., and Gregor W. Smith. 1995. "Business cycle theory and econometrics." *Economic Journal* 105 (433): 1597–608.

Grossman, Sanford J. 1976. "On the efficiency of competitive stock markets where traders have diverse information." *Journal of Finance* 31 (2): 573–85.

Grossman, Sanford J., and Joseph E. Stiglitz. 1980. "The impossibility of informationally efficient markets." *American Economic Review* 70 (3): 393–407.

Guégan, Dominique, and Xin Zhao. 2014. "Alternative modeling for long term risk." *Quantitative Finance* 14 (12): 2237–53.

Guillaume, Deffuant. 2004. "Comparing extremism propagation patterns in continuous opinion models." *Journal of Artificial Societies and Social Simulation* 9 (3): 8–14.

Gunaratne, Gemunu H., and Joseph L. McCauley. 2005. "A theory for fluctuations in stock prices and valuation of their options." *Proceedings of the SPIE* 5848: 131.

Gupta, Hari, and José Campanha. 1999. "The gradually truncated Lévy flight for systems with power-law distributions." *Physica A* 268: 231–39.

Gupta, Hari, and José Campanha. 2002. "Tsallis statistics and gradually truncated Lévy flight: Distribution of an economic index." *Physica A* 309 (4): 381–87.

Haavelmo, Trygve. 1944. "The probability approach in econometrics." *Econometrica* 12 (Supplement): iii–vi + 1–115.

Hacking, Ian. 1990. *The Taming of Chance*. New York: Cambridge University Press.

Hadzibabic, Zoran, Peter Krüger, Marc Cheneau, Baptiste Battelier, and Jean Dalibard. 2006. "Berezinskii-Kosterlitz-Thouless crossover in a trapped atomic gas." *Nature* 441: 1118–21.

Hafner, Wolfgang, and Heinz Zimmermann, eds. 2009. *Vinzenz Bronzin's Option Pricing Models: Exposition and Appraisal*. Berlin: Springer.

Hammer, Howard M., and Ronald X. Groeber. 2007. "Efficient market hypothesis and class action securities regulation." *International Journal of Business Research* 1: 1–14.

Hand, D. 1998. "Data mining: Statistics and more?" *American Statistician* 52 (2): 112–18.

Hankins, Frank Hamilton. 1908. "Adolphe Quetelet as statistician." Doctoral dissertation, Columbia University.

Hansen, Lars Peter, and James J. Heckman. 1996. "The empirical foundations of calibration." *Journal of Economic Perspectives* 10 (1): 87–104.

Harrison, J. Michael, and David M. Kreps. 1979. "Martingales and arbitrage in multiperiod securities markets." *Journal of Economic Theory* 20 (3): 381–408.

Harrison, J. Michael, and Stanley R. Pliska. 1981. "Martingales and stochastic integrals in the theory of continuous trading." *Stochastic Processes and Their Applications* 11 (3): 215–60.

Harrison, Paul. 1998. "Similarities in the distribution of stock market price changes between the eighteenth and twentieth centuries." *Journal of Business* 71 (1): 55–79. doi: 10.1086/209736.

Hartemink, Alexander J., David K. Gifford, Tommi S. Jaakkola, and Richard A. Young. 2001. "Maximum likelihood estimation of optimal scaling factors for expression array normalization." *Proceedings of SPIE* 4266: 132–40.

Hastie, Trevor, Robert Tibshirani, Jerome Friedman, and James Franklin. 2005. "The element of statistical learning: Data mining, inference and prediction." *Mathematical Intelligencer* 27 (2): 83–85.

Haug, Espen Gaarder, and Nassim Nicholas Taleb. 2011. "Option traders use very sophisticated heuristics, never the Black-Scholes-Merton formula." *Journal of Economic Behaviour and Organization* 77 (2): 97–106.

Hautcœur, Pierre-Cyrille, and Angelo Riva. 2012. "The Paris financial market in the nineteenth century: Complementarities and competition in microstructures." *Economic History Review* 65 (4): 1326–53.

Hendry, David F. 1995. "Econometrics and business cycle empirics." *Economic Journal* 105 (433): 1622–36.

Hendry, David F., and Mary S. Morgan, eds. 1995. *The Foundations of Econometric Analysis.* New York: Cambridge University Press.

Hoover, Kevin D. 1995. "Facts and artifacts: Calibration and the empirical assessmen." *Oxford Economic Papers* 47 (1): 24.

Houthakker, Hendrik S. 1961. "Systematic and random elements in short-term price movements." *American Economic Review* 51 (2): 164–72.

Huber, Michel. 1937. "Quarante années de la statistique générale de la France 1896–1936." *Journal de la Société Statistique de Paris* 78: 179–214.

Hughes, Robert I. G. 1999. "The Ising model, computer simulation, and universal physics." In *Models as Mediators: Perspectives on Natural and Social Science*, edited by Mary S. Morgan and Margaret Morrison, 97–145. Cambridge: Cambridge University Press.

Hurst, Harold Edwin. 1951. "Long-term storage capacity of reservoirs." *Transactions of the American Society of Civil Engineers* 116: 770–99.

Ilachinski, Andrew 2000. "Irreducible semi-autonomous adaptive combat (ISAAC): An artificial-life approach to land warfare." *Military Operations Research* 5 (3): 29–46.

Ingrao, Bruna, and Israel Giorgio. 1990. *The Invisible Hand: Economic Equilibrium in the History of Science.* Cambridge, MA: MIT Press.

Israel, Giorgio. 1996. *La mathématisation du réel: Essai sur la modélisation mathématique.* Paris: Le Seuil.

Ivancevic, Vladimir G. 2010. "Adaptive-wave alternative for the Black-Scholes option pricing model." *Cognitive Computation* 2 (1): 17–30.

Ivanov, Plamen Ch, Ainslie Yuen, Boris Podobnik, and Youngki Lee. 2004. "Common scaling patterns in intertrade times of U. S. stocks." *Physical Review E: Statistical, Nonlinear, and Soft Matter Physics* 69 (5.2): 056107. doi: 10.1103/PhysRevE.69.056107.

Izquierdo, Segismundo S., and Luis R. Izquierdo. 2007. "The impact of quality uncertainty without asymmetric information on market efficiency." *Journal of Business Research* 60 (8): 858–67.

Jensen, Michael C., ed. 1972. *Studies in the Theory of Capital Markets.* New York: Praeger.

Jensen, Michael C. 1978. "Some anomalous evidence regarding market efficiency." *Journal of Financial Economics* 6 (2–3): 95–101.

Jiang, Zhi-Qiang, Wei-Xing Zhou, Didier Sornette, Ryan Woodard, Ken Bastiaensen, and Peter Cauwels. 2010. "Bubble diagnosis and prediction of the 2005–2007 and 2008–2009 Chinese stock market bubbles." *Journal of Economic Behavior and Organization* 74 (3): 149–62.

Johansen, Anders, and Didier Sornette. 2000. "The Nasdaq crash of April 2000: Yet another example of log-periodicity in a speculative bubble ending in a crash." *European Physical Journal B* 17 (2): 319–28.

Johansen, Anders, Didier Sornette, and Olivier Ledoit. 1999. "Predicting financial crashes using discrete scale invariance." *Journal of Risk* 1: 5–32.

Jona-Lasinio, Giovanni. 2001. "Renormalization group and probability theory." *Physics Reports* 352: 439–58.

Jovanovic, Franck. 2000. "L'origine de la théorie financière: Une réévaluation de l'apport de Louis Bachelier." *Revue d'Economie Politique* 110 (3): 395–418.

Jovanovic, Franck. 2001. "Pourquoi l'hypothèse de marche aléatoire en théorie financière? Les raisons historiques d'un choix éthique." *Revue d'Economie Financière* 61: 203–11.

Jovanovic, Franck. 2002. "Le modèle de marche aléatoire dans la théorie financière quantitative." Doctoral dissertation, University of Paris 1, Panthéon-Sorbonne.

Jovanovic, Franck. 2004. "Eléments biographiques inédits sur Jules Regnault (1834–1894), inventeur du modèle de marche aléatoire pour représenter les variations boursières." *Revue d'Histoire des Sciences Humaines* 11: 215–30.

Jovanovic, Franck. 2006a. "Economic instruments and theory in the construction of Henri Lefèvre's 'science of the stock market.'" In *Pioneers of Financial Economics*, vol. 1, edited by Geoffrey Poitras, 169–90. Cheltenham: Edward Elgar.

Jovanovic, Franck. 2006b. "A nineteenth-century random walk: Jules Regnault and the origins of scientific financial economics." In *Pioneers of Financial Economics*, vol. 1, edited by Geoffrey Poitras, 191–222. Cheltenham: Edward Elgar.

Jovanovic, Franck. 2006c. "Was there a 'vernacular science of financial markets' in France during the nineteenth century? A comment on Preda's 'Informative Prices, Rational Investors.'" *History of Political Economy* 38 (3): 531–46.

Jovanovic, Franck. 2008. "The construction of the canonical history of financial economics." *History of Political Economy* 40 (2): 213–42.

Jovanovic, Franck, ed. 2009a. "L'institutionnalisation de l'économie financière: Perspectives historiques." Special issue of *Revue d'Histoire des Sciences Humaines* 20.

Jovanovic, Franck. 2009b. "Le modèle de marche aléatoire dans l'économie financière de 1863 à 1976." *Revue d'Histoire des Sciences Humaines* 20: 81–108.

Jovanovic, Franck. 2012. "Bachelier: Not the forgotten forerunner he has been depicted as." *European Journal for the History of Economic Thought* 19 (3): 431–451.

Jovanovic, Franck. 2016. "An introduction to the calculation of the chance: Jules Regnault, his book and its influence." In *The Calculation of Chance and Philosophy of the Stock Market*, edited by William Goetzmann, forthcoming. New Haven: Yale University Press.

Jovanovic, Franck, Stelios Andreadakis, and Christophe Schinckus. 2016. "Efficient market hypothesis and fraud on the market theory: A new perspective for class actions." *Research in International Business and Finance* 38 (7): 177–90.

Jovanovic, Franck, and Philippe Le Gall. 2001a. "Does God practice a random walk? The 'financial physics' of a 19th century forerunner, Jules Regnault." *European Journal for the History of Economic Thought* 8 (3): 323–62.

Jovanovic, Franck, and Philippe Le Gall. 2001b. "March to numbers: The statistical style of Lucien March." In *History of Political Economy*, annual supplement: *The Age of Economic Measurement*, edited by Judy L. Klein and Mary S. Morgan, 86–100.

Jovanovic, Franck, and Christophe Schinckus. 2013. "Towards a transdisciplinary econophysics." *Journal of Economic Methodology* 20 (2): 164–83.

Jovanovic, Franck, and Christophe Schinckus. 2016. "Breaking down the barriers between econophysics and financial economics." *International Review of Financial Analysis*. Online.

Kadanoff, Leo. 1966. "Scaling laws for Ising models near T_c." *Physics* 2: 263–72.

Kahneman, Daniel, and Amos Tversky. 1979. "Prospect theory: An analysis of decision under risk." *Econometrica* 47 (2): 263–91.

Kaiser, David. 2012. "Booms, busts, and the world of ideas: Enrollment pressures and the challenge of specialization." *Osiris* 27: 276–302.

Kaizoji, Taisei 2006. "On Stock-Price Fluctuations in the Periods of Booms and Stagnations." In *Proceedings of the Econophysics-Kolkata II Series*, edited by Arnab Chatterjee and Bikas K. Chakrabarti, 3–12. Tokyo: Springer.

Kaizoji, Taisei, and Michiyo Kaizoji. 2004. "Power law for the calm-time interval of price changes." *Physica A* 336 (3): 563–70.

Keen, Steve. 2003. "Standing on the toes of pygmies: Why econophysics must be careful of the economic foundations on which it builds." *Physica A* 324 (1): 108–16.

Kendall, Maurice George. 1953. "The analysis of economic time-series. Part I: Prices." *Journal of the Royal Statistical Society* 116: 11–25.

Kennedy, Robert E. 1966. "Financial analysts seminar." *Financial Analysts Journal* 22 (6): 8–9.

Kesten, Harry. 1973. "Random difference equations and renewal theory for products of random matrices." *Acta Mathematica* 131 (1): 207–48.

Keynes, John Maynard. 1936. *The General Theory of Employment, Interest and Money*. London: Macmillan.

Khinchine, A. Ya. 1933. *Asymptotische Gesetze der Warsheinlichekeitsrechnung*. Berlin: Springer.

Kim, Young, Svetlozar Rachev, Michele Bianchi, and Frank J. Fabozzi. 2008. "Financial market models with Lévy processes and time-varying volatility." *Journal of Banking and Finance* 32 (7): 1363–78.

King, Benjamin. 1964. "The latent statistical structure of security price changes." Doctoral dissertation, Graduate School of Business, University of Chicago.

Klass, Oren S., Ofer Biham, Moshe Levy, Ofer Malcai, and Sorin Solomon. 2006. "The Forbes 400 and the Pareto wealth distribution." *Economics Letters* 90: 90–95.

Kleiber, Max. 1932. "Body size and metabolism." *Hilgardia* 6: 315–51.

Klein, Julie Thompson. 1994. "Notes toward a social epistemology of transdisciplinarity." Paper presented to the First World Congress of Transdisciplinarity, Convento da Arrábida, Portugal.

Knorr-Cetina, Karin. 1981. *The Manufacture of Knowledge: An Essay on the Constructivist and Contextual Nature of Science*. Elmsford, NY: Pergamon.

Kolmogorov, Andrei N. 1931. "Über die analytischen Methoden in der Wahrscheinlichkeitsrechnung." *Mathematische Annalen* 104: 415–58.

Kolmogorov, Andrei N. 1941. "Dissipation of energy in isotropic turbulence." *Doklady Akademii Nauk SSSR* 32: 19–21.

Kolmogorov, Andrei N. 1942. "Equations of turbulent motion in an incompressible fluid." *Izvestiya Akademii Nauk SSSR Seriya Fizika* 6: 56–58.

Koponen, Ismo. 1995. "Analytic approach to the problem of convergence of truncated Lévy flights towards the Gaussian stochastic process." *Physical Review E* 52 (1): 1197–99.

Kou, Xiaodong, Lin Yang, and Lin Cai. 2008. "Artificial urban planning: Application of MAS." *Urban Planning Education* 1: 349–53.

Koutrovelis, Ioannis. 1980. "Regression-type estimation of the parameters of stable laws." *Journal of American Statistical Association* 75: 918–28.

Kreps, David M. 1981. "Arbitrage and equilibrium in economies with infinitely many commodities." *Journal of Mathematical Economics* 8: 15–35.

Krugman, Paul. 1991. *Geography and Trade*. Cambridge, MA: MIT Press.

Krugman, Paul. 1996a. "Confronting the mystery of urban hierarchy." *Journal of the Japanese and International Economies* 10: 399–418.

Krugman, Paul. 1996b. *The Self-Organizing Economy*. Cambridge, MA: Blackwell.

Kuhn, Thomas. 1962. *The Structure of Scientific Revolutions*. Chicago: University of Chicago Press.

Kuhn, Thomas. 1989. "Possible worlds in history of science." In *Possible Worlds in Humanities, Arts and Sciences*, edited by S. Allen, 9–32. New York: de Gruyter.

Kutner, Ryszard, and Dariusz Grech. 2008. "Report on foundation and organization of econophysics graduate courses at Faculty of Physics of University of Warsaw and Department of Physics and Astronomy of the Wrocław University." *Acta Physica Polonica A* 114 (3): 637–47.

Kydland, Finn E., and Edward C. Prescott. 1982. "Time to build and aggregate fluctuations." *Econometrica* 50 (6): 1345–70.

Kyle, Albert S. 1985. "Continuous auctions and insider trading." *Econometrica* 53 (6): 1315–35.

Lakatos, Imre. 1978. *Philosophical Papers*, vol. 1: *The Methodology of Scientific Research Programmes*. Cambridge: Cambridge University Press.

Larson, Arnold B. 1960. "Measurement of random process in futures prices." *Food Research Institute Studies* 1 (3): 313–24.

Le Gall, Philippe. 1994. "Histoire de l'econométrie, 1914–1944: L'erosion du déterminisme." Doctoral dissertation, University of Paris 1, Panthéon-Sorbonne.

Le Gall, Philippe. 1999. "A world ruled by Venus: On Henry L. Moore's transfer of periodogram analysis from physics to economics." *History of Political Economy* 31 (4): 723–52.

Le Gall, Philippe. 2002. "Les représentations du monde et les pensées analogiques des economètres: Un siècle de modélisation en perspective." *Revue d'Histoire des Sciences Humaines* 6: 39–64.

Le Gall, Philippe. 2006. *From Nature to Models: An Archaeology of Econometrics in FRANCE, 1830–1930*. London: Routledge.

LeBaron, Blake. 2001. "Stochastic volatility as a simple generator of power laws and long memory." *Quantitative Finance* 1 (6): 621–31.

LeBaron, Blake. 2006. "Agent-based computational finance." In *Handbook of Computational Economics*, vol. 2: *Agent-Based Computational Economics*, edited by Leigh Tesfatsion and Kenneth L. Judd, 1187–233. Amsterdam: North-Holland.

Lesne, Annick. 1998. *Renormalization Methods: Critical Phenomena, Chaos, Fractal Structures*. Chichester: John Wiley & Sons.

Lesne, Annick, and Michel Laguës. 2011. *Scale Invariance: From Phase Transitions to Turbulence.* Berlin: Springer.

Levy, M. 2003. "Are rich people smarter?" *Journal of Economic Theory* 110: 42–64.

Levy, Moshe H., Haim Levy, and Sorin Solomon. 1995. "Microscopic simulation of the stock market: The effect of microscopic diversity." *Journal de Physique I* 5 (8): 1087–107.

Levy, Moshe H., Haim Levy, and Sorin Solomon. 2000. *Microscopic Simulation of Financial Markets: From Investor Behaviour to Market Phenomena.* San Diego: Academic Press.

Lévy, Paul. 1924. "Théorie des erreurs: La loi de Gauss et les lois exceptionnelles." *Bulletin de la SMF* 2 (1): 49–85.

Li, Lun, David Alderson, John C. Doyle, and Walter Willinger. 2005. "Towards a theory of scale-free graphs: Definition, properties, and implications." *Internet Mathematics* 2 (4): 431–523.

Li, Sai-Ping, and Shu-Heng Chen, eds. 2012. "Complexity and non-linearities in financial markets: Perspectives from econophysics." Special issue of *International Review of Financial Analysis* 23.

Lillo, Fabrizio, and Rosario N. Mantegna. 2004. "Dynamics of a financial market index after a crash." *Physica A* 338 (1–2): 125–34.

Lintner, John. 1965a. "Security prices, risk and maximal gains from diversification." *Journal of Finance* 20 (4): 587–615.

Lintner, John. 1965b. "The valuation of risk assets and the selection of risky investments in stock portfolios and capital budgets." *Review of Economic Statistics* 47 (1): 13–37.

Lorie, James Hirsch. 1965. "Controversies on the stock market." Selected Papers, Graduate School of Business of the University of Chicago.

Lorie, James Hirsch. 1966. "Some comments on recent quantitative and formal research on the stock market." *Journal of Business* 39 (1.2: Supplement on Security Prices): 107–10.

Lotka, Alfred J. 1926. "The frequency distribution of scientific productivity." *Journal of the Washington Academy of Sciences* 16 (12): 317–24.

Louçã, Francisco. 2007. *The Years of High Econometrics. A Short History of the Generation That Reinvented Economics.* London: Routledge.

Louzoun, Yoram, and Sorin Solomon. 2001. "Volatility driven markets in a generalized Lotka Voltera formalism." *Physica A* 302 (1): 220–33.

Lowenstein, Roger. 2000. *When Genius Failed: The Rise and Fall of Long-Term Capital Management.* New York: Random House.

Lu, Zhiping, and Dominique Guegan. 2011. "Testing unit roots and long range dependence of foreign exchange." *Journal of Time Series Analysis* 32 (6): 631–38.

Lucas, Robert E., Jr. 1978. "Asset Prices in an Exchange Economy." *Econometrica* 46 (6): 1429–45.

Luttmer, E. 2007. "Selection, growth, and the size distribution of firms." *Quarterly Journal of Economics* 122: 1103–44.

Lux, Thomas. 1992a. "A note on the stability of endogenous cycles in Diamond's model of search and barter." *Journal of Economics* 56 (2): 185–96.

Lux, Thomas. 1992b. "The sequential trading approach to disequilibrium dynamics." *Jahrbücher für Nationaloekonomie und Statistik* 209 (1): 47–59.

Lux, Thomas. 1996. "The stable Paretian hypothesis and the frequency of large returns: An examination of major German stocks." *Applied Financial Economics* 6: 463–75.

Lux, Thomas. 2006. "Financial power laws: Empirical evidence, models, and mechanism." Working paper No12 from Christian-Albrechts-University of Kiel, Department of Economics.

Lux, Thomas. 2009. "Applications of statistical physics in finance and economics." In *Handbook of Research on Complexity*, edited by Barkley Rosser, 213–58. Cheltenham: Edward Elgar.

Lux, Thomas, and Michele Marchesi. 1999. "Scaling and criticality in a stochastic multi-agent model of a financial market." *Nature* 397: 498–500.

Lux, Thomas, and Michele Marchesi. 2000. "Volatility clustering in financial markets: A microsimulation of interacting agents." *International Journal of Theoretical and Applied Finance* 3 (4): 675–702.

Maas, Harro. 2005. *William Stanley Jevons and the Making of Modern Economics.* New York: Cambridge University Press.

Macintosh, Norman B. 2003. "From rationality to hyperreality: Paradigm poker." *International Review of Financial Analysis* 12 (4): 453–65.

Macintosh, Norman B., Teri Shearer, Daniel B. Thornton, and Michael Welker. 2000. "Accounting as simulacrum and hyperreality: Perspectives on income and capital." *Accounting, Organizations and Society* 25 (1): 13–50.

MacKenzie, Donald A. 2003. "An equation and its worlds: Bricolage, exemplars, disunity and performativity in financial economics." Paper presented to "Inside Financial Markets: Knowledge and Interaction Patterns in Global Markets," Konstanz, May.

MacKenzie, Donald A. 2006. *An Engine, Not a Camera: How Financial Models Shape Markets.* Cambridge, MA: MIT Press.

MacKenzie, Donald A. 2007. "The emergence of option pricing theory." In *Pioneers of Financial Economics*, vol. 2: *Twentieth Century Contributions*, edited by Geoffrey Poitras and Franck Jovanovic, 170–91. Cheltenham: Edward Elgar.

MacKenzie, Donald A., and Yuval Millo. 2009. "The usefulness of inaccurate models: Towards an understanding of the emergence of financial risk management." *Accounting, Organizations and Society* 34: 638–53.

Madan, Dilip B., Peter P. Carr, and Éric C. Chang. 1998. "The variance gamma process and option pricing." *European Finance Review* 2 (1): 79–105.

Madhavan, Ananth. 2000. "Market microstructure: A survey." *Journal of Financial Markets* 3 (3): 205–58.

Malcai, Ofer, Ofer Biham, and Sorin Solomon. 1999. "Power-law distributions and Lévy-stable intermittent fluctuations in stochastic systems of many autocatalytic elements." *Physical Review E* 60: 1299–303.

Malevergne, Yannick, Vladilen Pisarenko, and Didier Sornette. 2011. "Testing the Pareto against the lognormal distributions with the uniformly most powerful unbiased test applied to the distribution of cities." *Physical Review E* 83 (3): 036111.

Malevergne, Yannick, and Didier Sornette. 2005. *Extreme Financial Risks: From Dependence to Risk Management.* Vol. 1. Berlin: Springer.

Malevergne, Yannick, Didier Sornette, and Vladilen Pisarenko. 2005. "Empirical distributions of stock returns: Between the stretched exponential and the power law?" *Quantitative Finance* 5 (4): 379–401.

Malkiel, Burton G. 1992. "Efficient market hypothesis." In *The New Palgrave Dictionary of Money and Finance*, edited by Peter Newman, Murray Milgate and John Eatwell. London: Macmillan.

Mandelbrot, Benoit. 1957. "Application of thermodynamical methods in communication theory and in econometrics." Institut Mathématique de l'Université de Lille.

Mandelbrot, Benoit. 1960. "The Pareto-Lévy law and the distribution of income." *International Economic Review* 1: 79–106.

Mandelbrot, Benoit. 1962a. "Sur certains prix spéculatifs: Faits empiriques et modèle basé sur les processus stables additifs non gaussiens de Paul Lévy." *Comptes Rendus de l'Académie des Sciences* (Meeting of June 4): 3968–70.

Mandelbrot, Benoit. 1962b. "The variation of certain speculative prices." IBM Report NC-87.

Mandelbrot, Benoit. 1963a. "New Methods in Statistical Economics." *Journal of Political Economy* 71 (5): 421–40.

Mandelbrot, Benoit. 1963b. "The variation of certain speculative prices." *Journal of Business* 36 (4): 394–419.

Mandelbrot, Benoit. 1966a. "Forecasts of future prices, unbiased markets, and "martingale" models." *Journal of Business* 39 (1.2): 242–55.

Mandelbrot, Benoit. 1966b. "Seminar on the Analysis of Security Prices" held November 12-13, 1966 at the Graduate School of Business of the University of Chicago.

Mandelbrot, Benoit. 1997. *Fractals, hasard et finance.* Paris: Flammarion.

Mandelbrot, Benoit, and Richard L. Hudson. 2004. *The (Mis)Behavior of Markets: A Fractal View of Risk, Ruin, and Reward.* London: Profile Books.

Mantegna, Rosario N. 1991. "Levy Walks and enhanced diffusion in Milan stock exchange." *Physica A* 179 (1): 232–42.

Mantegna, Rosario N., and H. Eugene Stanley. 1994. "Stochastic process with ultra-slow convergence to a Gaussian: The truncated Lévy flight." *Physical Review Letters* 73 (22): 2946–49.

Mantegna, Rosario N., and H. Eugene Stanley. 2000. *An Introduction to Econophysics: Correlations and Complexity in Finance.* New York: Cambridge University Press.

March, Lucien. 1921. "Les modes de mesure du mouvement général des prix." *Metron* 1 (4): 57–91.

Mardia, Kanti V., and Peter E. Jupp. 2000. *Directional Statistics.* Chichester: Wiley.

Mariani, Maria Cristina, and Y. Liu. 2007. "Normalized truncated Lévy walks applied to the study of financial indices." *Physica A* 377: 590–98.

Markowitz, Harry M. 1952. "Portfolio selection." *Journal of Finance* 7 (1): 77–91.

Markowitz, Harry M. 1955. "Portfolio selection." MA thesis, University of Chicago.

Markowitz, Harry M. 1959. *Portfolio Selection: Efficient Diversification of Investments.* New York: Wiley.

Markowitz, Harry M. 1999. "The early history of portfolio theory: 1600–1960." *Financial Analysts Journal* 55 (4): 5–16.

Marsili, Mateo, and Yi-Chen Zhang. 1998. "Econophysics: What can physicists contribute to economics?" *Physics Review Letters* 80 (1): 80–85.

Maslov, Sergei. 2000. "Simple model of a limit order-driven market." *Physica A* 278 (3–4): 571–78.

Matacz, Andrew. 2000. "Financial modeling and option theory with the truncated Levy process." *International Journal of Theoretical and Applied Finance* 3 (1): 142–60.

Matei, Marius, Xari Rovira, and Nuria Agell. 2012. "Bivariate volatility modeling for stocks and portfolios." Working paper, ESADE Business School, Ramon Llull University.

Matsushita, Raul, Pushpa Rathie, and Sergio Da Silva. 2003. "Exponentially damped Lévy flight." *Physica A* 326 (1): 544–55.

Max-Neef, Manfred. 2005. "Foundations of transdisciplinarity." *Ecological Economics* 53: 5–16.

McCauley, Joseph L. 2003. "Thermodynamics analogies in economics and finance: Instability of markets." *Physica A* 329: 199–212.

McCauley, Joseph L. 2004. *Dynamics of Markets: Econophysics and Finance.* Cambridge: Cambridge University Press.

McCauley, Joseph L. 2006. "Response to 'Worrying Trends in Econophysics.'" *Physica A* 371 (1): 601–9.

McCauley, Joseph L. 2009. "ARCH and GARCH models vs. martingale volatility of finance market returns." *International Review of Financial Analysis* 18 (4): 151–53.

McCauley, Joseph L., and Gemunu H. Gunaratne. 2003. "An empirical model of volatility of returns and option pricing." *Physica A* 329: 178–98.

McCauley, Joseph L., Gemunu H. Gunaratne, and Kevin E. Bassler. 2007a. "Hurst exponents, Markov processes, and fractional Brownian motion." *Physica A: Statistical Mechanics and Its Applications* 379 (1): 1–9.

McCauley, Joseph L., Gemunu H. Gunaratne, and Kevin E. Bassler. 2007b. "Martingale option pricing." *Physica A* 380: 351–56.

McCauley, Joseph L., Bertrand M. Roehner, H. Eugene Stanley, and Christophe Schinckus, eds. 2016 (forthcoming). "Econophysics, where we are where we go." Special issue of *International Review of Financial Analysis*.

McCulloch, Hu. 1986. "Simple consistent estimators of stable distribution parameters." *Communications in Statistics: Simulation and Computation* 15 (4): 1109–36.

McGoun, Elton G. 1997. "Hyperreal finance." *Critical Perspectives on Accounting* 8 (1–2): 97–122.

McNees, Stephen. 1979. "The forecasting record for the 1970s." *New England Economic Review*, September–October, 33–53.

Mehrling, Perry. 2005. *Fischer Black and the Revolutionary Idea of Finance*. Hoboken, NJ: John Wiley & Sons.

Ménard, Claude. 1981. "La machine et le coeur: Essai sur les analogies dans le raisonnement économique." In *Analogie et connaissance*, edited by André Lichnerowicz, François Perroux, and Gilbert Gadoffre, 137–61. Paris: Éditions Maloine.

Ménard, Claude. 1987. "Why was there no probabilistic revolution in economic thought?" In *The Probabilistic Revolution*, vol. 2: *Ideas in the Sciences*, edited by Lorenz Krüger, Gerd Gigerenzer, and Mary S. Morgan, 139–46. Cambridge, MA: MIT Press.

Merton, Robert C. 1976. "Option pricing when underlying stock returns are discontinuous." *Journal of Financial Economics* 3 (1-2): 125–44.

Merton, Robert C. 1998. "Applications of option-pricing theory: Twenty-five years later." *American Economic Review* 88 (3): 323–49.

Meyer, Paul-André. 2009. "Stochastic processes from 1950 to the present." *Journal Electronique d'Histoire des Probabilités et de la Statistique* 5 (1): 1–42.

Miburn, J. Alex. 2008. "The Relationship between fair value, market value, and efficient markets." *Accounting Perspectives* 7 (4): 293–316.

Michael, Fredrick, and M. D. Johnson. 2003. "Financial market dynamics." *Physica A* 320: 525–34.

Mike, Szabolcs, and J. Doyne Farmer. 2008. "An empirical behavioral model of liquidity and volatility." *Journal of Economic Dynamics and Control* 32 (1): 200–234. doi: 10.1016/j.jedc.2007.01.025.

Miller, Merton H. 1988. "The Modigliani-Miller propositions after thirty years." *Journal of Economic Perspectives* 2 (4): 99–120.

Millo, Yuval, and Christophe Schinckus. 2016. "A nuanced perspective on *episteme* and *techne* in finance." *International Review of Financial Analysis* 46: 124–30.

Mills, Frederick Cecil. 1927. *The Behavior of Prices*. New York: National Bureau of Economic Research.

Mir, Tariq Ahmad, Marcel Ausloos, and Roy Cerqueti. 2014. "Benford's law predicted digit distribution of aggregated income taxes: The surprising conformity of Italian cities and regions." *European Physical Journal B* 87 (11): 1–8.

Mirowski, Philip. 1989a. "The measurement without theory controversy." *Oeconomia* 11: 65–87.

Mirowski, Philip. 1989b. *More Heat Than Light: Economics as Social Physics, Physics as Nature's Economics*. New York: Cambridge University Press.

Mirowski, Philip. 2002. *Machine Dreams*. Cambridge: Cambridge University Press.

Miskiewicz, Janusz. 2010. "Econophysics in Poland." *Science and Culture* 76: 395–98.

Mitchell, Melanie. 2009. *Complexity: A Guided Tour*. New York: Oxford University Press.

Mitchell, Wesley C. 1915. "The making and using of index numbers." *Bulletin of the United States Bureau of Labor Statistics* 173: 5–114.

Mitzenmacher, Michael. 2004. "A brief history of generative models for power law and lognormal distributions." *Internet Mathematics* 1 (2): 226–51.

Mitzenmacher, Michael. 2005. "Editorial: The future of power law research." *Internet Mathematics* 2 (4): 525–34.

Miyahara, Yoshio. 2012. *Option Pricing in Incomplete Markets: Modeling Based on Geometric Lévy Processes and Minimal Entropy Martingale Measures*. London: Imperial College Press.

Modigliani, Franco, and Merton H. Miller. 1958. "The cost of capital, corporation finance and the theory of investment." *American Economic Review* 48 (3): 261–97.

Moore, Arnold B. 1964. "Some characteristics of changes in common stock prices." In *The Random Character of Stock Market Prices*, edited by Paul H. Cootner, 139–61. Cambridge, MA: MIT Press.

Moore, Henry Ludwell. 1917. *Forecasting the Yield and the Price of Cotton*. New York: Macmillan.

Morales, Raffaello, Tiziana Di Matteo, and Tomaso Aste. 2013. "Non-stationary multifractality in stock returns." *Physica A: Statistical Mechanics and Its Applications* 392 (24): 6470. doi: 10.1016/j.physa.2013.08.037.

Morgan, Mary S. 1990. *The History of Econometric Ideas: Historical Perspectives on Modern Economics*. Cambridge: Cambridge University Press.

Morgan, Mary S., and Judy L. Klein, eds. 2001. *The Age of Economic Measurement*. Durham, NC: Duke University Press.

Morgan, Mary S., and Tarja Knuuttila. 2012. "Models and modelling in economics." In *Handbook of the Philosophy of Science*, vol. 13: *Philosophy of Economics*, edited by Uskali Mäki, 49–87. Amsterdam: Elsevier.

Morin, Edgar. 1994. "Sur l'interdisciplinarité." Paper presented to the First World Congress of Transdisciplinarity, Convento da Arrábida, Portugal.

Mossin, Jan. 1966. "Equilibrium in a Capital Asset Market." *Econometrica* 34 (4): 768–83.

Nadeau, Robert. 2003. "Thomas Kuhn ou l'apogée de la philosophie historique des sciences." In *Actes du colloque du Centre Culturel International de Cerisy-la-Salle sur "Cent ans de philosophie américaine"*, edited by Jean-Pierre Cometti and Claudine Tiercelin, 273–97. Pau: P.U. Pau et Pays de l'Adour – Quad.

Nakao, Hiroya. 2000. "Multi-scaling properties of truncated Levy flights." *Physics Letters A* 266: 282–89.

Newman, Mark. 2005. "Power laws, Pareto distributions and Zipf's law." *Contemporary Physics* 46 (5): 323–51.

Niederhoffer, Victor. 1965. "Clustering of stock prices." *Operations Research* 13 (2): 258–65.

Nolan, John P. 2005. "Modeling financial data with stable distributions." Working paper, American University.

Nolan, John P. 2009. "Stable distributions: Models for heavy tailed data." Working paper, American University.

O' Hara, Maureen Patricia. 1995. *Market Microstructure Theory*. Cambridge, MA: Blackwell.

O' Hara, Maureen Patricia. 2003. "Presidential address: Liquidity and price discovery." *Journal of Finance* 58 (3): 1335–54.

Officer, Robert Rupert. 1972. "The distribution of stock returns." *Journal of American Statistical Association* 340 (67): 807–12.

Okuyama, K., Misako Takayasu, and Hideki Takayasu. 1999. "Zipf's law in income distribution of companies." *Physica A* 269 (1): 125–31.

Olivier, Maurice. 1926. *Les nombres indices de la variation des prix*. Paris: Marcel Giard.

Orléan, André. 1989. "Mimetic contagion and speculative bubbles." *Theory and Decision* 27 (1–2): 63–92.

Orléan, André. 1995. "Bayesian interactions and collective dynamics of opinion: Herd behavior and mimetic contagion." *Journal of Economic Behavior and Organization* 28 (2): 257–74.

Osborne, Maury F. M. 1959a. "Brownian motion in the stock market." *Operations Research* 7 (2): 145–73.

Osborne, Maury F. M. 1959b. "Reply to 'Comments on "Brownian Motion in the Stock Market.'" *Operations Research* 7 (6): 807–11.

Osborne, Maury F. M. 1962. "Periodic structure in the Brownian motion of stock prices." *Operations Research* 10 (3): 345–79.

Pagan, Adrian R. 1996. "The econometrics of financial markets." *Journal of Empirical Finance* 3 (1): 15–102.

Pandey, Ras B., and Dietrich Stauffer. 2000. "Search for log-periodic oscillations in stock market simulations." *International Journal of Theoretical and Applied Finance* 3 (3): 479–82.

Pareto, Vilfredo. 1897. *Cours d'economie politique*. Geneva: Librairie Droz.

Paul, Wolfgang, and Jörg Baschnagel. 2013. *Stochastic Processes: From Physics to Finance*. Berlin: Springer.

Paulson, Alan, Edgar Holcomb, and Robert Leitch. 1975. "The estimation of the parameters of the stable laws." *Biometrika* 62: 163–70.

Pearson, Karl. 1905a. "The problem of the random walk." *Nature* 72 (1865): 294.

Pearson, Karl. 1905b. "The problem of the random walk (answer)." *Nature* 72 (1867): 342.

Pickhardt, Michael, and Goetz Seibold. 2011. "Income tax evasion dynamics: Evidence from an agent-based econophysics model." Working paper, University of Cottbus.

Pieters, Riek, and Baumgartner Hans. 2002. "Who talks to whom? Intra- and interdisciplinary communication of economics journals." *Journal of Economic Literature* 40 (2): 483–509.

Plerou, Vasiliki, Parameswaran Gopikrishnan, L. A. Nunes Amaral, Martin Meyer, and H. Eugene Stanley. 1999. "Scaling of the distribution of price fluctuations of individual companies." *Physical Review E: Statistical Physics, Plasmas, Fluids, and Related Interdisciplinary Topics* 60 (6.A): 6519–29.

Plerou, Vasiliki, and H. Eugene Stanley. 2008. "Stock return distributions: Tests of scaling and universality from three distinct stock markets." *Physical Review E: Statistical, Nonlinear, and Soft Matter Physics* 77 (3.2): 037101.

Poitras, Geoffrey. 2009. "From Antwerp to Chicago: The history of exchange traded derivative security contracts." *Revue d'Histoire des Sciences Humaines* 20: 11–50.

Poitras, Geoffrey, and Franck Jovanovic, eds. 2007. *Pioneers of Financial Economics*, vol. 2: *Twentieth-Century Contributions*. Northampton, MA: Edward Elgar.

Poitras, Geoffrey, and Franck Jovanovic. 2010. "*Pioneers of Financial Economics*: Das Adam Smith Irrelevanzproblem?" *History of Economics Review* 51 (Winter): 43–64.

Ponzi, Adam, and Yoji Aizawa. 2000. "Evolutionary financial market models." *Physica A*: 507–23.

Popper, Karl Raimund. 1959. *The Logic of Scientific Discovery*. New York: Basic Books.

Porter, Theodore M. 1986. *The Rise of Statistical Thinking, 1820–1900*. Princeton, NJ: Princeton University Press.

Potters, Marc, and Jean-Philippe Bouchaud. 2003. "More statistical properties of stock order books and price impact." *Physica A* 324: 133–40.

Preda, Alex. 2001. "The rise of the popular investor: Financial knowledge and investing in England and France, 1840–1880." *Sociological Quarterly* 42 (2): 205–32.

Preda, Alex. 2004. "Informative prices, rational investors: The emergence of the random walk hypothesis and the 19th century 'science of financial investments.'" *History of Political Economy* 36 (2): 351–86.

Preda, Alex. 2006. "Socio-technical agency in financial markets: The case of the stock ticker." *Social Studies of Science* 36 (5): 753–82.

Preda, Alex. 2007. "Where do analysts come from? The case of financial chartism." *Sociological Review* 55 (s2): 40–64.

Preis, Tobias, and H. Eugene Stanley. 2010. "Trend switching processes in financial markets." In *Econophysics Approaches to Large-Scale Business Data and Financial Crisis*, edited by Misako Takayasu, Tsutomu Watanabe, and Hideki Takayasu, 3–26. Tokyo: Springer Japan.

Press, S. James. 1967. "A compound events model for security prices." *Journal of Business* 40 (3): 317–35.

Press, S. James. 1972. "Estimation in univariate and multivariate stable distributions." *Journal of American Statistical Association* 67: 842–46.

Prietula, Michael, Kathleen Carley, and Les Gasse, eds. 1998. *Simulating Organizations: Computational Models of Institutions and Groups*. Cambridge, MA: MIT Press.

Quah, Danny T. 1995. "Business cycle empirics: Calibration and estimation." *Economic Journal* 105 (433): 1594–96.

Queiros, Silvio M. Duarte, and Constantino Tsallis. 2005. "Bridging the ARCH model for finance and nonextensive entropy." *Europhysics Letters* 69: 893–99. doi: 10.1209/epl/i2004-10436-6.

Quételet, Adolphe. 1848. *Du système social et des lois qui le régissent*. Paris: Guillaumin et Cie.

Rachev, Svetlozar T., John S. J. Hsu, Biliana S. Bagasheva, and Frank J. Fabozzi. 2008. "Bayesian methods in finance." In *The Oxford Handbook of Bayesian Econometrics*, edited by John Geweke, Gary Koop, and Herman van Dijk, 439–512. New York: Oxford University Press.

Rachev, Svetlozar T., Young Shin Kim, Michele L. Bianchi, and Frank J. Fabozzi. 2011. *Financial Models with Levy Processes and Volatility Clustering*. Hoboken, NJ: John Wiley & Sons.

Redelico, Francisco O., Araceli N. Proto, and Marcel Ausloos. 2009. "Hierarchical structures in the gross domestic product per capita fluctuation in Latin American countries." *Physica A: Statistical Mechanics and its Applications* 388 (17): 3527–35.

Reed, William J., and Barry D. Hughes. 2002. "From gene families and genera to incomes and internet file sizes: Why power laws are so common in nature." *Physical Review E* 66: 067103-1–067103-4.

Regnault, Jules. 1863. *Calcul des chances et philosophie de la bourse.* Paris: Mallet-Bachelier and Castel.

Renfro, Charles G. 2004. "The early development of econometric modeling languages." In *Computational Econometrics: Its Impact on the Development of Quantitative Economics,* edited by Charles G. Renfro, 145–66. Amsterdam: IOS Press.

Renfro, Charles G. 2009. *The Practice of Econometric Theory: An Examination of the Characteristics of Econometric Computation.* Heidelberg: Springer.

Richmond, P. 2001. "Power law distributions and dynamic behaviour of stock markets." *European Physical Journal B* 20 (4): 523–26.

Richmond, Peter, Jurgen Mimkes, and Stefan Hutzler. 2013. *Econophysics and Physical Economics.* Oxford: Oxford University Press.

Rickles, Dean. 2007. "Econophysics for philosophers." *Studies in History and Philosophy of Science* 38 (4): 948–78.

Rickles, Dean. 2008. "Econophysics and the complexity of the financial markets." In *Handbook of the Philosophy of Science,* vol. 10: *Philosophy of Complex Systems,* edited by John Collier and Cliff Hooker, 531–65. New York: North Holland Elsevier Editions.

Rimmer, Robert H., and John P. Nolan. 2005. "Stable distributions in Mathematica." *Mathematica Journal* 9 (4): 776–89.

Roberts, Harry V. 1959. "Stock-market 'patterns' and financial analysis: Methodological suggestions." *Journal of Finance* 14 (1): 1–10.

Robert, Shiller. 1981. "Do Stock Prices Move Too Much to be Justified by Subsequent Changes in Dividends." *American Economic Review* 3: 421–36.

Roehner, Bertrand M. 2002. *Patterns of Speculation: A Study in Observational Econophysics.* Cambridge: Cambridge University Press.

Rosenfeld, Lawrence. 1957. "Electronic computers and their place in securities analyses." *Analysts Journal* 13 (1): 51–53.

Rosenfield, Patricia L. 1992. "The potential of transdisciplinary research for sustaining and extending linkages between the health and social sciences." *Social Science and Medicine* 35 (11): 1343–57.

Ross, Stephen A. 1976a. "The arbitrage theory of capital asset pricing." *Journal of Economic Theory* 13 (3): 341–60.

Ross, Stephen A. 1976b. "Options and efficiency." *Quarterly Journal of Economics* 90 (1): 75–89.

Ross, Stephen A. 1977. "Return, risk and arbitrage." In *Risk and Return in Finance,* edited by Irwin Friend and James L. Bicksler, 189–217. Cambridge: Ballinger.

Rosser, Barkley. 2006. "The nature and future of econophysics." In *Econophysics of Stock and Other Markets,* edited by Arnab Chatterjee and Bikas K. Chakrabarti, 225–34. Milan: Springer

Rosser, Barkley. 2008. "Econophysics and economics complexity." *Advances in Complex Systems* 11 (5): 745–60.

Rosser, Barkley. 2010. "Is a transdisciplinary perspective on economic complexity possible?" *Journal of Economic Behavior and Organization* 75 (1): 3–11.

Roy, A. D. 1952. "Safety first and the holding of assets." *Econometrica* 20 (3): 431–49.

Rozenfeld, Hernán D., Diego Rybski, Xavier Gabaix, and Hernán A. Makse. 2011. "The Area and Population of Cities: New Insights from a Different Perspective on Cities." *American Economic Review* 101 (5): 2205–25.

Rubinstein, Mark. 2002. "Markowitz's 'Portfolio Selection': A fifty-year retrospective." *Journal of Finance* 62 (3): 1041–45.

Rubinstein, Mark. 2003. "Great moments in financial economics: II. Modigliani-Miller theorem." *Journal of Investment Management* 1 (2): 7–13.

Rutterford, Janette, and Dimitris Sotiropoulos. 2015. "Like the horses in a race': Financial diversification before modern portfolio theory." Paper presented to the 19th Annual Conference of the European Society for the History of Economic Thought (ESHET), Rome.

Rybski, Diego. 2013. "Auerbach's legacy." *Environment and Planning A* 45 (6): 1266–68.

Samorodnitsky, Gennady, and Murad Taqqu. 1994. *Stable Non-Gaussian Random Processes*. New York: Chapman and Hall.

Samuelson, Paul A. 1965a. "Proof that properly anticipated prices fluctuate randomly." *Industrial Management Review* 6 (2): 41–49.

Samuelson, Paul A. 1965b. "Rational theory of warrant pricing." *Industrial Management Review* 6 (2): 13–40.

Samuelson, Paul A. 1967. "Efficient portfolio selection for Pareto-Lévy Investments." *Journal of Financial and Quantitative Analysis* 2 (2): 107–22.

Savoiu, Gheorghe. 2013. *Econophysics: Background and Applications in Economics, Finance, and Sociophysics*. Boston: Academic Press.

Săvoiu, Gheorghe G., and Ion Iorga-Simăn. 2013. "Sociophysics: A new science or a new domain for physicists in a modern university?" In *Econophysics: Background and Applications in Economics, Finance, and Sociophysics*, edited by Gheorghe G. Săvoiu, 149–66. Oxford: Academic Press.

Scalas, Enrico, and Kyungsik Kim. 2007. "The art of fitting financial time series with Lévy stable distributions." *Journal of the Korean Physical Society* 50 (1): 105–11.

Schabas, Margaret. 1990. *A World Ruled by Number: William Stanley Jevons and the Rise of Mathematical Economics*. Princeton, NJ: Princeton University Press.

Schaden, Martin. 2002. "Quantum finance." *Physica A* 316: 511–38.

Schinckus, Christophe. 2008. "The financial simulacrum." *Journal of Socio-economics* 73 (3): 1076–89.

Schinckus, Christophe. 2009a. "La diversification théorique en finance de marché: Vers de nouvelles perspectives de l'incertitude." Doctoral dissertation, University of Paris 1, Panthéon-Sorbonne.

Schinckus, Christophe. 2009b. "La finance comportementale ou le développement d'un nouveau paradigme." *Revue d'Histoire des Sciences Humaines* 20: 131–57.

Schinckus, Christophe. 2010a. "Econophysics and economics: Sister disciplines?" *American Journal of Physics* 78 (1): 325–27.

Schinckus, Christophe. 2010b. "Is econophysics a new discipline? A neo-positivist argument." *Physica A* 389: 3814–21.

Schinckus, Christophe. 2010c. "A reply to comment on econophysics and economics: Sister disciplines?" *American Journal of Physics* 78 (8): 789–91.

Schinckus, Christophe. 2012a. "Financial economics and non-representative art." *Journal of Interdisciplinary Economics* 24 (1): 77–97.

Schinckus, Christophe. 2012b. "Statistical econophysics and agent-based econophysics." *Quantitative Finance* 12 (8): 1189–92.

Schinckus, Christophe. 2013. "How do econophysicists make stable Levy processes physically plausible." *Brazilian Journal of Physics* 43 (4): 281–93.

Schinckus, Christophe. 2017. "Econophysics and complexity studies." Doctoral dissertation, University of Cambridge.

Schoutens, Wim. 2003. *Lévy Processes in Finance.* New York: Wiley Finance.

Schwert, G. William. 2003. "Anomalies and market efficiency." In *Handbook of the Economics of Finance*, edited by George M. Constantinides, Milton Harris, and René M. Stulz, 939–74. Boston: Elsevier.

Seemann, Lars, Joseph L. McCauley, and Gemunu H. Gunaratne. 2011. "Intraday volatility and scaling in high frequency foreign exchange markets." *International Review of Financial Analysis* 20 (3): 121–26. doi: 10.1016/j.irfa.2011.02.008.

Shafer, Glenn, and Vladimir Vovk. 2001. *Probability and Finance: It's Only a Game!* New York: Wiley.

Shafer, Glenn, and Vladimir Vovk. 2006. "The Sources of Kolmogorov's Grundbegriffe." *Statistical Science* 21: 70–98.

Sharpe, William F. 1963. "A simplified model for portfolio analysis." *Management Science* 9: 277–93.

Sharpe, William F. 1964. "Capital asset prices: A theory of market equilibrium under conditions of risk." *Journal of Finance* 19 (3): 425–42.

Shefrin, Hersh. 2002. *Beyond Greed and Fear: Understanding Behavioral Finance and the Psychology of Investing.* New York: Oxford University Press.

Shinohara, Shuji, and Yukio Pegio Gunji. 2001. "Emergence and collapse of money through reciprocity." *Physica A: Applied Mathematics and Computation* 117 (1): 131–50.

Shleifer, Andrei, and Lawrence H. Summers. 1990. "The noise trader approach to finance." *Journal of Economic Perspectives* 4 (2): 19–33.

Shlesinger, Michael F. 1995. "Comment on 'Stochastic Process with Ultraslow Convergence to a Gaussian: The Truncated Lévy Flight.'" *Physical Review Letters* 74 (24): 4959.

Simkin, Mikhail V., and Vwani P. Roychowdhury. 2011. "Re-inventing Willis." *Physics Reports* 502: 1–35.

Simon, Herbert A. 1955. "On a class of skew distribution functions." *Biometrika* 42 (3–4): 425–40.

Sims, Christopher A. 1980a. "Comparison of interwar and postwar business cycles: Monetarism reconsidered." *American Economic Review* 70 (2): 250.

Sims, Christopher A. 1980b. "Macroeconomics and reality." *Econometrica* 48 (1): 1–48.

Sims, Christopher A. 1996. "Macroeconomics and methodology." *Journal of Economic Perspectives* 10 (1): 105–20.

Skjeltorp, Johannes Atle. 2000. "Scaling in the Norwegian stock market." *Physica A* 283 (3): 486–528.

Slanina, Frantisek. 2014. *Essentials of Econophysics Modelling.* Oxford: Oxford University Press.

Slanina, František. 2001. "Mean-field approximation for a limit order driven market model." *Physical Review E* 64 (5): 056136-1–056136-5.

Slutsky, Eugen. 1937. "The summation of random causes as the source of cyclic processes." *Econometrica* 5 (2): 105–46.

Sornette, Didier. 2003. *Why Stock Markets Crash: Critical Events in Complex Financial Systems.* Princeton, NJ: Princeton University Press.

Sornette, Didier. 2006. *Critical Phenomena in Natural Sciences: Chaos, Fractals, Self-Organization, and Disorder. Concepts and Tools.* 2nd ed. Berlin: Springer.

Sornette, Didier. 2014. "Physics and financial economics (1776-2014): Puzzles, Ising and agent-based models." *Reports on progress in physics* 77 (6): 062001–28.

Sornette, Didier, and Peter Cauwels. 2015. "Financial bubbles: Mechanisms and diagnostics." *Review of Behavioral Economics* 2 (3): 279–305.

Sornette, Didier, and Anders Johansen. 1997. "Large financial crashes." *Physica A* 245 (1): 411–22.

Sornette, Didier, and Anders Johansen. 2001. "Significance of log-periodic precursors to financial crashes." *Quantitative Finance* 1 (4): 452–71.

Sornette, Didier, Anders Johansen, and Jean-Philippe Bouchaud. 1995. "Stock market crashes, precursors and replicas." *Journal de Physique I* 6 (1): 167–75.

Sornette, Didier, and Ryan Woodard. 2010. "Financial bubbles, real estate bubbles, derivative bubbles, and the financial and economic crisis." In *Econophysics Approaches to Large-Scale Business Data and Financial Crisis*, edited by Misako Takayasu, Tsutomu Watanabe, and Hideki Takayasu, 101–48. Tokyo: Springer Japan.

Sprenkle, Case M. 1961. "Warrant prices as indicators of expectations and preferences." *Yale Economic Essays* 1 (2): 178–231.

Sprenkle, Case M. 1964. "Some evidence on the profitability of trading in put and call options." In *The Random Character of Stock Market Prices*, edited by Paul H. Cootner. Cambridge, MA: MIT Press.

Sprowls, Clay. 1963. "Computer education in the business curriculum." *Journal of Business* 36 (1): 91–96.

Standler, Ronald B. 2009. "Funding of basic research in physical sciences in the USA." Working paper.

Stanley, H. Eugene. 1971. *Introduction to Phase Transitions and Critical Phenomena*. New York: Oxford University Press.

Stanley, H. Eugene. 1999. "Scaling, universality, and renormalization: Three pillars of modern critical phenomena." *Reviews of Modern Physics* 71 (2): S358–S366.

Stanley, H. Eugene, Viktor Afanasyev, Luis A. Nunes Amaral, Serguey Buldyrev, Albert Goldberger, Steve Havlin, Harry Leschhorn, Peter Mass, Rosario N. Mantegna, Chung Kang Peng, Paul Prince, Andrew Salinger, and Karthik Viswanathan. 1996. "Anomalous fluctuations in the dynamics of complex systems: From DNA and physiology to econophysics." *Physica A* 224 (1): 302–21.

Stanley, H. Eugene, Luis A. Nunes Amaral, D. Canning, Parameswaran Gopikrishnan, Youngki Lee, and Yanhui Liu. 1999. "Econophysics: Can physicists contribute to the science of economics?" *Physica A* 269 (1): 156–69.

Stanley, H. Eugene, Xavier Gabaix, and Vasiliki Plerou. 2008. "A statistical physics view of financial fluctuations: Evidence for scaling universality." *Physica A* 387 (1): 3967–81.

Stanley, H. Eugene, L. A. Nunes Amaral, Parameswaran Gopikrishnan, Yanhui Liu, Vasiliki Plerou, and Bernd Rosenow. 2000. "Econophysics: What can physicists contribute to economics?" *International Journal of Theoretical and Applied Finance* 3 (3): 335–46.

Stanley, H. Eugene, and Vasiliki Plerou. 2001. "Scaling and universality in economics: Empirical results and theoretical interpretation." *Quantitative Finance* 1 (6): 563–67.

Stauffer, D. 2007. "Opinion dynamics and sociophysics." arXiv:0705.0891.

Stauffer, Dietrich. 2004. "Introduction to statistical physics outside physics." *Physica A* 336: 1–5.

Stauffer, Dietrich. 2005. "Sociophysics simulations II: Opinion dynamics." arXiv:physics/0503115.

Stauffer, Dietrich, and Didier Sornette. 1999. "Self-organized percolation model for stock market fluctuations." *Physica A* 271: 496–506.

Steiger, William Lee. 1963. "Non-randomness in the stock market: A new test on an existent hypothesis." MS thesis, School of Industrial Management, MIT.

Stigler, George J. 1964. "A theory of oligopoly." *Journal of Political Economy* 72: 44–61.

Stock, James H., and Mark W. Watson. 2001. "Vector autoregressions." *Journal of Economic Perspectives* 15 (4): 101–15.

Stumpf, Michael P. H., and Mason A. Porter. 2012. "Critical truths about power laws." *Science* 335 (6069): 665–66.

Sullivan, Edward J. 2011. "A. D. Roy: The forgotten father of portfolio theory." In *Research in the History of Economic Thought and Methodology*, edited by Jeff E. Biddle and Ross B. Emmett, 73–82. Greenwich, CT: JAI Press.

Takayasu, Hideki. 2002. *Empirical Science of Financial Fluctuations: The Advent of Econophysics*. Tokyo: Springer Japan.

Takayasu, Hideki, ed. 2006. *Practical Fruits of Econophysics*. Tokyo: Springer Japan.

Takayasu, Misako, Tsutomu Watanabe, and Hideki Takayasu, eds. 2010. *Econophysics Approaches to Large-Scale Business Data and Financial Crisis*. Tokyo: Springer Japan.

Tan, A. 2005. "Long memory stochastic volatility and a risk minimization approach for derivative pricing and hedging." Doctoral dissertation, School of Mathematics, University of Manchester.

Taqqu, Murad S. 2001. "Bachelier and his times: A conversation with Bernard Bru." *Finance and Stochastics* 5 (1): 3–32.

Teichmoeller, John. 1971. "A note on the distribution of stock price changes." *Journal of the American Statistical Association* 66: 282–84.

Theiler, James, Stephen Eubank, André Longtin, Bryan Galdrikian, and J. Doyne Farmer. 1992. "Testing for nonlinearity in time series: The method of surrogate data." *Physica D: Nonlinear Phenomena* 58 (1): 77–94.

Todd, Loreto. 1990. *Pidgins and Creoles*. London: Routledge.

Treynor, Jack L. 1961. "Toward a theory of market value of risky assets." Available at SSRN.

Tripp, Omer, and Dror Feitelson. 2001. "Zipf's Law Revisited." Working paper, School of Engineering and Computer Science, Jerusalem.

Tusset, Gianfranco. 2010. "Going back to the origins of econophysics: The Paretian conception of heterogeneity." Paper presented to the 14th ESHET Conference, Amsterdam.

Upton, David, and Donald Shannon. 1979. "The stable Paretian distribution, subordinated stochastic processes, and asymptotic lognormality: An empirical investigation." *Journal of Finance* 34: 1031–39.

van der Vaart, A. W. 2000. *Asymptotic Statistics*. Cambridge: Cambridge University Press.

Vitanov, Nikolay K., and Zlatinka I. Dimitrova. 2014. *Bulgarian Cities and the New Economic Geography*. Sofia: Vanio Nedkov.

Voit, Johannes. 2005. *Statistical Mechanics of Financial Markets*. 3rd ed. Berlin: Springer.

Von Plato, Jan. 1994. *Creating Modern Probability: Its Mathematics, Physics, and Philosophy in Historical Perspective*. New York: Cambridge University Press.

von Smoluchowski, Marian. 1906. "Zur kinetischen Theorie der Brownschen Molekularbewegung und der Suspensionen." *Annalen der Physik* 21: 756–80.

Walter, Christian. 2005. "La gestion indicielle et la théorie des moyennes." *Revue d'Économie Financière* 79: 113–36.

Wang, Jie, Chun-Xia Yang, Pei-Ling Zhou, Ying-Di Jin, Tao Zhou, and Bing-Hong Wang. 2005. "Evolutionary percolation model of stock market with variable agent number." *Physica A* 354: 505–17.

Wang, Yuling, Jing Wang, and Fengshan Si. 2012. "Conditional value at risk of stock return under stable distribution." *Lecture Notes in Information Technology* 19: 141–45.

Watanabe, Shinzo. 2009. "The Japanese contributions to martingales." *Journal Electronique d'Histoire des Probabilités et de la Statistique* 5 (1): 1–13.

Weber, Ernst Juerg. 2009. "A short history of derivative security markets." In *Vinzenz Bronzin's Option Pricing Models*, edited by Wolfgang Hafner and Heinz Zimmermann, 431–66. Berlin: Springer.

Weintraub, Robert E. 1963. "On speculative prices and random walks: A denial." *Journal of Finance* 18 (1): 59–66.

Welch, Ivo. 1992. "Sequential sales, learning and cascades." *Journal of Finance* 47 (2): 695–732.

Weron, Aleksander, Szymon Mercik, and Rafal Weron. 1999. "Origins of the scaling behaviour in the dynamics of financial data." *Physica A* 264: 562–69.

Weston, J. Fred 1967. "The state of the finance field." *Journal of Finance* 22 (4): 539–40.

Whitley, Richard Drummond. 1986a. "The rise of modern finance theory: Its characteristics as a scientific field and connection to the changing structure of capital markets." In *Research in the History of Economic Thought and Methodology*, edited by Warren J. Samuels, 147–78. Stanford, CA: JAI Press.

Whitley, Richard Drummond. 1986b. "The structure and context of economics as a scientific field." In *Research in the History of Economic Thought and Methodology*, edited by Waren J. Samuels, 179–209. Stanford, CA: JAI Press.

Wickens, Michael R. 1995. "Real business cycle analysis: A needed revolution in macroeconometrics." *Economic Journal* 105 (433): 1637–48.

Widom, Benjamin. 1965a. "Equation of state in the neighborhood of the critical point." *Journal of Chemical Physics* 43: 3898–905.

Widom, Benjamin. 1965b. "Surface tension and molecular correlations near the critical point." *Journal of Chemical Physics* 43: 3892–97.

Wiener, Norbert. 1923. "Differential-space." *Journal of Mathematics and Physics* 2: 131–74.

Williams, John Burr. 1938. *The Theory of Investment Value*. Cambridge, MA: Harvard University Press.

Willis, J. C. 1922. *Age and Area: A Study in Geographical Distribution and Origin of Species*. Cambridge: Cambridge University press.

Willis, J. C., and G. Udny Yule. 1922. "Some statistics of evolution and geographical distribution in plants and animals, and their significance." *Nature* 109: 177–79.

Wilson, Kenneth G. 1993. "The renormalization group and critical phenomena." In *Nobel Lectures in Physics (1981–1990)*, edited by Gösta Ekspong, 102–32. London: World Scientific.

Working, Holbrook. 1934. "A random-difference series for use in the analysis of time series." *Journal of the American Statistical Association* 29: 11–24.

Working, Holbrook. 1949. "The investigation of economic expectations." *American Economic Review* 39 (3): 150–66.

Working, Holbrook. 1953. "Futures trading and hedging." *American Economic Review* 43 (3): 314–43.

Working, Holbrook. 1956. "New ideas and methods for price research." *Journal of Farm Economics* 38: 1427–36.

Working, Holbrook. 1958. "A theory of anticipatory prices." *American Economic Review* 48 (2): 188–99.

Working, Holbrook. 1960. "Note on the correlation of first differences of averages in a random chain." *Econometrica* 28 (4): 916–18.

Working, Holbrook. 1961. "New concepts concerning futures markets and prices." *American Economic Review* 51 (2): 160–63.

Wyart, M., Jean-Philippe Bouchaud, J. Kockelkoren, Marc Potters, and M. Vettorazo. 2008. "Relation between bid-ask spread, impact and volatility in order-driven markets." *Quantitative Finance* 8: 41–57.

Yule, G. Udny. 1925. "A mathematical theory of evolution, based on the conclusions of Dr. J. C. Willis, F.R.S." *Philosophical Transactions of the Royal Society B* 213 (402–10): 21–87.

Zanin, Massimiliano, Luciano Zunino, Osvaldo A. Rosso, and David Papo. 2012. "Permutation entropy and its main biomedical and econophysics applications: A review." *Entropy* 14 (12): 1553–77. doi: 10.3390/e14081553.

Zhang, Qiang, and Jiguang Han. 2013. "Option pricing in incomplete markets." *Applied Mathematics Letters* 26 (10): 975.

Zipf, George K. 1935. *The Psychobiology of Language*. New York: Houghton Mifflin.

Zipf, George K. 1949. *Human Behaviour and the Principle of Least Effort*. Reading, MA: Addison-Wesley.

INDEX

Printed in the USA/Agawam, MA
September 6, 2017

658108.003